Pitt Series in
POLICY AND
INSTITUTIONAL
STUDIES

THE POLITICAL
PSYCHOLOGY OF THE
GULF WAR

■

LEADERS, PUBLICS, AND THE
PROCESS OF CONFLICT

Stanley A. Renshon, Editor

UNIVERSITY OF PITTSBURGH PRESS

Pittsburgh and London

DS
79.72
P64
1993

Published by the University of Pittsburgh Press, Pittsburgh, Pa., 15260
Copyright © 1993, University of Pittsburgh Press
All rights reserved
Manufactured in the United States of America
Printed on acid-free paper

Library of Congress Cataloging-in-Publication Data

The Political psychology of the Gulf War : leaders, publics, and the
    process of conflict / Stanley A. Renshon, editor.
        p.   cm. —(Pitt series in policy and institutional studies)
    Includes bibliographical references and index.
    ISBN 0-8229-3744-1 (alk. paper). —ISBN 0-8229-5495-8
(pbk. : alk. paper)
    1. Persian Gulf War, 1991.   2. Persian Gulf War, 1991—
Psychological aspects.   I. Renshon, Stanley A.   II. Series.
DS79.72.P64   1993
956.704'42—dc20   92-34182
                                                                          CIP
A CIP catalogue record for this book is available from the British Library.
Eurospan, London

CONTENTS

PART VI   *Epilogue*

FOREWORD

Fred I. Greenstein

Some historical episodes are of such intrinsic interest in and of themselves and are so fraught with larger implications that they elicit enormous quantities of research and writing, much of it taking place long before anything approximating a complete record can be available. A striking instance is the sequence of events provoked by the invasion, conquest, and annexation of Kuwait by Iraq in the summer of 1990 and the subsequent national and international decision making that ensued in the U.S.-led Gulf War of 1991. Dubbed even as it was under way as a slow-motion Cuban missile crisis, this episode, which was possible only because of the dramatic transformation of relations between the United States and the Soviet Union in the 1980s, spelled an end to the bipolar international politics of the post–World War II era and a beginning to whatever "new world order" might ensue.

This volume is a valuable contribution to what promises to be a rich first-cut scholarly literature on the causes, concomitants, and consequences of the Gulf War. The early studies of the Gulf War, like those of other episodes that immediately spawned extensive interpretive literatures, are bound to be emended as the historical record expands, but it need not follow that their intellectual contributions will be ephemeral. At their best, early analyses of an event as important and instructive as the Gulf War can prove to be of enduring importance. Much of what is central to many major historical episodes proves to have been present in or suggested by the contemporary public record. Precisely because the analysts who conduct early studies are without benefit of participants' memoirs and documents, they are likely to scrutinize the public record more intensely than do their data-rich successors. In doing this, they are helped by their immersion in the current historical context. Putting it negatively, first-cut analysts lack the *dis*advantages of hindsight: they are less likely than their successors to succumb to ahistorical assumptions about what the participants would or would not have considered politically feasible at the time.

ix

Above all, early analyses provide provisional lenses for further analyses. In this sense, they serve for the intellectual community some of
the same agenda-setting functions that the mass media perform for the
political community. The importance of establishing an early framework
for analysis of events of the vast magnitude of the Gulf War can be seen
by considering the vast early literature spawned by the Cuban missile
crisis itself, much of which was psychological in its implication but not
in its explicit emphasis.

Consider, for example, the most influential of the studies that explore the larger theoretical implications of the missile crisis—Graham
Allison's *Essence of Decision* (1971). Allison used the missile crisis as a foil
for identifying alternate intellectual prisms through which international
decision making might be interpreted. Decomposing the events of the
missile crisis into three accounts, each at a different level of analysis,
Allison noted that some analysts conceived of the United States and the
Soviet Union as if they were unitary rational actors, others conceived of
the two nations as if they were conglomerations of bureaucracies with
standard operating routines, and still others viewed them as governmental actors engaged in decision-making processes.

The "core" of the last (and seemingly most realistic) "level of close
political analysis is personality," Allison observed—that is "how each
man manages to stand the heat in his kitchen, each player's operating
style, and the complementarity and contradiction among personalities
and styles in the inner circle are irreducible pieces of the policy blend"
(1971, 166). Yet nowhere in his analysis did Allison discuss the actual
John F. Kennedy or allude to the personal characteristics of the flesh-
and-blood Nikita Khrushchev or, for that matter, those of either man's
principal associates.[1]

We now know, as a result of the declassification of American documents and a vast later oral record created by participants and observers
from both the United States and the Soviet Union, that many contemporary analysts underestimated the impact of the leaders' personalities
on the development and resolution of the missile crisis. The extent to
which the entire episode resulted from the personal proclivities of Nikita Khrushchev, much of whose political rise had depended on risk
taking, was underestimated at the time, as was the essential cautious-
ness of John (and Robert) Kennedy, who prove to have secretly assured
Khrushchev that U.S. missiles would be removed from Turkey.[2]

The lack of systematic attention to the significance of the two individuals whose trigger fingers were so obviously a matter of concern in
1962 is a reminder of the widespread tendency of students of politics to
underestimate, ignore, or even deny the psychological determinants of
major political outcomes. The reasons for such resistance (to borrow a

term from psychotherapy) are not fully clear. They probably include an ingrained lack of sensitivity to psychology on the part of individuals schooled in deterministic theories of history and politics and a more generalized reluctance on the part of political observers in all walks of life to acknowledge that momentous events can be determined by fallible human agents.

Whatever the case of the literature on the missile crisis, the existence of this explicitly psychological collection of early analyses helps ensure that future scholars will not be surprised by the psychological features of the later record of the Gulf War. More important, the chapters in this fascinating volume should help win converts to the study of political psychology from the fields of international relations and national security studies and contribute to valuable developments in the growing field of political psychology itself.

These chapters in no way reduce the Gulf War to the attitudes, personalities, and inner proclivities of its protagonists. Rather, the very fact that this volume is organized around a particular historical context serves to underline the fundamental premise of psychology in general and political psychology in particular, that human action is a joint function of the inner qualities of the actors and the outer circumstances of their political environments. The chapters that follow are full of reminders of the interdependence of the psychology of political actors and the contexts in which they take action. They also illustrate the extent to which the context of political action is itself psychological.

Thus, the accounts of traditional patterns of culture and political psychology in the Arab world by L. Carl Brown and Marvin Zonis characterize key elements in the settings in which the American and Iraqi decision makers operated, as do the characterizations of Arab mass publics during the war by Shibley Telhami and Israeli mass publics by Asher Arian and Carol Gordon. John Mueller's account of the responses to the war of the American mass public is particularly illuminating for its careful demonstration of how highly situation-specific mass opinion is likely to be. And Jarol Manheim's report of the battle to shape media messages about the Gulf crisis is a valuable reminder of the extent to which the battle for control of public opinion is a battle to mold the symbolic environment in which opinion is formed.

In a famous exercise of bravado, Secretary of State Dean Rusk is said to have described the Cuban missile crisis as an eyeball-to-eyeball confrontation in which the other side blinked. The image of two leaders (and to a lesser extent two leadership groups), neither of whom succeeded in staring the other down, is very much evident in the chapters of Janice Stein, Steven Wayne, Jerrold Post, and Stanley Renshon. Even more so than in the missile crisis, the Gulf War provided a spectacle of decision making in which individual psychology made such a clear difference that it should be evident even to committed environmental determinists.

When we say that an individual has made a difference in some historical outcome, we usually mean that three conditions have been met: the individual's actions were not ones we would have expected from any similarly situated actors, the actions were ones that made a difference for the outcome, and the outcome was substantively important. All three conditions were met in the first weeks of January 1991, when the world waited to see if Saddam Hussein would order an Iraqi withdrawal from Kuwait and if George Bush would ignore the option of relying on sanctions and order Operation Desert Storm. Each man held the power of national decision making. Neither man was compelled by circumstances to act as he did; Saddam Hussein was notable for his capacity to backtrack on commitments, and Bush operated in a political climate in which alternatives were available. A number of prominent figures with unimpeachable credentials for firmness (including former chairmen of the Joint Chiefs of Staff and former secretaries of defense) had publicly spoken out against military action. The outcome triggered by the two men, if not as apocalyptic as a nuclear exchange would have been in the missile crisis, was highly consequential—its results included the war itself, the still uncounted number of deaths, the despoiling of Kuwait and its environment, the costs incurred by the Shiite and Kurdish minorities, and the innumerable probable and possible changes in the circumstances of international politics about which Alexander George speculates.[3]

The chapters that follow are very much an exchange of preliminary insights. The authors sometimes reach different conclusions about important matters, and the editor has wisely not attempted to enforce conformity. Thus, one might infer from Brown's chapter that the Gulf War will inevitably exacerbate the intense distrust for the West in the Arab world, but Zonis's analysis suggests that there may be room for change. Similarly, Stein argues that Saddam Hussein could not have been deterred from invading Kuwait, but Post's analysis of Saddam's tactical flexibility suggests that different situational stimuli might have led him to act differently.

At this stage in the study of the Gulf War such disagreements are inevitable and constructive. Early analysts are limited in the firmness of what they conclude because the record is incomplete and the effects of the event they are studying continue to unfold. They also are hampered by the state of the art and science of the discipline of political psychology. But on this score disagreements and differences of emphasis by the contributors to this volume are to the good. From them will come more sharply focused hypotheses, fuller inquiry, and increasingly sound insight into not only the Gulf War but also the larger concerns of political psychology.

NOTES

1. On Allison's inattention to the U.S. president, see Krasner (1972).

2. For a valuable reconstruction of the Kennedy-Khrushchev relationship (including the missile crisis) on the basis of the full range of American and Soviet sources, see Beschloss (1991).

3. Early accounts of the events leading up to the Gulf War (including debates about whether such a war would be necessary) and of the war itself include Woodward (1991), Smith (1992), and U.S. News and World Report (1992).

REFERENCES

Allison, Graham. 1971. *The Essence of Decision: Explaining the Cuban Missile Crisis.* Boston: Little, Brown.

Beschloss, Michael R. 1991. *The Crisis Years: Kennedy and Khrushchev, 1960–1963.* New York: Harper Collins.

Krasner, Stephen D. 1972. "Are Bureaucracies Important? (Or Allison Wonderland)." *Foreign Policy* 7 (Summer): 159–79.

Smith, Jean Edward. 1992. *George Bush's War.* New York: Holt.

U.S. News and World Report. 1992. *Triumph Without Victory: The Unreported History of the Persian Gulf War.* New York: Random House.

Woodward, Bob. 1991. *The Commanders.* New York: Simon and Schuster.

PREFACE

The origins of this book began for me on August 2, 1990, while I was traveling in Egypt. That morning, I was at the front desk of my hotel when a young man rushed in carrying a stack of newspapers and began talking excitedly to the manager. I saw a banner headline in bold Arabic type and a photograph of tanks crossing the desert, and I knew that war had broken out in the Middle East.

From that moment, my attention was riveted by the drama, the stakes, the concern, and above all the questions that the invasion raised. Was George Bush serious when he said that this aggression will not stand? Would Saddam Hussein back away from his annexation of Kuwait in the face of the international resistance mobilized against him? Would there really be a war between Iraq and those who opposed Saddam Hussein's invasion?

By January we knew the answers to these questions, but there were many others. Why did Saddam Hussein decide to invade and then stay in Kuwait? Why did George Bush resolve to oppose him? What considerations—historical, cultural, strategic, or psychological—were involved in arriving at these decisions? How adequate were these judgments?

As the conflict began to unfold, other important questions were raised. It was clear that the crisis was taking place in a region with a particular history, culture, and psychology. And it was also clear that the United States and its president were a product of a particular history, culture, and psychology. How did these elements affect the crisis as it developed?

The war generated strong public sentiments that were carefully watched by all parties to the conflict. In many countries directly involved in the crisis, public response to the unfolding events was a key factor at each stage in the crisis. Attempts by Bush and Hussein to influence domestic and world public opinion were in many respects unprecedented. Rarely had the direct attempt to influence the understanding and actions of so many culturally, politically, and psychologically

diverse audiences been on such stark public display. Moreover, the conflict developed as the international system itself was undergoing profound change. The collapse of the Soviet Union and the dismantling of
the Warsaw Pact nations represented a fundamental change in the
structure and nature of the international system. The war, if not a defining event in a new world order, would certainly help codify rules.
The question was: What lessons and understandings would emerge?

All of these issues both troubled and stimulated me, and I thought it
worthwhile to bring together others with similar interests to discuss
these questions. The result was a conference on the political psychology
of the Gulf War held at the Graduate School and University Center of
the City University of New York in November 1991.

No one who analyzes this war, or the Middle East more generally,
can help being aware of the strong passions and politics that can be activated in discussions of these events. I did not know the particular political positions held by conference participants regarding the war, nor
was it my wish to develop the conference and this book around such
knowledge. For the conference and this book, my primary concern was
to bring together scholars who were distinguished by their contributions in one or more of the theoretical areas of political psychology that
were the conference's focus—that is, conflict, leadership, mass publics,
and Middle Eastern studies.

The rationale for this book, then, is not to be found in its adherence
to one or another political position, but in the light it casts on the processes that are central to our understanding of the Gulf War.

Most realizations are a collective effort, and this one is no exception.
A number of people were instrumental in this process and I would like
to express my appreciation to them. Steven M. Cahn, then acting president of the City University's Graduate School and University Center,
was very supportive of this work, for which I am extremely grateful.
Charles Strozier helped to clarify my thinking on various aspects of the
Gulf War, as did Asher Arian. Several students in the political science
program at the Graduate Center helped enormously with the conference, in particular, Grayson Williams, Carol Remond, Najib Ghadban,
and William Friedman.

I would also like to express my appreciation to a number of people at
the University of Pittsburgh Press. Bert Rockman, editor of the series in
which this book appears, was very supportive of this work. Frank
Moone, acquisitions editor for the press, was also very enthusiastic
about the project. My many helpful talks with both are sincerely appreciated. I would also like to thank Catherine Marshall, managing editor,
and Jane Flanders, senior manuscript editor, and Diane Hammond, editor. Finally, I would like to acknowledge the support of my family,
Judith, David, and Jonathan, which has helped to sustain and encourage me.

INTRODUCTION

Stanley A. Renshon

The Gulf War was in many respects a marker event in the Middle East and post–cold war world politics more generally. It was an event of substantial consequence, in which the risks to important personal and national interests were played out within a sharply bracketed time frame, by leaders whose direct involvement in propelling events was clear and well defined, and which resulted in a dramatic and seemingly incisive conclusion. It has, in short, many characteristics of a textbook case. It is thus the kind of historical experience that will generate discussions and research for many years to come.

These same sets of sharply etched circumstances also provide an important opportunity to examine some basic theoretical questions in the fields of political science and especially political psychology. Questions of leadership, motivation, effectiveness, and judgment are basic to understanding the Gulf War, as are questions of public psychology and response and the impact of the war on the region and the world. The Gulf War framed questions connected with these areas in ways that allow us to ask clear questions, even if we find the answers complex.

At the same time, political psychology has an important and unique role to play in understanding the conflict, drawing out its implications, and attempting to answer these questions. An appreciation of psychological process is essential for illuminating the elements that affected the conflict as it unfolded. What motivated the major actors to do what they did? How did they see themselves and their circumstances and those of the other actors? What elements went into the decisions that were made, and how adequate were these decisions?

Political psychology theory also has an important role to play in understanding the effects of the war. Has the Gulf War ushered in a new sense of reality in the Middle East, or have traditional patterns of myth and understanding been reinforced? Has the Gulf War resulted in a new world view in the international system in which new norms of international conduct are emerging, or is the Gulf War one more illustration of business as usual under the old norms?

Although most of the contributors have had previous scholarly interests in the Middle East, others better than we will be able to address the Gulf War through the traditional lens of regional history and politics. Our specific contribution to the understanding of the Gulf War is the examination of the role of psychological processes. This book, then, has a dual purpose. First, it is meant to address and illuminate the causes, the unfolding, and the consequences of the war. Second, in doing so it is meant to further refine our theoretical understanding of the psychology of conflict, leadership, decision-making, and consequences. The chapters in this book reflect this dual focus.

The Organization of the Book

The Political Psychology of the Gulf War proceeds developmentally. The book is divided into several parts, each addressing a major dimension of the war process. We begin by considering the origins (part 1), move on to the dynamics (parts 2, 3, and 4), and end by considering the consequences (parts 5 and 6).

Part 1, "The Origins of the Gulf War," dealing with the war's psychological origins, is essential to set the stage for a discussion and analysis of the war dynamics that follow. One accurate criticism of both the behavioral movement in political science and of some political psychology research is that it is historically and culturally insensitive. For political psychology in particular, this is a very difficult criticism not to take seriously, since so much of the psychological theory on which the field draws has a strong developmental component. Some background is necessary to provide a historical dimension to the events of the Gulf War and also because war takes place in a psychological as well as a historical context. L. Carl Brown's chapter provides this historical and psychological background, focusing on the patterns of belief that have shaped, and continue to shape, Middle East politics.

The Gulf War was, in major respects, a confrontation between two leaders, George Bush and Saddam Hussein. Each played a clear and fundamental role in the unfolding and shaping of events. Their views, calculations, beliefs, and ultimately their judgments were responsible for the events this book analyzes. The Gulf War thus provides a remarkably good context in which to analyze the psychology of leadership itself, the particular psychologies of these two leaders, and their relationship to each other.

The three chapters in part 2 ("Leaders, Leadership, and Decision Making") focus on George Bush, Saddam Hussein, and the nature of their leadership and judgment. Stephen Wayne analyzes the decision to go to war from the perspective of George Bush's own values and presidential style. Jerrold Post analyzes the political personality of Saddam Hussein and attempts to understand what motivated this leader before and during the war. I also examine the motivation and decision making of George Bush and Saddam Hussein, but from the perspective of the quality of their judgments before and during the war.

The two chapters that form part 3 ("The Conflict Process") focus on the unfolding of the Gulf War. Janice Stein's chapter examines the nature of the conflict process as it developed, with a view toward understanding why deterrence failed to accomplish its purposes in this particular case. Once the war began, it was fought in the arena of public perceptions and belief as well as on the battlefield. Each side invested substantial thought and resources to the management of how it and others were viewed. Jarol Manheim's chapter examines the attempts by the major actors in the conflict to influence and shape how the events were perceived and understood in the world at large and for particular targets of this strategic communication.

Part 4 ("Mass Publics") extends that focus and examines the ways in which publics both affected and were affected by the process of conflict. Shibley Telhami focuses on the complex and ambivalent responses of various publics in the Arab world to the events of the Gulf War, including an analysis of mass demonstrations. Asher Arian and Carol Gordon analyze Israeli public opinion and find that the war had important effects on that public's sense of security and its willingness to use force in the future. John Mueller addresses American public opinion during the Gulf War and provides some comparative evidence of the similarities to and differences from public responses to other conflicts.

The final sections (part 5, "The Consequences of Conflict," and part 6, "Epilogue") address the consequences of the war. These consequences were obviously felt mostly in the Middle East. Marvin Zonis's chapter details how the war called into question many of the myths and assumptions that had been the basis for Middle East politics for decades. But it was also clear that the consequences of this, the first major war in the post–Cold War period, might well have consequences for the structure of the emerging new international system. Alexander George traces the multiple consequences, some of them unanticipated and unintended, on the international system itself. Finally, in the "Epilogue," I examine some of the critical observations that have been made about the conduct of the war, both at the time and in light of subsequent events, and attempt an overall appraisal of it.

A Note on Time, Data, and Evidence

Some dilemmas of evidence and inference that arose in exploring the Gulf War and the concerns that frame this book should be noted. The obvious should be stated at the outset: wars are planned and conducted in secret. The Gulf War was no exception. Although all the participants had much to say in public, they thought, worried, and calculated in private. Moreover, any analysis of public events must be tempered by an appreciation that leaders involved in a conflict would be sensitive to the effect of what they said or did on others and on the unfolding situation. Even the overtly physical aspect of the war (as, for example, the reports on the performance of the Patriot missiles, which have been refined over time) alerts us not to assume that what we see is all there is.

Therefore, one makes use of public knowledge while appreciating that it will be supplemented and modified by the addition of what was heretofore private knowledge. This process has already begun. An example of this is the publication of the not-for-attribution interviews conducted by Bob Woodward (1991) on Gulf War decision making. Another is the series of for-the-public-record interviews conducted with American, British, and Arab officials at mid- and upper-level positions in the war deliberations and aired on national television on January 17, 24, and 31, 1992.[1] The Pentagon has completed and sent to Congress its interium report (U.S. Department of Defense 1992a), supplemented by its official three-volume study of the Gulf War (1992b). No doubt other data of this kind will emerge.

These data will not necessarily resolve the dilemmas of evaluating evidence, inference, and the drawing of conclusions. These and other new elements of information and sources of understanding benefit us in that they take the analyst one step closer to the events and the discussions that surrounded them. But they are no more inherently real or accurate than the public record. They are the views of specific individuals in particular locations looking back on specific and perhaps limited events with particular, perhaps multiple, interests.

Contemporaneously recorded deliberations for formally constituted decision groups like the National Security Council might well supplement or perhaps modify our understanding of the Gulf War, but here too there are limitations. The process of decision is only imperfectly captured even by written documentation. Much goes on outside of such meetings, and the meetings themselves may set some parameters for decision without necessarily arriving at final conclusions.

Finally, there is the element of comprehensiveness of understanding from the standpoint of the actors involved. The Gulf War involved a number of participants. Some were major, some were important, and many were peripheral. Some of the major participants responsible for policy during the Gulf crisis are unlikely to give in-depth interviews or provide contemporaneous documents of their deliberations. Without those, we are forced to rely solely on a public record. So we know less now, and may over time know less comparatively, about the assumptions, motives, concerns, and calculations of Iraq, Saudi Arabia, Israel, and others.

Correspondingly, it is likely that if and when more materials become available, they will result in modifications of our understanding of the origin, conduct, and aftermath of the war. The same process was evident in the scholarship that analyzed the Cuban missile crisis. The first set of analyses was based on the reflections of the key participants (e.g., Kennedy 1971; Macmillian 1973), the public record (Allison 1971), and later analysis of key contemporaneous documents, including previously top secret transcripts of the deliberations of the National Security Council (Bundy and Blight 1987–1988; Trachtenberg 1985), all from the American side. It is only recently that deeper appreciations of Soviet deliberations at the time of the crisis have come into focus and more recently still that the views of the Cubans and their relationship to the Soviets has emerged more clearly (Blight and Welch 1989; Blight 1990).

All of these points suggest caution but not paralysis. There is enough on the public record to support initial analyses of the issues that concern this book. The Gulf crisis stretched over a fairly extensive period, unlike the Cuban missile crisis. Many of the key actors spoke often and publicly about their views and understandings. The period between the invasion of Kuwait and the onset of the actual war was a period of intense concern and analysis by the press, public, and political leaders, and these all are important sources of information for understanding the psychological processes that developed and unfolded.

Finally, because the crisis extended over a substantial period and was played out in a particularly public way, with key participants trying to influence each other as well as regional and international community members, there is a wide range of observable behavior to analyze. This is important because, while public behaviors cannot be taken solely at face value, they do reflect and can illuminate goals, assumptions, strategies, and understandings.

Ultimately, the initial understandings of the political psychology of the Gulf War put forward in this book will stand or be modified in whole or part by a confluence of evidence from different sources. Each of these will have their own contributions to make, as well as their own limitations. Each datum or theoretical understanding will need to be judged by its reliability, its ability to help us comprehend and make sense of what we know and question, and its accord with other information and understandings. These tests are as relevant for future analyses as they are for those we have at present.

Yet, while accuracy, plausibility, and accord of new information or analyses with what is already known or understood are certainly relevant and important, they may not be enough. Successive understandings must also be judged not only by these criteria, but by the extent to which they deepen and extend our understanding. A model of theoretical understanding that seeks to uncover *the* truth about the Gulf War may therefore, be ill-advised. In the end, we may not arrive at one understanding of the political psychology of the Gulf War but, rather, a range of understandings.

The events of the Gulf War encompassed an enormous range of systemic, institutional, and individual activities, and its effects were just as wide and deep. For these reasons it is hard to think in terms of one understanding of the Gulf War. Perhaps a better model is the prism, which, when held up to the light and turned, reveals different aspects of a complex, differentiated, but still connected whole. This book represents a first turn of that prism.

NOTES

1. Those interviewed include National Security Council members and advisors, the secretaries of defense and state, and many other important participants both in the United States and among coalition allies. The project was conceived and arranged by the American Enterprise Institute and produced by Brian Lapping Associates for the Discovery Channel and BBC Television. Transcripts of the interviews can be obtained by writing to the American Enterprise Institute for Public Policy Research in Washington, D.C.

REFERENCES

Allison, G. 1971. *Essence of Decision: Explaining the Cuban Missile Crisis.* Boston: Little, Brown.

Blight, J. 1990. *The Shattered Crystal Ball: Fear and Learning in the Cuban Missile Crisis.* Savage, Md.: Rowman and Littlefield.

Blight, J., and D. Welch. 1989. *On the Brink: Americans and Soviets Examine the Cuban Missile Crisis.* New York: Hill and Wang.

Bundy, M., and J. Blight. 1987–88. "October 27, 1962." *International Security* 12(3): 30–92.

Kennedy, R. 1971. *Thirteen Days.* New York: Norton.

Macmillian, H. 1973. *At the End of the Day: 1961–1963.* New York: Harper and Row.

Tractenberg, M., ed. 1985. "White House Tapes and the Cuban Missile Crisis." *International Security* 10(1): 164–203.

U.S. Department of Defense. 1992a. *Conduct of the Persian Gulf Conflict: An Interim Report to Congress.* Washington, D.C.: Government Printing Office.

U.S. Department of Defense. 1992b. *Conduct of the Persian Gulf War.* 3 vols. Washington, D.C.: Government Printing Office.

Woodward, B. 1991. *The Commanders.* New York: Simon and Schuster.

PART I

THE ORIGINS OF
THE GULF WAR

1

Patterns Forged in Time:
Middle Eastern Mind-Sets
and the Gulf War

■

L. Carl Brown

> In a pattern called a war.
> Christ! What are patterns for?
> —*Amy Lowell*

TO WRITE of the psychology or the *mentalité* (to follow current fashion) of the Arabs or, indeed, of any entire people is an elusive enterprise. At the level of what we choose, perhaps too blithely, to label common sense we can readily agree that Americans, Egyptians, Saudis, Iraqis, Israelis, and so on differ in their attitudes toward politics and diplomacy.

Further, few would dispute that such differences are significantly shaped by a people's distinctive history plus—what is quite different— a people's perception of that history surviving as unconsciously accepted mind-sets even when the circumstances that once shaped them have been radically modified. A people's ideas about international politics will thus at any particular time be a composite of mind-sets developed generations or even centuries earlier alongside attitudinal responses to current events.

All this is obvious, but there is little scholarly agreement concerning how one discovers, describes, and measures such different group psychologies. There is no more agreement about the historical roots of such differences. After the Second World War, for example, scholars seeking to explain how totalitarian systems had come to prevail in parts of the presumably much more advanced Western world worked on what came to called national character studies. These studies soon fell out of favor. Few scientifically satisfactory—that is, verifiable—findings emerged. Not only that, but the several working hypotheses advanced often failed the fundamental test of being applicable in other cases.

Take early and strict toilet training, which, it was posited, would produce a society of uptight, or in the Freudian term, anal, characters.

3

Early and strict toilet training of Lebanese children, social psychologist Edwin Terry Prothro found, did not produce the classic Freudian character with "a miserly frugality, a petulant obstinacy, and a compulsiveness that expresses itself in 'orderliness, tidiness, punctuality, meticulousness and propriety.' " That list of traits, Prothro continued, is "startling in its inappropriateness" for those who know Lebanon. Instead, "the Lebanese are generous within their means (in a socially-determined fashion), flexible to the point of inconsistency, and non-compulsive to the point of fatalism. 'Anal character' would indeed be a poor way to describe the Lebanese modal personality" (1961, 92).

Even earlier, Bernard De Voto had punctured the balloon of national character studies when he observed that the more these scholars write about the United States the less we believe what they have been saying about Samoa.[1]

And yet the need to make sense of other people's attitudes toward politics, and thereby also to better understand the implicit political assumptions of one's own group, cannot be dismissed. Nor can the subject safely be left to those writers, including the hired pens, with political agendas designed to idealize or—more often—to demonize their subjects with the most egregious stereotypes.

Perhaps it is the beginning of wisdom to admit that the subject cannot be fitted into an all-embracing theoretical construct. Instead, a deliberately eclectic approach is adopted here, taking care to follow Spinoza, who insisted:

> My object in applying my mind to politics is not to make any new or unheard of suggestions, but to establish by sound and conclusive reasoning, and to deduce from the real nature of man, nothing save the principles and institutions which best accord with practice. Moreover, in order to investigate the topics pertaining to this branch of knowledge with the same objectivity as we generally show in mathematical inquiries, I have taken great care to understand human actions, and not to deride, deplore, or denounce them. (Spinoza 1958, 263).

The "Arab World": A Useful Unit of Analysis?

Our concern is to explore not the psychological makeup of leaders but the mind-sets of collectivities inhabiting the Arab world.

Diversity in the Arab World

Most, but not all, are Arabs in the sense that they speak Arabic and identify themselves with Arab culture. The Maghrib, however, boasts large numbers of Berbers, who constitute perhaps one-third of the population of Morocco, slightly less in Argeria, with only a handful in Tunisia and Libya. The population of southern Sudan is both non-Arab and non-Muslim. And as recent tragic events have made well known, about 15 percent of Iraq's population are Kurds.

Much more could be said about the diversity that characterizes this large Arab world covering an area from Morocco to the Gulf, roughly twice the area of the contiguous forty-eight states of the United States. For example, small Christian minorities are to be found in Egypt and all the states of the Fertile Crescent (Lebanon, Syria, Iraq, Jordan, and Israel). Christians are the politically and economically dominant group in Lebanon, although that dominance has been weakened by steady demographic change and by the Lebanese civil war beginning in 1975. Christians, along with even larger numbers of non-Muslim adherents to local religions, constitute a solid bloc in the southern third of the Sudan. On the other hand, the largest areas of the Arab world, the Arabian peninsula and the Maghrib, have no native Christian population at all. The once significant Jewish minorities in most Arab countries have, since the 1940s, been reduced to tiny remnant communities.

The great majority of those living in the Arab world are Muslim, of the majority Sunni persuasion. The Shiites constitute a small proportion of the total Arab world's population, but they are so concentrated as to form the majority in Iraq and the largest of Lebanon's many minorities. Shiites constitute significant minorities in several of the Gulf states as well.

Other significant minorities in the Fertile Crescent are the Alawis in Syria and the Druze, who are concentrated in a territory that includes Lebanon, Syria, and Israel. Nor should the appreciable Arab population living in Israel or in the territories occupied by Israel since 1967 be overlooked.

States in the Arab world vary in population from under 1 million to well over 50 million, in area from under 700 square miles to over 1 million square miles, and in per capita GNP from just over $600 to more than $18,000.[2] Arab diversity also reigns in the realm of oil. Over four-fifths of total Arab oil revenues go to states having less than 10 percent of the total Arab world's population.

Arabism

Given this diversity, can we speak meaningfully about the Arab world? Yes and no. Yes, in that the Arab world is a much more coherent psychological reality than, for example, the West or Western civilization and, obviously, more so than that other large mental construct—the Muslim world. That is to say, the sense of identification as Arab and as being part of the Arab world is firmly in place both as a collective self-perception from within the group and as an identifying rubric used by outsiders. Moreover, an Arabist historical pedigree is taught in the formal educational structures of the Arab world and is generally accepted even by those of little or no formal schooling.

To this extent one can talk meaningfully about an Arab world as grouping together a large number of peoples who, however much they differ in other ways, share a common collective self-image concerning who they are. Moreover, this collective self-image or myth is seen as being rooted in historical experience, even though professional historians might dispute many aspects of the resulting historical reconstruction.

A rough and ready gauge of this Arab myth might be by comparison with the Western myth in its Anglophone variety, which projects an almost linear historical development:

- from the earliest Jewish and then Christian experience in the Near East,
- blending in with the historical experience of the ancient Greek and then Roman civilizations,
- all moving westward to be further developed in the steady political institutionalization in Western Europe in the centuries to which we give such neat labels as *medieval* and *renaissance,*
- with special attention to Britain from Magna Carta onward,
- plus later special adaptations to explain the particularly American branch of the larger myth.

Stated so baldly, this Western myth, English-speaking variety, becomes a caricature. The purpose here is not to satirize, nor to trivialize but simply to emphasize that all peoples have "who we are" myths that are based on a selective ordering of the past. It is paradigmatic history, didactic history, not scientific history. It can be labeled as psychologically true insofar as it guides group perception of self and of other.

There is a similar "who we are" myth that binds together the Arab world, which I set out in general terms (and thus necessarily somewhat caricatured) below. It has not been around nearly so long as the Western myth, at least not in its fully elaborated present form, and those who would seek to discount the political importance of Arabism tend to stress its relative youth. Yet surely the psychological importance of group myths is best measured by the extent to which they are operative in any particular age, not by their longevity. By that standard, the Arab myth today has a more important impact on Arabs than does the Western myth on Americans.

Arabism can be properly compared to Zionism. Both adapt and nationalize sentiments of in-group togetherness that have existed for centuries but in quite different form. This comparison may serve as well to clarify another issue: those who insist that the ideological cement binding these people together is not so much Arabism as Islam are perhaps proposing a dichotomy that does not exist all that sharply in the collective mentality. Rather, Arabism and an Islamic identity coexist among the Arabs. One or another aspect of the protean Arabist myth may predominate at one time or another (e.g., secular Arabism in the heyday of Nasser during the 1950s and 1960s, a greater emphasis on Islam as both religion and state—Din wa Dawla—these days), but the essential notion of an Arab culture and Arabophone people remains remarkably stable, just as the sense of a common identity binds together Israelis and Zionists from the avowedly atheistic to the rigorously orthodox. This common ground of Arabism that incorporates Islam can be seen in the following examples:

- An eminent Christian Arab scholar advances the thesis that Muhammad is both the messenger of Islam and the unifier of the Arabs.
- Another Christian Arab intellectual presents Islam as part of his Arabist heritage.
- Pakistan, created as an Islamic state, cannot win Arab political support in opposition to India, especially in the critical early years following the independence of India and Pakistan.
- The Arab world gave less-than-wholehearted support to the Afghan resistance to the Soviet invasion of Afghanistan.
- Many Arabs supported Saddam Hussein as soon as he presented himself as an Arab and Muslim resistance leader in spite of his earlier secularist and anti-Islamic record (including the execution of an ayatollah).

Another comparison might be that of Arabism with the prevailing myth in South America. The sense of common Hispanic-American heritage has not eliminated disputes and even brutal warfare in South America. The same holds for the Arab world. Indeed, the overarching appeal to Arab togetherness is, like most myths, in large measure an effort to control the very real differences dividing the group. This moves the discussion to the negative aspect of our question about whether Arabs and the Arab world can be considered as a unity.

Arab World Regions

Certain of the important differences within the Arab world have already been noted. Another way to classify the diversity of these over 200 million people divided into twenty-plus states is by means of rough territorial boundaries delimiting four reasonably distinct cultural areas all within the Arab world: (1) the Arabian peninsula, (2) the Fertile Crescent, (3) the Nile Valley (Egypt and Sudan), and (4) the Maghrib. These are quite different areas. Their spoken Arabic is at least as different one from the other, in rhythm and vocabulary, as the English speakers in Mississippi are from their compatriots in Maine. Indeed, the furthest limits of diversity within the same Arabic language might be better compared with that distinguishing educated English speakers in Boston and Bombay, not to mention the greater gap dividing the dialects of the untutored.

Or to take a seemingly banal but in fact quite significant difference, even the educated Arabs of the Arabian peninsula tend to wear their distinctive indigenous dress, something long since abandoned by Arabs who have attained, or seek to "pass" as having attained, membership in the modern sectors of society.

As for Egypt, if ever there was a region destined to be a nation centuries before the word received its modern meaning it is surely this thin green strip of intensive settlement that Herodotus called "the gift of the Nile." Other Arab states have existed as politically autonomous units essentially within their present borders for longer than all but a handful of the world's nation-states. The Moroccan dynasty by one quite proper way of calculating is older than the British monarchy, and Morocco—never part of the Ottoman Empire as were most of today's Arab lands—boasts a distinctive political heritage. Tunisia has been a politically autonomous entity since the early eighteenth century and as the medieval *Ifriqiya* (adapted, of course, from the Roman *Africa*) has been a distinctive territorial and cultural unit for centuries. Nor should the Tunisian myth of being the heir to Carthage be overlooked.

The Arab region whose present political boundaries conform least well to a historical past is the Fertile Crescent. Ruled by the Ottoman Empire from the early sixteenth century until after the First World War, the Fertile Crescent not only had no political entity called *Palestine* (as Israel's Golda Meir and others have insisted) but no *Israel, Syria, Jordan,* or *Iraq* either. Lebanon comes closer to presenting a political and territorial continuity extending several centuries into the past, but historic Mount Lebanon was a much smaller and more culturally coherent entity than the greater Lebanon (created in 1920) of today's borders. Each of these contemporary political units can, of course, construct a myth of a national past, and that myth can be sustained, at least in part, by history.

The significant point is that, Israel aside, the political and intellectual leaders and opinion molders of the Fertile Crescent have been reluctant to accept the legitimacy of the present political arrangement. The prevailing opinion among Fertile Crescent Arabs can be compared to that in Italy or Germany before unification during the last century. There is a generalized desire to do away with existing "artificial" political borders and replace them with a political entity that is larger and stronger and that can command greater loyalty.

Yet this generalization does not do justice to the complex political and psychological reality. One must not overlook the Kurds, Druze, and

Alawites, and the several Christian minorities. Each such group, ever since that modern Western import, nationalism, arrived early in the nineteenth century, has been seized with the challenge of seeking political salvation either in a coherent but vulnerable small polity (for example, Kurdish or Druze or Shiite autonomy, a Palestinian state, a Christian "Zion" in Lebanon) or in a larger and more viable larger polity (Ottomanism yesterday, today Arabism or "greater Syria"). Saddam Hussein's Iraq has sought to develop a strictly Iraqi nationalism even while playing the card of defending Arabism against, first, non-Arab Iran and, then, the outside forces rallied to Operation Desert Storm (Baram 1991). Nor should the shifting currents of a narrowly Egypt-centered orientation as opposed to a larger Arabist approach among Egyptian political leaders and opinion molders throughout this century be overlooked.[3]

The result of these contradictory currents is that all Arabs, from the (Atlantic) Ocean to the Gulf (*min al Muhit ila al Khalij*), but especially those of the Fertile Crescent, have manifold reasons to see themselves as distinct from other Arabs. At the same time, all Arabs, especially those of the Fertile Crescent, are stirred by the myth of a greater unity that will restore tranquility at home and strength to confront the alien enemy. Before I suggest how these contradictions shaped the Arab response to the Gulf crisis, it is important to describe the Arab myth.

The Arab Myth

The broad lines of the Arab collective self-image can be presented in the following terms (with due allowance for the unavoidable distortion and potential for caricature in summarily depicting this or, for that matter, any group myth).

Well before the rise of Islam, the myth goes, in the seventh century of the common era, the Arabs existed as a people living in the Arabian peninsula and in important segments of the Fertile Crescent, bound together by their language and distinctive culture. Then God gave the final portion of his revelation (early parts of the revelation, consistent with what mankind was then able to absorb, included that which developed into Judaism and Christianity), choosing as messenger an Arab, Muhammad, who served as prophet to the Arabs first and foremost.

There followed the amazing spread of Arabism and Islam, bringing into existence a new culture, a new civilization—that of Dar al-Islam. Arabs—in the sense of all those who came to speak Arabic and embrace Arab culture—created the theological, philosophical, and political institutions underpinning Muslim civilization. This was the golden age, the centuries of the Prophet Muhammad, followed by the "rightly guided caliphs" and then the imposing political dynasties of the Umayyads (including the Umayyads of Spain) and the Abbasids.

This was a golden age in another important sense, for Arabs (still in the sense of Arabic speakers and those who had embraced Arab culture) translated into Arabic the best of the scientific and philosophical works of Greek and Eastern scholarship. It was, in turn, these Arabic translations, commentaries, and studies that medieval European scholars used in their effort to bring Europe out of the Dark Ages. Whatever borrowing the Arabs in modern times might take from the West can be seen as essentially repayment of an old loan.

In the centuries following the peaks of Abbasid power, however, political leadership passed from the Arabs to others, especially to various Turkic-speaking peoples who created several dynasties, the most long-lived of which was the Ottoman Empire. The Ottomans ruled over almost all of the Arab world for some four centuries, from the early sixteenth century until modern times. By the early nineteenth century, however, the Ottoman Empire had become "the sick man of Europe," no longer able to defend itself (including the Arab parts of the empire) against an advancing Europe. The Arabs, as a result, passed from one form of alien rule to another, from the Ottoman yoke to that of several different European empires. Only in modern times have the different parts of the Arab world been able to shake off the centuries of alien rule and achieve at least formal independence.

Even so, the myth concludes, the pattern in which the West seeks to divide and rule the Arab world continues. This is seen in the Western support of Zionism and the creation of Israel, a Western beachhead in the Arab world rather like that of the Crusades centuries earlier. It is seen as well in the way in which, since the Second World War, the United States has assumed the role of principal imperial overlord of the area (taking the mantle from the declining British Empire), resisting those who would unite the Arabs such as Nasser or those opposing Israeli domination such as the PLO or, in the eyes of many Arabs, those such as Saddam Hussein who threaten the Arab "puppets" of the West.

This Arab myth, like all myths, is a selective ordering of history. It is not scientific history. Some points are demonstrably false. For example, most Arabs during most of the long period of Ottoman rule did not see the Ottomans as aliens. For that matter they did not see themselves as Arabs groaning under alien Turkish rule. Such ethnolinguistic categories used as political labels were Western imports only slowly embraced, at first by a few members of the Westernized elites. Until quite recent times the more fundamental basis of social and political identification was according to religion. To the overwhelmingly Muslim Arab population the Muslim Ottoman dynasty could hardly be seen as alien. Even as late as the First World War, most Arabs of the Fertile Crescent identified politically more with the Ottomans than with forces of Sharif Hussein, leading the "Arab revolt" against "Turkish" rule.

Nevertheless, the Arab myth, like all such group myths, is not simply a fantasy. It offers a way of making sense of one's world based on a plausible and coherent interpretation of historical experience. As such, it serves to delimit the range of responses to any specific political crisis. In the context of the Iraqi invasion of Kuwait this works out as follows. The first response was that Saddam Hussein had violated a cardinal Arab precept. An Arab state must not attack another Arab state. This is enshrined in the charter of the Arab League, which, while hardly a powerful instrumentality for regulating inter-Arab politics, is of important symbolic value. Then it became increasingly apparent in the days following August 2, 1990, that the leader of the remaining superpower, President George Bush, was organizing resistance to the Iraqi invasion. Suddenly, the unacceptable behavior of an Arab despot, of a bully and a liar (Saddam Hussein having broken quite explicit commitments to various Arab leaders, such as Egypt's Hosni Mubarak), became obscured by actions of a powerful outsider seen as lining up Arabs against Arabs. This sufficed to bring the Arab myth into full play, triggering historical memories psychologically as fresh as yesterday. Let a few examples serve to evoke the resulting mind-set:

1. There were many American and Western efforts to line up opposition to Nasser, involving at different times President Camille Chamoun of Lebanon, King Saud of Saudi Arabia, Nuri al-Said of Iraq during the period of the monarchy, King Hussein of Jordan, and the Umma party leadership in Sudan. Equally, the entire thrust of the 1957 Eisenhower Doctrine was seen in the area, and rightly, as an effort to bring Nasser to heel.

2. America attempted, in cooperation with Israel and Iran, to support the Iraqi Kurds in the 1970s as a means of "disciplining" the Iraqi government.

3. American blandishments kept Anwar al-Sadat on track to a separate peace with Israel.

4. The American-brokered Israeli-Lebanese agreement of 1983 intended to present Syria and all other Arabs with a fait accompli, causing Lebanon also to break ranks with the Arab position and become virtually a client state of the Israeli-American combine.

5. The general American and Western tendency has been to favor the Arab haves against the Arab have-nots and also to support the more conservative Arab regimes that, without that outside backing, might well be pressured into implementing political reforms.

6. Often mentioned among Arabs during the time of the Gulf crisis was the historical parallel linking Muhammad Ali Pasha (who ruled Egypt from

the early nineteenth century until his death in 1849), Nasser, and Saddam Hussein, three Arab leaders whose strength and assertive policies induced the West to intervene.

It is irrelevant to observe that the above interpretations are not beyond challenge and that parts—in some cases major parts—of these interpretations are incorrect or at least inadequate. What does matter is that they are in accord with the Arab myth and sufficiently close to historical reality to be held without intellectual strain, not just by the masses but by the politically cosmopolitan and well informed.

Is it not possible to go one step further and suggest that emphasizing the intrusive outsider—a sort of *diabolus ex machina*—enabled many Arabs to avoid the psychic distress of sorting out difficult value judgments? The devil at home faded before the foreign devil. To some Arabs, Saddam Hussein ceased to be the bully and became Robin Hood. Others who realized that he continued to be a bully began to concentrate their concern, instead, on the more imposing outside bully.

From this point a number of subordinate interpretations become possible (and many were aired at the time throughout the Arab world):

- Given time, the Arabs would have been able to achieve a satisfactory Arab solution.
- The United States in a classic example of entrapment lured Saddam Hussein into attacking Kuwait so he could be destroyed.
- Saddam Hussein unmasked the true American motive by linking Iraqi withdrawal from Kuwait to withdrawal of foreign forces from Lebanon and the West Bank and Gaza. The United States is concerned only with protecting Israel, which means that no Arab power can be permitted to attain the strength to confront Israel.

This kind of thinking is explosively contradictory. On the one hand, by emphasizing the dominant role of the intrusive outsider this viewpoint pushes the responsibility onto that outsider, exonerating the Arabs of blame for their action or inaction. This can buttress political quietism. On the other hand, such thinking emphasizes the Arab perception of Arab impotence, which can only increase the desire to take, whenever possible, revolutionary action that can bring down the entire system. This brings us to yet another way of expressing the divergences, indeed the paradox, in Arab responses to the Gulf War. Is today's Arab world best described as beaten down by events into an enhanced sense of realism? Is the Arab world prepared to accommodate itself to the stubborn particularism and the limits on effective action that characterize the region? Or are the Arabs reacting in just the opposite fashion, becoming even more inclined to dream dreams—very revolutionary dreams?

The Arab Political Culture:
Yesterday and Today

Saddam Hussein's invasion of Kuwait came at a time when the legiti-macy of the Arab political order was at a very low ebb. At the interstate level, the Arab incapacity to achieve even a minimally acceptable solu-tion to the problem of the Palestinians was a constant and painful re-minder of failure. Arabs had fallen short time and again in confronting Israel militarily. Even the partial success of the October 1973 War (in which Egypt and Syria, although in the end militarily bested, fought courageously and well, inflicting casualties sufficient to show the en-emy that maintaining the status quo could be costly) was later wiped out. The 1982 Israeli invasion of Lebanon, culminating in the Israeli blockade and the bombing of a major Arab city, Beirut, unopposed by any Arab military action or threat, epitomized the futility of Arab diplomacy.

A History of Military Defeats

To the Arabs, Lebanon was merely the last in a long chain of military reverses at the hands of outsiders (and the Israelis, in Arab eyes, are clearly outsiders). Some of these defeats involved massive numbers, as in July 1967 or in the 1956 Suez War. Others were mere skirmishes but no less indicative of Arab impotence. These include Britain's ouster of the government of Rashid Ali in 1941 to return the Hashimite dynasty to Baghdad, and France's brushing aside of the brave but ill-prepared body of Arabs at Maysalun, which hoped to block the French drive from Lebanon against Damascus in 1920.

An educated Arab studying modern Arab history finds the entire nineteenth century almost too neatly divided by three cataclysmic Eu-ropean military victories over Arab forces: Napoleon's defeat of the Mamluks at the Battle of the Pyramids in 1798; French General Bugeaud's rout of the vastly larger Moroccan forces in the 1844 Battle of Isly (Isly became the Place d'Isly and a metro stop in Paris, as if to re-mind and taunt later generations of Arab students in France); and Kitch-ener's rout of the Mahdist forces in the 1898 Battle of Omdurman.

At one time the Arabs might have sought some solace for this string of military defeats in the knowledge that they were clearly outgunned by the technologically more advanced intrusive outsider, whose secure superiority was sharply etched in the bitter words of Hilaire Belloc: "Whatever happens, we have got / The Maxim gun, and they have not." What, however, can these later generations say about their military plight? They have been receiving the twentieth century's equivalent of

Maxim guns in abundance from both the Soviet bloc and the Western world since 1955—a long time ago. As a group, the Arabs have devoted a higher percentage of their gross national product to military expenditures than has any other region of the world. The bleak result has been virtually no change in the rough balance of military effectiveness between Arabs and their non-Arab potential or actual foes. Or if anything, it has become worse.[4]

That the perennial enemy, Israel, devotes an even higher percentage of GNP to the military[5] cannot ease the psychological pain—and there are just over 4 million people in Israel alongside over 200 million Arabs. Small wonder that Nasser grasped at the straw of claiming that the American air force secretly intervened in support of Israel on the first day of the June 1967 War.[6] Small wonder, as well, that whatever their other views Arabs could not but be heartened by the final ultimate victory of Iraq over Iran in that brutal eight-year war (even though the system-challenging Iranian revolution was not so easily demonized—especially among the have-nots—as were Israel and the United States).

The military denouement of Operation Desert Storm needs to be fitted into this historical legacy. Even those Arab leaders in the coalition against Iraq, even the other Arabs who had reason to believe that Saddam Hussein simply had to be brought to heel, must be haunted by the ghosts of past Arab military defeats. The categorical nature of that rout outstrips the battles of the Pyramids, Isly, and Omdurman. In psychological impact on the Arabs, only the June 1967 War would seem to be in the same league.

Of course, the armchair strategist can rightly say that the Arabs have never been united in any major military campaign, with the October 1973 War being only a partial exception that tests the rule. True. But the agonizing question for the Arabs remains. Why is this large Arab population, possessing the capital resources—thanks to OPEC oil wealth—needed to procure the requisite technology and with a not insubstantial cadre of highly educated elites, so divided? (Palestinians, for example, are reported to have the largest number of Ph.D. recipients, as a percentage of total population, of any group in the Middle East, including Israel.) Why this persisting weakness?

This question shifts the focus of attention from military to political performance, but the military establishment in many countries serves as a link between the two. Again, Nasser and the Nasser period provide a milestone. When the Egyptian Free Officers toppled Egypt's corrupt ancien régime in 1952, and—even more—after 1954–1955 as Nasser began to defy the West, it seemed to many Arabs and not a few outsiders that a modernizing praetorian guard might provide the kind of effective political leadership so clearly absent in earlier years. In 1958 a tangible step toward Arab political unity was taken with the union of Egypt and

Syria to form the United Arab Republic. The UAR's demise after three years shattered that dream. Nor does the performance of other regimes dominated by the military (such as the Syria of Hafiz al-Asad) provide a model that Arabs, given a choice, would follow.

The militarization of politics since World War II has consigned a number of civilian regimes to the dustbin of history (e.g., Iraq, Sudan, Libya, Syria, Egypt), but Arab experience would seem to confirm Napoleon's motto that one can do almost anything with a bayonet except sit on it.

Nor have the radical, populist parties of yesteryear worn well. Most sensitive Arabs in a position to express a free opinion would probably judge Baathism in practice as a terrible combination of murky nineteenth-century European romantic nationalism with twentieth-century fascism.

Arab Oil

Oil is a mixed blessing to the Arabs. It has made the Arab world a region that the outside world simply will not ignore, causing an updated "Eastern question" situation, in which regional disputes are internationalized. It was a favored arena of diplomatic jousting by proxy between the United States and the Soviet Union during the cold war, but the world after the cold war will continue to be involved. The political leadership in the area will continue to play off, line up, or seek to neutralize outside support.

Most of all, however, oil wealth in the past two generations has literally turned Arab world realities and perceptions upside down. Arabian peninsula Arabs were regarded with something approaching disdain by the urban and sedentary Arabs of the Nile Valley and the Fertile Crescent. Yet the Arabian peninsula Arabs were to some slight extent idealized in a time-warped way as a link to a long-lost past. It was the Arab equivalent of the American cowboy myth as exploited in fiction, films, and cigarette ads.

The Arab psychological reality is, however, better conveyed in the Arab nationalism that emerged during World War I, when Sharif Hussein and his family from the Hijaz assumed a leadership that Fertile Crescent Arabs thought rightly belonged to them. The reality is better conveyed in the sense of outrage Saad Zaghlul and his generation of Egyptians felt when comparing the political arrangements the British offered that same Sharif Hussein with what the British refused Egyptian nationalists. (That the arrangement with Sharif Hussein turned out badly for the Arabs is another matter.)

With oil wealth, those most "backward" Arabs of the Arabian peninsula were catapulted to the head of the queue. The most modern cities of the region sprang up in Riyadh, Jidda, Kuwait, Doha, and elsewhere, making the faded splendor of a Cairo look tawdry. Interestingly, in reaction, Cairenes—from taxi drivers to cabinet ministers—speak in unguarded moments with unconcealed bitterness about those "brother Arabs" who spend money with reckless abandon, "debauch our women," and generally make a nuisance of themselves.[7] Those same Cairenes seem capable of accepting with equanimity whatever outrageous behavior or plain bad manners Western tourists might display in public. There must surely be a psychological divide at work here. One pattern of wealth and its accompanying behavior (from Western tourists) is a given, the other (from Arabian peninsula Arabs) is not.

To get the full significance of these deep-rooted inter-Arab antipathies, it may well be necessary to bring to bear all that careful on-the-spot observation, plus insights gleaned from modern novels and psychological studies, can provide concerning who envies whom, the attitudes of declining old wealth toward parvenu wealth, and the like.

Moreover, Arabs outside of the Arabian peninsula have flocked to this modern El Dorado just as have millions of others from countries great and small, rich and poor. The psychological position of the Arab in this black gold rush is somewhat different, however. They, like the Americans and the Asians, are expatriates seeking a financial stake which will then be spent back home, but at the same time they are— according to the Arab myth—already at home. Unlike the Americans at the top of the privilege pyramid or the South Asian at the bottom, they measure themselves against their hosts. This, in turn, raises awkward questions that they have to suppress if they are to remain in the Arab El Dorado—Why should we be in service to them? Shouldn't the wealth from Arab oil be shared by all Arabs?

The Arabs of the Arabian peninsula, from their perspective, see themselves as sharing their wealth with their fellow Arabs but getting in return neither gratitude nor respect. They sense that many Arabs would be perfectly prepared, and deem it right, to strip them of their oil patrimony. The Iraqi invasion of Kuwait came as a surprise only because the Kuwaitis and others believed that the old regional and global power balances would prevent such action. Kuwaitis and, for that matter, Saudis and all members of the oil-rich Gulf Cooperation Council had no illusions about what other Arab leaders might do if they had the opportunity.

All this underlies the charade in which the oil-rich Arabs have been the most adamant in supporting Arab causes and have paid what amounts to ransom money to Arab states and political movements while at the same time keeping a watchful eye on their ally of last resort—the United States. Saddam Hussein's invasion of Kuwait and the resulting regional and world reaction exposed all these contradictions in their full nakedness.

The Arab reactions are best explained not logically but psychologically. Why would some or many (we remain poorly informed on this matter) Palestinians in Kuwait accept the Iraqi coup de main? Yes, the Iraqi invasion risked the very livelihood of Palestinians living in Kuwait. Yes, people in such a vulnerable position might be expected to hunker down and wait to see who wins. On the other hand, the invasion brought with it the immediate catharsis that comes from dropping all dissimulation. So too, the Palestinians in the occupied territories could welcome the fact that someone from the Arab side was actually doing something, even though the prospect that it would all turn sour was surely understood.

The Kuwaitis, for their part, and other Arabian peninsula Arabs will draw their own conclusions about the meaning of Arabism. This seems to suggest that the Arab world will never be the same after the Gulf War. We propose a more ambivalent outcome.

Farewell to Arabism?

Appraising the results of Saddam Hussein's invasion of Kuwait one year later, Bernard Lewis (1991) wrote:

> One myth that is being reluctantly relinquished concerns the strength and effectiveness of pan-Arabism. . . . No one could dispute the passionate belief of the Arabs in their common cultural identity; few would question the hatred for the West that still dominates much of their public life. Yet neither the passion nor the hatred has provided a usable political force. Time and time again the pundits have warned that this or that action or policy would raise the whole Arab world in arms against us—but it did not happen. . . . The Gulf crisis, which was essentially an interArab conflict into which outsiders were drawn, finally demonstrated the falsity of this belief, except perhaps for the most obdurate of pundits and the most amnesiac of audiences.[8]

By way of conclusion, I would answer the same ambivalent Yes, to some extent, balanced by No, not quite, to the Lewis formulation, as I have answered the question of whether the Arab world can be employed as a useful unit of analysis.

First, it is not quite clear just who these pundits are whose obduracy Lewis scathingly dismisses, but whoever they might be they must not be taking their cues from the Arabs involved, For at least since the 1960s a significant part of the Arab malaise has been the bitter realization that they cannot effectively unite against anybody or for any common purpose.

The Gulf crisis, I argue, exposed yet again the chasm separating Arabist imagery and Arab reality. Another chasm, well recognized in many quarters and at least suspected in others, was that separating the

policies and practices of Arab governments from the people over whom
they rule. This, all together, accounts for the confused and contradictory
reactions of the Arab public to Saddam Hussein's invasion and George
Bush's intervention.

Psychologists can help historians take the measure of especially dramatic moments when a whole people for a time seem smitten with a
strange combination of trauma and exaltation, of fear and hope. Comparative studies of such events suggest at least one common theme:
these are times when things become simplified into a Manichean struggle of good versus evil. And to the extent that the crisis became not Iraq
versus Kuwait but Saddam Hussein versus George Bush (and the crisis
was very much wrenched in that direction in public perception), many
Arabs either openly or quietly supported Hussein. They did so as an
outgrowth of frustrations with governments they do not respect, with
an unequal distribution of wealth, with a perception of being manipulated by outside powers, and with a feeling of impotence. Many Arabs,
at least in some part of their psyche, evinced a certain hope against
hope that this brutal man might transcend his past and become another
Saladin,[9] who succeeded in driving out the crusaders, not another
Nasser or Urabi Pasha or Rashid Ali.[10]

What now, after Saddam Hussein joins the ranks of those modern
Arab leaders cut down by outside force? (And in spite of the politically
important and militarily not insignificant contribution of several Arab
armies against Saddam Hussein, Operation Desert Storm was, in sheer
weight of numbers and leadership, an outside force.) Another tearing of
that already tattered garment we call Arabism? Yes, of course, but does
this mean that a new myth, or several different myths more attuned to
the political reality of inter-Arab divisions, will emerge? That is quite
possible.

Yet it should not be overlooked that the standard Arab myth fits
quite well an interpretation of the new political reality that began on August 2, 1990. The part of the myth that sees a divided Arab world unable
to work together and letting in outsiders all too eager to divide and
rule—favoring this or that Arab puppet and, in the process, exploiting
the Arab patrimony—accords with the pessimism and cynicism that af-
flicts the Arab world. If such tendencies prevail, then the myth will
emerge from the Gulf crisis strengthened in a way that can do harm not
just to Arabs but to others as well.

As such, it will be a "usable political force," alas, for all concerned.
It will be usable to future Saddam Husseins, usable to sincere but
no less dangerous peoples rendered fanatical by the gap between expectations and reality, usable also as a continuing check on pragmatic political leaders prepared to adjust to the world as it is, not as it
ought to be.

All of which is to suggest that it is important to be careful in interpreting the psychological patterns that explain the diverse Arab reactions to the Gulf crisis. It is no less important to be careful in evaluating the likely psychological patterns that remain after the crisis. Along with the risk of dangerous political leaders in this part of the world are other, more diffuse, more elusive risks, given the acute self-doubt, self-recrimination, and sense of impotence among these people. These risks are, at one extreme, continued terrorism and low-level, nihilistic violence and, at the other extreme, massive xenophobic outbreaks.

Policies now adopted by power wielders in the Middle East and in those parts of the world intimately involved in the Middle East will necessarily influence the next step of the collective Arab mind-set. Will it be a move toward pragmatic problem solving or a descent into a Hobbesian world of regional near anarchy with political life becoming increasingly "poor, nasty, brutish, and short"?

Epilogue

An eminent social scientists once noted, "Science might almost be defined as the process of substituting unimportant questions which can be answered for important questions which cannot" (Boulding 1977, 164). That whimsical statement consoles me. I cannot satisfactorily demonstrate the accuracy of the conclusions presented here. I am not aware of any important opinion polls of Arab publics in the period since August 2, 1990, and if such existed I would suspect the findings, given the political circumstances in most of the Arab states. Nor am I able to cite in-depth interviews or anthropological participant-observer studies specifically related to Arab attitudes concerning the Gulf crisis. My findings are based on what was available to me of publicly expressed or reported Arab opinion as conveyed by Arab publicists and opinion molders or reported by foreign journalists. The former also risk being obliged—if not indeed willing on their own accord—to follow the policy line of their government, whereas foreigners seldom have the time or the language aptitude to reach beyond official or quasi-official contacts.

Most of all, I rely on the indirect knowledge gained during thirty-eight years of following modern Arab history. Lord Palmerston once observed that when he wanted to be misinformed about a country he would ask the man who had lived there for fifteen years. What would he have said about someone who has lived in these countries for more than half of the period he specified and studied them and their inhabitants for more than double that?

"Important questions" that cannot be answered, but they need to be considered.

NOTES

1. After reading Margaret Mead's *And Keep Your Power Dry*. Cited by Clifford Geertz in Antoun and Harik (1972, 461).

2. According to the World Bank (1991, 204–05), Egypt has a per capital GNP of $640 as opposed to a whopping $18,430 for the United Arab Emirates. Sudan, for which 1991 data are not available, almost certainly has an even lower per capita GNP. The average 1991 per capital GNP for the oil-rich states of the Gulf Cooperation Council (Bahrain, Kuwait, Oman, Qatar, Saudi Arabia, and the United Arab Emirates) would be roughly $10,400 (per capita GNP for Bahrain and Qatar, not included in the World Bank report, is taken from the states of the world tables in the 1991 *Encyclopaedia Britannica Yearbook*).

3. The gyrations of Egyptian intellectual styles—not without impact on mass opinion—between the notion of Egypt as part of the Arab world and a more Egypt-centered ideological orientation, noted in passing in many works, would merit a specific in-depth study. Let a few hasty notations in chronological sequence serve to indicate the rich possibilities: Khedive Ismail in the 1860s proudly proclaiming that his country was no longer part of Africa but belonged to European civilization; the slogan Egypt for the Egyptians advanced by late nineteenth-century nationalists; Egyptian nationalist Saad Zaghlul's dismissal of the idea of cooperation with Arab nationalists in the early 1920s with the retort "Zero plus zero equals zero"; the Pharaonic Movement of the interwar years in Egypt; Nasser's moving Egypt to Arab world leadership, followed by the more narrowly Egyptocentric phase under Sadat, with a significant literary precursor in Husayn Fawzi, who wrote *Sindbad Al Masri* (the Egyptian Sindbad), which appeared late in the Nasser period. His book was a veiled criticism of Nasser's Arabism and a moving evocation of timeless Egyptianness in the form of short essays (or historical novellas) on Egyptian personalities and periods from the time of the pharaohs to the present.

4. Taking the annual military expenditures as a percentage of gross national product for the eleven years 1978 through 1988, as compiled in U.S. Arms Control and Disarmament Agency (1990), and compiling an average annual expenditure figure produce the following: Middle East, 12.8 percent; Africa, under 5 percent; NATO Europe, 8.7 percent; United States, just under 6 percent. Only the Warsaw Pact countries approached Middle Eastern expenditures during these years, with an average of 11.5 percent.

5. An average of 21.89 percent annual average for the same period. See U.S. Arms Control and Disarmament Agency (1990, 51).

6. It was Hosni Mubarak, then serving as an Egyptian air force officer, who when ordered to investigate the charge for the Luxor area truthfully reported that no non-Israeli aircraft had been sighted. See Al-Baghdadi (1977, vol. 2, 282).

7. This is based on personal observation and limited personal discussions with Egyptians in different walks of life at different time periods since the 1970s.

8. Lewis is, of course, here using "myth" in the sense of a misperception, not in the sociological sense of the presumably historically based explication of a group's belief system.

9. Saladin was a Kurd, an appropriate irony for this story, already shot through with irony.

10. The image of ultimate Middle Eastern success against the crusaders is often evoked in modern Arab political discourse in insisting that ultimately the Arab and Muslim world will again prevail against the intrusive Western and Israeli invader. See, for example, the earlier work by Emmanuel Sivan (1968). Urabi Pasha, a native Egyptian army officer resisting both the largely non-Egyptian ruling elite of the day and European pressures, had his movement brought to naught by the British military occupation of Egypt in 1882. Rashid Ali, as noted earlier, was ousted from power by British military intervention in 1941. And Nasser's imposing political ambitions were never successful militarily and ended in the crushing defeat at the hands of Israel in the June 1967 War.

REFERENCES

Al-Baghdadi, Abd al-Latif. 1977. *Mudhakkirat* (Memoirs). Cairo: Al-Maktab al-Masri al-Hadith.

Antoun, Richard, and Iliya Harik, eds. 1972. *Rural Politics and Social Change in the Middle East.* Bloomington: Indiana University Press.

Baram, Amatzia. 1991. *Culture, History and Ideology in the Formation of Ba'thist Iraq.* New York: St. Martin's.

Boulding, Kenneth. 1977 (1956). *The Image: Knowledge in Life and Society.* Ann Arbor: University of Michigan Press.

Lewis, Bernard, 1991. "What Saddam Wrought." *Wall Street Journal,* August 2.

Prothro, Edwin Terry. *Child Rearing in Lebanon.* Harvard Middle East Monograph Series. Cambridge: Harvard University Press.

Sivan, Emmanuel. 1968. *L'Islam et la Croisade: Ideologie et Propagande dans les Reaction Musulmanes aux Croisades.* Paris: Maisonneuve.

Spinoza, Benedict de. *Benedict de Spinoza: The Political Works.* Trans. and ed. A. G. Wernham. Oxford: Oxford University Press.

U.S. Arms Control and Disarmament Agency. 1990. *World Military Expenditures and Arms Transfers 1989.* Washington, D.C.

World Bank, 1991. *World Development Report.* Oxford: World Bank/Oxford University Press.

COMMENTARY ON PART I
Arab Perceptions of History and the Question of Identity

■

Dankwart A. Rustow

AS L. CARL BROWN rightly notes, there is a major difference between the actual course of history and the selective and interpretive way in which that history is perceived. In my comments I dwell specifically on factors in recent Arab history and some common interpretations of these factors that served as background both to Iraq's brutal attack on Kuwait and to some of the Arab and global responses to it.

The 1990–1991 Gulf War occurred in a unique global setting—the collapse of Soviet communism, a broad wave toward democracy from South America to East Asia, and an intensive process of international communication that tended to increase the concern of peoples, and hence of governments, with their standards of living and with human rights. And it may have been no coincidence that the first major international crisis to challenge the new global environment erupted among Arab countries.

One major feature of global change since World War II has been the exponential increase in foreign trade. Some of the most active aspects of that trade developed in petroleum and weapons—for which the Middle East happens to be the major exporting and one of the chief importing regions, respectively. The Middle East also had been a major focus of the Cold War ever since Stalin's 1945 threat to Turkey and Washington's response in the Truman Doctrine. The continuing conflict between Israel and its Arab neighbors also meant that the massive inflow of arms throughout the Cold War would be used not only for military coups (as in much of the Third World, including Arab countries) but also for actual military confrontations. And mounting OPEC oil profits only served to accelerate this militarization of the Middle East region.[1]

The global tide of democracy in the late twentieth century also emphasized the lingering problem of identity for Arab peoples from Morocco to Oman. For a people to be able to rule itself (which, after all, is the literal Greek meaning of *democracy*), there must be unquestioned agreement as to who are We, the people. In European countries, such as Britain, Sweden, France, and the Netherlands, the formation of nation-states generally preceded the transition from monarchy to oligarchy and democracy; and in overseas countries such as the United States, New Zealand, and Australia, the identity problem was solved by voluntary immigration and linguistic assimilation. By contrast, Italy and Germany in the midnineteenth century still found themselves divided into one or two dozen separate states each, and they were among the last European countries to develop representative government and the first to lapse into fascism and nazism.

Among Arabs, the emergence of solid feelings of national identity was delayed first by foreign rule—by the Turkish-Ottoman Empire until the nineteenth or early twentieth centuries and then by a long interval of Western domination. The fact that the Arab Middle East was the last major region to come under European imperial domination meant, on the one hand, that imperialism had become apologetic and hypocritical: Britain in 1882 established its "temporary" occupation of Egypt, which lasted until 1946; and the League of Nations mandates over Syria, Iraq, and Palestine supposedly were vehicles for training in self-government. It also meant that Western imperialism came to the Middle East at a time when ideas of modern nationalism had begun to take root throughout the region. And it is a tragic irony of history that the Palestinians, who early in the twentieth century were among the most nationally self-conscious Arabs, have remained the only Arab people without an independent country of their own.

Full independence for most Arab countries did not come until after World War II, and it left the Arab-speaking countries divided into more than twenty separate states, from Morocco to Oman and from the Sudan to Syria. When Spanish America was liberated from colonialism in the early nineteenth century, there was a brief dream of Simon Bolivar as "the liberator" and an attempt to establish a Gran Colombia including what today is Colombia, Venezuela, Ecuador, and Panama. Yet throughout the nineteenth century the absence of imperialist interference in most of South America helped to consolidate national identities despite the common links of language in the nine separate states, from Venezuela and Colombia to Chile and Argentina.

Among Arab countries, such a process of consolidation was prevented by involvement in the cold war and mounting militarization. Military leaders, such as Gamal Abdel Nasser in Egypt in the 1950s or Saddam Hussein in Iraq more recently, were not content to seize power at home but tempted to aggrandize their power further by appeals to anti-imperialism and Pan-Arabism—or, in the case of Hafez al-Assad, to a "greater Syria." Thus, not unlike Germany and Italy in the century before 1945, the Arab countries have been more inclined toward dictatorship and foreign aggression than democracy.

Recent Arab history also illustrates the psychological temptations to escape from intractable political problems of the present into past dreams of glory. Thus Saddam in the Gulf crisis alternately compared himself to Saladin, the Arab warrior who defeated the invasion of Christian crusaders, and Babylonian king Nebuchadnezzar. For the Arab people as a whole, of course, the centuries of the Arab-Islamic caliphate from the seventh to the fifteenth centuries A.D. represent the single most glorious phase of history. And indeed Arab linguistic identity was irrevocably shaped by the Koran, received as God's revelation by Muhammad. Hence, throughout the Arab world, Islamic movements retain a powerful appeal, particularly among the downtrodden poorer classes, compared to Pan-Arab or state-based nationalism.

The development of oil resources after the Second World War further accentuated inter-Arab divisions. Iraq and Algeria are the two Arab countries that have a sizable population as well as medium-sized oil reserves. But otherwise it happens that most of the oil was found in the least populated and most traditionally ruled countries, that is, the kingdom of Saudi Arabia and the coastal emirates from Kuwait to Oman. This meant that traditional monarchs were able to perpetuate their outdated systems of government, paying off both their own subjects and some of their envious neighbors with part of their accumulating oil money—whereas more populous Arab countries such as Egypt and the Sudan sank deeper and deeper into poverty. It also meant that the monarchies had to rely on foreign workers to run their booming oil economies—a circumstance that explains the deep resentment against Kuwait felt by many Palestinians and the pro-Iraq stance taken in the Gulf conflict by the PLO, Jordan (with its Palestinian majority), and Yemen. Note that, in contrast to the emirates, Saudi Arabia has been trying to avoid such problems by giving preference to non-Arab Muslim foreign workers, such as Bangladeshis.

These latent social tensions and contradictions provided much of the background for the Gulf crisis, which, as Brown notes, exposed once more the chasm separating Arabist imagery and Arab reality. The further question of whether developments in response to Iraq's attack on Kuwait will help bridge this chasm and provide an impetus for the ultimate integration of Arab states into a new regional and global order is one to which I shall return in my concluding comments on the chapters by Marvin Zonis and Alexander George.

NOTE

1. For the correlation between the petroleum profits and arms imports of Middle Eastern governments, see Rustow (1982), 278f, 282f.

REFERENCE

Rustow, Dankwart A. 1982. *Oil and Turmoil: America Faces OPEC and the Middle East*. New York: Norton.

PART II

∎

LEADERS, LEADERSHIP, AND DECISION MAKING

2

President Bush Goes to War: A Psychological Interpretation from a Distance

■

Stephen J. Wayne

THEY WERE momentous decisions: to defend our friends, to liberate Kuwait, and to do so with military force, if necessary. They were decisions that could make or break his presidency. Yet they did not seem difficult for Bush. In fact, they seemed easy in comparison to his delayed and timid response to the collapse of the Soviet empire in Eastern Europe in 1989, to his indecision and inaction during the failed Panamanian coup attempt in October of that same year, and to his equivocation and eventual retreat from his pledge not to raise taxes during the budget deficit negotiations conducted in the summer of 1990. And they seemed almost out of character for a cautious, calculating, politician, for a person who always prided himself on his ability to get along, for an individual who made reason and compromise into a strategy for achieving his policy objectives, for a pragmatist who never jumped far ahead of public opinion, and for a president who tended to react to events rather than anticipate them.

What explains Bush's decisiveness, boldness, steadfastness? Why did he respond so quickly, forcefully, and deliberatively to the events in the Gulf? How was he able to exercise such skillful leadership within the international community? Why was he so stable and steady throughout the crisis? In the words of Defense Secretary Richard Cheney, "He [Bush] was clear-headed when the future was murky. He never, ever wavered. He knew that he was going to get Saddam out of Kuwait one way or another" (Weymouth 1991).

Answering these questions requires us to look at the multiple influences on presidential decisions. Others have examined these generic factors in some detail and in doing so have contributed substantially to our understanding of decision-making theory (see especially, George 1980; Janis 1982; and Burke and Greenstein 1989). Their work frames many studies of presidential decision making, including this one.

My concern here, however, is not with decision-making theory per se. Nor do I examine all of the variables that affect presidential

29

decisions. Rather I focus on those that have directly impinged on Bush's decisions that culminated in the Persian Gulf War: his personality, his conceptual framework, his decision-making style, and his advisory apparatus. Obviously, I must also be sensitive to the environment in which events unfolded and for which the decisions were made. Taken singly and together, these factors go a long way toward explaining why a consensus-oriented president with a penchant for seeking approval through compromise would act so boldly and decisively in the Gulf.

There are several problems with this type of analysis in general and with mine in particular. It is likely to exclude or deemphasize nonpsychological factors that may have contributed to the president's decisions and actions. Similarly, it may also place the subject in an altogether too neat psychological framework in explaining his behavior. In the pursuit of brevity and simplicity, I have perpetrated both of these intellectual sins, omitting a detailed discussion of the politics and reducing Bush's psyche to a few dominant tendencies.

There is another obvious difficulty with my analysis: it was written at a distance. I was not privy to any of the president's private conversations, decisions, or reminiscences of them. Nor did I have the opportunity to interview those who *were* privy to them. As a consequence, my interpretation is based largely on public information in the print media, much of it impressionistic. To the extent that this information is incomplete or inaccurate, my analysis obviously suffers.

Finally, my interpretation of this information is obviously subjective. I had to decide what to include and what to exclude. In general, I have relied on firsthand reports of those who participated in the presidential advisory and decision-making process. Where this information was inadequate, I turned to the accounts of those who covered these decisions for the media (these secondary accounts are cited in the text). Readers should thus take my interpretation for what it is—a simplified and subjective psychological interpretation at a distance.

The Environment

The events in the Persian Gulf occurred within the context of both the end of the cold war and the persistence of deep, seemingly intractable, conflicts in the Middle East, both within the Arab world and between it and Israel. The Bush administration had little success in ameliorating these conflicts before the Persian Gulf War began. It may in fact have exacerbated them by its failure to develop and articulate a clear, consistent Middle East policy as the cold war was ending.

For Bush this environment was both liberating and constraining. It was liberating in the sense that the Soviet role was markedly reduced. No longer did the United States have to calculate Soviet interests, intentions, and military capabilities so carefully, if at all, when making its own Middle East policy decisions. Moreover, Soviet support in the United Nations, combined with China's decision not to oppose sanctions against Iraq, enabled the president to cloak U.S. policy in a UN flag, fashioning an international response under its auspices.

The collapse of the Soviet economy, the crumbling of its empire in Eastern Europe, and the unwillingness and incapacity of the Soviet Union to provide aid to client states in the Third World radically changed the balance of power in the Middle East. Although this change allowed, indeed required, the United States to exert more influence, it also heightened instability, perhaps encouraging Saddam Hussein to take advantage of a political vacuum in the area to try to achieve his territorial ambitions. The threat posed by the Iraqi invasion to moderate Arab states, to Israel, and to the American interests in that part of the world required an effective response if the United States was to continue to be influential in the Gulf and benefit from its superpower status. In other words, ignoring the Iraqi invasion was not a viable option for the president.

Moreover, the lack of discernible progress in the administration's diplomatic efforts in the Middle East, combined with ambiguity in its official policy pronouncements, contributed to the pressure on Bush to do something tangible. That the United States ambassador to Iraq, April Glaspie, may have inadvertently led Saddam Hussein to believe that the United States would not involve itself in a dispute among Arab states by her statement to him, "We have no opinion on the Arab-Arab conflicts like your border disagreement with Kuwait" (Woodward 1991, 212) increased this pressure.

In short, the ball was in Bush's court. He had to act, but he also had more leverage in responding, given the Soviet Union's weakness and its willingness to back U.S. efforts. This international environment created conditions that were conducive to a forceful U.S. response, conditions that were a necessary but not sufficient condition for understanding the president's decisions that ultimately culminated in war.

Personal Attributes

The Iraqi invasion of Kuwait presented Bush with a challenge from which he could not retreat. It was similar to those he had undertaken in the past, challenges he had used to prove himself to himself and, of course, to others.

The challenge facilitated Bush's decision making in the Gulf dispute and oriented him toward action. Not only did it play to his strengths—his experience and knowledge in foreign affairs, his contacts and personal relationships among world leaders, and his ability to engage in behind-the-scene diplomacy, much of it out of the range of public view—but it forced him to be more decisive and more assertive than he would have been under normal, noncrisis, less personally threatening circumstances.

For Bush, challenge has always been a critical, self-defining mechanism, which he has used to reinforce positive feelings about himself and to compensate for whatever self-doubts he may have. Personal challenges thus serve both ego-defensive and ego-supportive modes of adoptive behavior in Bush. Political scientist James David Barber (1989) describes these tendencies as Bush's mission orientation. Bush provides a similar description of his propensity for undertaking challenges in his acceptance speech to the 1988 Republican nomination convention. "I am a man who sees life in terms of missions . . . missions defined and missions completed" (Address to the Republican Convention 1988).

Bush's personal challenges have been recurrent throughout his life and have been self-generated. They include volunteering for the military upon graduation from high school rather than going directly to college, trying to make it on his own in Texas rather than going into his father's business, requesting a tough diplomatic assignment to China rather than a plush European ambassadorship, running for elective office in the Democratic state of Texas, and most important, persevering and remaining an active candidate for the presidency after two defeats for the Senate and one for the Republican presidential nomination.

Challenge for Bush becomes particularly critical to his self-image when doubts about his strengths (will and forcefulness in particular), his vision, or his decisiveness have been raised. My guess is that being assertive—his own man—has always been an issue, perhaps because Bush had such an opinionated, controlling, and economically and politically successful father, Prescott Bush. The challenge presents the son, George Bush, with the opportunity to demonstrate those traits that he believes his father had but he fears he himself may lack.

Moreover, in situations in which the challenge has occurred in full public view, Bush has tended to overreact by exaggerating these traits in his observable behavior. This overreaction occurred during the Persian Gulf crisis, but it wasn't the first time. During the 1988 presidential primary campaign *Newsweek* magazine raised the "wimp" issue in a cover story that questioned whether Bush was strong enough and tough enough to be president. The then vice president responded to that charge by launching a highly negative campaign, which many of his aides said was out of character with his usually friendly, agreeable style. There were hard handshakes, forceful pats on the back, and a more assertive tone in his voice. To reporters whose questions put him on the defensive, he would bristle with a frustrated "Look!", jabbing his left hand forward, often with a finger pointing toward the menacing journalist as if the beleaguered candidate were about to pull the trigger. Nor could Bush even bring himself to say the word *wimp*, referring to it as the unspeakable W word. When threatened, Bush tends to arch his back and play the tough guy.

The challenge may take on an added macho dimension when women are involved. Two meetings with Margaret Thatcher, which occurred during the very early stages of the Persian Gulf crisis when the president was still formulating his response, seemed to have a powerful impact on the president and his policy decisions. The first, a previously planned meeting in Aspen, Colorado, took place on August 2, following news of the invasion. According to reports, Thatcher told Bush that Saddam Hussein had to be stopped, and the only way to convince him that the West meant business was to send military forces to the Persian Gulf (Mathews 1991, 58). National Security Adviser Brent Scowcroft, who attended this meeting, stated in a television interview that Thatcher's advice reinforced Bush's inclinations to hang tough: "The president was ready for what Mrs. Thatcher came with, which was the same idea, that this is more than just another case of a border incursion or something, this has great significance. So there was a meeting of minds of the two. They were both heading in the same direction, and they tended to reinforce each other" (American Enterprise Institute 1992, program 1, 7).

In their second meeting, four days later, Thatcher reiterated her advice. It was during this meeting, held in the Oval Office and attended by other presidential advisors, that Secretary of Defense, Cheney telephoned the president from Saudi Arabia to tell him that King Fahd had agreed to the presence of U.S. forces in his country. One day later, Bush announced that he was ordering 125,000 troops to the Gulf.

From a psychological perspective, Mrs. Thatcher's presence and her advice to the president in the company of others had to be a powerful inducement for him to take a strong, unequivocal stand against Saddam Hussein. It certainly would have made it more difficult for Bush to have responded moderately and cautiously had he been so inclined. Thatcher's admonition to be tough helped toughen Bush. In 1984 he also felt obligated to demonstrate his macho character following a meeting with another woman, Geraldine Ferraro. The day after their televised debate, Bush told some longshoremen, "We tried to kick a little ass last night" (Drew 1985, 700).

The issue of whether Bush is sufficiently forceful and decisive had been raised by the media at least twice during his presidency prior to his actions in the Gulf. The first occurred during and after the failed coup attempt in Panama in October 1989. The United States had been asked by the rebels, who wanted to overthrow dictator Manuel Noriega, to give sanctuary to the families of the coup leaders and to prevent Noriega's forces, who were stationed outside Panama City, from returning to put down the rebellion. Bush decided to grant sanctuary but to use U.S. forces only to block access to or across U.S. military bases. When the coup failed, Bush was heavily criticized for his failure to take effective actions in support of the coup.

Less than three months later, following several incidents involving Americans living in Panama, including the killing of an unarmed marine, the beating of a navy lieutenant and the threatening of his wife with sexual abuse by Panamanian defense forces, the president ordered a full-scale military invasion, replete with 24,000 U.S. troops, to remove Noriega.

The second accusation of indecisiveness occurred during the summer of 1990. The issue at that time concerned the budget deficit and whether the president would support a tax increase as part of a bipartisan compromise. Bush vacillated in public, wanting neither to repudiate his campaign pledge of no new taxes nor kill the compromise. During this period of indecision when "Read my lips" became "Read my hips"—a humorous quip uttered by a jogging president to avoid a reporter's question of whether or not he would raise taxes—Bush's approval rating began to decline. Criticism by conservative Republicans after he made his decision further accelerated the drop in the president's popularity.

It was probably more than coincidental that Bush was strong and steadfast in foreign affairs during and after the period when he was perceived as weak and equivocal in domestic affairs. Whether he would have been as decisive and steadfast in the absence of a major domestic confrontation is, obviously, impossible to say. My guess, however, is that the criticism of the president at home, particularly from the Right, and his inability to respond successfully to that criticism within the domestic political context in which he found himself, led to compensatory behavior that reinforced his need to appear decisive and resolute in his Gulf decisions.

Of course, as president, Bush was in a much stronger position to respond to an international crisis than to a domestic political problem, which for most Americans had not assumed crisis proportions. A president has greater latitude as foreign policy leader and greater constitutional authority as commander in chief than he does within the domestic policy realm. Moreover, in national security affairs, and especially at the onset of a crisis, interest group pressures tend to be muted and public support magnified. All of this works to the initial advantage of the president.

In addition, his foreign policy stance in the Gulf offered the president some political dividends. It enabled him to increase his public approval, deflect conservative Republican criticism, and divert the media's focus from domestic issues and partisan political gridlock to national security issues, bipartisan policy, and presidential leadership.

From the beginning of the Persian Gulf crisis, the normally cautious, compromising Bush did not waver from his resolve to get Iraq out of Kuwait. In a meeting with senior aides the day after the invasion, the president reportedly responded to Treasury Secretary Nicholas Brady's assertion that the United States could adjust to the higher oil prices that were expected by saying, "Let's be clear about one thing: We are not here to talk about adapting. We are not going to plan how to live with this" (Friedman and Tyler 1991). On Sunday afternoon, August 5, Bush reiterated his determination to get Iraq to withdraw, but this time he did so in public. Pressured by reporters to discuss how he was going to accomplish an Iraqi withdrawal, the president, waving his finger, replied angrily, "Just wait. Watch and learn. I view very seriously our determination to reverse this aggression. . . . This will not stand. This will not stand, this aggression against Kuwait" (Woodward 1991, 260). In listening to the president's reaction, one senior presidential advisor remarked to a *Newsweek* reporter that "he heard a tone that he hadn't heard before" (Mathews 1991, 59).

Bush's spontaneous public comments limited his options, which on an unconscious level, he may have wished to do. Both Powell and Scowcroft were surprised that he had been so specific so quickly (Woodward 1991, 260; American Enterprise Institute 1992, program 1, 15). But it was not the first time that Bush had used categorical language or made impulsive decisions from which he found it difficult to retreat. His selection and then unwavering support of Dan Quayle, John Tower, and more recently, Clarence Thomas, his damning description of Manuel Noriega, and his "Read my lips—no new taxes" pledge during the 1988 presidential campaign are other illustrations. Although the president later toned down his public reaction to the Iraqi invasion, undoubtedly on the recommendation of some of his principal advisors, he did not retreat from his stated goal of liberating Kuwait.

In addition to the assertiveness evident in the tone and substance of his words, Bush also exhibited extremely high energy levels during this initial phase of the crisis. Determined not to be a prisoner of the White House as Jimmy Carter had been during the early months of the Iranian hostage crisis, Bush frantically recreated during a planned August vacation in Maine with "nonstop golf and horseshoes, iron-man jogs, marathon sets of tennis, relentless trolls for bluefish aboard his speedboat, Fidelity" (Mathews 1991, 60).

It is difficult to know how much of this frenzied activity was abnormal for Bush, given the activity he usually displays at work or play (he is not a person who likes to sit alone or be idle). Some of it may also have been the consequence of an overactive thyroid. Nonetheless, the frustration of being unable to reverse the Iraqi action during this early period, particularly in light of political disappointments and setbacks at home, may have contributed to his near manic activity during the early stages of the crisis. Leaving Kennebunkport for Washington on August 10, eight days after the invasion, Bush told reporters, "Life goes on. Gotta keep moving. Can't stay in one place all the time" (Trafford 1991).

In summary, Bush's psychological defense mechanisms, particularly those associated with challenges to his strength and decisiveness, exacerbated by the public dimensions of the issue, drove him toward the military option as an instrument of diplomacy. Angry at Saddam Hussein and probably at himself for being duped, for believing that it was just bluff, Bush reacted to the invasion of Kuwait as if he had been personally challenged by Saddam. His reaction quickly took on the character of a personal vendetta, replete with mean and nasty rhetoric, revealing an underlying personality response that "nice guy" Bush had also exhibited in his past.

Bush's negative campaign against Michael Dukakis, to which he assented after being shown clips of Democrats mocking him at their convention, his rage against Noriega after the failed coup and the state of war that the Panamanian legislature declared against the United States,[1] even the planned personal attack against Dan Rather during their live interview illustrate a tendency of Bush to personalize confrontations when he feels that his back is against the wall. Dick Cheney, who had known Bush for over twenty years, described this aspect of the president's personality to Admiral Crowe, chairman of the Joint Chiefs of Staff, in a private conversation. "You know the President has got a long history of vindictive political actions," Cheney warned, indicating to Crowe the names of a few individuals who had crossed Bush and paid for it (Woodward 1991, 89).

Not only did Bush's personal rancor toward Saddam Hussein color his rhetoric—he couldn't or wouldn't even pronounce the Iraqi leader's name correctly—it also quickened his reaction and hastened his resolve not to let the bully get away with it. It energized an already energetic president to initiate an incredible amount of personal diplomacy. And it contributed to Bush's no-nonsense response.

Ironically, some of the same personality needs that led Bush to his decisions that culminated in war may also have contributed to his abrupt decision to end it. Having struck at the villain and taught him a lesson, humiliating him on the battlefield, Bush became increasingly sensitive to the additional human suffering that would have occurred had the war continued. Thus when General Norman Schwarzkopf indicated in a news conference that Iraqi forces were in full retreat and at the mercy of the military coalition, Bush abruptly called a halt to the hostilities. He had made his point; he had proved himself. He did not want to be a conquering hero; he did not want to be responsible for unnecessary loss of life.[2]

From a military perspective, the war had been won. There did not seem to be much more to accomplish. From a political perspective, the achievements were substantial: Kuwait had been liberated and the coalition held together under the leadership of the United States; but Saddam Hussein remained in power. Bush had met his challenge but had not removed his challenger. This result, from a psychological perspective, was unsatisfying. In his first news conference held after the war, Bush appeared to be depressed, prompting one reported to ask him why he seemed so somber. The president replied: "Well, to be very honest with you, I haven't yet felt this wonderful euphoric feeling that many Americans feel. I feel much better about it today than I did yesterday. But I think it's that I want to see an end. You mention World War II. There was a definite end to that conflict. And now we have Saddam Hussein still there, the man that wreaked this havoc upon his neighbors. We have our prisoners still held. We have people unaccounted for." (News Conference 1991). Bush's attention and energy level dissipated quickly after the termination of hostilities.

Observable Emotions

The president experienced significant mood swings throughout the period that began with the Iraqi invasion and continued through the commencement of hostilities. The emotions may indicate some of the internal conflicts he was experiencing and trying to resolve during this period.

Roller coaster emotions are not abnormal in a situation in which rapidly changing international events build and then destroy hopes for achieving political objectives peacefully. In Bush's case, these mood swings also occurred during the period when he was diagnosed as having Graves' disease. According to endocrinologist Dr. Terry Taylor of the Georgetown University Medical Center, people with Graves' can feel very good and then very bad. Their emotions fluctuate. "There are a lot of ups and downs" (Trafford 1991).

Three periods in particular evidenced mood swings in addition to the mixed feelings he displayed at the end of the war.[3] The first occurred in August when the crisis began. During that period the president's mood shifted from anger, perhaps at being tricked by Saddam Hussein, to determination that the aggression must be reversed, to sober recognition that the events could culminate in war, to happiness on August 6 when King Fahd approved the presence of U.S. armed forces in Saudi Arabia (Woodward 1991, 273), to euphoria when the UN Security Council voted on August 25 to authorize the use of force to enforce an international trade blockade with Iraq (ibid., 285).

The second series of mood swings occurred in November after the president approved the deployment of an offensive force in the Gulf. Decided on October 30 during a two-hour White House meeting, it was announced two days after the midterm elections to try to depoliticize the reaction to the decision. Nonetheless, what followed was a barrage of criticism from Democratic members of Congress and increased public apprehension as shown by public opinion polls. Bush seemed bewildered by the criticism, perhaps because the decision seemed like such an obvious one to him. He reacted incredulously and defensively to the reservations and objections that were raised. "What am I doing wrong?" he asked a group of friends and advisors in a White House meeting (Mathews 1991, 64).

Bush became more subdued following his Thanksgiving trip to Saudi Arabia to visit American troops. *Newsweek's* Tom Mathews reports that the president's breezy style gave way to shortness and tenseness with his staff, a product perhaps of the emotions he felt when talking directly to young men and women whose lives would be affected by his decisions (ibid.). Bush had been visibly moved by his visit. Kenneth T. Walsh (1990–1991, 25) senior foreign policy editor of *U.S. News and World Report,* writes that "he was misty-eyed at nearly every stop." On three occasions, Walsh states, "Bush deleted from speeches a story he found particularly heartrending, the tale of a woman soldier recently sent to the desert. A TV reporter had rushed up to her and demanded to know, 'Do you know why you're in the Gulf?' The soldier replied, 'I'm here for my kids.' Managing a weak smile, Bush told aides, 'I can't handle this,' and excised the passages."

By the end of December, Bush had made peace with himself. In meetings with friends and senior White House staff following a twelve-day Christmas vacation at Camp David, the president indicated that he had resolved the matter in his own mind and was content with his decision. "If I have to go, it's not going to matter to me if there isn't one congressman who supports this, or what happens to public opinion. If it's right, it's gotta be done," he said. Mathews writes, "As the January 15 deadline approached, the old Bush was back, friendly, confident, almost eerily serene" (Mathews 1991, 65).

Conceptual Framework

Bush's mind-set, his interpretation of events, and his understanding of his responsibilities as president reinforced his decision to respond force-

fully to the Iraqi invasion. The cognitive framework in which he interpreted and evaluated the events in the Persian Gulf was World War II.
It was the good war, fought for the right reason—and it was successful.

Bush's participating in World War II had to be one of the most formative experiences of his life, his rite of passage into manhood. Volunteering upon graduation from preparatory school, Bush was the
youngest naval aviator in the war. Shot down over the Pacific, he faced
capture and possible death but was rescued; his crew, however, was
lost. Bush explained his own rescue and his buddies' deaths as divine
fate. "In my own view," he stated, "there's got to be some kind of destiny and I was being spared for something on earth" (Hyams 1990–1991,
31). This powerful personal experience seems to have strengthened his
conviction in the righteousness of the war, the importance of patriotism, the inevitability of sacrifice, and the ultimate triumph of good
over evil.

Bush saw and rationalized Saddam Hussein as the embodiment of
evil and Hussein's actions as blatant aggression that needed to be reversed. He believed concessions to Hitler at Munich were a fundamental cause of World War II and saw a similar danger in the Gulf if the
United States did not demonstrate its determination to stand firm
against the aggressor (Walsh 1990–1991, 25). As one unnamed presidential advisor put it: "He is deathly afraid of appeasement. His generation
had to fight a war over it, and he feels that if he blinks today, he will be
leaving a real mess for the next generation to clean up. You have an aggressor and if you let him take over Kuwait, he will take over Saudi Arabia and become the paramount power in the Middle East" (ibid.). Bush
said as much himself, soon after the Iraqi invasion. To a friend during
his vacation in Kennebunkport, he said, "We are going to try to do this
without war. But if the choice were war or appeasement, I would opt for
war and risk losing the '92 election" (Weymouth 1991).

Bush saw military force as a legitimate and effective instrument of
foreign policy, one that he had used successfully three times during his
first year in office: to free American military advisors threatened by a
rebel capture of the hotel in which they were staying in El Salvador, to
demonstrate support for Corazon Aquino's government in the Philippines, which was threatened by a military coup, and to remove Manuel
Noriega from power in Panama. Each successful use of military force by
the president, combined with the criticism he received for not aiding a
failed coup attempt in Panama in October 1989, seemed to reinforce his
judgment that the military option was viable, could be employed to further U.S. interests, and would be tolerated by the international community and supported by the American people.

Moreover, Bush believed, as did many of his advisors, that Saddam
Hussein would not be foolish enough to oppose the military might of

the United States and its coalition partners.[4] Until the outbreak of hostilities, he thought there was a reasonable chance that the U.S. buildup would cause Saddam Hussein to back down. But the threat had to be credible. "We saw it as part of the Big Bluff," was the way one of his aides put it (Mathews 1991, 64). Up to the end he hoped that the threat of force would work. To a reporter in December he said: "My gut says he will get out of there" (Friedman and Tyler 1991). Obviously, the president and his advisors seriously misjudged Saddam Hussein.

In addition to perceiving the events in the Persian Gulf within the context of World War II, Bush reinforced his perspective by removing all ambiguity from the situation and reducing it to a simple case of good versus evil. In an interview with *U.S. News and World Report* conducted approximately one month before the commencement of hostilities, Bush stated: "I've got it boiled down very clearly to good and evil. And it helps if you can be that clear in your own mind" (Walsh 1990–1991, 24). He used much the same language with David Frost in a December 16, 1991, interview in which he defended the need to stand firm against Saddam Hussein. "It won't happen if we compromise. When you have such a clear sense of good and—good versus evil. We have such a clear moral case. . . . It's that big. It's that important. Nothing like this since World War II. Nothing of this moral importance since World War II. (Woodward 1991, 343–44).

To a senior staff meeting in January, following his decision to commence hostilities if Iraq did not withdraw by the middle of the month, he noted, "For me it boils down to a very moral case of good versus evil, black versus white" (Mathews 1991, 65) And to the Congress in his address after the war, Bush reiterated his rationale. "The recent challenge could not have been clearer. Saddam Hussein was the villain, Kuwait the victim. To the aid of this small country came nations from North America and Europe, from Asia, South America, from Africa and the Arab world—all united against aggression" (Address to Congress 1991).

If simplification was one technique Bush used to impel and justify his decision to liberate Kuwait with force, if necessary, his sense of the inevitability of confrontation with Iraq was another. As early as August 1990, he told one of his aides, "One of these days, there's going to be a provocation, and we are going to have to go" (Mathews 1991, 60). Restoring the balance of power in the Middle East was of primary concern to the president, who was upset by Iraq's military buildup, territorial ambitions, and increasingly bellicose actions.

Throughout the crisis, Bush's rhetoric reinforced his perception of the nature and gravity of the problem, the inevitability of conflict, and the morality of using force to achieve his ends. He was sensitive to the human costs and to the personal sacrifices that war required. What helped him accept and justify these costs, however, was the suffering that had occurred and, he thought, would continue to occur in Kuwait[5] and potentially in other countries threatened by Iraq, if its aggression was not reversed. He cited the Amnesty International report on Iraqi human rights abuses in Kuwait, calling it "devastating, absolutely devastating. It helps one come to a recognition that the right must prevail" (Walsh 1990–1991, 24).

The president became even more emotional in his recorded interview with David Frost. Describing the Amnesty report, Bush said:

> Oh David, it was so terrible, it's hard to describe. . . . The torturing of a handicapped child. The shooting of young boys in front of their parents. The rape of women dragged out of their homes and repeatedly raped and then brought into the hospital as kind of basket cases. The tying of those that are being tortured to ceiling fans so they turn and turn. The killing of a—of a Kuwaiti and leaving him hanging—this is a picture of this one— leaving him hanging from a crane and so others will see him. Electric shots to the private—shocks to the private parts of men and women. Broken glass inserted in—jabbed into people. I mean, it—it is primeval. And I—I'm afraid I'd get very emotional if I described more of it. (Woodward 1991, 343)

To the Reverend Edmond Browning, presiding bishop of the Episcopal church, who came to the White House in early January to urge patience, Bush said: "You should read the Amnesty International report. Then you tell me what I should do" (Mathews 1991, 64).

Bush had reacted in a similar way to the killing of a military officer and to the harassment of another officer and his wife in Panama prior to the U.S. invasion. "This guy [Noriega] is not going to lay off. It will only get worse," he said, in approving the military operation to remove him from power (Woodward 1991, 171).

In short, it was Bush's sensitivity to innocent human suffering and his anger against the perpetrators of that suffering that helped him rationalize a war in which thousands of others, both civilian and military, would likely be hurt or lost. As noted earlier, it was also that sensitivity to needless violence and injury that contributed to his decision to end the war quickly, after Kuwait had been freed, and not decimate the retreating Iraqi army.

To minimize American casualties during the war, the president accepted the recommendations of his military advisors that a large, technically superior U.S. force had to be employed. The Panamanian experience indicated the tactical advantage that could result from overwhelming force and firepower. In contrast, the slow buildup of U.S. armed forces in Vietnam and the limits that were imposed on the air operations in Southeast Asia indicated to Bush the danger of doing too little, too late. In his *U.S. News and World Report* interview Bush recounted the lessons of Vietnam: "Never fight a war with a hand tied behind your back. Never send a kid into a battle unless you're going to give him total support. Don't send a mission in undermanned. Don't send them in where you tell commanding officers what they can't do" (Walsh 1990–1991, 24). Bush believed U.S. involvement in Vietnam had been justified but that the strategy and tactics were wrong.

Meeting with congressional leaders in the White House on November 30, Bush heard strong reservations about the huge buildup of U.S. forces in the Gulf and the potential resort to force to oust Iraq from Kuwait. Replying to these fears, the president said: "We don't need another Vietnam War. World unity is there. No hands are going to be tied behind backs. This is not a Vietnam. . . . I know whose backside's at stake and rightfully so. It will not be a long, drawn-out mess" (Woodward 1991, 339). He repeated this to congressional leaders in a January 3 White House meeting: "There is no Vietnam parallel" (ibid., 335).[6]

In summary, Bush's understanding of recent history, reinforced by his own experiences in World War II, provided him with a cognitive framework for perceiving and interpreting events. It also helped him arrive at a very unambiguous judgment—that aggression had to be stopped, by force if necessary.

What this framework did not clarify for Bush, however, was the seemingly irrational behavior of Saddam Hussein. In the face of such a large, unified world force, how could Hussein hope to prevail? Throughout the crisis, the president and his aides never seemed to appreciate the non-Western culture and mentality that lay behind Saddam's actions. To Bush, Saddam was an Adolf Hitler pure and simple, a ruthless dictator bent on extending his territory, his resources, and his influence, and he was doing so by brutalizing those who stood in his way.

This same cognitive framework did not provide direction or facilitate decisions for Bush after the war. The vanquished were hurt but not decimated. There was no unconditional surrender, no war trials. Saddam remained in power, suppressing the internal uprisings that the coalition's victory and Bush's rhetoric had helped to encourage. The administration spoke hopefully, even whimsically, of Hussein's removal by elements in the Iraqi armed forces, but to no avail. Bush had underestimated Saddam's staying power in Iraq much as he had underestimated it in Kuwait.

The good-evil dichotomy, which helped Bush justify military action, gave way to the ambiguities and machinations of Middle East politics and behind-the-scenes diplomacy, while American public opinion, which had coalesced over the war and become euphoric in victory, reasserted its traditional anti-interventionist posture. With his World War II analogy less relevant for the postwar period, Bush returned to the intrigues of Middle East politics and to demands of the population in the

United States that its military forces be withdrawn and that the president address concerns that were closer to home. In a speech before Congress and to the American people, Bush declared victory and began the pullout.

Decision-Making Style

Presidents are expected to be chief policy makers. They are expected to make the final decisions that set their course of action. In most cases they do so with the help of an array of political advisors and policy experts. Over the course of their administrations they tend to interact with a designated group on designated issues. Their patterns of interaction vary, however, with their styles and personalities.

Dwight Eisenhower met with his cabinet and National Security Council to set administration policy. John Kennedy did not like meetings of formal bodies, preferring instead to discuss issues with those White House aides and department heads whom he knew and trusted and whose advice he valued. Richard Nixon met even less regularly with groups of policy experts. He depended on Henry Kissinger, his national security advisor, to inform and advise him in foreign affairs and to oversee the operation of the White House's national security policy mechanism. Gerald Ford also relied on Kissinger, who had become secretary of state in 1973, for policy advice but relieved him of day-to-day responsibilities as Assistant for National Security Affairs, appointing Kissinger's deputy, Brent Scowcroft, to that position. Jimmy Carter's advisory mechanism was more ad hoc. Carter relied on National Security Advisor Zbigniew Brzezinski and to a lesser extent on Secretary of State Cyrus Vance for information and advice, with other White House aides, such as presidential assistant Hamilton Jordan, also participating in presidential-level discussions.

Much has been written about Ronald Reagan's national security advisory system: the turnover of his White House advisors (he had seven in eight years), the tensions between those advisors and his two secretaries of state, and the president's dependence on his staff and his lack of oversight of them. The Iran-contra affair painfully illustrated the dangers of a dependent, hands-off president.

Bush's decision-making style and advisory system contrasted markedly with his predecessor's. Whereas Reagan was underinformed, disengaged, and a reluctant and slow learner with little foreign policy experience, Bush was well informed, knowledgeable, experienced, and involved. Unlike Reagan, Bush's primary interest and policy emphasis during the first years of his presidency had been foreign affairs. He conceded little to his advisors and did not delegate the making of middle-level strategic decisions to them nearly as much as Reagan did.

Not only did Bush's style differ from Reagan's but so did the composition and internal relationships of his advisory group. Reagan depended on a group of advisors in national security affairs whose personalities often clashed with one another, whose institutional allegiances were allowed to dominate their policy advice, and who were not close friends with one another or with the president, although they were loyal to him. Bush's advisors were cut from a different cloth. Pragmatists, friends, men who had worked with Bush in the past, they respected his knowledge of world events, deferred to his policy inclinations and judgments, and easily adapted to his conciliatory style. Institutional allegiances were downplayed. Harsh words and personal confrontations gave way to a group ethos of congeniality and consensus.

Journalist Bob Woodward describes the early meetings of Bush's Persian Gulf advisors as follows: "When the principals met, Bush liked to keep everyone around the table smiling—jokes, camaraderie, the conviviality of old friends. Positions and alternatives were not completely discussed. Interruptions were common. Clear decisions rarely emerged. Often Powell and Cheney returned from these gatherings and said to each other, now what did that mean? What are we supposed to do? Frequently, they had to wait to hear the answer later from Scowcroft or the television" (Woodward 1991, 302). Woodward also recounts Colin Powell's frustration with the unfocused atmosphere of these White House strategy meetings. "The mood in the Oval Office was too relaxed, too convivial—the boys sitting around shooting the shit before the weekend. . . . It was a general problem with these kinds of meetings, Powell felt. Often they had no beginning, middle or end. They would kick the ball around. Feet would be up on the table, cowboy boots gleaming" (ibid., 41).

There were also allegations from others outside the inner circle that departmental staff were not adequately consulted and that a formal process in which options were systematically examined and consequences weighed was not followed (ibid., 320). Although it is unclear whether the tight-knit group that advised the president limited the range of information he received, there is some evidence that the decision-making environment worked to narrow the options that were presented to the president and to mute the passions with which those options that lay outside the group's consensus were articulated. There were no devil's advocates.

The discussion in late October on whether to continue to rely solely on the economic sanctions or additionally introduce an offensive capability is a case in point. As reported by Woodward, Colin Powell, chairman of the Joint Chiefs, favored containment and reliance on the sanctions to force Iraq out of Kuwait but was either unable or unwilling to state his personal opinion to the president. Rather, Powell presented the containment strategy as one option, first to individuals within the inner circle and then to the group itself with the president in attendance. No one in the group voiced support for containment. The president seemed to preempt further discussion by his comment, "I don't think there is time politically for that strategy" (ibid., 41–42, 229–302).

The decision to end the war was apparently made even more quickly. It occurred at a meeting in the Oval office in which the president and his principal advisors all agreed that the major military objectives of the war had been achieved (American Enterprise Institute 1992, program 3, 18). According to Brent Scowcroft, a critical factor that affected that decision was how the world would react to continued hostilities. "The picture that would have come of the carnage on the road and fighter planes and tanks and artillery blasting people who were simply trying to get away would have been—would have left a bad taste on what was otherwise a brilliant military operation" (ibid.).

Bush's strong public statements and his personal resolve to stand firm seem to have streamlined group discussions, casting them within the framework of the president's inclination to hang tough. There was not a careful, systematic analysis of Bush's predispositions, assumptions, and attitudes. On the question of sanctions, for example, Scowcroft made it clear to other members of the inner circle that the president had made up his mind and that his views could not be changed (Woodward 1991, 301). Although Bush was reported to be a good listener in the strategy sessions of the group, his personal experience and knowledge in foreign affairs, which exceeded that of most of the participants with the possible exception of Scowcroft, may have worked to intimidate those who might have fundamentally disagreed with the president, if there was anyone who did fundamentally disagree. On the issue of tactics, however, particularly military tactics, the president seemed more open to recommendations.[7]

Of all the president's advisors, Scowcroft seemed to be the most influential. He was also the person most clearly on the president's wavelength. He briefed Bush daily, coordinated the administration's response on the Persian Gulf, and spoke for the president. He also had Bush's ear. Scowcroft's conservatism, his military background, and his previous national security experience oriented him toward a tougher posture in dealing with Saddam Hussein than some of the president's other advisors, especially Secretary of State James Baker.

The close-knit composition and operation of Bush's advisory group did not challenge but reinforced the president's psychological inclinations and cognitive perspective. The group provided the president with an informational and psychological support mechanism, one that enabled him to act more quickly, more decisively, and more confidently than he might otherwise have acted had there been serious internal disagreements and dissent.

Obviously, by keeping the group small, homogeneous, and friendly, Bush minimized additional stress that might have been generated by a multiple-advocacy approach, one that could have questioned his judgments. In the end, he reconfirmed his judgment more or less alone, secluded at Camp David without meetings of his advisory group.

What the gang of eight (Bush, Scowcroft, Baker, Cheney, Powell, Dan Quayle, John Sununu, and Robert Gates) did not provide, however, was a basis for understanding Saddam Hussein and for anticipating the American public's reaction to the doubling of U.S. forces in the Gulf and Congress's hesitation in authorizing the president to use force. The president continued to express surprise and anger at Saddam Hussein and surprise and resentment at the opposition at home, dismissing the former as irrational, delusionary, and dictatorial and the latter as ill informed and partisan. Bush also claimed that, as commander-in-chief, he did not need a congressional authorization to use armed forces in the Gulf, but he obviously needed political support at home to maintain the international coalition abroad.

Once hostilities began, the success of the effort, measured in military terms—the liberation of Kuwait from Iraqi occupation with a minimum loss of American lives—silenced most of the opposition. Consensus among his advisors helped to produce a favorable military strategy, although it seemed less able to aid the president in determining U.S. objectives in the aftermath of the war, much less in achieving them. Policy objectives became muddled; mixed signals were given to Iraqi dissidents; for a time, Kuwaiti revenge on Palestinians was ignored. It was only after repeated attempts by Iraq to thwart the United Nations' inspection of its biological, chemical, and nuclear facilities that the prewar Bush returned to issue a veiled warning to cooperate or else.

Conclusion

Understanding Bush's personality, cognitive framework, and decision-making apparatus is critical to explaining the president's decisions that culminated in war in the Persian Gulf. Bush's psychological needs, his worldview, and his advisory system all contributed to his strong, steadfast, and decisive response to Iraq's invasion of Kuwait, a response somewhat at variance to his normal, cautious, conciliatory style. This response resulted in a policy that enabled the president to achieve some of his principal objectives: the liberation of Kuwait, the reduction of

Iraq's military capacity, and the reestablishment of the balance of power in the Middle East. However, that same personality, cognitive structure, and decision-making apparatus may have also inhibited the achievement of other goals, namely the removal of Saddam Hussein and the securing of a more permanent peace in the region in which the rights, interests, and needs of minorities were protected.

NOTES

I wish to thank the following individuals for their thoughtful critiques of the draft of this chapter: Jeff Fishel, Alexander George, Fred Greenstein, Erwin Hargrove, Barbara Kellerman, Lawrence Korp, Robert Lieber, and James Pfiffner.

1. As vice president, Bush had headed the Reagan administration's effort to combat illegal drug trafficking into the United States. His frustration with Noriega was undoubtedly heightened during this period and reinforced during the campaign, when Bush's Democratic rival, Michael Dukakis, made the administration's continued backing of Noriega an issue.

2. There were, obviously, strategic and military considerations involved that affected his decision as well. Reports (which later turned out to be exaggerated) indicated that much of Iraq's military equipment had already been damaged or destroyed, and thus the Iraqi military no longer seemed to be a threat to others in the region. Moreover, the president did not want the U.S. military to become an occupying force in Iraq and a target for terrorists. Nor did he want to decimate that country so that a vacuum would be created in the region in which other countries might vie for power.

3. The evidence here is sketchy and anecdotal. The mood swings discussed are those reported in the print media. At this writing I am not aware of any systematic analysis of the president's moods during this period.

4. The president had lost confidence in economic sanctions by the end of the September, when he received a secret CIA report indicating that the sanctions would not remove Saddam Hussein "in the short or medium term" (Mathews 1991, 62). That William Webster, director of the CIA, was later to testify that the economic sanctions were having an impact did not seem to alter Bush's judgment that sanctions alone would not be sufficient to get Iraq to withdraw from Kuwait within a reasonable time frame.

5. Bush's special feeling for the people of Kuwait strengthened his resolve. The company with which he associated in Texas was the first American one to drill oil wells in Kuwait. Bush has maintained contacts with some of the Kuwaitis he knew from his Texas days.

6. Geopolitical factors, prevalent in the Gulf crisis, were very different from those that affected the Vietnam confrontation. Vietnam was a guerrilla war; the Persian Gulf was not. Enemy forces in Vietnam proved to be less vulnerable to air attack than they were in the Persian Gulf. The Soviet Union and China supported the North Vietnamese; no major country, much less a superpower, supported Iraq.

7. It is interesting to note that in the area of military affairs, where the president lacked detailed knowledge and experience, he deferred to his commanders. Other than issuing the directive to commence hostilities, approving the overall plan and its timing, and declaring certain targets to be off-limits, Bush left the conduct of the war to the military.

REFERENCES

Address to Congress. 1991. Transcript. *New York Times,* March 7.

Address to the Republican Convention. 1988. Transcript. *New York Times,* August 19.

American Enterprise Institute. 1992. *The Gulf Crisis: The Road to War.* Washington, D.C.: American Enterprise Institute. Transcript of three-part television series aired in January 1992.

Barber, James David. 1989. "George Bush: In Search of a Mission." *New York Times,* January 19.

Burke, John P., and Fred I. Greenstein. 1989. *How Presidents Test Reality.* New York: Russell Sage.

Drew, Elizabeth. 1985. *Campaign Journal: The Political Events of 1983–1984.* New York: Macmillan.

Friedman, Thomas L., and Patrick E. Tyler. 1991. "From the First, U.S. Resolves to Fight." *New York Times,* March 3.

George, Alexander L. 1980. *Presidential Decisionmaking in Foreign Policy: The Effective Use of Information and Advice.* Boulder: Westview.

Hyams, Joe. 1990–1991. "Excerpt from *Flight of the Avenger.*" *U.S. News and World Report,* December 31–January 7, 26–31.

Janis, Irving L. 1982. *Groupthink.* Boston: Houghton Mifflin.

Mathews, Tom. 1991. "The Road to War." *Newsweek,* January 28, 58–65.

News Conference. 1991. Transcript. *New York Times,* March 2.

Trafford, Abigail. 1991. "Me, Bush, and Graves' Disease." *Washington Post,* March 31.

Walsh, Kenneth T. 1990–1991. "Commander in Chief." *U.S. News and World Report,* December 31–January 7, 22–25.

Weymouth, Lally. 1991. "How Bush Went to War." *Washington Post,* March 31.

Woodward, Bob. 1991. *The Commanders.* New York: Simon and Schuster.

3

The Defining Moment of Saddam's Life: A Political Psychology Perspective on the Leadership and Decision Making of Saddam Hussein During the Gulf Crisis

■

Jerrold M. Post

■ AFTER A LONG, defiant, and self-justifying speech by Iraq's pre-eminent leader in October 1991, one of Saddam Hussein's syco-phantic subordinates proclaimed "Iraq is Saddam; Saddam is Iraq." This characterization accurately captures one of the most unusual aspects of the Gulf crisis: the degree to which the personality and political behavior of key individual actors played crucial roles in the decision to enter the war. This political psychological analysis of Saddam Hussein first summarizes his basic political personality as demonstrated throughout his stormy political career.[1] It then considers the manner in which the unfolding crisis engaged Saddam's political psychology and contributed to his decision to enter the war. It also considers the effects of the personalization of the conflict between Saddam Hussein and President Bush.

Iraq's invasion of Kuwait produced a torrent of inflammatory rhetoric concerning the irrationality of its president, Saddam Hussein, who was characterized as "the madman of the Middle East." In fact, irrationality in the seat of power is inconsistent with sustained leadership. An examination of Saddam's life and career reveals a judicious political calculator who is by no means irrational but is dangerous in the extreme. While not a psychiatrically disturbed individual out of touch with psychological reality, he is often out of touch with political reality. Although he is a rational political calculator, it is because of his often flawed perception of political reality that he frequently miscalculates.

A Flawed Perception of Political Reality

There is a dual contribution to Saddam's flawed perception of political reality. His worldview is narrow and distorted, and he has scant experience out of the Arab world. He reportedly has traveled out of the Arab world on only two occasions: a trip to Moscow and one brief trip to Paris

49

in 1976. His only sustained experience with non-Arabs was with his Soviet military advisors.

More important, he is surrounded by sycophants who are cowed by
Saddam's well-founded reputation for brutality and are afraid to contradict him. He has ruthlessly eliminated perceived threats to his power
and equates criticism with disloyalty.[2] One criticizes a policy or decision
of Saddam at great peril, for to criticize Saddam is to be disloyal, and to
be disloyal is to lose one's job or one's life.[3]

Thus he is deprived of the check of wise counsel from his leadership
circle. This combination of limited international perspective and a sycophantic leadership circle has led him to miscalculate on a number of
occasions. But when he has miscalculated, he has demonstrated a pragmatic bent and has been able to reverse his course if it was proving to be
counterproductive. When circumstances forced him to reverse his
course, it did not mean the end of his drive for increased power, however, but merely a temporary delay.

Unbounded Drive for Power

In fact, Saddam epitomizes Lasswell's *homo politicus* or power seeker
who displaces a private need onto a public object and rationalizes it as
being in the public good (Lasswell 1960). Saddam has explained the ex-
tremity of his actions as president of Iraq as justified by the "exceptionalism of revolutionary needs." But this is the ideological rationalization
for a lifelong pattern: all actions are justified if they are in the service of
furthering Saddam Hussein's drive for power and messianic ambition.

Saddam's entrance into this world could scarcely have been more
traumatic. When Saddam's mother was pregnant with him, Saddam's
father died. Information from an Israeli source indicates that Saddam's
one-year-old brother also died, of cancer, during the pregnancy. Saddam's mother became seriously depressed and may have attempted
suicide. She subsequently married her husband's brother, according to
tradition. He reportedly was abusive both psychologically and physically to Saddam. Such painful early experiences strongly suggest that
underlying Saddam's grandiose facade is a foundation of insecurity,
what Heinz Kohut (1971) characterizes as "the wounded self."

After this extremely traumatic early childhood, at the age of ten Saddam fled his family home to the sanctuary of his maternal uncle Kairallah. Kairallah, a fiery Iraqi nationalist, was to steep young Saddam in
dreams of glory and inculcate in him the belief that he was destined to
follow in the path of Nebuchadnezzar, the king of Babylonia who con-
quered Jerusalem (586 B.C.) and Saladin, who regained Jerusalem in
1187 by defeating the Crusaders. Kairallah tutored his young charge in

his view of Arab history, a view consistent wi.
Baath party. In this view, the problems of the Arab
by divisions within the Arab world and oppression by
the hands of the Ottomans, then by the Western mana.
monarchies ruled by Western interests, and finally by the es.
of the Zionist entity. The justice that the Arab people deserve.
come when a strong leader unified the Arab world and expelled th.
eigners. Saddam was destined to fill that role.

Kairallah not only instructed his young charge in his role in history;
he also taught him to hate. In 1981, Saddam republished a pamphlet
written by his uncle entitled *Three Whom God Should Not Have Created:
Persians, Jews, and Flies.* Saddam's grandiose dreams were given further
shape during his adolescence. He was fifteen when Gamal Abdel
Nasser led the Free Officers' Revolution, displacing the corrupt King
Farouk and providing a heroic model of an Arab strongman and Pan-
Arab leader. From Nasser, Saddam learned that only by courageously
confronting imperialist powers could Arab nationalism be freed from
Western shackles. Nasser was to become Saddam's hero and model.
This is of crucial importance in understanding the dynamic of the con-
flict in the Gulf.

Revolutionary Opportunism

A matter of continuing significance throughout the Gulf crisis and its
aftermath has been the question of Saddam's trustworthiness and how
he lives up to or breaks commitments. An examination of the historical
record demonstrates a convincing pattern. The 1968 coup in which the
Baathists seized control of Iraq could not have succeeded without the
crucial secret assistance of the military intelligence chief, Abdul Razzaz
al Nayef. In gratitude for services rendered, within two weeks Saddam
had arranged for the capture and exile of Nayef, and subsequently he
ordered his assassination.

This act is a paradigm for the manner in which Saddam has rewarded loyalty and adhered to commitments throughout his career.
Commitments and loyalty are matters of circumstance, and circumstances change. If an individual or a nation, no matter how loyal, is perceived as an impediment or a threat that individual or nation will be
eliminated violently without a backward glance, and the action will be
justified by "the exceptionalism of revolutionary needs."

Saddam's practice of revolutionary opportunism has another important characteristic. Just as previous commitments must not be permitted
to stand in the way of Saddam's messianic path, neither does he persist
in a particular course of action if it proves to be counterproductive for

the ideology of the
rld were caused
'siders, first at
, then the
ishment
would
for-

es a course of action he pursues it
ce he struggles all the harder, con-
gments. But if circumstances dem-
ich he often has—he is capable of
nces Saddam does not acknowledge
elf as adapting flexibly to a dynamic
logical flexibility concerns his vow
Arab waterway. In 1988, the bloody
inconclusive end when a cease-fire
g an advantage, retaining control of
rritory and the strategic Shatt al Arab
ed 500,000 troops on the disputed
llow Iran sovereignty over any part of
the waterway. Until Iran ag___ ɔ forgo its claim to the disputed waterway, Saddam declared he would not agree to an exchange of prisoners nor would he withdraw from Iranian territory.

But revolutionary pragmatism was to supersede this vow. Shortly after invading Kuwait, Saddam desperately needed the 500,000 troops
tied up in the dispute to reinforce his troops in Kuwait against the anticipated military reaction. On August 15, 1990, Hussein agreed to meet
Iranian conditions, promising to withdraw from Iranian territory, agreeing to an exchange of prisoners and, most important, agreeing to share
the disputed Shatt al Arab waterway. "Never" is a short time when revolutionary pragmatism dictates.

The decision to release all foreign hostages in December 1990 also fit
this pattern. As with other misdirected policies in the past, Saddam initially pursued his hostage policy with full vigor, despite mounting evidence that it was counterproductive. When it became clear to him that
it was not protecting him from the likelihood of military conflict, as initially conceived, but was actually unifying the international opposition,
he reversed the policy. The announcement that he would release the
hostages followed an especially strong statement by Secretary Baker
concerning the use of "decisive force," but the anger of his former ally,
the Soviet Union, was undoubtedly important as well. Moreover, the
timing was designed to play on both perceived internal divisions within
the United States as well as to magnify differences in the international
coalition—a demonstration of the sense of timing of the shrewdly manipulative Saddam.[4]

Dreams of Glory

Saddam's pursuit of power for himself and Iraq is boundless. In fact, in
his mind, the destiny of Saddam and Iraq are one and indistinguish-

able. His exalted self-concept is fused with his Baathist political ideology. Baathist dreams will be realized when the Arab nation is unified under one strong leader. In Saddam's mind, he is destined for that role. Nothing must be permitted to stand in "the great struggler's" messianic path as he pursues his.(and Iraq's) revolutionary destiny, as exemplified by this extract from Saddam Hussein's remarkable "Victory Day" message of August 8:

> This is the only way to deal with these despicable Croesuses who relished possession to destroy devotion . . . who were guided by the foreigner instead of being guided by virtuous standards, principles of pan-Arabism, and the creed of humanitarianism. . . . The second of August . . . is the legitimate newborn child of the struggle, patience and perseverance of the Kuwaiti people, which was crowned by revolutionary action on that immortal day. *The newborn child was born of a legitimate father and an immaculate mother. Greetings to the makers of the second of August, whose efforts God has blessed.* They have achieved one of the brightest, most promising and most principled national and pan-Arab acts.
>
> Two August has come as a very violent response to the harm that the foreigner had wanted to perpetrate against Iraq and the nation. The Croesus of Kuwait and his aides became the obedient, humiliated and treacherous dependents of that foreigner. . . . What took place on 2 August was inevitable so that death might not prevail over life, *so that those who were capable of ascending to the peak would not be brought down to the abysmal precipice,* so that corruption and remoteness from God would not spread to the majority. . . . Honor will be kept in Mesopotamia so that Iraq will be the pride of the Arabs, their protector, and their model of noble values. (FBIS, Middle East Report, August 9, 1990)

An Extremely Dangerous Political Personality

There is no evidence that Saddam is constrained by conscience in pursuing his messianic dreams; his only loyalty is to Saddam Hussein. In pursuing his goals, Saddam uses aggression instrumentally. He uses whatever force is necessary and will, if he deems it expedient, go to extremes of violence, including the use of weapons of mass destruction. His unconstrained aggression is instrumental in pursuing his goals, but it is at the same time defensive aggression, for his grandiose facade masks underlying insecurity.

While Hussein is not psychotic, he has a strong paranoid orientation. He is extremely suspicious, ready for retaliation, and not without reason, sees himself as surrounded by enemies. But he ignores his role in creating those enemies and righteously threatens his targets. The conspiracy theories he spins are not merely for popular consumption in the Arab world but genuinely reflect his paranoid mindset.[5] He is convinced that the United States, Israel, and Iran have been in league for the purpose of eliminating him and finds a persuasive chain of evidence for this conclusion. His minister of information, Latif Nassif Jassim, who was responsible for propaganda and public statements, probably helped reinforce Saddam's paranoid disposition and in a sense was the implementer of his paranoia. Saddam's conspiracy theory has been printed in a glossy pamphlet, the publication and dissemination of which preceded the invasion of Kuwait.[6]

It is this political personality constellation—messianic ambition for unlimited power, absence of conscience, unconstrained aggression, and a paranoid outlook—that make Saddam so dangerous. This constellation of personality traits has been conceptualized as malignant narcissism by Otto Kernberg (1975). It is the personality configuration of the destructive charismatic who unifies and rallies his downtrodden supporters by blaming outside enemies. While Saddam is not charismatic in the classical sense of the term, this psychological stance is the basis of Saddam's particular appeal to the Palestinians, who came to see him as a strongman who shared their intense anti-Zionism and would champion their cause.

Ranks Himself as One of the Great Leaders of History

Saddam Hussein genuinely sees himself as one of the great leaders of history, ranking himself with Nasser, Castro, Tito, Ho Chi Minh, and Mao Zedong, each of whom he admires for adapting socialism to his environment, free of foreign domination. Saddam sees himself as transforming his society. He believes youth must be "fashioned" to "safeguard the future" and that Iraqi children must be transformed into a "radiating light that will expel" traditional family backwardness. Like Mao, Saddam has encouraged youths to inform on their parents' antirevolutionary activity. Just as giant pictures and statues of Mao were placed throughout China, so too giant pictures and statues of Saddam abound in Iraq. Asked about this cult of personality, Saddam shrugs and says he "cannot help it if that is what they want to do."

Saddam Hussein is so consumed with his messianic mission that he probably overestimated the degree of support for him in the rest of the Arab world. He may have assumed that many in the Arab world, especially the downtrodden, shared his views and saw him as their hero. He was probably genuinely surprised at the nearly unanimous condemnation of his invasion of Kuwait in the Arab world and may have indeed persuaded himself of his oft repeated assertion that the moderate Arab leaders and the United Nations are controlled by the United States but that the people support him.

The Quintessential Survivor

It is not by accident that Saddam Hussein has survived for more than two decades as his nation's preeminent leader in this tumultuous part of the world. While he is driven by dreams of glory, and while his political perspective is narrow and distorted, he is a shrewd tactician with a capacity for patience. Able to justify extremes of aggression on the basis of revolutionary needs, if the aggression is counterproductive he has shown a pattern of reversing course when he has miscalculated, waiting until a later day to achieve his revolutionary destiny. His drive for power is not diminished, only deflected, by these reversals.

Saddam Hussein is a ruthless political calculator who will go to whatever lengths are necessary to achieve his goals. But his survival in power—with dignity intact—is his highest priority. Saddam was characterized by Soviet Foreign Minister Primakov and others as suffering from a *Masada complex*, preferring a martyr's death to yielding. This is assuredly *not* the case, for Saddam has no wish to be a martyr, and survival is his number one priority. A self-proclaimed revolutionary pragmatist, he did not want a conflict in which Iraq would be grievously damaged and his stature as a leader destroyed.

While Saddam's advisors' reluctance to disagree with Saddam's policies contributes to the potential for miscalculation, nevertheless, by providing information and assessments, his advisors are able to make significant inputs to the accuracy of Saddam's evaluation of Iraq's political-military situation.

As the crisis escalated, despite their reluctance to disagree, several officials expressed their reservations about remaining in Kuwait. Saddam dismissed them, replacing them with family members and known loyalists. It was as if he were drawing in the wagons. A measure of the stress on Saddam, it suggested that his siege mentality was intensifying. The fiercely defiant rhetoric was another indicator of the stress on Saddam, for the more threatened Saddam feels, the more threatening he becomes.

Under Saddam's opulent palace was a mammoth bunker fortified with steel and prestressed concrete. The architecture of this complex is Saddam's psychological architecture: a defiant, grandiose facade resting on the well-fortified foundation of a siege mentality. Attacked on all sides, on the eve of the conflict Saddam remained besieged and defiant.

Although throughout his career he has used whatever aggression was necessary to consolidate his control and ensure his survival, the key to his survival in power for twenty-two years is his capacity to reverse course when events demonstrate that he has miscalculated. Saddam is by no means a martyr; he is, indeed, the quintessential survivor.

How can it be, then, that this self-described revolutionary pragmatist, faced by an overwhelming array of military power that would surely deal a mortal blow to his nation, entered into and persisted in a violent confrontational course?

Why the Revolutionary Pragmatist Did Not Reverse Course

Throughout his twenty-two years at the helm of Iraq, Saddam Hussein had languished in obscurity, overshadowed by the heroic stature of other Middle Eastern leaders such as Anwar Sadat and the Ayatollah Khomeini. With the invasion of Kuwait, for the first time in his entire career Saddam was exactly where he believed he was destined to be, a world-class political actor at center stage commanding world events, with the entire world's attention focused upon him. When his rhetoric was threatening, the price of oil rose precipitously and the Dow Jones average plummeted. He was demonstrating to the Arab masses that he was an Arab strongman with the courage to defy the West and expel foreign influences.

Saddam was at the center of international attention, his appetite for glory was stimulated, and he would not easily yield the spotlight. But even though he wanted to remain at center stage, he would not do so at the expense of his power and prestige. Saddam would withdraw only if he calculated that he could do so with his power and honor intact and ensure that the drama in which he was starring would continue.

Honor and reputation must be interpreted in an Arab context. Saddam had already achieved considerable honor in the eyes of the Arab masses for having the courage to stand up to the West. It should be remembered that even though Egypt militarily lost the 1973 war with Israel, Sadat became a hero to the Arab world for his willingness to attack—and initially force back—the previously invincible forces of Israel. Qaddafi mounted an air attack when the United States crossed the so-called line of death. Even though his jets were destroyed in the ensuing conflict, Qaddafi's status was raised in the Arab world. Indeed, he thanked the United States for making him a hero to the Third World.

Thus Saddam could find honor on the eve of conflict. He could claim that he had already stood up to the united forces of the imperialist West for five months and had forcibly called attention to the Palestinian question. His history reveals a remarkable capacity to find face-saving justification when reversing his course in very difficult circumstances. But this time he did not reverse himself. Why?

An analysis of his political personality and his past pattern of reversals indicates that he could again reverse himself if he concluded that *unless* he did so his power base and reputation would be destroyed and *if* by so doing he could preserve his power base and reputation. This is a double conditional, and neither condition was fulfilled.[7]

In the first place, given the psychological rewards Saddam was obtaining from the crisis, he would need to be convinced to a fare-thee-well that destruction of his power base was certain unless he withdrew. It is by no means clear that he was so convinced. Again, cultural factors may well have contributed to his underestimating the seriousness of President Bush's expressed intentions. Defiant rhetoric was a hallmark of this conflict and lent itself to misinterpretation across cultural boundaries. The Arab world places great stock in expressive language. The language of courage is a hallmark of leadership, and there is great value attached to the very act of expressing brave resolve against the enemy, in and of itself. There is no necessary connection between courageous verbal expression and the act threatened. Nasser gained great stature from his fiery threats to make the sea red with Israeli blood.

Even though a statement by Saddam was made in response to the United States, when Saddam spoke it was to multiple audiences; much of his language was solipsistic and designed to demonstrate his courage and resolve to the Iraqi people and the Arab world. By the same token, Saddam probably heard the Western words of President Bush through a Middle Eastern filter. When a public statement of resolve and intent was made by President Bush, Saddam may well have discounted the expressed intent to act and calculated that President Bush was bluffing. It is also possible he downgraded the magnitude of the threat, likening the threatened response to the characteristic Arab hyperbole.

The Fulfillment of His Messianic Dreams of Glory

More important, the dynamic of the crisis affected Saddam. What began as an act of naked aggression toward Kuwait was transformed into the defining moment in the drama of his life. Although he had previously shown little concern for the Palestinian people, the shrewdly manipulative Saddam had wrapped himself and his invasion of Kuwait in the Palestinian flag. The response of the Palestinians was overwhelming. They saw Saddam as their hope and their salvation, standing up defiantly and courageously to the United States to force a just settlement of their cause. This caught the imagination of the masses throughout the Arab world and their shouts of approval fed his already swollen ego.

Intoxicated by the elixir of power and the acclaim of the Palestinians and the radical Arab masses, Saddam may well have been on a euphoric high and optimistically overestimated his chances for success, for Saddam's heroic self-image was engaged as never before. He was fulfilling the messianic goal that had obsessed him—and eluded him—throughout his life. He was actualizing his self-concept as leader of all the Arab peoples, the legitimate heir of Nebuchadnezzar, Saladin, and especially Nasser.

His psychology and his policy options became captives of his rhetoric. He became so absolutist in his commitment to the Palestinian cause—to not yielding Kuwait until there was justice for the Palestinian people and UN Security Council Resolutions 242 and 338 had been complied with—that it would have been extremely difficult for him to reverse himself without being dishonored—and to lose face in the Arab world is to be without authority.[8] Unlike past reversals, these absolutist pronouncements were in the full spotlight of international attention.

The Bush administration's insistence on "no face-saving" only intensified this dilemma. It was extremely important not to insist on total capitulation and humiliation, for this could drive Saddam into a corner and make it impossible for him to reverse his course. He could withdraw from Kuwait only if he believed he could survive with his power and his dignity intact, but the highly personalized confrontation between President Hussein and President Bush increasingly converted this contest into a zero-sum game.

The personal aspect of the confrontation, often waged through the media, was to play a major role in the spiraling dynamic of the conflict and was to become the defining moment in the drama of Saddam Hussein's life. It was the long-delayed ascension to the pantheon of heroic world leaders; Saddam was finally receiving the recognition he deserved, and the leadership mantle of Nasser was finally his. Each time President Bush portrayed the conflict in highly personal terms, it gave Saddam an opportunity to emulate Nasser and to demonstrate his courage in defying the hated outsiders, a strong value in his Baath ideology.

When the conflict was presented as the civilized world versus Saddam, as the United Nations versus a rogue nation, it hit a tender nerve in Saddam, who has always sought respect as a major world leader. He in turn would try to diminish the international consensus and instead attempt to cast the conflict as a struggle between Iraq and the United States and, even more personally, as a struggle between the gladiators: Saddam Hussein versus George Bush. When the struggle became thus personalized, it enhanced Saddam's reputation as a courageous strongman willing to defy the imperialist United States.

More often than not, President Bush accepted Saddam's invitation to personal combat, insufficiently stressing the role of the international coalition he had so painstakingly assembled. It has been suggested by several scholars of the American presidency that the Gulf crisis represented a defining moment for President Bush, the climax of the drama of his political life, the moment to finally put a lie to the accusations concerning the indecisive nature of his leadership that had followed—and haunted—him throughout his career.

Thus it may be that a remarkable and crucial aspect of the unfolding dynamic of the crisis in the Gulf was that it represented for the two principal actors—President Saddam Hussein and President George Bush—the defining moment of their leadership careers, and as such neither protagonist could back down or be seen as weak and indecisive. Saddam would have experienced backing down as capitulating, anathema in his political psychology.

Might Saddam have pulled back if he had a graceful way out, if he could have preserved a degree of dignity? What if the United States had not rejected the French compromise? What if the United States, rather than insisting on "no linkage," had made it clear that after Iraq withdrew the United States would take the lead in initiating peace talks between the Palestinians and the Israelis, so that Saddam could in effect say that he had fulfilled his public commitment? Saddam's range of responses was sharply limited by the nature of the struggle. He perceived that his adversary was demanding unconditional surrender—and that Saddam could not do.

Moreover, Saddam probably did not believe that his power base would be preserved if he left Kuwait. Saddam doubted that the aggressive intention of the United States would stop at the border of Iraq. For years he had been convinced that a U.S.-Iran-Israeli conspiracy was in place to destroy Iraq and remove Saddam from power. The tenor of the inflammatory rhetoric issuing from Washington and the revelation by Air Force Chief of Staff General Michael Duggan (subsequently dismissed) of the plan to personally target Saddam would have done nothing to diminish his doubts. The administration's assurances that their aggressive intentions stopped at the borders of Kuwait, that their only goal was to enforce Iraq's withdrawal from Kuwait, would have fallen on deaf ears even if Saddam did not have a paranoid orientation. Just because he was paranoid doesn't mean they weren't out to get him.

By late December any semblance of diplomatic flexibility had disappeared, and Saddam seemed intent on challenging the coalition's ultimatum. Saddam had concluded that he needed to enter the conflict to demonstrate his courage and to affirm his claim to Pan-Arab leadership. Saddam expected a massive air campaign and planned to survive it. In the succeeding ground campaign, he hoped to engage the U.S. "Vietnam complex." He believed, as he had demonstrated in the Iran-Iraq War, that his battle-hardened troops could absorb massive casualties, whereas the weak-willed United States would not have the stomach for this, and a political-military stalemate would ensue.

By demonstrating he had the courage to stand up against the most powerful nation on earth, Saddam's credentials as Pan-Arab leader would be consolidated, and he would win great honor. Having the courage to fight a superior foe can bring political victory in the Arab world, even though a military defeat follows. Sadat had won great honor in 1973 by leading the attack against previously invincible Israel, even though Egypt lost the military conflict. Indeed, his enhanced prestige permitted him to approach Israel as an equal negotiating partner and ultimately led to the Camp David Accords. Saddam's political hero and model Nasser gained great honor for attacking the imperialists in the 1956 Suez campaign, even though he lost.

Saddam hoped to consolidate his place in history as Nasser's heir by bravely confronting the U.S.-led coalition. On the third day of the air campaign, his minister of information, Latif Jassim, declared victory. To the astounded press he explained that the coalition had expected Iraq to crumble in two days. Having survived the massive air strikes for three days, the Iraqis were accordingly victorious, and each further day would only magnify the scope of their victory.

The preceding discussion has attempted to address the following conundrum: in the face of unambiguous signals that his already war-ravaged nation would be subjected to overwhelming force, why did the rational calculator Saddam Hussein, who prided himself on being a revolutionary pragmatist, not realistically appraise the destructive consequences of entering the conflict and at the eleventh hour reverse himself, as he had so often in the past? An attempt has been made to identify the psychological motives that were engaged in Saddam by the confrontation. It is far too simple to characterize Saddam as only a rational calculator, a revolutionary pragmatist. In trying to make sense of Saddam's political calculus, one cannot consider any of the decisions on a wholly cognitive basis, apart from the emotional loading of each of the reasoned calculations. To say that Saddam is a rational political calculator is not to say that the alternatives he considers do not tap into deeply held and conflict-laden values. And as the conflict played out, some of those values were to take precedence over others.

A Schematic Map of
Saddam's Political Psychology

Students of political psychology will recognize that leaders may be entirely objective in their decision making for most classes of decisions but that certain issues are salient for their political personality and, in effect, hook, or engage, them psychologically, as do certain circumstances. Person schema theory suggests that salient psychological issues and circumstances are those that engage particular leader person schemas. Applying person schema theory may help to clarify the impact of Saddam's powerful personality drives upon his reasoning.[9] The activation of particular leader schemas, some of which were contradictory, may account for some of the shifts and departures from objective decision making by Saddam during crucial moments of the Gulf crisis. The following is an attempt to draw a schematic map of Saddam's political psychology and how his schemas became activated during the conflict in the Gulf.

It is reasonable to infer from his traumatic background that a dreaded schema for Saddam is that of the *abandoned helpless victim of the persecutor with superior strength*. Saddam defends against this schema with aggressive actions as *the aggressive combatant*. A particularly powerful schema, inculcated by his uncle and compensating for the underlying insecurity, was that of the *heroic charismatic leader of the Arab masses* (in the model of Nasser). Using time as a weapon and demonstrating a gift for patience, Saddam was not headstrong in pursuing his grand ambitions. He demonstrated a pattern of reversing his course of action when it proved counterproductive on a number of important occasions, deferring the actualization of his dreams of glory to a later time and defining himself as a *revolutionary pragmatist*.

The Schematic Dynamics of the Conflict

Having little to show for the bloody eight-year war with Iraq, Saddam characteristically was unable to take responsibility himself for a failure of leadership judgment. Rather, he saw himself as the *victim* of a conspiracy among Iran, Israel, and the United States. In Saddam's view, when this conspiracy to destroy Saddam and Iraq was unable to succeed through military means, the United States, in league with Great Britain, decided to destroy Iraq by economic means, using the Gulf states as their agents. Kuwait's economic aggression against Iraq, in this view, was a further stage in the plot to destroy Iraq. Saddam's invasion of Kuwait was not aggression but a *required response to his own victimization*. It was self-defense against economic aggression by Saddam *the aggressive combatant*. He was demonstrating to the Arab masses that he was an *Arab strongman* with the courage to defy the West and expel foreign influences.

Intoxicated by the elixir of power and the acclaim of the Palestinians and the radical Arab masses, Saddam's heroic self-image was engaged as never before. He was fulfilling the messianic goal that had obsessed him—and eluded him—throughout his life. When the struggle between Saddam Hussein and George Bush became personalized, it further fueled this schema, for it enhanced Saddam's reputation as a *courageous combatant willing to defy the imperialist United States.* At the same time, Saddam *could not be seen as giving in to a superior enemy.* The Bush administration's insistence on "no face-saving" confronted Saddam with the dreaded schema of *the helpless victim capitulating to superior force.*

Thus the characteristic schema of *revolutionary pragmatist* was overwhelmed by two powerful schemas—the final activation of Saddam's self-schema as *heroic leader of the Arab masses,* and his need to avoid the humiliation of replaying the dreaded schema of *helpless victim capitulating to superior force.*

Aftermath

After the war, with his remarkable capacity for historic revisionism, which was abetted by his control over the Iraqi media, Saddam predictably proclaimed the courage of the Iraqi people (and himself) in withstanding and surviving the U.S.-led aggression, portraying himself in heroic terms. Never one to acknowledge personal error in the wake of defeats, he replaced a number of senior officials, a pattern that can be expected to continue. Gravely—but not fatally—wounded, Saddam retains the core of his power base. The quintessential survivor survives. His self-concept was wounded, but his aggressive dreams of glory have not been destroyed.

Saddam's "agreement" to the UN conditions did not represent an agreement but a humiliating forced capitulation. His intensified pursuit of a nuclear weapons capability was restitutive, a demonstration to his leadership circle that Saddam had not capitulated, that Iraq under Saddam would remain a powerful force in the Arab world. It should be clear that the blocking of his nuclear adventurism is by no means the end of his unbounded drive for power and that continual close monitoring by the international community will be required. Moreover, as his overt aggression is blocked, covert expression of aggression through increased international terrorism can be expected.

Just as the Middle East has been transformed by this conflict, so too has Saddam Hussein. Having tasted glory for a brief, intoxicating moment, he will not rest until he and Iraq again have the power and international recognition he has sought throughout his life, and he can be expected to continue to resist the efforts of the international community to curb him. The central question concerning Saddam's maintaining a hold on power will be the degree to which he can sustain the loyalty of his followers, especially as they increasingly realize that Iraq will be a pariah among nations, denied access to the international community, as long as it remains under the highly personalized leadership of Saddam Hussein.

NOTES

1. I developed a comprehensive political psychology profile of Saddam Hussein in late August 1990. Initially published in the *Boston Herald*, the profile became the object of widespread attention from the electronic and print media because of the intense interest in the personality and political behavior of Saddam. The profile was presented in testimony to the House Armed Services Committee and the House Foreign Affairs Committee hearings on the Gulf crisis in December 1990. This chapter summarizes the principal features of the profile, which was published in full in *Political Psychology* (Post 1991a). The psychobiographic and personality analysis was based on some six political biographies, a review of speeches over a twelve-year period, interviews with a number of senior government and business officials who had personal contact with Saddam, and focused analysis of critical junctures in his career. Supportive evidence is not provided in this chapter, but it should be emphasized that the patterns described are quite pronounced and extremely consistent throughout his political career. Because the profile was presented in the midst of the crisis and attempted to assess Saddam's current political psychology, I employ the present tense in this chapter. An analysis of Saddam's decision making immediately before and during the conflict was published in Post (1991b).

2. Saddam's first act on fully assuming the reins of power in 1979 had a lasting impact on his subordinates. Suspecting the loyalty of twenty-one senior officials, he coerced a "confession" to a plot through a combination of torture and threats to the family of one of the suspected officials. At a meeting of all of his senior leadership, while Saddam smoked a cigar, the name of each individual in the room was read. The confessed "traitor" would then identify whether or not he was a plotter. Security guards immediately seized the identified "traitors." The next day, the officials who had not been singled out formed execution squads for the disloyal twenty-one.

3. In 1982, when the war with Iran was going very badly for Iraq and Saddam wished to terminate hostilities, Khomeini, who was by then obsessed with Saddam, insisted there could be no peace until Saddam was removed from power. At a cabinet meeting, Saddam asked his ministers to candidly give their advice, and the minister of health suggested that Saddam temporarily step down, to resume the presidency after peace had been established.

There are two versions of Saddam's reaction to this advice, one more brutal than the next. According to one version, Saddam thanked him for his candor and ordered his arrest. His wife pleaded for her husband's return. The next day, Saddam returned her husband's body to her in a black canvas bag, chopped into pieces. The other version is reminiscent of a Mafia movie. In this "milder" version, Saddam thanked his minister for his candor and then took him out into the corridor and shot him in the head. In either case, Saddam's violent reaction powerfully concentrated the attention of the other ministers, who were unanimous in their insistence that Saddam remain in power.

Such stories circulate among the Iraqi military and civilian elite. The fear of Saddam's violent reactions clearly inhibits constructive criticism. A former U.S. ambassador to Iraq, David Newton, stated that if Saddam's house is on fire, and he asks you if his house is on fire, you had better find out what answer he wishes to hear before you answer.

4. While Saddam can be extremely patient and uses time as a weapon, his tendency to rely on his own instincts can lead him to "miss the moment."

5. This is not to say that Saddam does not adroitly manipulate the Arab population's readiness to subscribe to a conspiracy theory. But on a number of occasions his espousal of a conspiracy served no useful political purposes and indeed led him to positions that were contrary to his political interests. This was particularly the case when the U.S. tilt was pro-Iraq.

6. According to this document, the United States, Iran, and Israel were involved in a secret conspiracy to overthrow the Iraqi government and eliminate Saddam. The document cites the Irangate documents as proving that this conspiracy was orchestrated by Vice President George Bush. When, despite the best efforts of this group, Iraq prevailed in the Iran-Iraq War, the conspiracy shifted from military warfare to economic warfare. Saddam's other archenemy, Margaret Thatcher, joined George Bush in plotting Iraq's economic destruction. They planned for an economic embargo. Thus the invasion of Kuwait was seized upon by George Bush and Margaret Thatcher as a convenient excuse to implement an embargo they had already agreed upon. In pursuing the economic destruction of Iraq, they recruited the Gulf states as their agents. Kuwait's economic aggression against Iraq was, according to this theory, in the service of this conspiracy. Moreover, because Kuwait's economic aggression was an act of warfare, Saddam's invasion of Kuwait was defensive and a justifiable response to Kuwait's economic aggression, which he saw as in the service of the overall goals of the conspiracy.

7. In the epilogue to *Avoiding Inadvertent War*, Alexander George comments upon the influence of my profile of Saddam on the administration (1991, 567–76). He observes that the administration appeared to pay attention to the first part of the evaluation—that is, that Saddam needed to be met with firm resolve and no ambiguity about the likelihood of forceful response if he did not withdraw. But, George observes, the administration did not seem to attend to the second part of the evaluation—that is, that it was important that he not be backed into a corner with no way out whereby he could preserve his power base and his honor. In this book and in *Coercive Persuasion* (1992) George contrasts the dynamic of the Gulf crisis with the Cuban missile crisis, in which Kennedy took pains to ensure that Khruschev had a way of reversing his course while preserving his honor.

8. The importance of honor, pride, dignity, and avoiding humiliation cannot be overemphasized. These themes are mentioned in nearly every speech and clearly were of paramount importance in Saddam's political psychology.

For example, in the official Iraqi transcript of the meeting between President Saddam and Ambassador April Glaspie, Saddam is quoted as saying, "You can come to Iraq with aircraft and missiles, but do not push us to the point where we cease to care. And when we feel that you want to injure our pride and take away the Iraqis' chance of a high standard of living, then we will cease to care and death will be the choice for us. Then we would not care if you fired 100 missiles for each missile we fired. Because without pride, life would have no value" (Meeting between President Saddam Hussein and U.S. Ambassador April Glaspie 1990).

9. The *schema* is a generalized knowledge structure about a domain that provides selection criteria for regulating attention and lends a focus and structure to encoding, storage, and retrieval of information. As enduring psychological structures, schemas tend to persist in the face of contradictory evidence.

Person schemas are enduring representations of the self and others. The interdisciplinary research bearing on the development of new relationships indicates that they develop according to a mixture of situational appraisals and internal repertoires of self concepts and models of relationship roles and scripts.

The *self-concept* can be viewed as the aggregate of self-schemas. For some individuals, there is not as coherent an organization for self-schemas as for others, and contradictory self-schemas may coexist and can be elicited by similar situation triggers. These schemas, which are triggered both by situational and internal stimuli, are associated with states of mind and affective states. They are seen as controlling ideas and feelings.

In a useful heuristic, Mardi Horowitz et al. (1991) define a *role relationship model* (R-R-M) as consisting of a schema of self, a schema of other, and a script of transactions between them. Individuals have repertoires of multiple-person schemas and multiple R-R-Ms. Dreaded role relationship models represent current replays of past traumas. They must be avoided at all costs.

REFERENCES

George, A. 1992. *Coercive Persuasion*. Washington, D.C.: United States Institute of Peace.

George, A., ed. 1991. "Epilogue." In *Avoiding Inadvertent War*, ed. A. George. Boulder: Westview.

Horowitz, M., T. Merluzzi, M. Ewert, J. Ghannam, D. Hartley, and C. Stinson. 1991. "Role-Relationship Models Configuration." In *Person Schemas and Maladaptive Intersonal Patterns*, ed. M. Horowitz. Chicago: University of Chicago Press, 115–54.

Hussein, Saddam. 1990. "Victory Day Message." FBIS *Middle East Report*, August 9.

Kernberg, O. 1975. *Borderline Conditions and Pathological Narcissism*. Northvale, N.J.: Jason Aronson.

Kohut, H. 1971. *The Analysis of the Self*. New York: International University Press, 1971.

Lasswell, H. D. 1960. *Psychopathology and Politics*. New York: Viking.

Meeting Between President Saddam Hussein and U.S. Ambassador April Glaspie. 1990. Excerpts from Iraqi transcript. *New York Times,* September 23.

Post, J. M. 1991a. "Saddam Hussein of Iraq: A Political Psychology Profile." *Political Psychology* 12 (Spring): 279–87.

——— . 1991b. "Afterword." *Political Psychology* 12 (December): 723–25.

4

Good Judgment, and the Lack Thereof During the Gulf War: A Preliminary Psychological Model with Some Applications

■

Stanley A. Renshon

■ NO POLITICAL decision is more consequential than the decision to go to war. Sometimes decisions can be made in the fullness of time,[1] but occasionally the stakes are high and the time short. In these circumstances, leadership skills and the quality of decision making are directly and severely tested.[2]

These situations compel our attention not only because of their consequences, but because they disclose in sharp relief the adequacies or inadequacies of a leader's judgment and leadership. Both are closely connected. At the heart of leadership lies choice, and at the heart of choice lies judgment.

The judgment of political leaders has seldom directly preoccupied political psychologists. Recent studies of political decision making have focused more on procedures than the decisions themselves or the leaders who make them. Instead, a theoretical concern with judgment examines qualities of mind, temperament, and character that underlie decisions. In short, it seeks to place an individual's psychology within a specific context and faced by a specific set of problems.

We expect to see evidence of good judgment, or its lack, when the importance of the decisions and the price for being wrong are likely to arouse a leader's personal concern and involvement. Moreover, an analysis of good judgment is facilitated by examining situations in which leaders' judgments have a direct and observable relationship to an unfolding situation and its consequences. The Gulf War provides just such a set of sharply etched circumstances in which the risks to important interests and values were played out within a limited time frame, by actors whose direct involvement was clear and well defined, and which had a dramatic conclusion.

In this chapter I examine the policy judgments made by George Bush and Saddam Hussein in the period leading up to and during the Persian Gulf War of 1991. I argue that while good judgment is necessary for satisfactory policy decisions, it is not sufficient for executing successful policy, which entails the relationship between good judgment and effective political leadership. Good judgment can answer the question "What should be done?" but only effective political leadership accomplishes policy purposes.

I begin by examining procedural models of decision making and theories of cognitive functioning that have been used to analyze the making of high-quality decisions. I then consider the nature of good judgment and develop a psychological model of its elements and dynamics in political decision making. The model links character functioning and cognitive heuristics with situational circumstances. It also focuses on the relationship between good judgment and political leadership. I then apply this model to the Gulf War with special focus on two major framing decisions, Saddam Hussein's decision to invade Kuwait and George Bush's decision to respond. (Chapter 13 analyzes Saddam Hussein's decision to stay in Kuwait after the January 19 deadline.)

Three caveats should be made. First, there is some overlap between the models of procedural decision making I critique and the psychological model of good judgment I present. In some respects, the psychological model examines procedural adequacy from the inside out. One purpose is to account psychologically, and specifically in relation to character, for the willingness and capacity to use procedures that lead to good decisions. I am concerned with the personal traits, skills, and circumstances that inhibit or facilitate their use.

Second, while the psychological model of good judgment attempts to be comprehensive, my explication of the model within the Gulf War context is necessarily selective; exploring all aspects of the model would require more information than we have, information that may never be known.

Third, my analysis of good judgment implies that judgments must be assessed in part by reference to outcomes. Such assessments are likely to be controversial; outcomes themselves are very complex, and it is difficult to establish lines of causality and intent, as well as connections between causes and multiple effects. Moreover, the Gulf War is politically controversial. Attempts to evaluate the decisions surrounding the war and its outcomes, especially in relation to a theory of good judgment, are therefore doubly difficult. Nonetheless I will attempt some assessments of the war's outcomes in relation to the process of judgment.

The Procedural Model of Political Decision Making

The study of political decision making has been approached from two directions. One approach examines the individual decision maker, the other the decision-making processes that shape policy consideration. Rather than focusing on leaders' unconscious barriers to effective decision making,[3] more recent analyses (Lasswell 1956; Janis and Mann 1977; George 1980) have stressed the procedural requirements for making good decisions. We know, for example, that better decisions are based on a valid and complete diagnosis of a problem (George, 1980, 10), after a careful weighing of the costs and risks associated with each option (Janis & Mann, 1977, 11).

The guidelines developed through the procedural model are neither wrong nor useless.[4] Their difficulties lie elsewhere. First is the danger that decisions will be considered adequate not because they effectively address difficulties, but merely because they adhere to certain routines. The procedural model does not claim that following procedures alone will guarantee good results, but by not specifying what else is necessary, it implies it.

A second concern is the cognitive limits on a leader's ability to make effective use of the procedures identified in the model. Janis and Mann characterize their procedural model as "ideal" (1977, 11). This suggests that the model may not accurately reflect either what decision makers do or what they are capable of doing.[5]

The possibly idealized nature of procedures requirements raises the question of what other factors are operating. Often decision makers do not fully use the procedures described in the model, yet their decisions may be good ones, for reasons yet to be closely examined. I argue in this chapter that good judgment may be the key missing variable in understanding how good decisions get made.

It is also true that even an ostensibly sound decision may have mixed or modest results. It could be that the decision was flawed in some way or that circumstances did not permit a positive result. Or even when a decision and its implementation are of high quality, there is often strong resistance by other actors with different interests. A judgment that succeeds despite adverse circumstances gains increased respect.

Procedural models have difficulty with such factors because they do not often attempt to assess independently why one set of outcomes is better than another. Indeed, emphasizing procedures runs the danger of diverting attention from outcomes. Thus, it is difficult to know whether adherence to procedure alone necessarily results in better decisions. It would be useful to have a model of high-quality decisions and decision making that takes into account the problem at hand and assesses their adequacy by criteria of specific needs and outcomes.

One should also note here the theoretical affinity of the procedural and rational-actor models of decision making. The list of procedural requirements for high-quality decisions looks remarkably like those for acting "rationally."[6] In the rational-actor model, the decision maker considers all relevant values at stake, compares all possible responses in terms of their costs and benefits, and selects the option that maximizes crucial values. In the procedural model, the decision maker explicitly does the first and second, and implicitly does the third.[7]

But perhaps the most significant drawback is that these models tend to neglect the personal qualities and skills of the individual making the decisions.[8] The suggestion is that the procedures themselves, rather than the person using them, produce higher-quality decisions. The procedural model thus raises in modified form the question of "actor dispensability" (Greenstein 1987, 46–57).

An important aspect of decision making that is not addressed in the procedural model is judgment. Nor is the basis of good judgment—a leader's understanding of the problem and its dynamics and implications—carefully examined. In short, the procedural model does not capture well the dynamic aspects of reaching a decision.

A leader not only gathers information, but must also put it into a appropriate framework for understanding and action. Without good judgment based on an accurate appreciation of the circumstances and their implications, good procedures do not necessarily lead to good decisions. The procedural model also does not pay sufficient attention to political leadership and policy implementation. Making good decisions lies in the province of thought; carrying them out belongs to action. A leader must excel at both.

Nor does the procedural model adequately consider the decision maker's leadership style and capacities and their relation to outcomes. The seventh procedural rule for high-quality decisions outlined in Janis and Mann (1977, 11) is that the decision maker "makes detailed provisions for implementing or executing the chosen course of action with special attention to contingency plans that might be required if various known risks were to materialize." George's fourth rule for high-quality decisions notes that the decision maker must "provide for careful consideration of the problems that may arise in implementing the options under consideration" (1980, 10).

Both of these suggestions, although accurate, are limited. In both, the leader appears to think more about implementation rather than doing much about it. A decision maker's leadership skills may be highly important in effecting a desired outcome, and indeed may produce a successful outcome even if the quality of judgment has not been exceptional. Finally, the means selected by the leader to accomplish policy goals, especially when compared with other available options for accomplishing the same or similar purposes, deserve closer attention. They can provide important information about a leader's judgment, values, and way of relating to the world.

The psychological model of good judgment presented herein does not resolve all of these difficulties. Nor does it dispute the view that, in general, effective procedures will bring about better decision outcomes. Rather, I ask what intrapsychic and interpersonal capacities help to account for the willingness and capacity to follow good procedures. In that respect, the procedural model and the psychological model of good judgment are complementary.

Our analysis also asks two further questions. First, how are good judgments linked to good outcomes? And second, what relationships, if any, exist between the capacity for good judgment and effective political leadership?

Psychological Functioning in Political Decision Making: The Cognitive Model

High-quality decisions reflect not only the capacities and limitations of the person who makes them, but also the procedures used. The two are related. Even the best procedures will not produce good decisions if the decision maker is not inclined or able to make good use of them. The question is how best to conceptualize and study the personal characteristics of the decision maker that shape the use of these procedures. Several answers have been proposed. Each approach has theoretical and practical drawbacks. We have already discussed the "first-generation" psychodynamic models (see note 3). Let us now turn to the "second-generation" cognitive decision-making models.

The second group of models stress cognitive frames and processes. These models fit nicely with the procedural model of decision making that focuses on the acquisition and use of information. The potential advantages of such models for understanding good judgment seem obvious, since judgment is dependent in some measure on cognition.

Research in cognitive psychology has underscored the importance of decision heuristics (Nesbitt and Ross 1980)—that is, how the decision maker frames and processes information. In the experiments of Tversky and Kahneman (1981; see also Kahneman and Tversky 1984), the same problem is presented within a different frame, which appears to—but in reality does not—alter the payoff matrix. They are able to demonstrate that how a problem is framed has substantial consequences for the choices selected.[9]

The framing of a problem, however, marks the start of a complicated information-gathering and assessment processes. Cognitive theorists see perception itself as a process that both frames the definition of a problem and subsequent decision evaluations. Misperceptions can occur both for motivational and informational reasons (see Jervis 1976). Their net result, however, is to introduce biases into the decision process that impede high-quality decisions. Many factors can lead to such difficulties, and the defenses against such errors are generally thought to be located in institutionalized procedural remedies (George 1972).

Framing the problem is not the only cognitive operation that can go askew. Interpretations of another's intentions or of a causal chain of effects, can be distorted or misinformed. One can for example misattribute cause, thinking a particular actor or state is responsible for events (in both the political and causal sense), when in fact that actor's contribution relative to other causal factors might be negligible. This *fundamental attribution error* is one of many difficulties that accompany the attempt to disentangle complex layers of causality and evaluate the motives and understandings that lie behind perception.

Cognitive models of decision making also make another important contribution by focusing on the qualities of thought that go into high-quality decision making. Early research analyzed "black or white thinking" (Rokeach 1960; Glad 1983), the tendency for individuals to frame questions and view information in strong *either-or* terms. Tetlock (1985) focuses on another set of cognitive abilities, the capacity to deal with complexity in political thinking.[10]

Cognitive models of decision making focus on important concerns. But like their psychodynamic counterparts, cognitive models also have limitations, the most important of which is their failure to develop theoretical links to other areas of psychological functioning, even though they are apparently relevant. Consider for example the framing of problems. Surely even if the framing of a problem is not a given (see note 9), and sometimes even when it is, it reflects a complex amalgam of a leader's feelings, experiences, and understandings. The same appears to be true of judgment heuristics like attribution.

The importance and persistence of the fundamental attribution error (ascribing too much causal importance to persons at the expense of circumstances) is deeply rooted in the individual psyche, and its origins do not lie solely in the complexity and ambiguity of "reality." Some attributions are strongly psychologically driven in another more directly political sense. Interpretations of each other's behavior by Arabs and Israelis, for example, are strongly driven by beliefs, experiences, and feelings about themselves and each other (Heradstveit 1979). Even schemes, the cognitive categories into which persons (and by extension leaders) encode and process information, are themselves *constructions* and can have as much to do with motivation and socialization as with cognition.

The point is that *composite*, not partial, theories of psychological functioning are needed for studying political decision making. Such theories should focus on the affective elements in the decision process that often accompany information and influence what cognitive categories it is placed in. Or they may address such feelings as hope, which Janis and Mann (1977) demonstrate is strongly associated with effective decision making and which is rooted in basic character structures, developmental experiences, and belief systems. Finally, theories of cognitive processing should be integrated with more general psychological theories of character function. To do otherwise is to run the risk of specifying factors but not refining syndromes. A concern with good judgment may help to facilitate that integration.

Good Judgment in Political Decision Making

What is good judgment? How does it differ from poor judgment, and how do both differ, if they do, from misjudgment? Is good judgment a quality of mind, of temperament, of character? Does it also derive from other sources? Is there a relationship between good judgment and effective leadership? And, finally, how can we evaluate George Bush and Saddam Hussein and their decisions in the Gulf War along these dimensions?

In a political context, judgment is the quality of analysis, reflection, and insight that informs the making of politically consequential framing decisions. Only decisions that pose significant questions and therefore have significant consequences for decision makers and their areas of responsibility raise the issue of the quality of judgment.[11] These *framing decisions* are crucial because they represent key, and starkly contrasting, choice points, each of which could result in very different alternatives.

The exercise of good judgment first depends on seeing the framing decision as a crucial choice point and appreciating its implications. But good judgment itself does not guarantee good outcomes, for several reasons:

1. A framing decision may be decided with good judgment, but subsequent decisions that flow from it may be flawed. In making an overall assessment, the good judgment that went into making the right framing decision receives more weight than the flaws in a secondary decision unless they were so pervasive and serious as to undermine the basic framing judgment itself.

2. Without the capacity to realize the fruits of one's judgments, good judgment alone will not result in high-quality outcomes. The required link here is political leadership, the capacity to act on the implications of one's judgments and achieve results.

3. The complex process leading from good judgment to good outcomes also features other actors who may act to thwart or otherwise deflect the impact of a good judgment. A judgment is not made in a static world, but in a world in which others are actively striving to modify or reverse the effects of judgments.

Consequences, often unintended or unforeseen, also shape our assessments of good judgment. Whereas good judgment does not require foresight of all the consequences of a framing decision, we expect a leader to anticipate the major consequences that could flow from a framing decision and act accordingly. Indeed, one mark of poor judgment is that a leader failed to appreciate what he could and should have known, or realized but failed to act accordingly. Good judgment entails the capacity to understand and act on consequences.

The analysis of good judgment focuses on three factors: the problem itself, the decisions made, and their results. To analyze a problem, we must know what fundamental issues it raises. In analyzing decisions, we need to understand what factors were weighed and with what results. And last, analyzing outcomes depends on appreciating the consequences of the decision on the leader, those the leader represents, and the larger community beyond the leader's own state.

What then is good policy judgment in international politics? It is the quality of analysis, reflection,[12] and insight that results in finding solutions to problems that raise significant issues (that is, framing decisions). These problems directly affect (1) a nation's geographical integrity, (2) its political-institutional integrity, (3) its economic well-being, or (4) its strategic security.

A solution produced by good judgment protects the important values and interests at risk in one or more of the four areas just noted, while causing minimal harm to the interests of others with legitimate differences from one's own and inflicting the least possible harm on adversaries. It is therefore important to assess the alternatives that might have accomplished the same goal against the option actually chosen.

Poor judgment is reflected in a leader's failure to adequately appreciate the risks to himself, the community (institutions or traditions) he or she represents, or the wider regional or international community, or failure to defend the four substantive interests noted above. It also occurs when a leader realizes these risks but is not deterred.

Good judgment entails both analysis and reflection. It is only partially cognitive. Good judgment does require the ability to comprehend and process information, as well as to compare facts with each other and within other frames of reference—all cognitive skills. But one must integrate this information and place it in a framework that makes intellectual, experiential, and emotional sense not only to the leader but to those whom the decisions affect. Reflection therefore requires not only cognitive skills but also the ability to place analysis within a framework of understanding, values, and action. This depends on maturity of character.

By character I mean an one's basic psychological stance toward experience. It is found in a leader's sense of self as an able, honorable person and reflects beliefs and feelings about the self and the world following from this awareness. Feelings of capacity and worth, and the psychological structures that support them, are linked to good judgment in a number of ways. So too, feelings of inadequacy (or hyper-adequacy) or low (or too high) self-regard, and the psychological structures in which they are embedded, are linked with poor judgment.

Maturity refers to the degree to which an individual's character structure has evolved, consolidated, and integrated the diverse demands with which it must deal.[13] Among these are the capacity to both modulate but satisfy basic (developmentally normal and appropriate) wishes for accomplishment and recognition. It also consists of having consolidated a personal and professional identity (including a set of values that provide the leader with an internal compass for evaluation), which provides a vehicle for the expression of oneself and ambitions in the world and which is in turn voluntarily recognized and validated by others.

Maturity also reflects having satisfactorily resolved the sometimes conflicting needs for interpersonal connectedness and personal autonomy. The ability to make emotional connections to others reflects a number of important accomplishments. It reflects a capacity to go beyond self-interest and to empathize with and understand the concerns and feelings of others. This capacity is a fundamental element of political empathy and good policy judgment as well.

Good Judgment and the Nature of the Problem to be Solved

Good judgment is a joint function of the match between the leader's analytical, reflective, and character strengths on the one hand, and the nature of the problem to be faced on the other. Procedural, cognitive, and psychodynamic models of decision making tend to treat the problem at hand as a given rather than as a variable.[14] Obviously, knowing the nature of a problem is crucial to deciding what is at issue and what solutions are viable. But it also affects the understanding and experience that a leader brings to a problem.

Every problem is to some degree sui generis, but to facilitate understanding and reduce ambiguity and its associated anxieties, individuals search for appropriate frameworks within which to place events (May 1973). There is a danger that the wrong analogy may be used or inappropriate lessons drawn. But using personal and historical experience is a necessary device to bring one's experience and knowledge to bear on an issue. The key question is always to what extent the analogy holds in its crucial respects, and to what degree appropriate lessons are taken, *reformulated for the present*, and applied.

Does good judgment depend on the situation? Certainly the general character elements at the core of good judgment (a sense of capacity and self-regard) develop over time. One could argue that good judgment enjoys certain universal characteristics; yet it is also very closely tied to particular domains and issues. A leader's range and depth of understanding of a problem is related to experience with and understanding of problems of this sort.[15] A president could have very good judgment on domestic issues and politics, for example, but lack the experiential frame to make good judgments in certain international circumstances, and vice versa.

Even within one domain—say, international affairs—different kinds of problems can generate different levels of judgment in response. A president might be well positioned to exercise good judgment regarding political competition and conflict but not well prepared if the major international challenge were primarily economic.[16] This is not to contend that good judgments cannot be reached in unfamiliar areas, only that good judgment is facilitated by understanding refined by experience.

While good judgment is to some degree specific to each context, poor judgment tends to be systematic. The reason is to be found in the psychological elements, particularly those associated with character function, that both impede and facilitate good judgment.

Psychological Elements of Good Judgment

Good judgment reflects a set of composite skills. Among them are the ability (1) to understand the essential elements of a problem including their significance and implications, (2) to weigh complex, frequently discordant facts, which requires tolerance of both ambiguity and anxiety, (3) to use, but not be subservient to, feeling or impulse,[17] (4) to consider and appreciate the range of issues and values raised by the situation for oneself and others, to deal adequately with the various interests (political, social, and psychological) involved, (5) to place these considerations in a framework of understanding that adequately assesses the nature of the problem and points to responses that preserve, and perhaps advance, the values and interests at risk to develop a fitting solution, (6) to draw on the understanding of the past and present (point 1) to consider how alternatives might shape the future (the extrapolation of implications), and (7) to embark on steps to accomplish, with minimal harm, purposes consistent with one's understanding of the issues raised and values at risk.

Analytic abilities in the judgment process include the ability to discern the essential nature of a problem, potential responses and their implications, and how goals might be accomplished. *Reflective abilities* include the capacity to consider and evaluate analytical information from a series of perspectives. These include the leader's (or other leaders') values and views, those of other actors involved, and both long- and short-term political/strategic considerations. Finally, leadership skills are essential to translating good judgment into effective policy. The personal and political *means* a leader has at his disposal, and which ones he selects, weigh heavily on whether policy ends can be met.

In focusing on means, one may consider the adequacy of a decision maker's leadership skills to implement the decisions reached. But a second important dimension of means concerns the type of action chosen as a response. Does a leader choose to talk, to threaten, to fight? Are the means adequate and appropriate? Could less costly means accomplish the same ends? The means selected reveal important information about a leader's character as well as judgment.

Some capacities associated with good judgment are clearly cognitive. Others are more clearly affective, and at least one is more closely linked to leadership skills. But all are to some degree shaped by character. We now turn to these linkages.

Character and Analytic Skills

A leader must first recognize a problem. Not all leaders are able to do this equally well. Some have difficulty discerning the facts; others can discern them but refuse to accept them; while others feel that they can afford to ignore them. The inability to grapple with problems can have complex and varied roots in character. Difficulties can come either from a meager or inflated sense of capacity and self-regard. Leaders may be too inhibited to respond boldly and directly to an issue, or prefer optimism over realism. Similarly, the optimistic weighing of sobering information (wishful thinking), a dislike of conflict, a strong sensitivity to criticism, and a strong need to be liked all play inhibiting roles.

On the other hand, an inflated sense of capacity and self-regard can lead to equally damaging results. The sense that "it can't happen here" can inhibit the accurate appreciation and diagnosis of problems. So too can a leader's conviction of being unusually competent, invulnerable— of being special, powerful, and beyond the reach of ordinary circumstances.[18] In such cases, a leader may discount the significance of obvious facts. Or he may fail to appreciate the difficulties of carrying out plans because the possibility of failure is foreign to his view of himself.

Second, a leader must be able to diagnose a problem. This is not just a matter of having a high I.Q., but of being able to discern and appreciate the essential issues raised. This skill requires the ability to appreciate implications and in turn to extract significance from incomplete or massive amounts of information.[19] Finally, a leader must place this information in an analytically useful framework.

Character Functioning and Reflective Skills

Good judgment leads to high-quality decisions because information is assembled into an understanding that both correctly diagnoses the situation and points toward adequate responses. High-quality decisions require the leader to evaluate and place information into a framework that relates elements to one another and to a larger context. So, too, the leader must be able to extrapolate implications from limited data and to anticipate possible results. These skills go beyond cognition; they entail creative insight and construction.

The leader's personal and political experience is instrumental in this process. One basic problem of dictators is that they are often shielded from the results of their mistakes; thus they are denied experiences that might ameliorate their policy and decision thinking. Major political decisions generate intense emotions as well as calculation. Especially in times of crisis, the leader must control and delay impulses toward premature closure or action.[20] In the Gulf War these pressures included the potential costs of delay, which might have placed the situation beyond even difficult solutions. Persistence in seeking solutions in the face of personal and public anxiety, criticism, and demands for action is crucial. This requires that the leader have confidence in himself and in his abilities as well as a conception of a possibly adequate response.

When a leader weighs alternatives, simple national or individual self-interest is a poor criterion for adequate policy. Obviously, pursuit of the national interest frequently requires considering the concerns and feelings of others. Leaders with little empathy find it difficult to include this important element into the policy deliberation process. One way is to "take the role of the other." This involves more than political calculations or "strategic empathy."[21] From a psychological standpoint, realistic empathy rests on the capacity to make real interpersonal connections.

This is not a matter of imagining what one would do or feel if one were in another's situation—an approach presupposing that the other is fundamentally similar to oneself. Rather, realistic empathy involves an attempt to enter into a different frame, one starting from different assumptions and perhaps leading to different conclusions. This is difficult even when the other shares a similar culture. It is all the more so when, as in the Gulf War, two leaders faced each other across cultures as well as conflicting policy interests.

Ultimately, a leader must be guided by his personal and political identity. Values, policy aspirations, and feelings regarding a policy issue are appropriate and legitimate tools of policy choice, if the leader recognizes them as such. The ability to draw on the past, confront the present, and follow these analyses to a conclusion requires a personal and political vision and a strong sense of purpose, effectiveness, and direction.

Judgments Made During the Gulf War

Thousands of decisions were made during the Gulf War, but I focus in this essay on two major framing decisions: the decision of Saddam Hussein to invade Kuwait and the decision of George Bush to respond. First we must consider the issues raised by the invasion for each leader.

The Nature of the Issue—Iraq

On August 2, 1990, over 100,000 Iraqi troops invaded Kuwait. The Iraqi government's first explanation for the invasion was that the colonialist powers had divided Arab lands so that "it separated civilization with its high strong state of preparedness due to the rich culture and demographic density from the resources of the new wealth, petroleum, and other minerals, [and put them] where there is a small population, a lack of cultural depth and a weak state of preparedness." Second, this policy had resulted "in colonialism divesting [Iraq] of a dear part of it, namely Kuwait, and kept Iraq away from the waters to prevent it from acquiring part of its tactical and strategic abilities."[22]

On August 16, 1990, Iraq's Foreign Minister Tariq Aziz raised a third issue: Kuwait's failure to stick to its oil production quota, thereby depriving Iraq of needed revenue. Aziz accused the Kuwait government of "trying not only to destabilize . . . [but also] to impoverish Iraq."[23] Karsh and Rautsi view this element as extremely important and argue that the "fundamental predicament underlying the invasion" had been "a desperate attempt to shore up [Hussein's] regime in the face of dire economic straits" (1991, 239). Among these difficulties were the enormous costs of the war with Iran, which had been partially financed by accumulating a large national debt, and the need to address delayed improvements in the lives of Iraqi citizens.[24]

Hussein also accused Kuwait of waging "economic war" against Iraq because it had not maintained its oil-producing quota. He further charged Kuwait with oil theft (by horizontal drilling) from Iraqi land (Rumaila) and demanded repayment of $2.4 billion. Like Aziz, Hussein demanded that Kuwait forgive the massive debt that Iraq had incurred in the war with Iran, a war he insisted had been fought in part to protect the conservative Gulf states, Kuwait among them. He also wanted wealthy Arab nations to contribute to a substantial aid program to help rebuild his country.

But while economic concerns may have been important, they were not the only considerations at issue. Karsh and Rautsi note:

> By adding Kuwait's fabulous wealth to the depleted Iraqi treasury Hussein hoped to slash Iraq's foreign debt and launch the ambitious reconstruction programs he had promised his people in the wake of the war with Iran.

Given Iraq's historic claim to Kuwait, its occupation would enhance Hussein's national prestige by portraying him as a liberator of usurped Iraqi lands. Furthermore, the capture of Kuwait could improve Iraq's access to the Gulf and give it a decisive say in the world market. (1991, 213)

To these points one might add that a successful invasion of Kuwait would improve Hussein's standing among Iraqis after a long, difficult war and would also have consequences in the Gulf. It would demonstrate that Iraq's wishes were not to be taken lightly. Saudi Arabia, the United Arab Emirates, and others in the region would come under severe pressure. Moreover, a successful invasion would boost Saddam's position as an Arab leader, perhaps especially at the expense of his bitter rival, Syrian leader Hafiz Asad. Last, it seems clear that the money and reputation (for being bold, decisive, and successful) associated with a successful invasion would have made Saddam a player of major consequence in international as well as regional politics.

The Nature of the Issue—The United States

Iraq's invasion of Kuwait raised important economic political, strategic, and psychological issues for the United States. It threatened to change the regional balance—precisely why Saddam undertook it. For the United States, it raised the possibility that a shrewd, calculating, and aggressive leader would add substantial economic, political, and military resources to his arsenal. Saddam Hussein would become a formidable force in the Gulf and elsewhere. He would be in a very strong position to influence oil pricing and production, thus able to exert economic leverage on the United States, which is heavily dependent on imported oil. The same would be true of a number of close allies who are even more dependent on external sources oil.[25]

The United States was also faced with the possibility that Iraq might be on its way beyond Kuwait into Saudi Arabia. Egypt's President Hosni Mubarak reported in a televised address to his country that he had been told by Saddam that the latter would not invade Kuwait: "You said you would not strike and you struck. And now you are turning to Saudi Arabia and saying, 'I will not strike.' They will not believe you. Do you think that they will wait until disaster strikes them?"[26] The loss of Saudi Arabia would have dramatically magnified the economic, strategic, and psychological consequences discussed above. Therefore it was not surprising that Bush publicly raised this concern as early as his August 8 news conference.[27]

The United States would have been most concerned about the stability of the Gulf region if Saddam had established hegemony. In general, a highly armed, rich, and aggressive leader with a history of initiating and supporting violence does not bode well for the security of any region. This concern about regional stability appeared to have at least two elements.

The first was a concern with Iraq's acquisition and use of "weapons of mass destruction." In a speech given on August 28, 1990, Bush noted that his concern about Iraqi nuclear research had led him to issue orders "stopping the export of furnaces that had the potential to contribute to Iraq's nuclear capabilities."[28]

Bush raised the issue again in a September address to Congress[29] and elaborated on it the following month: "Those who would measure the timetable for Saddam's atomic program in years may be seriously underestimating the reality of that situation and the gravity of the threat."[30] A week later, the nuclear issue was raised more specifically: "Imagine his ability to blackmail his neighbors should he possess a nuclear device."[31]

Although Bush did not ever publicly base his policy on it, a second major concern must have been the distinct possibility that Iraq, one of the so-called rejectionist states, would go to war with Israel. Were that to occur, the United States would have been faced with painful choices. Even if armed conflict did not come, if Iraq could establish its hegemony through a combination of threats, power, and inclination to use force, the tortuously slow progress toward resolving major Middle East conflicts would have been at risk.

Bush also had to consider that a number of U.S. presidents had expressed the view that the stability of the Middle East and Western access to oil was a "vital interest" that the United States would be defend and protect. To do nothing in the face of the threats just described would have sent a message that the United States was unwilling to defend what it had defined as its vital interests. Just as Saddam Hussein had to consider the consequences to his reputation of Kuwait's unfavorable response to his charges and demands, so too the United States had to consider these effects.

Finally, a last important issue for the United States was how to respond when a country with whom it had a working relationship was invaded by a larger, more powerful neighbor. The issue was not simply that of assisting a friendly country; also at stake was how to respond to the use of invasion as a policy instrument. The decline of Soviet-sponsored dictatorships in Eastern Europe and the changing nature of the Soviet Union itself from enemy to possible ally opened up vast new possibilities of restructuring world politics. Bush had frequently spoken of the prospect of a "new world order" and specifically contrasted the invasion of Kuwait to "the shape of the postwar world" very early in the crisis.[32] Saddam's Hussein's invasion of Kuwait seemed more like the politics of the old world order, not the new.

Judgment and National Interests in the Gulf War

To analyze the process of judgment for each leader, we must first consider the issues that each faced within a modified framework of national interest. This is a difficult concept that governments have often interpreted so as to justify and rationalize their own behavior. Before we proceed, it may be useful to examine various approaches to this concept.

George argues that "irreducible national interests" should be separated from other national interests (1980, 224–31). For the United States, he suggests three: physical survival, liberty, and the ability to provide economic subsistence. While one could disagree with some aspects of this minimalist list,[33] it outlines the basic interests of any state.

No one could argue that Iraq's irreducible interests were at stake in its argument with Kuwait. Its physical survival was not at issue, nor were its cultural, political, social, or economic institutions. Indeed, they were put at risk by Saddam's invasion. Still, one must still consider the Iraqi concerns expressed in their demands and accusations.

White suggests that we need to empathize with Saddam Hussein in order to understand him; by this he means "simply understanding how a situation looks to another person or group" (1991, 296). White acknowledges that Saddam is a ruthless dictator who yet may have real goals that need to be understood, if not addressed. Chief among these is economic gain, but they also include realistic national security concerns, given the nature of the Middle East and its deadly rivalries, and the goal of increasing his national power. White adds to these Saddam's concern with being a "great tough champion of the Arab world" (1991, 300–01).

White's analysis points to the difference between a leader's goals and his "irreducible national interest." There were other means to settle the issues that Saddam Hussein had raised: one was to place the charge of theft from the Rumaila oil fields before the Arab League, or even the World Court. Indeed, at a meeting of the Gulf oil ministers in Jedda on July 10, 1990, under pressure from Saudi Arabia and Iran as well as Iraq, Kuwait agreed to abide by its oil quotas (Miller and Mylroie 1990, 15).[34]

Hussein's failure to understand that he could have achieved much of what he wanted without the invasion, thus not threatening his country's irreducible national interests, directly raises the issue of poor judgment. Yet if, following White's interpretation, one looks at the invasion as a way to satisfy Saddam Hussein's goals, a different view emerges. The invasion increased his economic gains, his national power, his national security, and his stature as a "great tough champion of the Arab world."

So even if the decision to invade Kuwait cannot be justified in terms of irreducible national interest, it can be from Saddam's view of his own self-interest as well as Iraq's. In these ways he fits the model of the rational actor. But that is precisely the difficulty with that concept. It may well be that from his own point of view Saddam Hussein was a rational actor, but he still displayed poor judgment.

What of George Bush? At first glance, the invasion of Kuwait did not seem to threaten the physical security of the United States or its political institutions. Thus the U.S. response does not appear justifiable as a defense of irreducible national interests. But this view deserves closer examination.

Certainly George Bush saw basic American interests at stake and acted accordingly. Very early in the crisis he stated that the Iraqi attack threatened "our jobs, our way of life, our own freedom and the freedom of friendly countries around the world would all suffer if control of the world's great oil reserves fell into the hands of Saddam Hussein" (Apple, 1990). Iraq's control over a substantial part of the world's oil reserves could have threatened the nation's standard of living and the economy, given U.S. dependence on foreign oil. It is true, as George notes, that small raises in a country's standard of living cannot be justified as an irreducible national interest (1980, 224). Yet perhaps avoiding a precipitous decline in a country's standard of living, especially if brought about willfully by an outside party, might be cause for thinking differently.

But another consideration is much closer to George's explication of a country's irreducible national interests. The extremely well-developed Iraqi nuclear and biological weapons program, coupled with Iraqi attempts to build a long-range missile system capable of delivering these weapons, was enormously threatening to regional security. Nuclear or biological weapons blackmail, subtle or not-so-subtle, is consistent with the behavioral history and character of both the Iraqi state and its leader (al-Kahli 1989; Post 1991).

Having two nuclear-armed countries facing each other would be difficult enough. However, the confrontation of two enemies, one sworn to the annihilation of the other and the other dedicated "never again" to be victimized, would pose a Middle East situation of unprecedented danger and draconian choices for U.S. security interests.

A further element to consider is not covered by George's discussion of irreducible national interest. Countries with legitimate international obligations must also counter attempts to erode their "degrees of freedom" in the international system, not because they should be able to "do what they want," but because they have responsibilities and others depend on them to carry them out. Any threat to that freedom, either through manipulation of oil markets or other kinds of pressure, is a serious concern.

The Iraqi invasion did not raise these issues in an absolute or unqualified way. But the issues raised did appear to touch directly our national and international interests. To have done nothing would have shown very poor judgment indeed.

The Process of Decision:
Rational Actors or Good Judgment?

Was Saddam a "rational actor"? Yes. But this type of question simply asks whether he had reason to believe that his actions would further his self-interest. This is a minimalist requirement given that a leader (or an outside observer) can almost always find some justification for action on the basis of self-interest. A more appropriate question is what his actions suggest about the nature and quality of his thinking. Suggesting that Saddam Hussein was a rational actor does not imply very much about his judgment.

Saddam Hussein grossly miscalculated the impact of his actions. He clearly underestimated George Bush. But the problem really begins in his choice of invasion to gratify his economic and political ambitions. To use violent means to obtain his ends is very consistent with his past behavior.[35] But this choice cost him dearly. Was it necessary?

As already noted, there were other means to accomplish his purposes. The Kuwaitis had already agreed (albeit reluctantly) to keep to their quotas. The allegations made about the oil fields could have found a forum for resolution. Saddam Hussein had not repaid any major share of the debts owed to Kuwait, and likely could have avoided paying them for many years, and so on. For someone who is said by analysts to be a patient man (Post 1991; Karsh and Rautsi 1990), the choice of means in this case suggests that impulse triumphed over prudence.

And what of George Bush? Bush was faced with a "do it or lose it" situation. Doing nothing immediately after the invasion would have narrowed the range of available alternatives for action. Decisions needed to be made, and quickly, if only to preserve future options.

In these highly uncertain, volatile, and time-pressured circumstances, Bush's response was psychologically active. By most accounts, Bush was the driving force behind the policy and its implementation. His decisive response indicates that any doubts and uncertainties he may have had did not inhibit him.[36] His response was consistent with Bush's active—one can say peripatetic—style. This trait has a long developmental history.[37]

Bush's reaction also suggests another dimension of the process of his judgment in this case. Whether one agrees with the action Bush took, his immediate response indicates the quick nature of his understanding of some major implications of the invasion. First and most immediate was the threat to Saudi Arabia and the oil fields. We do not know whether Saddam Hussein intended to cross Kuwait into Saudi Arabia; it would have been very tempting had there been no response to his invasion into Kuwait. But the introduction of even limited numbers of U.S. troops raised the certainty of direct armed confrontation with the United States and thus raised the stakes of such a move considerably.

As the conflict progressed, Bush voiced a number of reasons for his strong response. Many have already been discussed. Bush has been criticized for seeming to add new reasons and change his emphasis at times. At one point, for example, Bush declared, "This is not about oil, its about aggression" (Friedman 1990, 9). Yet earlier he had warned about the consequences of allowing Saddam Hussein to gain control over these vast oil reserves (Apple, 1990, 14).

Bush advanced most of the reasons for his response in some form during the first days of the crisis.[38] But he clearly considered the implications of the invasion more fully as time passed. There is nothing sinister in this; further consideration in a crisis is beneficial. Indeed, had personal outrage been the sole driving force behind Bush's policy it would have been questionable indeed.

Clearly the invasion galvanized Bush; his response was strong, visceral, and unequivocal. Thomas Friedman reports that "by all accounts it is President Bush's gut instincts that drove the rapid American commitment of forces to Saudi Arabia" (1990b). On August 5, 1990, returning from Camp David "visibly angry," he made the following statement to reporters: "I view very seriously our determination to reverse this aggression . . . this will not stand. This will not stand, this aggression towards Kuwait" (ibid., 1). This is a very strong public statement; it committed the president and the United States to action—indeed, it literally promised it.

Bush's repeated assertion that this invasion "will not stand" is also interesting in another, more psychological sense. It certainly appears to reflect a sense of decisional optimism that Janis has identified with high-quality decisions and also accords with our discussion of the sense of capacity and effectiveness as two important psychological characteristics underlying good judgment.

Bush's anger about the invasion, which clearly fueled his determination and which was prominently and publicly displayed from the first, should also be examined more closely. Three factors fueled Bush's anger.

First, Bush felt betrayed by Saddam Hussein's action. He had failed to influence Saddam by a series of military and economic relationships (see chapter 13). Another aspect of the betrayal was the reassurance given to Egypt's President Mubarak (and thus to others) by Saddam Hussein that he would not use force with Kuwait. Bush values loyalty, which in part relies on doing what you say you will do.

A second source of Bush's anger were his feelings regarding a large nation invading a smaller one. This had a parallel to earlier experiences. There is a story in several of Bush biographies that tells of Bush intervening when a bully was harassing a schoolmate at Andover. Psychologically in these situations, two dynamics seems to be operating for Bush.

Not only was Bush apparently genuinely upset about the reported atrocities committed by the Iraqi army in Kuwait, but also he felt a "duty to intervene." A strict sense of right and wrong was stressed in Bush's early family experience, especially associated with the teaching of his mother (Hyams 1991, 68). This strong sense of propriety continued to be emphasized by his mother in latter life, even when Bush was running for president.[39]

Finally, Bush may have been angered by Saddam's assertion of the old politics exactly when Bush was trying to construct his new world order. Whatever the exact cause of the anger, it clearly fed Bush's determination, galvanized him, and pushed him toward action. It clearly illustrates how feeling can not only shape, but also inform decision. There is no cool, unemotional, rational actor here, but neither is there a response driven solely or even primarily by emotion.

Good Judgment and Political Leadership in the Process of Policy Implementation

I have suggested that in assessing judgment it is not only important to examine elements of character and cognition in a decision judgment, but also behavioral ones, in particular actions of leadership. The psychological model of good judgment suggests two areas to examine: first, the actual responses that the leader selects and, second, how he carries through on his decisions.

Bush's first response to the invasion was to forge an economic boycott while dispatching troops to Saudi Arabia. Some have observed that the commitment of troops set the stage for a strictly miliary approach to the problem, and it is true that without the commitment of troops at this point it would have been difficult (if not impossible) to pursue a military option later. But it is also accurate that forging economic sanctions put into place a mechanism that allowed the possible resolution of the issues without military action.

Did Bush use the second approach only to cover his intention to use military force? To answer that question, one must know what was really in Bush's mind, a difficult task. We need perhaps to distinguish the readiness to use force from the determination to use it under any circumstances.

It seems clear that Bush was ready to use force from the start, but this is not the same as a determination to use it regardless. The latter implies that Bush was committed to sacrificing lives even if there was no reason for it. It would reflect a deeply cynical, exploitative view of human relations, a view of which we have seen no evidence. It would in addition go against Bush's highly moral, even idealized view of human behavior.

In contrast to Saddam Hussein, whose major policy tool both before and after the invasion was a resort to force, Bush had a more sophisticated response.[40] In effect he put into effect a two-pronged, parallel approach that gave him a range of options. In terms of our discussion about fitting solutions, a dual approach has obvious advantages.

A last point about leadership is how Bush carried out his judgments, fitting together skills, the actions chosen, and the capacity to move toward a solution. Bush's leadership style is clearly collegial. In Barber's terms, he specializes in "interpersonal relations" (1992, 6), a trait with a long developmental history (Hymes 1991). Of the two actions that Bush chose, one—the economic sanctions—clearly depended on building and maintaining a coalition.[41] This would have been simply impossible without his long history and skill at personal diplomacy. Moreover, however one may judge George Bush's actions in the Gulf, building and holding together that unprecedented coalition, for that cause (the defense of a faraway small state), in those circumstances, remains an impressive act of political leadership.

The Process of Good Judgment During the Gulf War: Facilitating and Inhibiting Factors

How leaders view each other in a crisis is almost as important, and not unrelated to, how they view the situation. In a crisis situation, a key question is "Who intends what?" An answer requires knowledge of the adversary's history and culture, to be sure, but it also rests on knowledge about the person who has internalized that culture and history, and the meaning of his acts within those contexts.

One important key to Bush's handling of the crisis was that he came to a quick understanding of Saddam Hussein. Conversely, Saddam Hussein misread and continued to misjudge George Bush. In part, he failed to fully appreciate aspects of George Bush's character. But he also misread history and misapplied his own cultural experience.

Saddam Hussein

Saddam Hussein misread and misunderstood George Bush from the start. Moreover, he *continued to do so*. Why he did so is one of the major questions of political psychology that emerges from the Gulf War. One can argue that the administration's "mixed signals" and in particular the Glaspie-Hussein discussion[42] may have misled Hussein before the invasion, but they can not plausibly be seen as reasons to continue to misjudge and miscalculate.

Limiting myself to why Saddam misjudged George Bush's response to the invasion itself, I believe first that he correctly read history but misapplied his knowledge. He told Ambassador Glaspie at their July 25 meeting, "Yours is a society which can not accept 10,000 dead in one battle."[43] Later, in an address taped and delivered to American audiences on network television (Kamen 1990, 30) he warned that President Bush "is repeating the Vietnam experience, only this time [it will be] more violent and [there will be] more casualties." I think he correctly read our society's dislike of war and especially the painful experiences associated with Vietnam.

However, Saddam Hussein did not sufficiently appreciate George Bush's willingness to use force, even though the possibility should have been evident from Bush's decision to invade Panama. Saddam Hussein may also have also underestimated George Bush's determination and political skill. Hussein clearly counted on U.S. public opinion to exert restraints on the president, and it did. But Bush was able to mobilize the public and international support to a degree that was not anticipated.

Last, I think that Saddam Hussein was in some ways a victim of his own success. Experience teaches lessons through consequences. Yet when a leader is answerable to no one, and there is no political mechanism confronting a leader with the direct effects of ill considered decisions, less learning will take place.

Saddam's Advisors: Real Advice?

Saddam Hussein's has maintained power in Iraq over several decades by a skillful use of incentives and force. He has been flexible as well as brutal (Karsh and Rautsi 1991, 57–109; al-Khalil 1989, 46–72). Yet he has made some very critical and costly policy misjudgments while in power. These include the 1974 war against the Kurds (Karsh and Rautsi 1991, 80–82) and of course the disastrous decision to invade Iran.

In each case, the decisions resulted in enormous political, social, and economic costs to Iraq. But they did not harm Saddam Hussein personally or politically for evident reasons: there were no public mechanisms to hold Saddam Hussein accountable; there were no legislative or judicial inquiries; nor were there publicly articulated demands for an accounting. On each occasion, the regime put the best possible interpretation on events, and there was no individual and no institution to contradict the official view.

Moreover, there appear to be no private mechanisms available that might have required Saddam Hussein to confront directly and perhaps learn from costly policy mistakes. Saddam Hussein's circle of advisors consists of relatives, military leaders, and political advisors from his early days with the Baath party, many of whom are from his hometown (Sciolino 1990; 1991). His inner circle consists of "like-minded men," "extreme loyalists" who can hardly be unaware that Saddam Hussein has consolidated his position by "killing his enemies."

Sciolino describes his rule as "total" (1990; see also al-Khalil, 1989; Karsh and Rautsi, 1991) and reports:

> Arab leaders and Western diplomats who have dealt with him say that a conversation with Mr. Hussein is not a dialogue. They say he states a position and then asks questions that he then proceeds to answer himself.[44] He runs meetings with his commanders like a tribal leader or an arrogant corporate chairman, and those who murmur in private about his decisions, or who are perceived to have failed in their duty, are either retired or executed. (Sciolino, 1991)

Not surprisingly, "when it comes to political maneuvering or military strategy, Saddam Hussein is his own best advisor."[45] Yet it seems unlikely these decisions of Hussein's were strongly debated or contested before they were implemented. They certainly were not afterward, even though they proved to be costly errors.

We do not exactly what lessons Saddam Hussein took from these experiences. One might be that while violence can be costly, it is not necessarily self-defeating. This possibly helps to account for Saddam Hussein's willingness to stay in Kuwait when a more prudent and advantageous path would have been a partial tactical withdrawal coupled with calls for a conference.

George Bush

A key ingredient of Bush's response to the crisis was his understanding of Saddam Hussein.[46] At a very early stage Bush characterized Hussein in ways parallel to scholarly and well-researched views. Even those who ask us to empathize with Saddam Hussein (White 1991) characterize him as "aggressive," "dangerous," and "ruthless." Others are less kind (Post 1991; Karsh and Rautsi 1991; al-Khalil 1989). But what is striking in terms of our model of judgment is how quickly and early Bush came to a similar view.

For example, in one of the first news conferences after the invasion, Bush raised the issue of Saddam Hussein's past violent behavior and coupled it with the assertion, "Iraq may not stop using force to advance its ambitions."[47] In addressing Congress, Bush referred to Saddam Hussein's "ruthlessness" as one reason for a strong response.[48]

I have argued that the exercise of good judgment requires not only placing information in a framework that provides accurate understanding, but also drawing implications for action. The basic question before us (and the question that confronted George Bush) is how to respond to a leader who has seized and maintained power though violence, who has repeatedly used violence to settle conflicts, and who is described (evidently accurately) as aggressive, dangerous, and ruthless.

The answer is not as self-evident as it may appear. White observes that Saddam Hussein's use of violence may be in large part defensive—that he uses violence not because he likes it, but because it is instrumental in addressing realistic fears about Iraqi's national security interests in a turbulent area and his own hold on power (1991, 298–90). If so, White argues, the best policy would be one that, while maintaining strength, addresses some of Saddam Hussein's concerns—for example, "exchanging a corner of Kuwait for elimination of Saddam's chemical, biological, and nuclear weapons (ibid., 304–08). The U.N. would give up something it wants less (a corner of Kuwait) for something it wants more (drastically reducing Saddam's military power)."[49]

The "defensive violence" theory is an attractive argument, made even more so because it is accurate to some degree. The Middle East is a dangerous and turbulent place (Friedman 1989, 76–105), and there are internal and external threats to both Iraq and Saddam Hussein. The problem with the argument is that it does not fully appreciate the implications of the psychological analysis it begins by accepting.

To say that someone is aggressive, dangerous, and ruthless means that a person is not stopped by conventional boundaries or interpersonal concerns in pursuit of a goal. I will not speculate about the early origins of these characteristics which have been widely described (see the chapter in this volume by Post). But it seems clear that the lessons of violence have been firmly etched in Hussein's character and pervade his stance toward life. He is suspicious and violence-prone partly because these character elements have been required and successful tools for him. Even the unsuccessful use of violence has not reversed this pattern, because he has not been held accountable.

The defensive violence theory fails to appreciate that a violent arena (such as Middle Eastern or Iraqi politics) may *combine* with an adult political career made successful by a mastery of violence and cunning. After decades of using violence to survive in a violent place, a leader's character structure may parallel and reinforce rather than conflict with the domestic or regional political culture. Therefore, it is difficult to expect that a few gestures in the midst of an intense international crisis directed toward easing these realistic fears could reverse a pattern developed over many years. It is all the less likely when those patterns are constantly maintained by the very domestic and regional characteristics that (as White argues) led to Saddam Hussein's uses of violence in the first place.

Ruthless people make use of their surroundings as well as being affected by them. In the leader's view, a violent world justifies and requires the use of violence in return. If the Kuwaiti government wages economic war, that justifies waging military war in response. If one's opponents are out to get you, one is thoroughly vindicated in getting them first. The problem is that such justifications fail to account for other, less violence-prone responses to the same environment. In Egypt and Saudi Arabia, the use of external and internal violence, while not totally absent, are nonetheless of a different magnitude than that exercising by Saddam Hussein and others in the area.

Finally, the defensive violence theory also fails to appreciate that a ruthless individual often mistrusts attempts at compromise, when he does not see them as weakness. Suspicion and experience would cause him to be wary, if not to reject such initiatives outright. More frequently an attempt at compromise is viewed as a signal that toughness is working, as usual. If so, why stop?

Indeed, Bush's much critized policy of attempted accommodation with Iraq before the war was just the kind of policy initiative that White suggests would be fruitful. But it failed because Saddam took advantage of the overtures and used them as an opportunity to get more weapons and increase his military and political power. It was this experience, I believe, that caused Bush to use the Munich analogy.[50] He had tried, by selective accommodation, to influence Saddam's behavior. The invasion of Kuwait had betrayed that attempt.

Bush personalized the Gulf War (as did Saddam Hussein),[51] just as he did when ordering the invasion of Panama to remove General Noriaga from power. Bush is clearly more comfortable in personalizing conflict than in generalizing it. In part, separating the Iraqi people from their leader is a tested way of preparing for an eventual resumptions of relations. But is also serves other functions as well for Bush.

It is related I think to Bush's strong sense of the importance of moral behavior, and correspondingly the importance of duty and propriety. The strong moral emphasis in Bush's formative development has, I believe, led him to see the world in somewhat idealized form—not that he is an idealist (although this is possible), but rather than he has an idealized sense of how the world should be, even as he "harbors no illusions."

Saddam Hussein, the leader of a big powerful country, not only invaded and overran a smaller neighbor, but also violated George Bush's strong sense of propriety. In his news conference of August 30, 1990, Bush said, "I'd like to think that out of this dreary performance by Saddam Hussein there could now be an opportunity for peace all through the Middle East."[52] A few days latter at a news conference, the following exchange occurred:

> Q: Sir, what do you make . . . of the piecemeal approach that Saddam has been taking releasing a few women and children?
> A: I don't like that. Yeah. I don't like it. I don't like it. I don't think the world likes it; . . . there's a certain brutality, a certain tawdry performance in all of this.[53]

Bush's Advisors: A Consensus-Minded In-Group?

If, as suggested, Saddam may have failed to learn important lessons from his past mistakes, in part because of timidity and fear among his advisors, what is the role of George Bush's advisors? According to Woodward, the Bush decision-making group was strongly collegial (1991, 302). Moreover, it was headed by a president experienced in foreign affairs who had publicly and private stated his strong views.[54] When "accommodation" to the invasion was raised as an option by one advisor, the president quickly and decisively ruled it out and it was not seriously considered again. This is not ordinarily a combination that leads to wide-ranging discussion. Moreover, at least one participant expressed reservations about the coherence of the deliberations.

There was general agreement among the major advisors that a quick and direct response to the invasion was necessary (Friedman and Tyler 1991; Friedman 1990b). Yet one cannot assume therefore that the decision was necessarily flawed or that no differences were present or expressed. Friedman notes, "By all accounts, it is President Bush's gut instincts that drove the rapid American commitment of forces to Saudi Arabia and if anything, it is Mr. Baker, with Defense Secretary Dick Cheney and Gen. Colin L. Powell . . . who take turns playing cautionary roles (1990b, 6).

Woodward notes that at least one of these participants, General Powell, was unhappy about the lack of consistent focus in discussions at formal meetings. However, transcripts of other National Security meetings (for example, now declassified Cuban Missile Crisis EXCOM meetings) suggest that few issues are sharply focused and subjected to sustained examination before another is brought up. Crisis meetings tend to be free flowing. Issues are raised, put aside, and raised again. In such meetings, perhaps reflecting the nature of the crisis itself, consideration of one thing often leads to another.

There are some suggestions that General Powell favored containing Saddam Hussein rather than removing him from Kuwait, but did not argue forcefully for his view. His reasons are somewhat unclear. Powell says that he saw his role as giving a balanced assessment of the options available to the president, implying that he voiced his reservations. However, we do not know how strong his reservations were. Woodward reports that even though harboring private misgivings about the military buildup, Powell supported the recommendations of General Schwartzkopf, who did advise a contingency buildup. If he did feel strongly, it is unclear why Powell declined to press his views. It would be a cause for concern if Powell had felt inhibited by the cohesion or actions of the group, and was prevented from offering them, or was pressed to alter them, or was marginalized, or that other mechanisms of groupthink were in evidence.

There is another factor to consider: emphasizing the president's close advisors tends to understate other consultation during the crisis. Bush was in frequent personal contact with a range of world leaders, not all of whom shared his views or favored his plans. Bush's consultation decision making and leadership style suggest that alternative points of view could easily have been presented and forcefully pressed.

The Consequences of Judgment

To assess the judgments made during this war using the model presented at the outset, we must consider the issues raised by the invasion and the consequences of decisions that were made. Whereas the final three chapters of this book examine the consequences of the Gulf War in detail, I will anticipate those analyses with some general theoretical considerations.

Our analysis of decision-making models emphasized that a concern with procedure was necessary partly because judging outcomes was exceedingly difficult. Judgments about outcomes must be made against criteria that are often theoretically complex and influenced by political views;[55] moreover, outcomes of decisions may take unintended or surprising forms and may vary in important respects over time.[56] Hence few have grappled with the difficult question of outcomes. Those who have focused on "national interest" have sometimes done so without a clear explication of that term. Herek et al. (1987) focus on outcomes, such as increases in international tension, which, while they should not be foolishly sought, may be an inevitable result of any crisis regardless of the quality of the procedures used to resolve conflict.

How then should we judge the outcomes of the Gulf War? The approach I have chosen is to assess the consequences of the invasion for the United States and Iraq, to understand what interests were at stake, and to determine whether those interests could not have been served by other means.

Even granting that Iraq's concerns had a legitimate basis does not lead to the position that the invasion of Kuwait was either necessary or justified. Certainly, the strong and unequivocal response of the United States and its allies threatened Iraq with enormous losses to what Alexander George has called irreducible national interests. To place those interests at such risk was itself problematic.

Further, Saddam Hussein had a viable strategy for both standing up to George Bush and removing his country from harm. What if, in the hours after the deadline had passed, Saddam Hussein had announced that he had not caved in, but in the interests of peace and at the urging of many nations was taking the following steps: (1) he was going to begin an orderly withdrawal from Kuwait, and (2) after taking clear and verifiable steps, he would call for a conference to address his nation's concerns. Of course, George Bush might have refused to participate in a conference until all troops were removed, but given the public sentiment in favor of talks during the countdown this might have been a difficult step to take.

Why Saddam Hussein did not do something like this is one of the major puzzles of the war. Instead he chose to stay, for reasons that are not yet clear. But this assumes that Saddam Hussein should weigh the factors involved in ways that are appropriate to *our* understanding of his circumstances. This he clearly did not do.

In the end, Saddam Hussein lost much, but not all. He survives to fight another day, and as recent events indicate, is doing so already. Still, his regional power has been dealt a severe blow, and with it his personal and political ambitions. He has paid a severe price, but regrettably required his country to pay also. If good judgment consists of finding a way to accomplish purposes that preserve or even advance the national interest, Saddam Hussein clearly failed in this regard.

What of George Bush? Two of his nation's three irreducible national interests did not appear to be immediately challenged by the invasion, although several may have been at risk over time. Yet, given what we now know about the advanced status of Saddam Hussein's nuclear program and his attempts to obtain technology for long-range missiles, even a threat to the United States' physical survival cannot be totally ruled out as an issue. Saddam Hussein's position in the Middle East is a cause for concern and does affect strategic U.S. interests. As the international system undergoes a structural transformation, it is important to pay attention to the development of new rules. One hopes that one of the lessons of the Gulf War is that no leader can use force for personal and territorial aggrandizement without risk.

A major consequence of the war was the loss of life on both sides. The war was a terrible and traumatic event—no evaluation of the judgments involved can fail to address that fact. But the suffering enduring must be balanced against options and finally accomplishments, among which and I would suggest these:

1. A dangerous despotic leader with a history of using violence to further his personal position and regime was dealt a severe blow.
2. A program of nuclear weapons development, which in Saddam Hussein's hands would have been a powerful instrument of intimidation, and perhaps war, was also dealt a decisive blow.
3. The cooperation between the former Soviet Union and the United States, coupled with the latter's strong and unequivocal response to the invasion has changed the climate of the Middle East, and made it possible to develop new alignments and arrangements. Obviously, the chief reflection of this process is to be seen in the peace conference convened after the war. This is of course the start of a long process, but a real step toward peace.
4. Aggression was confronted and defied by an unprecedented collective process linking a number of world powers.

Any judgment process poses risks and results in some unfavorable outcomes. This one is no exception. But overall, there is much to be learned about the process of good judgment in Bush's response, just as there is to learn about its opposite in the initial and subsequent decisions of Saddam Hussein.

NOTES

I would like to express my appreciation to colleagues who provided helpful comments on this paper: John Fiscalini, Alexander L. George, Fred I. Greenstein, Noel Kaplowitz, Mohammad-Mahmoud Mohamedou, and Philip Tetlock. This article builds on and extends the analysis presented in Renshon, 1992.

    1. Decisions also vary in their time frames. Some decisions, like the basing mode for U.S. ICBMs, have been debated for years with no final decision in sight. Others, like how to rid Cuba of offensive missiles in 1962, had to be decided in a matter of days. Finally, decisions vary in their location along a public-private continuum. Some presidential decisions are made in the context of public debate, more often they are the product of small decision groups, and occasionally decisions are made by the president acting alone.

    2. The term *political decision making* here refers to those decisions that affect the substance and nature of political institutions and practice. *Political* is not meant to refer to more narrowly focused partisan politics.

    3. Early psychoanalytic formulations of political decision making emphasized unconscious motivations and ego defenses. This proved unsatisfactory for several reasons. As George writes:

Some years ago, when political scientists were exposed to early developments in ego psychology, they were struck by the fact that arousal of a leader's anxieties and ego defenses could severely impair his ability to deal rationally with a situation. As a result, political scientists—and some psychiatrists and psychologists as well—tended to regard any display of ego defenses (such as denial, projection, or rationalization) by a political leader in a stressful situation that his ability to cope rationally and effectively with that situation had been impaired. Decisions made under these circumstances were regarded with suspicion, and any inadequacy perceived in the substance of the decision was explained as being the unfortunate by-product of the leader's resort to ego defenses to cope with his anxieties. *Explanatory hypotheses of this kind often oversimplified and distorted the role of unconscious emotional factors in decision making.* (George, 1980, 8–9, emphasis added)

George is not arguing that unconscious elements play no role in decision making, but rather that the use made of them is often problematic. Consider for example the assumption that unconscious elements are always injurious to high-quality decision making. True, unconscious conflicts or associations can distort the process, but as a counter example, the triggering of anticipatory guilt may signal that a particular choice may violate some important and problem-relevant normative standard.

The difficulty of using unconscious elements in analyzing decision making (wishes, feelings, associations, motivations—covering a wide range of psychological territory) is that they are difficult to discern and it is difficult to know which elements are involved in any given decision.

The unconscious contains residues of later experiences that are neither repressed nor fully conscious, as well as memory traces that have lost their emotional valence because of maturation (see Waelder 1960, n.5). The unconscious also contains feelings associated with particular kinds of experience. Thus certain events might elicit feelings that are then experienced as contemporaneous with ongoing events. These could form the basis of unconscious "lessons from the past."

Analysts can infer the presence and influence of the unconscious only from a leader's observed behavior. This is difficult unless one knows what the leader is "usually like," knows of previous patterns into which current behavior fits, can distinguish cognitive distortions from those having other psychological roots, and has detailed information about how and why the leader approached a problem in a particular way.

Moreover, even if one acknowledges the influence of unconscious elements, and even if one could discern which (if any) were operative, what use can be made of this knowledge? How can it contribute toward improvement? Unless one wishes to suggest, as some have, that every leader be psychoanalyzed to be rid of unconscious conflicts, it is hard to see a practical payoff. Elsewhere (Renshon 1990) I have suggested some techniques and examined the possibilities of integrating such experiences into leadership development education.

The psychological (and even psychodynamic) factors that affect a leader's decision making go beyond the unconscious. The old psychoanalytic models need to be supplemented by other models of psychological functioning in decision making.

4. There is some evidence that following decision-enhancing procedures does lead to better outcomes. Herek, Janis, and Huth (1987) studied nineteen major crises since World War II. Using content analysis of bibliographic sources, they rated the decision procedures used (1987, 211). Experts then rated the outcomes on two dimensions, increased (decreased international tension, and favorable (unfavorable) outcomes for U.S. interests. They found that "quality of decision-making process is related to the decision's outcome" (218).

5. A number of contextual or cognitive limitations accompanying high-level political/executive roles may inhibit adherence to the requirements of an ideal model. Most leaders confront many complex decision problems at a time. This fact tests the limits of the cognitive capacity and the ability to fully follow through on procedural requirements.

6. Compare the list of procedural requirements contained in Janis and Mann (1977, 11) with Allison's (1971, 32–35).

7. After all, why follow these procedures if not to pick the option that enlarges one's share of the crucial values at stake, even if one cannot realistically expect to maximize them? Adherents of the procedural model accept the modification of rational-actor theory that notes that decision makers may be content to satisfice rather than maximize (Simon, 1957). Yet they are still bound by the basic logic of the accumulation calculus, that is, more is better than less; the question is how much more.

8. One exception is Janis (1989, 203–29).

9. One can note some drawbacks to such experiments. For example, the payoff matrix is fairly clear (if you think about it), the choices limited, and the consequences of failure (or success) not substantial. But for our purposes the major problem is that the problem is essentially defined by the experimenter. In real life, the definition of the problem is not a given but a variable and can therefore reveal substantial information about the views and psychology of the definer.

10. It is not clear that cognitive complexity is necessarily related to high-quality decisions—the issue Tetlock raises. Obsessive thinkers, for example, usually exhibit highly complex ideation, yet it may lack depth and sophistication. This leads to the issue of understanding: more complex thinking may not necessarily lead to better policy judgment. The real issue may be rather the amount of reflective capacity and insight, which are apparently related to, perhaps dependent on, some form of complex thinking.

11. Any decision can reflect a judgment, but minor or routine decisions do not ordinarily raise issues regarding the basic adequacy of judgment. Misjudgment from this perspective then would represent a flawed judgment on a relatively small matter, or one in which the information to make adequate judgments is not available.

12. I differ somewhat from Tetlock (1992), who examines good judgment primarily in terms of predictive capacities. In my view, the issue is less the ability to predict than the capacity to understand. Predicting specific outcomes in politics is so difficult as to preclude defining good judgment solely in this way.

13. Psychological maturity does not mean freedom from conflict. Well-developed persons have conflicts and emotional and interpersonal difficulties like everyone else, but these difficulties exist in a general context of psychological accomplishment, rather than vice versa.

14. The closest theorists have come to examining the impact of the problem itself have been to discuss the leader's definition of the problem (Pruitt 1965), which has implications for both decision making and political process. But perception operates within factual and historical as well as personal frames.

15. Sophisticated handling of information such the ability to draw on past and present, to extrapolate to possible futures, and to shift among perspectives requires cognitive and emotional flexibility. These too are affected by character. Barber (1992) argues that active-positive presidents, characterized by high self-esteem, are better able to learn from experience.

This relationship is supported by Sniderman's study of several samples of adults, including one of party and political leaders, to examine the impact of self-esteem on political orientation. He suggests that "low self-esteem clearly inhibits the acquisition of political knowledge" (1975, 161). In both studies, low self-esteem is associated with inhibitions to learning and less adequate decisions.

16. This possibility is raised by Gelb's analysis of George Bush's mishandling of his January 1992 meeting in Japan with executives of major automobile manufacturers (1992: 15).

17. The importance of affect in decision making is becoming more widely recognized, but its exact roles are not clear. Abelson (1959) introduces the concept of "hot cognition" to account for the finding that in some areas cognition becomes suffused with affect and thus more salient and powerful in shaping behavior. Janis and Mann's emphasis on the important of feelings of hope in being able to reach optimal political decisions represents a further attempt to integrate the two domains (1977).

Traditional "rational-actor" theorists of decision making viewed affect as interfering with calculations of "value maximizing," which was, in their view, the essence of rational decision making. Affect can interfere in two ways. First, it can result in leaders giving inappropriate weight to some consideration and, second, some feelings like empathy for example would appear to undercut a totally self-interested calculation.

Full rational actor models have given way to "bounded rationality" (Kinder and Weiss 1978) models, in which place a number of constraints on the assumptions of the "rational actor." Most these constraints have to do with the cognitive requirements of the full rational model. The role of affect in these models is still somewhat unclear.

In some models of self-interest, feelings are viewed as simply another datum to be factored into the overall self-interest evaluation. This solves the problem of accounting in some way for affect, and perhaps preserving the (self-interest) model, but whether it provides a theory of the relationships of affect to decision is another issue.

Psychoanalytically inclined theorists on the other, tend to emphasize affect, especially as it presents itself in the form of impulse. This has the virtue of examining how and why affect effects decisions, but appears to limit the role to affect primarily to the expression of unconscious wishes.

18. A leader's grandiosity and accompanying sense of invulnerability and entitlement often reflect an underlying masked anxiety and or an insufficiently consolidated sense of self-esteem. This anxiety may arise from the direct per-

sonal and political implications of events themselves or may be related to the steps that might need to be taken if events are viewed clearly and seriously.

19. Interestingly, the Herek et al. (1987) study of the relation between procedures and outcomes noted that one of the most frequent procedural failures was not faulty information search, but rather failure *to use* new information, which also was the procedural deficiency most empirically associated with negative outcomes.

20. This does not mean that one's immediate feelings are necessarily wrong, only that one must supplement the information they supply.

21. I use this term for attempts at empathy whose purpose is advantage rather than an understanding that might moderate competitive pressures. For an example of this kind of empathy in the context of the rational-actor model of managing international conflict, see Allison (1971, 256).

22. Transcript, "Statement Issued by Iraq's Revolutionary Command Council," *New York Times*, August 9, 1990, p. 8.

23. Transcript, "Excerpts from TV Interview with Iraqi Official," *New York Times*, August 17, 1990, p. 9.

24. Karsh and Rautsi report a figure of $230 billion in war reconstruction costs (1991, 201).

25. Whereas greater oil independence for the United States would reduce the need to intervene to protect the supply of foreign oil, it should be noted that (1) reduced dependency is not the same as independence; (2) shutting off oil and related commerce would have serious political, military, economic, social and psychological effects, some of which would damage U.S. interests in the Middle East; (3) the dependence of several important U.S. allies on imported oil would still exert pressure to become involved in a crisis such as the invasion of Kuwait and the possible invasion of Saudi Arabia. And there could be other policy reasons, even assuming oil independence, to intervene.

26. Transcript, "Excerpts from the TV Talk by Mubarak to the Egyptians," *New York Times*, August 9, 1990, p. 8.

27. Transcript, "Excerpts from Bush's Statement on U.S. Defense of the Saudis," *New York Times*, August 9, 1990, p. 15.

28. Transcript, "Excerpts from Bush's Speech on Iraq Policy," *New York Times*, August 29, 1990, p. 14. A closer examination of the Bush administration policy toward Iraq immediately before the war, including its policy regarding nuclear materials, is found in chapter 13.

29. Transcript, "President's Address to Joint Session of Congress," *New York Times*, September 12, 1990, p. 20.

30. Transcript, "Excerpts from Speech by Bush at Marine Post," *New York Times*, November 23, 1990, p. 14.

31. Transcript, "Excerpts from President's News Conference on Crisis," *New York Times*, December 1, 1990, p. 6.

32. Transcript, "Excerpts from President's News Conference on the Gulf Crisis," *New York Times*, August 31, 1990, p. 11.

33. The list apparently recognized no irreducible interest other than domestic. Nor does it recognize that a major power also has international interests, although satisfying them is not essential to maintaining irreducible national interests. On the other hand, in a world where others have the ability to inflict

severe economical and political damage, a concern about maintaining some "degrees of freedom" in the international system is not inappropriate. Further, although a nation's continued existence can be minimally defined as being able to survive physically and economically, is minimal economic subsistence consonant with the maintenance of democratic institutions? Last, does physical survival include the forced dismemberment of a country? If so, to what degree?

34. In the transcript of the Glaspie-Hussein meeting (*New York Times*, September 21, 1990, p. 9), Hussein acknowledged that agreement had been reached at this meeting, but went on to assert, "We have received some intelligence that they were talking of sticking to the agreement for two months only." This implies of course that the Kuwaiti government was, at the time of the invasion and at least as of the Jedda meeting, complying with a major Iraqi demand.

35. It is relevant that that Saddam Hussein's "first independent political success" (Barber, 1992) and a marker event in his adult political socialization (Renshon, 1989), was to take part in an assassination attempt (Karsh and Rautsi, 1991, 16–18; al-Khalil, 1989, 118).

36. One must distinguish a leader's approach to decision making and the effects of what is chosen. Deliberative approaches to decision making are no bar to decisive, consequential action. Nor does a quick response necessarily result in extreme action. Nor should taking decisive action be confused with acting on impulse. Bush appears to have a deliberative, not an impulsive style. Like Saddam Hussein, he takes things carefully. Indeed, his careful approach to his previous public service roles, and the bureaucratic nature of the roles themselves, were probably responsible for his image as a man "who left no marks."

37. Bush reports in his autobiography that as a young man working in Texas to build an oil company he worked "eighteen hours a day to build a company from the ground up." His doctor called him "a classic ulcer case . . . a young businessman with only one speed, 'all out.' " The doctor also told him, "You try to do too much and you worry too much" (1987, 12).

38. Compare the explanation before August 15 (Apple 1990, 14) with that put forward in the president's news conference of August 30 (*New York Times* transcript, August 31, 1990, p. 11), which uses similar language, but goes further. However, this is possibly only a more systematic statement of what had been implicit earlier. It differs dramatically from the kinds of statements that crop up later in the conflict. For example, in a talk at a marine post in Saudi Arabia (*New York Times* transcript, November 23, 1990, p. 8), Bush argued, "We're here to protect freedom," a generalized extension of the more specific goals that he had enunciated previously.

39. Bush recalls his mother saying to him after a campaign speech, "You're talking too much about yourself too much, George . . . try to retrain yourself" (1987, p. 27).

40. After the invasion, Saddam elaborated a secondary strategy that broadened the issues (e.g., past and present colonial practices, sharing of oil wealth), called for a *jihad* against the coalition members, and suggested attacking Israel as a way to split the alliance. It is interesting to note the degree of violence even in these secondary strategies, developed in response to strong opposition to Saddam's primary strategy, the invasion.

41. The military option in theory could have been carried through by the United States alone. But just as Bush's dual response (economic sanctions and

commitment of troops) developed along two alternative but parallel tracks, so too did his building of a coalition. The coalition that imposed and maintained sanctions would be available should sanctions fail.

42. Karsh and Rautsi characterize Ambassador Glaspie as "servile" in this encounter (1991, 216). A more contextual analysis, which is nonetheless critical, may be found in Gelb (1991, 28). Tariq Aziz is quoted as saying, "She was summoned suddenly. We knew she was acting on available instructions. She spoke in vague diplomatic language, and we knew the position she was in. *Her behavior was a classic diplomatic response, and we were not influenced by it*" (Viorst 1991, 66–67, emphasis added).

43. Transcript, *New York Times*, September 21, 1990, p. 9.

44. One gets a sense this from the transcript of the Hussein-Glaspie meeting (*New York Times* transcript, September 23, 1990, p. 9). Hussein began by giving a strong, detailed, and extensive lecture to Ambassador Glaspie. Exchanges between them at the end of the meeting were relatively brief.

45. Sciolino 1991. These descriptions raise the issue of the impact of *groupthink* (Janis, 1972; 't Hart, 1990), which evidence suggests was at work here. Janis and others (George, 1972) note that advisors must have a certain independence and the capacity to speak their minds before they can present a range of alternatives from which the leader can select the wisest course. Wayne (1991) suggests that George Bush too may have surrounded himself with too many like-minded advisors and raises the issue of groupthink.

46. I do not refer to Bush's personalization of the conflict and his remarks comparing Saddam Hussein to Hitler, calling him a liar, etcetera, but to his attunement to the psychology (motivation, world view, developmental history, etc.) that appear to characterize Saddam Hussein. Bush's understanding reflects an empathy with the nature of the man, at least as far as can be determined. But it is a limited form of empathy: Bush seems particularly sensitive to the nature of bullies, as noted, and was genuinely concerned with the plight of the Kuwaitis during the invasion. But Bush's empathy is not absolute, as evidenced by his failure to respond to Iraq's attacks on the Kurds following the war—a disturbing lapse, even given his public explanations. Bush also seems to have less appreciation of those who are not attacked, but who suffer nonetheless—those at the margins and even in the mainstream of our society who suffer because of economic or political circumstances.

47. Transcript, "Excerpts from Bush's Statement on U.S. Defense of the Saudis," p. 15.

48. Transcript, "President's Address to a Joint Session of Congress," p. 20.

49. The idea of the United Nations disposing of a sovereign state's territory does have difficulties. Moreover, one wonders how the Kuwaitis would feel about losing their land.

50. In addition, the Munich analogy no doubt sprung from Bush's own very powerful World War II experiences.

51. Saddam Hussein's speeches make it clear that he too personalized the war. See for example, excerpts from his "Open Letter to Bush" (*New York Times* transcript, August 17, 1990, p. 9), in which he calls Bush a liar and contemptuous of Arabs.

52. Transcript, "Excerpts From President's News Conference on the Gulf Crisis," p. 11.

53. Transcript, "Excerpt from the President's News Conference on Meeting with Gorbachev," *New York Times*, September 2, 1990, p. 18.

54. General Scowcroft reports (AEI 1992, p. 10) that at the second National Security Council meeting on August 3, 1990, he asked to begin the meeting by framing the larger significance of the invasion. Bush replied that perhaps he should take this role himnself. Scowcroft responded, "No, I think its better that I do and you sit back and let the debate develop."

55. For example, Herek et al. find that in judging outcomes (increased world tension, advances for U.S. interests) "the conservative expert was inclined to see more of the outcomes as favorable or neutral, while the liberal saw more of them as negative" (1987, 215). This suggests how political views may frame the evaluation of outcomes even for scholarly observers.

56. Herek et al. find that raters of decision outcomes agreed much more about short-term than long-term effects, which were considered so unreliable that they were omitted from the analysis (1987, 213 n.3).

REFERENCES

Abelson, R. P. 1959. "Models of Resolutions of Belief Dilemmas." *Journal of Conflict Resolution* 3: 342–52.

al-Khali, S. 1989. *Republic of Fear.* Berkeley and Los Angeles: University of California Press.

Allison, G. 1971. *Essence of Decision: Explaining the Cuban Missile Crisis.* Boston: Little, Brown.

American Enterprise Institute. 1992. *Transcript, The Gulf Crisis: The Road to War, a Three Part Television Series.* Washington, D.C.: American Enterprise Institute.

Apple, R. W., Jr. 1990. "Bush Says Iraqi Aggression Threatens 'Our Way of Life.' " *New York Times*, August 16, p. 14.

Aspin, Les. 1991. "Winning the War and Losing the Peace in Saddam Hussein's Iraq." U.S. House of Representatives Committee on Armed Forces. Memorandum, December 12.

Baquet, Dean. 1992a. "Investigators Say U.S. Shielded Iraqis from Bank Inquiry." *New York Times*, March 20, p. 1.

Barber, J. D. 1992. *Presidential Character.* 4th ed. Englewood Cliffs, N.J.: Prentice-Hall.

Bush, G. 1987. *Looking Forward: An Autobiography.* New York: Bantam.

Friedman, T. L. 1989. *From Beirut to Jerusalem.* New York: Anchor.

——— . 1990a. "Iraqi Assault 'Will not Stand.' " *New York Times*, August 8, p. 1.

——— . 1990b. "Baker Seen as Balance to Bush on Crisis in Gulf. *New York Times*, November 3, pp. 1, 6.

——— . 1990c. "No Compromise on Kuwait, Bush Says." *New York Times*, October 25, 1990, p. 9.

Friedman, T. L., and P. E. Taylor. 1991. "From the First, U.S. Resolve to Fight." *New York Times*, January 1, pp. 18–19.

Gelb, L. 1991. "Mr. Bush's Fateful Blunder." *New York Times*, July 19, p. 28.

——— . 1992. "Three Whine Mice." *New York Times*, January 12, p. 15.

George, A. L. 1972. "The Case for Multiple Advocacy in Making Foreign Policy." *American Political Science Review* 66: 751–58.

———. 1980. *Presidential Decisionmaking in Foreign Policy: The Effective use of Information and Advice.* Boulder, Colo.: Westview Press.

Glad, Betty. 1983. "Black and White Thinking: Ronald Reagan's Approach to Foreign Policy." *Political Psychology* 4: 33–76.

Greenstein, F. I. 1987. *Personality and Politics: Problems of Evidence, Inference and Conceptualization.* Princeton, N.J.: Princeton University Press.

Heradstveit, D. 1979. *The Arab-Israeli Conflict: Psychological Obstacles to Peace.* Oslo: Universitetsforlaget.

Herek, G., I. Janis, and P. Muth. 1987. "Decision Making during International Crises: Is Quality of Process Related to Outcome?" *Journal of Conflict Resolution* 31: 203–26.

Hymes, J. 1991. *Flight of the Avenger.* New York: Harcourt, Brace, Javanovich.

Janis, I. L. 1972. *Victims of Groupthink.* Boston: Houghton Mifflin.

———. 1989. *Crucial Decisions: Leadership in Policymaking and Crisis Management.* New York: Free Press.

Janis, I. L., and L. Mann. 1977. *Decision Making: A Psychological Analysis of Conflict, Choice, and Commitment.* New York: Free Press.

Jervis, R. 1976. *Perception and Misperception in International Relations.* Princeton, N.J.: Princeton University Press.

Kahneman, D., and A. Tversky. 1984. "Choices, Values and Frames." *American Psychologist* 29: 341–50.

Kamen, A. 1990. "Iraqi Warns U.S. of Heavy Casualties." *Washington Post,* September 26, p. 30.

Karsh, E., and I. Rautsi. 1991. *Saddam Hussein: A Political Biography.* New York: Free Press.

Kinder, D. R., and J. A. Weiss. 1978. "In Lieu of Rationality: Psychological Perspectives on Foreign Policy Decision Making." *Journal of Conflict Resolution* 22: 707–75.

Lasswell, H. D. 1956. *The Decision Process: Seven Categories of Functional Analysis.* College Park: University of Maryland Press.

May, E. 1973. *"Lessons" of the Past: The Uses and Misuse of History in American Foreign Policy.* New York: Oxford University Press.

Miller, J., and L. Mylroie. 1990. *Saddam Hussein and the Crisis in the Gulf.* New York: Times Books.

Nesbitt, R. E., and L. Ross. 1980. *Human Inference: Strategies and Shortcomings of Social Judgment.* New York: Appleton-Century-Crofts.

New York Times. August 9, 1990. "Statement Issued by Iraq's Revolutionary Command Council," p. 8.

———. August 9, 1991. Transcript, "Excerpts from Bush's Statement on U.S. Defense of Saudis," p. 15.

———. August 9, 1990. Transcript, "Excerpts from the TV Talk by Mubarak to the Egyptians," p. 8.

———. August 17, 1990. Transcript of Saddam Hussein's "Open Letter to Bush," p. 9.

———. August 17, 1990. Transcript, "Excerpts from TV Interview with Iraqi Official," p. 9.

————. August 29, 1990. Transcript, "Excerpts from Bush's Speech on Iraq Policy," p. 14.

————. August 31, 1990. Transcript, "Excerpts From President's News Conference on the Gulf Crisis," p. 11.

————. September 2, 1990. Transcript, "Excerpt from the President's News Conference on Meeting with Gorbachev," p. 18.

————. September 11, 1990. Transcript, "President's Address to a Joint Session of Congress," p. 20.

————. September 12, 1990. Transcript, "President's Address to Joint Session of Congress," p. 20.

————. September 21, 1990. Transcript, "Excerpts from Iraqi Document on Meeting with U.S. Envoy," p. 9.

————. November 23, 1990. Transcript, "Excerpts from Speech by Bush at Marine Post," p. 14.

————. December 1, 1990. Transcript, "Excerpts from President's News Conference on Crisis," p. 6.

Post, J. 1991. "Saddam Hussein of Iraq: A Political Psychology Profile." *Political Psychology* 12: 279–89.

Pruitt, D. G. 1965. Definition of the Situation as a Determinant of International Action. In *International Behavior: A Social-Psychological Perspective*, ed. H. C. Kelman. New York: Holt, Rinehart and Winston.

Renshon, S. 1989. "Psychological Theories of Adult Development and the Political Socialization of Leaders." In *Political Learning in Adulthood*, ed. R. Sigel. Chicago: University of Chicago Press.

————. 1990. "Educating Political Leaders in a Democracy." In *Political Socialization, Citizenship Education, and Democracy*, ed. O. Ichilov. New York: Teacher's College Press.

————. 1992. "The Psychology of Good Judgment: A Preliminary Model with Some Applicaitons to the Gulf War." *Political Psychology* 13: 477–96.

Rokeach, M. 1960. *The Open and Closed Mind*. New York: Basic Books.

Sciolino, E. 1990. "In Saddam Hussein's Iraq, All Real Power Settles at the Top." *New York Times*, August 26, p. 18.

————. 1991. "Very Tight Inner Circle Surrounds Iraq's President." *New York Times*, January 27, p. 16.

Simon, H. 1957. *Models of Man: Social and Rational*. New York: Wiley.

Sniderman, P. 1975. *Personality and Democratic Character*. Berkeley and Los Angeles: University of California Press.

Tetlock, P. E. 1985. "Integrative Complexity of American and Soviet Foreign Policy Rhetoric: A Time-Series Analysis." *Journal of Personality and Social Psychology* 49: 1565–85.

————. 1992. "Good Judgment in International Politics: Three Psychological Perspectives." *Political Psychology* 13: 517–39.

't Hart, P. 1990. *Groupthink in Government: A Study of Small Groups and Policy Failure*. Rockland, Maine: Swets and Zeitlinger.

Tversky, A., and D. Kahneman. 1981. "The Framing of Decisions and the Rationality of Choice." *Science* 221: 453–58.

Viorst, M. 1991. "Report from Baghdad." *New Yorker*, June 24.

Waelder, R. 1960. *The Basic Theory of Psychoanalysis.* New York: International Universities Press.

White, R. K. 1991. "Empathizing with Saddam Hussein." *Political Psychology* 12: 291–308.

Woodward, B. 1991. *The Commanders.* New York: Simon and Schuster.

COMMENTARY ON PART II

Personality and Leadership in the Gulf War

■

David G. Winter

MORE THAN MOST dramatic political events, the Iraqi invasion of Kuwait and the resulting Gulf War invite personalistic attributions of cause. Thus, for example, in the earliest weeks of the crisis President George Bush focused on the role of the Iraqi president: "Saddam has claimed that this is a holy war of Arab against infidel—this from the man who . . . invaded Iran . . . and who now plunders Kuwait. . . . It is Saddam who lied to his Arab neighbors. It is Saddam who invaded an Arab state. And it is he who now threatens the Arab nation" (Woodward 1991, 282). Stephen Wayne in chapter 2 recounts that earlier, on August 2, 1990, British Prime Minister Margaret Thatcher had told Bush that Saddam Hussein (not Iraq) had to be stopped, while Bush reacted as if he had been personally challenged by Saddam and went on to compare Hussein to Adolf Hitler, the classic example of a leader whose personality shaped history (but see the dissenting voice of the historian Taylor 1961).

Saddam Hussein, for his part, also came to personalize his adversary, as in the January 30, 1991, interview with CNN correspondent Peter Arnett: "*He* had decided on war. . . . *Bush* . . . struck at Baghdad. . . . Has *Bush* gained victory? . . . *He* crosses the Atlantic Ocean, the oceans, the seas to attack a nation of 18 million" (FBIS 1991, 22–23, emphasis added). The chapters in this volume by Jerrold Post, Stephen Wayne, and Stanley Renshon suggest that, in their analyses of the Gulf War, scholars also have looked for personalistic causes.

Let us acknowledge at once that seeking to explain political events as the result of the personalities of leaders is always a risky intellectual venture. It is easy to neglect situational pressures, institutional forces, and above all, history. (For example, Saddam Hussein's August 1990 claim that "Kuwait is joining the motherland" was not the first of its kind. Twenty-nine years before, Iraq's Prime Minister Abd al-Karim Qasim also announced a claim to Kuwait, then newly independent from

Britain, and appeared to be mobilizing troops for an invasion; see Gott 1965). For this reason, many social psychologists label the search for personal, individual causes of social events as the "fundamental attributional error" (Ross 1977).

But is it always an error? Surely the events of 1990–1991 are a case where the two principal leaders' personalities *were* important, even decisive. The situation posed by the Iraqi invasion was new, ambiguous, and highly uncertain. (In F. I. Greenstein's terms, "the environment admit[ted] of restructuring.") Hussein and Bush occupied strategic locations in their national and international political structures. The events and issues at stake strongly resonated with the deepest images and themes of their respective personalities. Thus the invasion and subsequent Gulf War fit most of the criteria offered by Greenstein (1969, 40–61) for identifying instances where leaders' personalities make a difference.

Renshon identifies three key points, or framing decisions, in the Gulf War story that seem especially to call for explanation in terms of the personality dynamics and cognitive styles of the key actors. Post and Wayne give detailed and sensitive personality portraits of Saddam Hussein and George Bush that enable us to pinpoint some of those dynamics and to observe how, by interacting with events, advisors, the political climate, and (above all) adversaries, they set the course toward war, cease-fire, and an ambiguous peace.

My task in this commentary is twofold: (1) to place these portraits in the broad framework of variables and structures developed in systematic research studies of personality (originally in the laboratory but now more and more often in field studies of political leaders; see Winter 1992a, 1992b); and (2) to explore how these personality studies of the Gulf War may reflect more general relationships between leaders' personalities and the escalation of crisis to armed conflict and war.

The Psychological Dynamics of the Two Leaders

Saddam Hussein

Post interprets Saddam Hussein's behavior during the Gulf War crisis in terms of an unbounded drive for power and prestige. This drive has many components. In psychoanalytic terms, it is characterized as extreme narcissim, manifested in messianic dreams about himself and his nation. Thus even before the Gulf War, Hussein's exalted and extravagant rhetoric was filled with references to cultural heroes ancient (Nebuchadnezzar) and modern (Nasser). He sees himself as a strong leader who will unify the entire Arab nation. In the quest to realize

TABLE A. MOTIVE PROFILES OF SADDAM HUSSEIN AND GEORGE BUSH

	Standardized Motive Imagery		
	Achievement (Concern with standards of excellence, success in competition, or innovation)	Affiliation (Concern with interpersonal warmth, and close, friendly relations)	Power (Concern with impact and prestige)
Saddam Hussein	39	55	57
George Bush	58	83	53

Sources: Hussein: transcripts of ten interviews between 1974 and 1991. The comparison sample is sets of interviews with 22 world leaders. Bush: January 1989 inaugural address. The comparison sample is first inaugural addresses of all U.S. presidents (see Winter et al. 1991). Note: All scores are expressed in standardized form, with sample means of 50 and standard deviations of 10.

these dreams, he has readily resorted to aggression as an instrument of policy, seemingly unconstrained by conscience, moral code, or even religious principles. Finally (and not without reason, perhaps), he often displays a paranoid fear of being surrounded by enemies, to which he responds with intensified aggression.

Each of these themes or characteristics is associated with power motivation, which is operationally defined as a concern for impact or prestige (McClelland 1975; Winter 1973; Winter and Stewart 1978), especially in the absence of a sense of responsibility (see Winter and Barenbaum 1985). Thus people whose words are saturated with power motive imagery are verbally and physically aggressive. They are prone to quick and great sympathetic nervous system arousal (McClelland 1982); thus power motivation may take on some attributes of an addiction, requiring ever stronger jolts to maintain what Post describes as the euphoric high of power intoxication. In setting policy, they are prone to ignore or neglect moral considerations (Fodor and Smith 1982). To adapt the words of Lord Acton's famous dictum: power motivation corrupts.

Some preliminary data on Saddam Hussein's motives, based on content analysis of press conference transcripts, show that he is indeed relatively high in power motivation. Compared to a sample of twenty-two world leaders, his standardized power motive score of 57 is a little less than one standard deviation above average, as shown in table A.[1] Power motivation, then, is a concept from the domain of personality research that can bring together some of the observations and analyses of Post and Renshon about the behavior and judgment of Saddam Hussein before and during the Gulf War.

Can the concept of power motivation help us understand Saddam Hussein's curious combination of flexible pragmatism yet rigid defiance in the face of obvious misjudgment? (As Renshon points out, Hussein's miscalculation of George Bush's response to the invasion of Kuwait was presaged by his misjudgment about fighting the Kurds in 1974 and his disastrous decision to invade Iran in 1980.) Much of the Western fascination with the drive for power is connected to the ancient Greek notion of hubris—that power sows the seeds of its own destruction. In terms of the results of his Kuwaiti venture (if not necessarily—at this writing—the overall results of the Gulf War), Saddam Hussein certainly displayed the hubris of power.

Laboratory research on power motivation suggests some of the mechanisms of hubris. First, power motivated people enjoy taking extreme risks in the pursuit of prestige, but they may confuse feelings of power and omnipotence with the reality of genuine social power. As a result, they may overestimate their chances of success. Next, power motivated people are vulnerable to ingratiation, so that they end up surrounded by sycophants, who will not tell them the truth (Fodor and Farrow 1979). For them, success breeds future creativity and further success; but when they fail, their reserves of creative innovation seem to desert them (Fodor 1990). (In contrast, achievement motivated people are able to learn from their mistakes by paying attention to negative results. Table A shows that Saddam Hussein's achievement motivation score is almost two standard deviations below the mean for world leaders.)

Each of these mechanisms can be seen in the analyses by Post and Renshon. While Saddam Hussein is capable of rational calculation, his narrow cultural outlook and vulnerability to sycophantic ingratiators has often led him to make disastrous misjudgments and mistakes. And in the sway of a euphoric power high, he seems to have overestimated his chances of success by underestimating Bush's reaction. And yet, from the perspective of power motivation, even the ultimate defeat in Kuwait and the terrible destruction of the Gulf War may not signify failure, since the goal of power is to compel—at least attention, if not behavior. As the ancient Greeks knew, the hubris of power makes for much more compelling theater than do sober tales of rational calculation. Thus as Post suggests, for Saddam Hussein even defeat in the Gulf War was the defining act of the drama of his life. (And are we so certain that it was a defeat?)

Table A also shows that Saddam Hussein scores above the mean for world leaders in affiliation motivation. At first this seems to contradict his behavior as described by Post and Renshon. When were his concerns for warm friendly relationships ever in evidence? They certainly did not check his aggressive behavior toward his internal opponents, toward the Kurds, or toward Iran and Kuwait. Actually, laboratory research suggests that affiliation motivation is more complicated than that. People high in affiliation motivation are drawn into warm, friendly, and cooperative relationships *but only with people they perceive as similar and only when they feel safe.* Under threat, they are often quite prickly and defensive. In the turbulent and dangerous world of Iraqi politics, Saddam Hussein has acted like an affiliation motivated person under threat: he has surrounded himself with like-minded people (as Renshon points out, literally people from his own village and family). At the same time, he has fused his affiliative brotherhood concerns with the power-saturated messianic message to the wider Arab community.

Post qualifies his analysis of Saddam Hussein's power drives and aggression by arguing that they are, at the same time, defensive, since his grandiose facade masks underlying insecurity. This suggests ego-defensiveness in the classic psychological sense, in which manifest behavior is often the opposite of (in psychoanalytic terms, a reaction formation to) underlying feelings and wishes. In a classic study, A. L. George (1968) suggests as a general principle that power is a compensatory value for political leaders. (The analysis of Woodrow Wilson, by George and George 1954, applies this principle to a case.) No doubt the roots of this claim lie in Alfred Adler's concept of overcompensation for perceived inferiority.[2] In a slightly different sense, R. K. White (1991) makes this same point in his claim that Saddam Hussein's use of violence is at least in part defensive, based on realistic fears about dangers to Iraq's national security in a hostile world.

Claims of this sort have their strong supporters and, equally, their strong skeptics and critics. When applied to someone as apparently brutal and insensitive as Saddam Hussein, do they represent the reductio ad absurdum of psychoanalytic logic, in which everything is really its opposite? What would it take for us to label brutal and tyrannical power strivings as, simply, nondefensive and brutal power strivings? And is the real basis of Saddam Hussein's power strivings defensive or offensive, compensatory or direct? How can we tell?

I cannot pretend to answer any of these questions in the present commentary. However, I will cite evidence concerning a more limited question, namely, is power motivation fundamentally defensive and compensatory? Are the children who grow up with high levels of power motivation the ones who were denied power as children (power as compensation), or were they the children who were indulged and humored in their childish power strivings (power as directly trained)? D. C. McClelland and D. A. Pilon (1983) measured power motivation in a sample of seventy-eight men and women, aged thirty-one and thirty-two years old, whose mothers had been interviewed about their child-rearing practices more than twenty five-years earlier, when the children were five years old. McClelland and Pilon found that adult power motivation scores were positively associated with parental permissiveness for sex and aggression, including especially aggression toward parents. Parental emphasis on the inhibition of children's impulses, as (possibly) reflected in the child-rearing variable "praise for good behavior at dining table," was significantly *negatively* correlated with the child's power motivation score as an adult.

Of course, these results are from one study of white middle-class intact American families at one point in time, so that we should be very cautious about generalizing to the roots of Saddam Hussein's power motivation. Nevertheless, the McClelland and Pilon results, as far as they go, were clear-cut and the opposite of what would be predicted by the power-as-compensation hypothesis. Power motivation, at least as measured by available scoring systems, is not a compensatory reaction to early experiences of weakness or being deprived of power. Rather, it appears to grow out of simple reinforcement—indulgence, if you will—of early power behavior, particularly in the domains of sex and aggression. Taking these results seriously, what can we say about power as compensation? In a culture like the United States, with considerable ambivalence about power (see McClelland 1970), such a concept could offer a convenient rationalization for present power strivings, projected on to the mythic past of childhood. Here it is important to remember that the McClelland and Pilon results, for all their contextual boundedness, were based on a contemporary (rather than retrospective) assessment of parental patterns of childrearing. Alternatively, White's "power-as-a-way-to-be-safe" (1991, 299) may involve motivations other than power—for example, the defensive and prickly aspect of affiliation motivation under threat, discussed below. (As shown in table A, Hussein's affiliation motivation is slightly above average.)

With the McClelland and Pilon finding in mind, it is worthwhile to look once again at Post's account of Saddam Hussein's childhood. Post reports that Saddam's father and his older brother both died before he was born and that his mother then married his father's brother. We are told that this uncle was reportedly abusive to Saddam. According to Heinz Kohut's theory, this abuse should have created a permanent wounded self in the young child (Kohut 1966). Beyond this presumption, little direct evidence for a traumatic childhood is cited. At the age of ten, Saddam left home and went to live with a maternal uncle, who, according to Post, steeped the young Saddam in dreams of glory and inculcated in him the belief that he was destined to follow the path of Nebuchadnezzar. Perhaps in examining the early years of Saddam Hussein, we have made too much of his stepfather's abuse and not enough of his uncle's indulgence, not to mention his mother's possible favoritism toward him as the youngest—and only surviving—child (cf. Rank 1975, 83, 94).

Thus I do not believe that the evidence permits us to decide whether Saddam Hussein's power drives are compensatory or direct. As a guide to policy, the power-as-compensation principle has its dangers as well as its virtues. In situations where people are genuinely afraid and arm themselves out of fear—what R. Jervis (1976) calls the spiral model—understanding and applying this principle can lead us away from conflict and toward a relaxation of tension. Applied inappropriately in situations of direct aggression (the deterrence model, in Jervis's term), however, the power-as-compensation principle can leave us naked before a real enemy.[3]

George Bush

Wayne emphasizes the role of challenge in George Bush's response to the Iraqi invasion of Kuwait. In his early years, Bush met challenges by enlisting in the army air force right after graduating from preparatory school and then striking off on his own in the Texas oil fields. Restless and energetic ("Gotta keep moving. Can't stay in one place all the time"), flexible in his pursuit of a goal, and a successful entrepreneur, Bush seems the quintessential achievement motivated person (see McClelland 1961, esp. chap. 8). And as table A shows, he scores almost one standard deviation above the average of American presidents.

Wayne also points out that sometimes Bush responds to challenge with aggression. Called a wimp in 1988, he lashed out with a negative campaign that recalled the Watergate era. Humiliated over his handling of the 1989 Panama coup, he unleashed a full-scale military invasion to arrest and extradite Manuel Noriega. Forced to retract his "Read my lips—no new taxes" pledge during the 1990 budget negotiations, he was primed to mount Desert Shield, Desert Sword, and finally Desert Storm to reverse the Iraqi annexation of Kuwait. Normally (as in his 1988 announcement of candidacy speech and his 1989 inaugural address) Bush displays only average levels of power motivation, but on these occasions of aggressive response to challenge, Bush's power motivation scores climbed sharply, as shown in table B. Thus we find the aggressive images of the Gulf War still echoing in his 1992 announcement of candidacy speech.

When does Bush follow an aggressive path in response to challenge? What sets him off? Wayne suggests several factors: the threat of humiliation, doubts about his strength, a hint that he is not liked, perhaps competition with a woman. At least one of these precipitating factors, the fear of being disliked, may result from his extraordinarily high

TABLE B. Motive Profiles of George Bush over Time

	Standardized Motivation Imagery		
Bush Speech	*Achievement (Concern with standards of excellence, success in competition, or innovation)*	*Affiliation (Concern with interpersonal warmth, and close, friendly relations)*	*Power (Concern with impact and prestige)*
1988 announcement of candidacy	61	62	51
1988 nomination acceptance	46	43	62
1989 inaugural address	58	83	53
1991 announcement of candidacy	63	69	71

Note: Comparison samples for the four speeches are, in order, candidacy announcements of all major 1988 presidential candidates, 1988 nomination acceptance speeches of all major party nominees, first inaugural addresses of all U.S. presidents, and candidacy announcements of all 1992 major candidates. All scores are expressed in standardized form, with sample means of 50 and standard deviations of 10.

affiliation motivation (see table B, especially). Normally, this motive is reflected in his congenial relations with those advisors and colleagues whom he trusts, as documented by Wayne and Renshon. Sensitive—highly sensitive—to dislike, disagreement, and dissimilar people, Bush responds to such threats not with a constant high level of power motivation but rather with sudden and impulsive outbursts of power. (Is this perhaps the true motivational root of A. L. George's power as compensation, discussed above?) Different from Bush in culture, social class, family background, religion, language, goals, interests, and personal style, Saddam Hussein was the ideal potential target for an aggressive response.

To this list of precipitating factors, we can probably now add the sense of being taken advantage of or tricked. As the Glaspie interview intimates and as recently disclosed documents attest, Bush actively and energetically supported Saddam Hussein with military, economic, and intelligence assistance right up to his invasion of Kuwait. Perhaps Bush thought that, in spite of all their differences, he could deal with Hussein as a friend (as he later was able to deal with many of the coalition leaders). If so, then the sudden and surprising invasion dashed those hopes, and Bush impulsively responded with aggression. Wayne documents the peculiar quality of vindictive personalization in Bush's response: Hell hath no fury like an affiliation motivated person scorned—or being double crossed.[4] (It is tempting to speculate that affiliation motivated people respond to threats and deception with power-as-compensation behavior; without further studies, however, this is only speculation.)

The Psychological Roots of War

Psychologically speaking, how do wars happen? A model developed by D. C. McClelland (1975, chap. 9) suggests that conflicts escalate into war when levels of power motivation are high (or rising) and affiliation motivation is low (or falling). In contrast, conflicts tend to be peacefully resolved when power motivation is low or falling and affiliation motivation is high or rising. D. G. Winter (1991b) confirms this model in a study of the outbreak of World War I and the Cuban missile crisis. In 1914, as the crisis that began in Sarajevo grew worse, the statements and communications between the British and German governments showed increased power motivation and decreased affiliation motivation over time. In the Cuban missile crisis, on the other hand, the letters and statements of John Kennedy and Nikita Khrushchev showed decreased power motivation and increased affiliation motivation as the crisis grew worse. In the Gulf War crisis, one leader, Saddam Hussein was dispositionally high in power motivation. In contrast, the power motivation of his counterpart, George Bush, was not usually high but rather was subject to situational arousal, especially when his affiliation motivation was threatened.

Wars have many causes, ranging from geography and resources, through economic growth and competition, down to the structure of military alliances. Political psychologists account for only a small part of the variation in outcomes, and an even smaller part of that variation can be attributed to the personalities of leaders. And yet in the end, all of the external factors leading to war and peace are filtered through the minds of the individual people in a position to opt for war or peace. As they perceive, interpret, and decide, they are guided by the "unspoken assumptions" (Joll 1968) in which their motives, goals, worldview, and styles are embedded. Conflict may be inevitable, but war is not. Sometimes, as in the case of the Gulf War, those unspoken assumptions in leaders' personalities can make all the difference.

NOTES

1. The figures for Saddam Hussein in table A should be interpreted with more than the usual amount of caution. Transcripts of interviews with Saddam Hussein are rare, and those available show signs of heavy editing. Nevertheless, his power motive score is essentially the same for the more versus less spontaneous interviews, for early interviews (before 1980), and for the July 1990 interview with U.S. Ambassador April Glaspie.

2. In its everyday version, we find this principle applied—somewhat indiscriminately—to playground bullies, that they are only seeking attention because they are insecure.

116 *David G. Winter*

3. In *The Firebugs* (1963), the Swiss playwright Max Frisch illustrates the disaster of continued reassurance and accommodation to power drives that are (wrongly) presumed to be only defensive in nature.

4. Even so, the "kinder, gentler" side of Bush's affiliation motivation led him to make one more attempt at reconciliation, when he forgot the "lesson of Vietnam" and overruled his on-the-scene military commander, ordering a halt to the war.

REFERENCES

FBIS (Foreign Broadcast Information Service). 1991. "Baghdad Radio Airs Saddam Interview with CNN." *FBIS Daily Report.* FBIS-NES-91-021, 20–24.
Frisch, M. 1963. *The Firebugs: A Learning Play Without a Lesson.* New York: Hill and Wang.
Fodor, E. 1990. "The Power Motive and Creativity of Solutions to an Engineering Problem." *Journal of Research in Personality* 24: 338–54.
Fodor, E., and D. L. Farrow. "The Power Motive as an Influence on Use of Power." *Journal of Personality and Social Psychology* 37: 2091–97.
Fodor, E., and T. Smith. 1982. "The Power Motive as an Influence on Group Decision Making." *Journal of Personality and Social Psychology* 42: 178–85.
George, A. L. 1968. "Power as a Compensatory Value for Political Leaders." *Journal of Social Issues* 24 (3): 29–50.
George, A. L., and J. L. George. 1954. *Woodrow Wilson and Colonel House.* New York: John Day.
Gott, R. 1954. "The Kuwait Incident." In *Survey of International Affairs 1961,* ed. D. C. Watt. London: Oxford University Press.
Greenstein, F. I. 1969. *Personality and Politics: Problems of Evidence, Inference, and Conceptualization.* Chicago: Markham.
Jervis, R. 1976. *Perception and Misperception in International Relations.* Princeton: Princeton University Press.
Joll, J. 1968. *1914: The Unspoken Assumptions.* London: Weidenfeld and Nicolson.
Kohut, Heinz. 1966. "Forms and Transformations of Narcissim." *Journal of the American Psychoanalytic Association* 14: 243–72.
McClelland, D. C. 1961. *The Achieving Society.* Princeton: Van Nostrand.
——— . 1970. "The Two Faces of Power." *Journal of International Affairs* 24: 29–47.
——— . 1975. *Power: The Inner Experience.* New York: Irvington.
——— . 1982. "The Need for Power, Sympathetic Activation, and Illness." *Motivation and Emotion* 6: 31–41.
McClelland, D. C., and D. A. Pilon. 1983. "Sources of Adult Motives in Patterns of Parent Behavior in Early Childhood." *Journal of Personality and Social Psychology* 44: 564–74.
Rank, O. 1975 (1924). *The Don Juan Legend.* Princeton: Princeton University Press.
Ross, L. 1977. "The Intuitive Psychologist and His Shortcoming: Distortions in the Attribution Process." in *Advances in Experimental Social Psychology,* vol. 10, ed. L. Berkowitz. New York: Academic Press.

Taylor, A. J. P. 1961. *The Origins of the Second World War*. London: Hamish Hamilton.

White, R. K. 1991. "Emphathizing with Saddam Hussein." *Political Psychology* 12: 291–308.

Winter, D. G. 1973. *The Power Motive*. New York: Free Press.

———. 1991a. "Measuring Personality at a Distance: Development of an Integrated System for Scoring Motives in Running Text." In *Perspectives in Personality*, ed. A. J. Stewart. London: Jessica Kingsley.

———. 1991b. "Power, Affiliation, and War: Three Tests of a Motivational Model." Unpublished paper, University of Michigan.

———. 1992a. "Content Analysis of Archival Data, Personal Documents, and Everyday Verbal Materials." In *Thematic Content Analysis in Personality and Motivation Research*, ed. C. P. Smith. New York: Cambridge University Press.

———. 1992b. "Personality and Foreign Policy: Historical Overview of Research." In *Political Psychology and Foreign Policy*, ed. E. Singer and V. Harper. Boulder: Westview.

Winter, D. G., and N. B. Barenbaum. 1985. "Responsibility and the Power Motive in Women and Men." *Journal of Personality* 53: 335–55.

Winter, D. G., M. G. Hermann, W. Weintraub, and S. G. Walker. 1991. "The Personalities of Bush and Gorbachev Measured at a Distance: Procedures, Portraits, and Policy." *Political Psychology* 12: 215–45.

Winter, D. G., and A. J. Stewart. 1978. "The Power Motive." In *Dimensions of Personality*, ed. H. London and J. Exner. New York: Wiley.

Woodward, B. 1991. *The Commanders*. New York: Simon and Schuster.

PART III

■

THE CONFLICT PROCESS

5

Threat-Based Strategies of Conflict Management: Why Did They Fail in the Gulf?

■

Janice Gross Stein

■ EARLY ON THE morning of August 2, 1990, Iraqi troops poured across the border into Kuwait. Within a few hours, Kuwait's limited resistance had collapsed, the emir had fled, and Iraq's forces occupied and controlled all of Kuwait. The invasion and occupation of Kuwait was preceded by a confused and half-hearted attempt by the United States to deter Iraq from using force against Kuwait and to reassure Iraq of its benign intentions; it is not surprising that both deterrence and reassurance failed.[1] The intriguing question is whether, had the United States tried seriously to deter Iraq before it invaded Kuwait, deterrence would have succeeded in preventing the attack.

After Iraq's invasion, occupation, and annexation of Kuwait, the United States assembled a broad international coalition that signaled its determination to go to war in order to compel Iraq's withdrawal from Kuwait, if Iraq failed to remove its forces voluntarily. The coalition had unquestioned military supremacy and deployed sufficient military forces in Saudi Arabia to signal its resolve. Yet the deadline set for Iraq's withdrawal passed, and on January 16, 1991, the international coalition led by the United States began a large-scale military campaign to expel Iraqi forces from Kuwait. The second puzzle is why compellence failed.[2] The two failures are interconnected.

Three different explanations can be advanced for the twin failures. All rest on counterfactual reasoning. First and most obvious is the failure of the United States to mount an effective strategy of deterrence in the period preceding the invasion of Kuwait. This explanation assumes that had deterrence been implemented properly, Saddam Hussein might have been deterred. A second related argument suggests that Saddam Hussein systematically miscalculated the capabilities and resolve of the United States, even after large numbers of American forces were deployed in Saudi Arabia. The fault here lies not so much with the strategy as with Saddam's tactical miscalculations. If he had correctly calculated the power balance, the war might have been avoided.

The third explanation argues that Saddam Hussein could not have been deterred. He was unstoppable because of the strategic judgment he had made, late in 1989, that the United States was determined to undermine his regime through economic sabotage and covert action. Once he had developed a strong image of an enemy bent on his destruction, he was almost immune to any evidence that challenged that image. Under these conditions, neither deterrence, nor reassurance before the invasion, nor compellence after the invasion stood much of a chance. This explanation challenges the argument that deterrence might have succeeded had it been practiced more effectively. It is not wholly inconsistent, however, with the proposition that deterrence and compellence failed because Saddam misperceived relative capabilities. The two are interconnected.

To establish the relative weight of these two explanations, we compare American and Iraqi estimates of military and political capabilities made before the war began. On most dimensions, there are surprising similarities between the two sets of estimates. This similarity in estimates across most dimensions of political and military capability suggests that Saddam's estimates of the relative military and political balance were not prima facie unreasonable. The critical difference was the broad strategic judgment President Hussein made early in the process.

One important caveat is in order. This argument rests not only on a counterfactual argument but also on the limited evidence we have of Saddam Hussein's calculations.[3] With the exception of Tariq Aziz, who was foreign minister at the time, and a senior Iraqi diplomat with access to the Iraqi president, no one of the inner circle around Saddam has spoken publicly about the thinking that governed the decisions of President Hussein and the Revolutionary Command Council. Tariq Aziz gave several interviews after the war that are revealing of Saddam's thinking. However, they may well be tainted both by his fear of the consequences of public statements and by the impact of the war, which may have colored his reconstruction of earlier decisions.[4] The speeches Saddam gave from October 1989 until January 1991 therefore provide the principal source of evidence for the reconstruction of his images. Even though his image of the enemy is remarkably consistent throughout the period, any conclusions must remain tentative until more varied and better quality evidence is available.

The Failure to Deter

Evidence that a confrontation was brewing in the Gulf first became available at the end of May 1990. During an Arab summit meeting convened in Baghdad to condemn the increased flow of Soviet immigrants to Israel, Saddam Hussein privately denounced the Arabs of the Gulf who, he claimed, were keeping the price of oil artificially low, thereby engaging in economic sabotage of Iraq (1990b). On July 10, the oil ministers of Iraq, Kuwait, Saudi Arabia, Qatar, and the United Arab Emirates met in Jidda and agreed to limit production in order to get the price back up to $18 a barrel. In announcing the agreement the next day, however, Kuwait added the stipulation that it would review and possibly reverse its commitment in the fall. At an OPEC meeting a few days later, Kuwait repeated its intention to observe the limitation on production only until the autumn.

As the impasse deepened, Iraq escalated its demands. On July 16, at Saddam's request, Foreign Minister Tariq Aziz sent a memorandum to Kuwait demanding $2.4 billion in compensation for oil that he claimed Kuwait had pumped from the disputed Rumaila oil field; $12 billion in compensation for the depressed oil prices brought about by Kuwait's overproduction; forgiveness of Iraq's war debt of $10 billion; and a lease on the strategic island of Bubiyan that controlled access to Iraq's only port, Umm Qasr.[5] In a speech on Iraq's Revolution Day on July 17, Saddam again attacked those who were stabbing Iraq in the back with "a poison dagger" by overproducing oil as part of a plan "inspired by America to undermine Arab interests and security." Kuwait and the United Arab Emirates were part of a "Zionist plot aided by imperialists against the Arab nation," and Sheikh Sabah al-Ahmad, the foreign minister of Kuwait, was "an American agent." Iraq, he said, had become the Arabs' one reliable defender: because of Iraq's advanced weaponry, the imperialists no longer dared to attack but were resorting to economic warfare through their agents, the Gulf rulers (1990c).

As Iraq began to mass troops along its border with Kuwait, King Fahd of Saudi Arabia, President Hosni Mubarak of Egypt, and King Hussein of Jordan attempted to mediate a solution. President Mubarak arranged a meeting on July 31 in Jidda between Izzat Ibrahim, the vice-chairman of the Revolutionary Command Council in Iraq, and Crown Prince Saad al-Sabah of Kuwait, with a second session scheduled for Baghdad.[6] The meeting ended the next day with no progress. Early on the morning of August 2, two Iraqi armored divisions spearheaded the attack against Kuwait.

While the crisis was intensifying, Washington's signals to Iraq were ambiguous and contradictory. On July 19, Secretary of Defense Richard Cheney affirmed that an American commitment made during the Iran-Iraq War to come to Kuwait's defense was still valid: "Those commitments haven't changed" (Sciolino with Gordon 1990). Later that day, Pentagon spokesperson Pete Williams qualified the statement by noting that the secretary had been quoted by the press "with some degree of liberty" (Sciolino with Gordon 1990).

On July 21, the Central Intelligence Agency (CIA) reported the first Iraqi troop movements near the border with Kuwait. Two days later, the United States sent two KC-135 aerial tankers and a C-141 cargo transport to the Gulf for joint exercises with the United Arab Emirates and moved six warships in the area closer to Kuwait and the Emirates in order, in the words of a Pentagon official, to "lay down a marker for Saddam Hussein" (Gordon 1990a). However, when Navy Secretary H. Laurence Garnett told the House Armed Services Subcommittee on Seapower, "Our ships in the Persian Gulf were put on alert status," an aide later told the press that the secretary had misspoken (ibid.).

On July 24, as Saddam escalated his threats against the Gulf states, Pentagon spokesperson Pete Williams said, "We remain strongly committed to supporting the individual and collective self-defense of our friends in the Gulf with whom we have deep and long-standing ties." When asked whether the United States would provide help if Kuwait were attacked, he declined to answer (ibid.). That same day, the State Department asked Ambassador April Glaspie in Baghdad to stress the friendship of the United States toward Iraq but also to warn that the United States had made a commitment "to ensure the free flow of oil from the Gulf and to support the sovereignty and integrity of the Gulf states. We will continue to defend our vital interests in the Gulf. [We are] strongly committed to supporting the individual and collective self-defense of our friends in the Gulf" (Gelb 1991).[7] This was the strongest and least ambiguous warning sent by the United States in the weeks preceding the invasion. It would be followed by less clear and less forceful statements.

The senior State Department spokesperson added to the confusion. On July 24, the same day that the CIA reported the movement of two Iraqi divisions to the frontier, she was asked whether the United States had any commitment to defend Kuwait. Margaret Tutwiler replied, "We do not have any defense treaties with Kuwait, and there are no special defense or security commitments to Kuwait." Asked explicitly whether the United States would come to the assistance of Kuwait if it were attacked, she added, "We also remain strongly committed to supporting the individual and collective self-defense of our friends in the Gulf with whom we have deep and long-standing ties" (Gordon 1990a).

On July 25, Saddam Hussein asked to meet with Ambassador Glaspie within the hour. The request was extraordinary. In her two years as ambassador, she had never met with President Hussein privately.[8] Glaspie had been seeking a meeting with high-level Iraqi officials since July 17, when she met with the deputy foreign minister, Nizar Hamdoon, and asked for clarification of Iraq's intent following its explicit threats against Kuwait and the United Arab Emirates.[9] Angered by the announcement on July 24 that the United States was conducting joint military exercises with the United Arab Emirates, Saddam suddenly requested the meeting.

President Hussein complained that U.S. maneuvers with the United Arab Emirates were encouraging the Emirates and Kuwait to disregard Iraq's rights (Iraqi transcript 1990).[10] In response, Ambassador Glaspie assured the president: "I know you need funds. But we have no opinion on the Arab-Arab conflicts, like your border disagreement with Kuwait. I was in the American Embassy in Kuwait during the late 'sixties. The instructions we had during this period were that we should express no opinion on this issue and that the issue is not associated with America. James Baker has directed our official spokesmen to emphasize this instruction" (ibid.).

Glaspie then asked, in light of Iraq's troop movements to the border with Kuwait yet "in a spirit of friendship," "What are your intentions?" Saddam Hussein informed Ambassador Glaspie that he had just told President Mubarak "to assure the Kuwaitis . . . that we are not going to do anything until we meet with them. When we meet and we see that there is hope, then nothing will happen. But if we are unable to find a solution, then it will be natural that Iraq will not accept death, even though wisdom is above everything else" (ibid.).

Despite the conditional quality of Saddam's statement, the ambassador herself was reassured of Iraq's intentions. "His emphasis that he wants peaceful settlement is surely sincere," she concluded. "Iraqis are sick of war."[11] In a cable to Washington, Glaspie recommended that "we ease off on public criticism of Iraq until we see how the negotiations develop" (Hoffman and Dewar 1991). Consistent with Glaspie's advice, on July 28 President Bush cabled Saddam, "We believe that differences are best resolved by peaceful means and not by threats involving military force or conflict. My administration continues to desire better relations with Iraq" (ibid.). No reference to the deployment of 100,000 Iraqi troops on Kuwait's border was made in the president's message to Saddam Hussein.[12]

In testimony before the Senate Foreign Relations Committee, Ambassador Glaspie claimed that she delivered strong oral warnings to President Hussein against the use of force. "I told him orally we would defend our vital interests, we would support our friends in the Gulf, we would defend their sovereignty and integrity," the ambassador insisted. Although she acknowledged that she had indeed told Iraq's president that the United States had no opinion on its conflict with Kuwait, she claimed that she preceded that comment with the repeated warning that "we would insist on settlements being made in a nonviolent manner, not by threats, not by intimidation, and certainly not by aggression" (Friedman 1991).

No such warnings appear in either the Iraqi transcript or Ambassador Glaspie's summary of the meeting cabled to the State Department. It is possible that in conformity with standard practice, her cabled summary concentrates on what Saddam Hussein said, rather than on any warnings she was instructed to deliver.[13] Tariq Aziz, then foreign minister of Iraq, who was present at Glaspie's meeting with Saddam, affirmed, however, that no strong warnings against military action were delivered:

> Having been a Foreign Minister, I understand the work of an ambassador and I believe Miss Glaspie's behavior was correct. She was summoned suddenly. The President wanted to tell her that the situation was worsening and that our government would not waive its options. . . . We knew she was acting on available instructions. *She spoke in vague diplomatic language* and we knew the position she was in. Her behavior was a classic diplomatic response and we were not influenced by it. (Viorst 1991b, 66–67, emphasis added)

In the forty-eight hours preceding the invasion, as intelligence agencies in Washington received evidence of heightened Iraqi military preparations, the United States made no additional attempt at deterrence.[14] Not until August 1, when the CIA warned that Iraq would attack within twenty-four hours, did Assistant Secretary of State John Kelly summon Iraq's ambassador in Washington to warn that the situation was "extremely serious."[15] The previous day, Iraq and Kuwait had met in Jidda for the abortive negotiating session. Tariq Aziz insists that Saddam decided to invade on August 1, after the collapse of the negotiations (ibid., 67). Saddam could not have received Kelly's warning before he made his decision. Early on the morning of August 2, Iraqi tanks rolled across the border into Kuwait.

Ambassador Glaspie argued in her testimony to the Senate Foreign Relations Committee that deterrence failed because President Hussein "was stupid—he did not believe our clear and repeated warnings that we would support our vital interests. Like every other government, we did not understand that he would be impervious to logic and diplomacy" (Friedman 1991). But her allegation does not bear the weight of the evidence. The diplomacy of deterrence in the critical two weeks preceding the invasion was inconsistent, incoherent, and unfocused. Given the confusing signals from Washington, had Saddam been deterrable, it is unlikely that he would have been stopped.

That deterrence did not receive a fair test is clearly established by the evidence. Insofar as it was not seriously attempted, two intriguing questions remain. If deterrence had been practiced seriously and well, could the invasion of Kuwait have been prevented? Second, could the United States have mounted an effective strategy of deterrence? The answer to the first question hinges on the assessment of Saddam's motives and intentions. Was Saddam Hussein an opportunity-driven aggressor or a vulnerable leader motivated by need? This judgment is critical because it determines the appropriate mix of deterrence and reassurance.

The Motives and Intentions of Saddam Hussein

The motives and intentions of Saddam Hussein were then and are now the subject of intense controversy. Iraq had unquestioned military capability to engage in expansionism in the Gulf; it was by far the preeminent military power in the region.[16] Iran was recovering from its eight-year war with Iraq, and no coalition of Arab states in the Gulf could conceivably match the battle-tested and battle-hardened Iraqi army. During its war with Iran, Baghdad had also received substantial amounts of financial aid from the Gulf states and sophisticated military technology and equipment from the Soviet Union and the Western world, who all felt threatened, albeit in different ways, by the revolution wrought by the Ayatollah Khomeini in Iran. Especially for the Sunni governments in the Gulf, Iraq was the first line of defense against the export of the Shia revolution from Iran. The Gulf states, as well as Egypt, were willing to pay in loans and military assistance to reinforce Iraq's military capability against Iran. Overwhelming local military superiority does not, however, necessarily lead to crisis and war unless the motive and the intention to use force are also present.

Saddam's repeated threats against the Gulf states from mid-May 1990 are consistent with the argument that he saw an opportunity to assert Iraq's longstanding claim to Kuwait and to control oil pricing. The strongest version of the proposition that Saddam Hussein was an opportunity-driven aggressor suggests that the invasion of Kuwait was not primarily provoked by the specific issues in dispute between the two countries. Rather, Saddam was determined to assert Iraq's historic claim to Kuwait, to establish control over the oil-producing Gulf, and to secure for Iraq a commanding voice in the determination of oil pricing and production for the rest of the decade. Although intentions cannot be inferred directly from capabilities, Iraq's heavy investment in the development of nuclear capabilities is also used to substantiate charges of Iraq's aggressive intent.[17] The logic of these arguments suggests that the invasion could have been avoided only if the United States had deterred forcefully or if Kuwait had appeased Iraq.

The United States did not deter effectively, and Kuwait did not concede. On the contrary, the al-Sabah family was unwilling to accommodate Iraq and make major concessions on the issues in dispute.

Immediately after the OPEC meeting in July, Kuwait's statement that it would reconsider its willingness to observe OPEC quotas in the autumn signaled major buyers to wait for October, when the price would drop again; in the opinion of Iraqi officials, "Kuwait killed the agreement" (Viorst 1991b, 66). Tariq Aziz, then the foreign minister of Iraq, observed that at the meeting in Jidda on August 31, "the Kuwaitis were very strange, very pompous, very obstinate" (ibid.). Mohammed al-Mashat, Iraq's ambassador to the United States, subsequently maintained that "[the Kuwaitis] were arrogant. They were conducting themselves like small-time grocery store owners. The gap was irreconcilable, so the meeting collapsed" (Miller and Mylroie 1990, 20).[18]

The Iraqi reconstruction of Kuwaiti behavior at the meeting is largely consistent with evidence from American and Kuwaiti officials. Sheikh Salim al-Sabah, the minister of interior in Kuwait before the war, observed: "By the time the crisis with Iraq began last year, we knew we could rely on the Americans. There was an exchange of talks on the ambassadorial level just before the invasion. No explicit commitments were ever made, but it was like a marriage. Sometimes you don't say to your wife 'I love you' but you know the relationship will lead to certain things" (Viorst 1991a, 72).[19] The United States indeed did not encourage the al-Sabah family to be forthcoming in the negotiations. In late June, Ambassador Nathan Howell cabled Washington for instructions. He proposed that Kuwait be encouraged to make concessions but was advised by the State Department to reiterate the American commitment to defend Kuwait.[20] If Saddam was "another Hitler," driven largely by the opportunity he saw to control oil pricing, then the absence of effective deterrence or meaningful concessions made the invasion of Kuwait very likely.

A somewhat different construction of the motives and intentions of Saddam Hussein, one that emphasizes need, is also plausible. For eight years, Iraq had been the frontline participant in a bitter and protracted war against Iran. Although Iraq had initiated the war, it did so because of the threat posed by the revolutionary Shiite government of Ayatollah Khomeini to Sunni governments throughout the Gulf. The war had cost Iraq over $500 billion, and throughout most of the conflict Iraq had spent about 40 percent of its gross domestic product on military procurement.

After the war ended, Iraq owed Western governments some $40 billion and Arab governments the equivalent.[21] Before the war with Iran, Iraq had had a net surplus of $30 billion, but by early summer 1990 inflation raged in Iraq and the dinar had fallen to one-twelfth its official value. The Iraqi economy was severely strained by the cost of financing its large debt and by the sharply lower price of oil, its principal export and source of hard currency. Between January and June 1990, the average price of a barrel of oil dropped from $20.50 to $13.00. A one-dollar drop in the price of oil cost Iraq $1 billion annually in lost revenue. The loss of revenue was a severe strain on Iraq's economy and its capacity to finance imports of essential foodstuffs.

After the invasion, Foreign Minister Tariq Aziz drew a direct link between Iraq's deteriorating economy and the invasion of Kuwait:

> The economic question was a major factor in triggering the current situation. In addition to the forty billion dollars in Arab debts, we owe at least as much to the West. This year's state budget required seven billion dollars for debt service, which was a huge amount, leaving us with only enough for basic services for our country. Our budget is based on a price of eighteen dollars a barrel for oil, but since the Kuwaitis began flooding the world with oil, the price has gone down by a third.
>
> When we met again—in Jidda, at the end of the July—Kuwait said it was not interested in any change. We were now desperate, and could not pay our bills for food imports. It was a starvation war. When do you use your military power to preserve yourself? (Viorst 1990, 90)

The foreign minister is explicit that Iraq had no long-term intention to invade and that the deployment of troops along the border was designed to compel concessions from Kuwait at the bargaining table:

> President Saddam had no intention of invading—he didn't even think of it before the end of June. It was never discussed at any level of government. . . . The issue of the Rumaila oil field and our border demands became a part of our talks with the Kuwaitis only in late June, by which time we had concluded that they had joined some sort of conspiracy to destroy our regime. Finally, in mid-July, we decided to dispatch troops to the Kuwaiti border, hoping it would make the Kuwaitis change their minds. (Viorst 1990, 66)

Aziz contends that on July 17, President Hussein warned Kuwait that he would use force if Kuwait violated its production quotas. One week later, when President Mubarak of Egypt visited Baghdad, Saddam pledged to take no military action as long as negotiations were ongoing but warned Mubarak: "Don't comfort the Kuwaitis." Aziz alleges that Mubarak informed Kuwait that there would be no invasion, thereby encouraging their inflexibility during the negotiating session (ibid.).[22] Saddam decided to invade only at the last minute, Aziz maintains, after the negotiations in Jidda broke down (ibid., 67). The foreign minister insists that a frustrated and desperate Iraq first tried compellence and resorted to force only when coercive diplomacy failed and it saw no other way to meet its fundamental needs.

The two interpretations of Saddam Hussein's motivations and intentions are not wholly incompatible. It is likely that Saddam, angered by

Kuwait's unwillingness to guarantee higher oil prices and frustrated by the reluctance of the al-Sabah family to compensate Iraq for its huge expenditures incurred during the war with Iran, was initially driven by the acute economic weakness of Iraq and its inability to finance basic imports. In this context, he saw an opportunity to reassert Iraq's long-standing claim to Kuwait.[23] Under these conditions, a vigorous attempt at deterrence combined with some attempt to address the refinancing of Iraq's debt might have prevented the invasion.

Was an Effective Strategy of Deterrence Possible?

Could the invasion of Kuwait, as distinct from a limited attack against the disputed oil field and strategic islands, have been deterred? To answer this question, we must first determine whether the United States could have mounted an effective strategy of deterrence. The answer must of necessity be the product of limited evidence and counterfactual reasoning.

The limited evidence that is available suggests that it would have been very difficult for the United States to deter forcefully in the period preceding the invasion. A few days before the attack, members of the Policy Planning Staff at the State Department were uncertain of and divided about the likely American response to an Iraqi attack.[24] As late as the afternoon of August 1, the general expectation in Washington was that Saddam was engaging in coercive diplomacy and that, at most, he would occupy the disputed oil fields and the strategic islands.[25] At a meeting of the interagency Deputies Committee at the State Department to consider the Iraqi military buildup, CIA Deputy Director Richard Kerr estimated that Iraqi troops would cross Kuwait's border, but he would not predict whether Iraq's forces would go farther than the disputed oil field and Bubiyan island (Oberdorfer 1991, 40).[26] Senior American officials were uncertain until the invasion began about Iraq's intentions. "We were reluctant to draw a line in the sand. I can't see the American public supporting the deployment of troops over a dispute over 20 miles of territory and it is not clear that local countries would have supported that kind of commitment. There would have been a lot of fluttering if there had been a partial invasion. The crucial factor in determining the American response was not the reality but the extent of the invasion" (Sciolino with Gordon 1990).

The logic of the United States is difficult to understand: a deterrent commitment could not be defined before it was massively violated. The United States could not "draw a line in the sand" because unless the line was crossed in a large-scale invasion, officials doubted Arab as well as domestic support for military action against a limited incursion. American officials felt constrained by both Arab and domestic opinion. These political judgments made an effective strategy of deterrence virtually impossible.

Even if an effective strategy of deterrence had been politically possible, it is questionable whether it would have succeeded. Saddam's motives and intentions developed within the larger context of his strategic image of the United States as an unrelenting enemy determined to destroy his regime through economic warfare and covert action. This image made both deterrence and reassurance immeasurably more difficult, if not impossible.

Saddam's Image of the United States as Enemy

As early as October 6, 1989, when he met with Secretary of State Baker in Washington, Foreign Minister Aziz accused the United States of being hostile to Iraq and of "mounting a campaign" to punish Iraq (Oberdorfer 1991, 21). His accusation followed charges by investigators from the Department of Agriculture that Iraq had systematically misused funds granted for the purchase of food to acquire "sensitive nuclear technologies."[27] Aziz subsequently revealed that his government was also informed early in 1989 that the CIA was telling Iraqis inside and outside the country that Saddam's regime had to be overthrown (Viorst 1991b, 64).

A few months later, Saddam was infuriated by an editorial aired by the Voice of America. The February 15, 1990, editorial explicitly criticized Iraq's repressive record as well as that of other "police" states and called for the overthrow of dictatorial governments.[28] Ambassador Glaspie cabled Washington that Saddam "read the editorial as USG [United States Government] sanctioned mudslinging with the intent to incite revolution" (Oberdorfer 1991, 22).[29] She wrote immediately to Tariq Aziz that the VOA editorial had been incorrectly interpreted in Baghdad: "It is absolutely not United States policy to question the legitimacy of the government of Iraq nor interfere in any way with the domestic concerns of the Iraqi people and government" (ibid.).

This reassurance was not credible to Saddam. He did not accept the disclaimer that the Voice of America, which explicitly claimed to represent the views of the U.S. government, did not in fact reflect administration policy. At his meeting with Ambassador Glaspie on July 25 in Baghdad, he told her: "Then the media campaign against Saddam Hussein was started by the official American media. The United States thought that the situation in Iraq was like Poland, Rumania, or

Czechoslovakia. We were disturbed by this campaign. . . . The media campaign continues. And it is full of stories" (Iraqi transcript, 1990).

In a speech later that month to the Arab Cooperation Council in Amman, Iraq's president made explicit his image of the United States as an imperialist power bent on economic warfare against the Arab world through its agents in the Gulf states. He predicted that because of the decline of Soviet power, the United States would exercise hegemonic power in the Middle East unless challenged by Arab governments:

> The [United States]. . . . will have the greatest influence in the region, through the Arab Gulf and its oil, [and] will maintain its superiority as a superpower without an equal to compete with it. This means that if the Gulf people, along with all Arabs, are not careful, the Arab Gulf region will be governed by the wishes of the United States. . . . [Oil] prices will be fixed in line with a special perspective benefiting American interests and ignoring the interests of others. (Hussein 1990a)

In the post-cold war world, the United States was no longer constrained and contained by the Soviet Union. The only answer, Saddam argued, was the assertion of Arab power. If Arab states did not assert their power, the United States would dictate the economic and political shape of the region through its agents in the Arab world for five years to come. President Mubarak of Egypt was so angered by Saddam's explicit attack on the United States and the implicit charges against Egypt that he walked out of the meeting.[30]

In March 1990, Gerald Bull, the inventor of the supergun, who had been advising Iraq on artillery, was assassinated in Brussels. Iraq blamed agents of the Mossad (Israel's intelligence agency), alleging that they were engaged in a conspiracy with the United States against Iraq. Shortly thereafter, a shipment to Baghdad of devices suitable for triggering nuclear weapons was intercepted in London. Saddam's image of a growing American-led conspiracy was reinforced. On April 1, he announced that Iraqi scientists had developed binary chemical weapons and threatened that "we will make the fire eat up half of Israel, if it tries to do anything against Iraq" (Cowell 1990). Washington finally took notice: the State Department called the threat "inflammatory, irresponsible, and outrageous," and the White House termed Saddam's speech "deplorable and irresponsible" (ibid.).[31]

On April 12, directly following Saddam's threat against Israel, five senators, headed by Senate Minority Leader Robert Dole, met with Iraq's president in Baghdad. Saddam again voiced his complaint that the United States was conspiring against Iraq. Senator Dole reassured him of President Bush's benign intentions (Woodward 1991, 199–204). On April 16, the interagency Deputies' Committee met at the White

House for the first time to reconsider U.S. policy toward Iraq, and after heated discussion some $500 million in agricultural loan credits to Iraq were suspended. As Tariq Aziz observed, "[Baker] got half the deal [on soft-loan guarantees] through, but in April of 1990, it was suspended, just when we critically needed barley." From that moment, Aziz continued, "as Foreign Minister, I was convinced that in April the Americans had stopped listening to us and had made up their minds to hit us" (Viorst 1991b, 64–65, 67). Policy was uncoordinated, and the mixed signals only confirmed Saddam's suspicions of American intent.

The image of the United States bent on conspiratorial action against Iraq remained constant right up to the invasion of Kuwait. In his meeting with Ambassador Glaspie, Saddam reviewed the history of U.S.-Iraq relations and returned again to the attempt by the United States to undermine his regime: "I don't say the President himself—but certain parties who had links with the intelligence community and with the State Department. . . . Some circles are gathering information on who might be Saddam Hussein's successor." Glaspie reported that he complained as well that such circles "worked to insure no help would go to Iraq" from the Export-Import Bank and Commodity Credit Corporation. He recalled the "U.S.I.A. campaign against himself and the general media assault on Iraq and its President" (U.S. transcript 1991).

Despite the dramatic improvement in relations between the United States and Iraq during the war with Iran, Saddam still recalled with anger the secret sales of equipment to Iran in 1986 and remained acutely suspicious of American intentions. He told Ambassador Glaspie on July 25:

> The worst of these [rifts] was in 1986, only two years after establishing relations, with what was known as Irangate. . . . But when interests are limited and relations are not that old, then there isn't a deep understanding and mistakes could leave a negative effect. Sometimes the effect of an error can be larger than the error itself. . . . And we shouldn't unearth the past except when new events remind us that old mistakes were not just a matter of coincidence (Iraqi transcript 1990).

In addition to the image of the United States as enemy, Saddam gave voice in his two-hour conversation with Ambassador Glaspie to the powerful impact of pride and honor on his calculations: "You can come to Iraq with aircraft and missiles, but do not push us to the point where we cease to care. And when we feel that you want to injure our pride and take away the Iraqis' chance of a high standard of living, then we will cease to care and death will be the choice for us. Then we would not care if you fired 100 missiles for each missile we fired. Because without pride, life would have no value" (ibid.). Saddam asked that the United

States not force Iraq to the point of humiliation at which logic must be disregarded (U.S. transcript). Pride and the avoidance of humiliation, shame, and dishonor loom far larger in Arab culture and calculations than they do in Western culture.

Saddam was also infused with a sense of the legitimacy of Iraq's claims and anger at Kuwait. An estimate of legitimacy and entitlement generally increase the propensity of leaders to commit themselves to a risky strategy and to ignore information that suggests that their preferred option is dangerous. A deeply embedded image of a powerful enemy, a strong sense of pride, acute frustration, and a keenly felt sense of legitimacy and entitlement all contributed to Saddam's decision to invade Kuwait.

American attempts at reassurance were uneven, unpersuasive, and ineffective in addressing Hussein's growing suspicion that the United States was masterminding a plot against his regime. Nor did they address the economic issues that Saddam voiced with growing urgency in the late spring of 1990. Although President Mubarak, King Hussein of Jordan, and Yasir Arafat all warned Kuwait to negotiate seriously with Iraq, the United States, as we have seen, did not urge the al-Sabah family to be more forthcoming in its negotiations with Iraq on debt forgiveness. Rather, the United States strengthened Kuwait's resolve to resist.

Was it reasonable or justified for Iraq's leadership to conclude, judging by American actions, that the United States was determined to sabotage their regime? Washington had no intention, before the invasion of Kuwait, to destabilize the regime of Saddam Hussein; on the contrary, the Bush administration intervened repeatedly to block congressional attempts to end loan guarantees and suppressed investigations of irregularities in Iraq's use of American aid.[32] Its flawed strategy was in large part a function of the expectation that it could "reform" and "resocialize" Saddam, encourage moderate behavior by him, and build Iraq as a regional counterweight to Iran.[33]

On a superficial level, Iraq's Revolutionary Command Council did not distinguish carefully between public comment and private commentary in the United States and had difficulty decoding the cacophony of signals that emanated from multiple American sources. More fundamentally, the United States had been portrayed for so long as an imperialist power, conspiring against the Arab people and populist Arab leaders, that it was all too easy for Saddam to interpret information as consistent with this deeply rooted and easily available stereotype.[34] Given the strength of the stereotype, it was extraordinarily difficult to reassure Iraq of the benign intentions of the United States in the period preceding the decision to invade Kuwait. The cultural and political divide across which the two sides communicated was simply too great for each to assess the other's intentions accurately. Whether or not it was reasonable for Saddam to draw this conclusion about American intentions is beside the point. Once Saddam concluded that the United States was determined to undermine his regime, reassurance and deterrence became virtually impossible, even had the United States clearly defined its commitments and consistently communicated its benign intentions.

Could Saddam Hussein Have Been Deterred?

Had an effective strategy of deterrence been possible, would it have been successful in preventing the full-scale invasion? Again, the answer to this question must be based on counterfactual reasoning. To the extent that Hussein was motivated principally by the opportunity to establish a commanding regional presence, claim Kuwait, and control oil pricing, only a clear and unequivocal commitment combined with an explicit threat of the consequences of the use of force against Kuwait stood any chance of preventing the invasion. Deterrence had to be forcefully executed. If Saddam was driven primarily by Iraq's economic vulnerability, then a strategy of reassurance had to address the issues, both directly and indirectly through Kuwait, that were central to easing its acute economic crisis. If the United States was uncertain of Iraq's motives and intentions, as its senior leaders and seasoned diplomats were, then a mixed strategy of a strong and unequivocal commitment to come to Kuwait's defense and reassurance of its determination to address Iraq's pressing economic concerns was appropriate. As we have seen, the United States could not deter.

Nor could the United States reassure Saddam, given his image of Washington as bent on his destruction through economic sabotage and covert action. Tariq Aziz reported that from April on, not only Saddam but the rest of the senior leadership of Iraq was convinced that the United States was trying to destabilize the regime through economic warfare waged by its agents in the Gulf. He put it bluntly:

> The decision [to occupy all of Kuwait] was predicated on Saddam's belief that it would make no difference whether Iraq chose to take part or all of Kuwait. The Americans had decided long before August 2nd to crush Iraq, and there was nothing [our] government could do to stop them. . . . We expected an American military retaliation from the very beginning. Within the leadership we had no dispute—we agreed that we had to go all the way. (Viorst 1991b, 67)

Aziz suggested that the overarching judgment of an American-inspired conspiracy against Iraq made the choice between a limited attack along the border and a full-scale invasion largely inconsequential.

Several intriguing inferences can be drawn from the limited evidence that is available. Evidence uncovered after the war suggests that Iraq was within a few years of developing a primitive nuclear capability; in such a position, an opportunistic aggressor logically should have waited to invade Kuwait until its capability was operational. This anomaly in Iraq's behavior is understandable only if Saddam and members of the Revolutionary Command Council were firmly convinced that the United States was trying to destabilize their regime. Under these circumstances, they had little to lose by precipitating a confrontation that they expected would eventually come in any case. They were clearly aware of superior American military capability, but in their view they faced a choice between overt and covert conflict. Deterrence was unlikely to have succeeded, given the way Iraqi leaders had framed the problem.[35]

The proposition that the invasion could have been prevented by stronger warnings may well be overly optimistic. Given the premise of Saddam's decisional calculus, he may well have been unstoppable. His judgment of American intentions was deeply rooted in the political and cultural context that reinforced the long-standing image of the United States as an imperialist power working through its wealthy agents in the Gulf against the interests of Arab states like Iraq.[36] During the height of the cold war in 1961 and 1962, similar but reciprocal images of the United States and the Soviet Union led to serious mutual miscalculation of intent and precipitated intense crises in their relationship.[37] Similarly, in the summer of 1990 it was extraordinarily difficult for deterrence or reassurance to cross the cultural and political divide.

Saddam's strategic image of an adversary bent on his destruction through economic and covert action is not inconsistent with his estimate that the United States, given its distaste for large numbers of casualties, might not retaliate for the invasion of Kuwait with large-scale military force. A senior Iraqi official explained that the decision to invade all of Kuwait rather than only the disputed areas was in part an attempt to deny the United States the opportunity to deploy large numbers of ground forces in the area.[38] Saddam chose to occupy all of Kuwait, rather than only the disputed oil field and the strategic islands, after information reached him that, should Iraq attack, Kuwait intended to invite a U.S. expeditionary force to land and establish bases in the unoccupied part of the country.[39] Convinced that the Saudi royal family could not survive the political consequences of a deployment of Western forces on its territory and that, therefore, it would neither invite nor permit the deployment of U.S. forces, Saddam chose at the last moment to occupy all of Kuwait and deprive the United States of the opportunity to establish landing facilities there for its ground forces (Viorst 1991b, 67).[40] If this reconstruction of Saddam's calculations is correct, it suggests that he hoped to avoid a massive American military response and contradicts Aziz's statement that the Revolutionary Command Council expected military retaliation by the United States.[41]

Saddam's reasoning was, however, fraught with tactical miscalculations. The only major airport in Kuwait capable of providing landing facilities for the huge American transports is on the outskirts of Kuwait City. If Iraqi troops had advanced no farther than Kuwait City, large numbers of American troops could have arrived only by sea, a process that would have taken months. Kuwait, moreover, has only one good harbor; if Iraq had occupied the port of Kuwait City, it would have been extraordinarily difficult for the United States to deploy forces to Kuwait, even by sea. Had they attempted to do so, they would have been within range of Iraqi missiles and artillery.[42]

By moving large numbers of troops to the border with Saudi Arabia and by briefly deploying these forces in offensive configuration to discourage King Fahd from shutting down the pipeline that carried Iraqi oil, Saddam created the very condition he wanted to avoid: a frightened Saudi leadership and a sense of alarm and urgency in Washington, which culminated in Saudi acquiescence to the deployment of American troops. Moreover, during the critical days immediately after the invasion, Saddam made little effort to reassure King Fahd of his benign intentions. This was Hussein's most serious tactical miscalculation.

However, even with Iraqi troops deployed in offensive formation along the Saudi border, President Bush and Secretary of Defense Richard Cheney experienced considerable difficulty in persuading King Fahd to agree to the deployment of large numbers of American forces on Saudi soil.[43] Saddam's initial judgment that the Saudi royal family would fear the consequences of a large deployment of Western forces was correct. Only the offensive deployment along the Saudi border persuaded King Fahd to agree to the deployment that neither he nor Saddam—for quite different reasons—wanted. Without access to Saudi bases and logistics, U.S. military action to compel Iraq to withdraw from Kuwait would have been infinitely more complicated. Saddam also badly misjudged the likely American reaction to a limited invasion, as distinct from a full-scale occupation of Kuwait. Ironically, as we have seen, American and Iraqi judgments of the domestic political consequences in the United States of the use of force against Iraq differed only on the issue of the magnitude of the provocation.

King Hussein of Jordan has provided an alternative explanation of Saddam's decision to invade and occupy all of Kuwait. He reports that Saddam told him that he did not intend to stay but "that he believed he would be in a stronger position . . . if he eventually withdrew to a point that left Iraq with the disputed territories only" (Miller 1990). If indeed Saddam intended to use most of occupied Kuwait as a bargaining chip,

it was imperative that he begin a withdrawal before serious military opposition began to coalesce. Saddam did the reverse: in a speech on
August 12, he attached political conditions to the withdrawal that would
have taken months to meet.[44] In so doing, he persuaded many Arab
leaders that he intended to occupy Kuwait permanently.[45]

My analysis of the failure to prevent a full-scale attack against Kuwait and the ensuing crisis points to three distinct but not mutually exclusive explanations: a poorly designed strategy by the United States
that would have confused a fully rational adversary bent on expansion;
an adversary motivated by a mixture of opportunity and need who
made serious tactical miscalculations about the scope of military
action; and an adversary who framed the problem in such a way that
the choice was between open confrontation and long-term sabotage.
Any one of these conditions could have defeated deterrence and reassurance. Together, they made deterrence of the attack against Kuwait
hopeless. Only two of these conditions were present, however, when
compellence failed.

The Failure of Compellence

Unlike the practice of deterrence, the orchestration of coercive diplomacy by the United States after the invasion of Kuwait met textbook requirements. President Bush, working through the United Nations,
imposed a stringent embargo and economic sanctions against Iraq, marshaled an impressive international coalition, deployed hundreds of
thousands of troops as well as the latest generation of aircraft equipped
with precision-guided munitions in Saudi Arabia, set a deadline for
withdrawal, and threatened to use force to compel Iraq to withdraw
from Kuwait if it did not do so voluntarily. Unlike the period preceding
the invasion, presidential attention was now focused overwhelmingly
on the Gulf. The Soviet Union and France, although not the United
States, offered Iraq considerable inducements to withdraw from Kuwait.

Yet the attempt to manage the crisis short of war failed. Saddam
Hussein ignored the international ultimatum, and the coalition went to
war on January 16. The failure of a carefully crafted strategy of coercive
diplomacy serves as a useful comparison in explaining the earlier failure
of deterrence. Unlike the period preceding the invasion, the failure of
coercive diplomacy to compel Iraq to withdraw cannot be traced to
flawed strategy, ineptly executed. We must look elsewhere for the
explanation.

One argument holds that the United States did not want coercive diplomacy to succeed and planned to trap Saddam into war. Seeking to
destroy his regime, it sought international legitimacy to wage war and

did not provide the inducements necessary to persuade Saddam to concede and ease the withdrawal. Successful coercive diplomacy depends not only on credible threat but on inducement as well. Tariq Aziz lamented that his government had tried repeatedly to find a diplomatic exit but had invariably found itself trapped by the determination of the United States to wage war (Viorst 1991b, 67).

The evidence does not support this proposition. Some powerful members of the administration certainly welcomed the opportunity to go to war to curtail the power of Saddam in the Gulf. Senior military officials, National Security Advisor Brent Scowcroft, and Secretary of Defense Cheney grew increasingly confident by November that they could eject Iraq from Kuwait with a tolerable number of American casualties.[46] Such a policy was constrained, however, by the terms of the resolutions and by the vigorous attempts of a large number of mediators to provide Saddam Hussein with an honorable exit. In September and October, French, Arab, and Soviet mediators put forward a series of proposals that went some distance toward meeting the terms outlined by Saddam in his speech of August 12.[47] Saddam rejected all these offers.

It can be argued, however, that compellence did not really begin until November 8, when President Bush announced the deployment of an additional 150,000 troops. Until that time, the military forces assembled in the Gulf were there primarily to deter and defend against an attack on Saudi Arabia. Only with the large increase in the number of forces, and the decision announced two days later by Secretary of Defense Cheney not to rotate American forces stationed in the Gulf, did the American commitment to compel an Iraqi withdrawal from Kuwait become clear (Gordon 1990b). After that point, some U.S. officials described negotiations and a partial Iraqi withdrawal from Kuwait as a "nightmare scenario" (Apple 1990). Nevertheless, as the risk of war grew, others outside the United States redoubled their efforts to resolve the crisis.

In mid-November, President Hassan of Morocco (1990) proposed a special summit to find an Arab solution to the crisis. President Gorbachev, before he agreed to UN Resolution 678, which authorized the "use of all necessary means" to eject Iraq from Kuwait, invited Foreign Minister Tariq Aziz to Moscow on November 28 for a final attempt to mediate the conflict; no progress was made. On December 4, King Hussein of Jordan, Yasir Arafat, and Ali Salim al-Bid, the vice-chairman of the Presidential Council of Yemen, met with Saddam in Baghdad. In mid-December, President Chadli Benjedid (1990) announced his intention to work with Iraq to find a negotiated solution.[48] Saddam took none of these opportunities to begin a negotiating process. If he had, the willingness of the international coalition to use force would have fractured, and there likely would have been no war. Irrespective of the wishes of some members of the Administration, Saddam was not trapped into war.[49]

There remains only one plausible explanation for the failure of coercive diplomacy. It is clear in retrospect that Saddam Hussein preferred to retain Kuwait without war but preferred war to unconditional withdrawal from Kuwait. The puzzle is why Saddam ranked his preferences that way. His preference ordering can be explained by a series of tactical calculations that were generally plausible and surprisingly similar to those made by American officials at the time.

Saddam's Calculations

Saddam made a series of tactical judgments that led him to question first the likelihood, but more important the duration and the outcome, of war, should it occur. His most important judgments were political rather than military: he was not certain that the United States would use force, but more to the point he was persuaded that, if it did, Iraq would win a political victory in military defeat. Many of these political judgments were shared by senior officials in Washington. It is difficult to conclude, as April Glaspie did, that Saddam was stupid or irrational; if he was either, so were many others.

Yevgenni Primakov (1991b) reports that Saddam was surprised by the Soviet reaction to Iraq's invasion of Kuwait. Saddam believed that the Soviet Union would not endorse American coercion nor agree to resolutions at the United Nations authorizing the use of force. Saddam's estimate was not completely unrealistic: Gorbachev did press vigorously for a peaceful resolution to the crisis, to the evident discomfort of senior members of the Bush administration. It is not easy, however, to reconcile Saddam's expectation of Soviet behavior with his analysis in February 1990 of the decline of the Soviet Union and the emergence of unchallenged American hegemony (1990a). His strategic analysis was not fully consistent with his tactical expectation that the declining Soviet Union would stand apart from the hegemonic United States in the international effort to compel Iraq to withdraw from Kuwait. Moreover, even after he saw the pattern of Soviet-U.S. cooperation, he took none of the opportunities for exit provided by Gorbachev.

Saddam also behaved at times as though he were not certain that the United States would attack. His decision to release the hostages, for example, is difficult to reconcile with an expectation of a large-scale American attack.[50] Saddam subsequently acknowledged that Western diplomats who had come to Baghdad had convinced him that a release of the hostages would prevent war (Hussein 1991b). The judgment that the United States might not respond with massive force was also not inherently implausible. After the fact, action often appears predetermined; but there was an intense domestic debate within the United States, almost until the last moment, about the appropriateness of the use of force to drive Iraq out of Kuwait.

More important, Saddam calculated that Iraq could survive the military consequences of the war and win a political victory. Saddam was warned repeatedly by Primakov of the vastly superior American military capabilities, but he remained confident that Iraq would survive the air and missile attacks and prevail through superior staying power in the ground fighting to follow (1991b). In a speech to the Islamic Conference in Baghdad in January 1991, Saddam argued,

> Under all circumstances, one who wants to evict a fighter from the land will eventually depend on a soldier who walks on the ground and comes with a hand grenade, rifle, and bayonet to fight the soldier in the battle trench. All this technological superiority, which is on paper, will eventually be tested in the theater of operations. We are not people who speak on the basis of books; we are people with experience in fighting. (Hussein 1991a)

Saddam significantly underestimated the impact of air power. It is not surprising that he did so, because air power had figured so little in the eight-year Iran-Iraq War. Moreover, even American analysts, who were convinced of the decisive impact of air power, were also persuaded that, regardless of how successful the air campaign might be, a ground war would be necessary.[51]

Saddam also doubted the resolve of the United States to sustain the large numbers of casualties expected in ground fighting. As he told Ambassador Glaspie even before the invasion of Kuwait, "Yours is a society which cannot accept ten thousand dead in one battle" (Iraqi transcript 1990). This judgment was not inherently unreasonable: division ran deep within the United States, and American military analysts were estimating a considerable number of casualties should the war go to a ground battle.[52] Saddam was persuaded that the United States would not have staying power, as it had demonstrated when it withdrew its marines from Beirut after an attack on the marine compound in October 1983.

Far more important than his military calculations was the weight Saddam gave to political factors in the Arab world. He expected that Arab governments aligned with the United States would not survive the political consequences if they went to war and that the coalition arrayed against him would fracture. Indeed, he worked actively to engineer the downfall of the coalition in the period preceding the outbreak of war. Saddam again and again enjoined the Arab people to launch a "jihad" against the "imperialist aggressors" and their "agents" in the Arab world and explicitly called for the overthrow of Fahd and Mubarak (1990e, 1990f, 1990h). Saddam described the American decision in November to enlarge the deployment of its forces as evidence that it was losing the battle among the Arab masses (1990g). Again, Saddam's estimate was not wholly unrealistic: senior American officials worried as well that friendly Arab governments could be destabilized by images of Western forces killing Iraqis.[53]

Planning to attack Israel as soon as war began, Saddam hoped that Arab governments would be unable to survive the political consequences of a tacit alliance with the "Zionist enemy" (1990i). In late December, after the United Nations had imposed a deadline for withdrawal, Saddam argued that escalation to war would ignite a Pan-Arab and Pan-Islamic reaction that would eradicate the evil imperialist and Zionist conspiracies along with their illegitimate Arab agents (1990i). He was persuaded that soon after war began, if he could draw Israel into the battle, he would triumph in the "street" and force negotiation on his terms. This too was a concern shared by senior American officials who worked hard to prevent a retaliation by Israel, should Iraq attack.[54]

Saddam calculated relative capability not only in traditional military categories but also in larger political terms measured on longer time horizons. His political calculations weighed heavily in his decision to stand firm in Kuwait despite his obvious vulnerability to American power in the air. Saddam misjudged his fellow Arabs badly, but so did many analysts of the Middle East in Washington and elsewhere. Although there were widespread demonstrations in North Africa, in Yemen, and in Jordan during the war, no Arab government was overthrown, and the Arab coalition did not fracture, even when it appeared that Israel might retaliate for the missile attacks against its cities.

These political as well as military judgments governed Saddam's decision to stand firm. Almost all of these judgments were not inherently implausible; other than the underestimation of the impact of air power, many were widely shared by Western analysts before the war. They proved, however, to be wrong, and cumulatively they doomed the prospects of coercive diplomacy.

Could War Have Been Avoided?

The difference in the way the two strategies of deterrence and compellence were crafted and implemented is striking. The attempt at deterrence was flawed, inept, and incredible, while the attempt at coercive diplomacy drew on carefully assembled political and military forces to signal unequivocally to Baghdad that the coalition would go to war if Iraqi forces were not withdrawn voluntarily from Kuwait. Despite the differences in the execution of the two strategies, they led to similar outcomes—failure. An effectively designed strategy is a necessary but insufficient component of successful crisis prevention and management.

It can be argued that deterrence is generally easier than compellence, given the costs of retreat once Saddam had occupied and annexed Kuwait.[55] The argument is not convincing: the multiple opportunities provided by French, Soviet, and Arab mediators for a face-saving exit, which would have given Saddam almost all of what he wanted, should have compensated for the additional costs of withdrawal. Nor is Saddam's "stupidity" a satisfying explanation for the failure of compellence. Many of his military and political calculations were widely shared by sophisticated leaders and analysts in the Western world. The explanation for the failure to avoid war lies largely in the strategic judgment of Saddam Hussein.

Foremost was Saddam's conviction that the United States and its agents were determined to destroy his regime. Convinced that if he retreated the conspiracy against Iraq would be strengthened, he saw no alternative but political resistance, even in military defeat.[56] Saddam's isolation and inexperience with the West facilitated his easy acceptance of the conspiracy theory, prevalent in Arab political culture, that placed the United States at the center of both power and evil in the Middle East.

Saddam's serious error was not the narrow, technical miscalculation of the impact of air power but the initial, fundamental misjudgment of the intentions of the United States. American leaders could not imagine that Saddam believed that the United States was determined to destroy him. When Aziz first met Baker in October 1989, he accused the United States of hostility toward Iraq and of "mounting a campaign" to punish Baghdad; Baker was surprised and puzzled.[57] It was extraordinarily difficult for the United States to design a strategy of reassurance to deal with a contingency they found incredible and knew to be false. From Saddam's central belief in an American conspiracy, it appears that most if not all else followed. His expectation that the United States sought to destroy him became a self-fulfilling prophecy.

His strategic conviction was reinforced by anger and frustration toward Kuwait, given the costs Iraq had borne during the war with Iran, a war Iraq fought for the Gulf states as well as on its own behalf. King Hussein of Jordan asserts that Saddam was embittered because leaders in the Gulf seemed indifferent to the fact that Iraq had protected them and their people with "the blood of Iraqis" during the war with Iran (Miller 1990). The bitterness was increasingly dominant from May 1990 through to January 1991.[58]

Reinforcing his bitterness and anger was Saddam's strong sense of entitlement. Again and again during his meeting with Ambassador Glaspie, he spoke in the language of "rights": "I say to you clearly that Iraq's rights, which are mentioned in the memorandum [delivered to Kuwait], we will take one by one. . . . We are not the kind of people who will relinquish their rights. There is no historic right, or legitimacy, or need, for the U.A.E. or Kuwait to deprive us of our rights" (Iraqi transcript 1990). Within the context of Saddam's conviction that the United States sought his destruction, this sense of entitlement, magnified by the judgment of inequity at Kuwait's behavior, fueled the anger and frustration that contributed heavily to the decision to invade and then to stand firm.

The failure of compellence is explained by a complex and interacting set of political, cultural, and emotional factors that led Saddam to prefer war to retreat in the face of conspiracy. Although he preferred to retain Kuwait without war, he believed that, should war come, it would be the catalyst for the fundamental change he expected and wanted in the political landscape of the Middle East. My analysis suggests further that, within the framework of his judgment of American hegemony and conspiracy, Saddam was inflamed by anger and frustration and that he was driven by his sense of Iraq's legitimate rights, however these may have appeared to others. Within this context, he saw both the need to address Iraq's looming economic crisis and the opportunity to assert Iraq's longstanding claim to Kuwait. Given these multiple incentives, even finely crafted and optimally designed strategies of deterrence and compellence stood little chance of success. The conclusion is sobering. My analysis suggests that the invasion of Kuwait was probably unstoppable, short of major concessions by Kuwait not only on oil prices but on the other issues in dispute, and irreversible, short of the use of force to compel withdrawal.[59]

NOTES

An earlier version of this chapter was published in *International Security* 17 (Autumn 1992). I would like to acknowledge the helpful comments of Alexander L. George, Robert Jervis, Richard Ned Lebow, and David Welch. I am grateful for the generous support of the United States Institute of Peace, the Social Science and Humanities Research Council of Canada, the Connaught Senior Fellowship, and the Center of International Studies at the University of Toronto.

1. Deterrence threatens punishment or denial in order to prevent an adversary from taking unwanted action. It is most effective against an adversary that is opportunistic and seeking to make gains. Reassurance seeks to reduce the incentives for adversaries to use force by reducing the fear and insecurity that

are so often responsible for escalation to war. It is most effective against a vulnerable adversary that fears loss. For detailed analysis of the factors that contribute to the failure of deterrence as a strategy of crisis prevention, see George and Smoke (1974), Jervis, Lebow, and Stein (1985), and Lebow and Stein (1990b). For an analysis of strategies of reassurance, see Stein (1991, 8–12).

2. For a detailed anlaysis of the requirements of successful compellence, see Schelling (1966), George, Hall, and Simons (1971), George (1991), and George (forthcoming).

3. There are good historical and biographical studies of Saddam Hussein, but they do not treat the period under investigation. See, for example, al-Khalil (1989) and Matar (1981).

4. The interviews with Tariq Aziz may also be contaminated by the bias of hindsight, which leads people after the fact to consider as certain events they had earlier seen as contingent.

5. Boustany and Tyler (1990) and Theodoulou (1990) report the comments of the private memorandum.

6. At the meeting, Iraq demanded $10 billion in new loans from Kuwait. Kuwait and Saudi Arabia agreed to grant the loans, but Kuwait insisted that the boundary question must first be addressed. Iraq refused. See Cooley (1991, 128), citing private interviews with King Hussein and Foreign Minister Malway al-Kassem of Jordan.

7. These documents were released to the Senate Foreign Relations Committee for its investigations in spring 1991.

8. Author's interview with a senior member of the Policy Planning staff, State Department, Washington, D.C., April 1991.

9. Testimony of Ambassador April Glaspie before the Senate Foreign Relations Committee, March 20, 1991, reported in Friedman (1991).

10. The official U.S. version of Ambassador Glaspie's cable of July 25, 1990, reporting on the conversation, released to the Senate Foreign Relations Committee in summer 1991, differs from the Iraqi transcript only in minor details. It is hereafter cited as U.S. transcript (1991).

11. The cables between the embassy in Baghdad and Washington are reprinted in Hoffman and Dewar (1991).

12. No one in authority remembers who approved the cable or indeed if President Bush saw it before it was sent (Gelb 1991).

13. Author's interview with a member of the Policy Planning staff, State Department, Washington, D.C., August 1991.

14. On the contrary: on July 31, Assistant Secretary of State John Kelly went to testify before the Middle East Subcommittee of the House Foreign Affairs Committee against the cutoff of loan guarantees to Iraq. When asked what the U.S. position would be with respect to the use of force should Iraqi forces cross the border into Kuwait, Kelly replied: "That, Mr. Chairman, is a hypothetical or contingency question. Suffice it to say that we would be extremely concerned." Pressing further, the subcommittee chair, Congressman Lee Hamilton, asked explicitly whether, under those circumstances, it would be correct to say that the United States did not have a treaty commitment that would obligate Washington to engage U.S. forces. Kelly replied: "That is correct." Testimony of

Assistant Secretary of State for Near East and South Asian Affairs John Kelly to the Middle East Subcommittee of the House Foreign Affairs Committee, July 31 1990, reported in Cockburn (1990).

During this period, King Hussein of Jordan telephoned President Bush and assured him that Saddam would not resort to military force. President Mubarak of Egypt and King Fahd also told the president that the problem was being handled in an Arab way and asked Bush to do nothing to upset the process. See Oberdorfer (1991, 40). These requests from Jordan, Egypt, and Saudi Arabia may explain the quiescence of the United States in the forty-eight hours before Iraq's invasion.

15. Kelly told Ambassador al-Mashat: "Mr. Ambassador, we know you have at least 100,000 troops on your border. This is extremely serious. It looks as though you are preparing aggressive action against Kuwait." He reiterated that any differences must be solved peacefully and asked Iraq to pull its forces back from the border. Al-Mashat denied any aggressive intentions whatsoever. See Oberdorfer (1991, 40).

16. Iraq had some 700 combat aircraft, 6,000 tanks, 5,000 artillery pieces, and approximately 1 million men under arms. The figures are misleading in that only 165 of the aircraft were advanced fighters and bombers, and the Republican Guards, the crack fighting units, constituted less than a third of the total armed forces. See International Institute for Strategic Studies (1990).

17. UN investigators after the war concluded that Iraq could have produced an atomic bomb within one to three years. See Broad (1991) and Lewis (1992).

18. Egyptian Ambassador-at-large Tahseen Bashir reported that Kuwait was very "difficult" in the negotiations. Author's interview with Tahseen Bashir, Los Angeles, August 15, 1990.

19. When he made these comments, Sheik Salim al-Sabah was the foreign minister and second in the line of succession.

20. Author's interview with a senior member of the Policy Planning staff, State Department, Washington, D.C. April 1991.

21. Saddam Hussein claimed a debt of $40 billion to Western governments during his meeting with Ambassador Glaspie (Iraqi transcript 1990).

22. In his interview with Viorst, Aziz charges, "Mubarak was the Americans' man. After the invasion, Mubarak accused Saddam of having lied about his intentions. It was actually Mubarak who was the liar and whose lie speeded up the race to disaster." Aziz's reconstruction of what Saddam told Mubarak is consistent with the U.S. transcript of his meeting with U.S. Ambassador April Glaspie, where he used the same phraseology. It is unlikely, however, that Mubarak would have deliberately sought to fuel the crisis, since he was vigorously attempting to mediate a peaceful solution. Egyptian officials subsequently expressed frustration with the negotiating position of Kuwait's representative at the talks.

23. Iraq's leaders have long held that the border between the two countries was imposed by Britain in 1922 and thus lacked legitimacy. They considered Kuwait part of the Ottoman vilayet of Basra, which was severed by Britain to deny Iraq easy access to the Gulf. The claim of entitlement is counterbalanced by Kuwait's autonomous status within the Ottoman empire, by the continuous al-Sabah rule there since the middle of the eighteenth century, and by its status as

a British protectorate since 1899. Iraq accepted the official status of the border in 1932, when it became independent, and again in 1963, when the Baath came to power. However, it challenged the legitimacy of the border whenever it saw an opportunity to do so: in 1961, when Kuwait became independent from Britain; in 1969, when Iraq deployed forces in Kuwait to defend Umm Qasr from an alleged Iranian attack; and again in March 1973, when Iraqi troops occupied a border outpost close to Bubiyan.

24. Author's interview with a senior member of the Policy Planning staff, State Department, Washington, D.C., August 1990.

25. Author's interview with a senior member of the National Security Council staff, Washington, D.C., August 1990.

26. Charles E. Allen, testifying at the confirmation hearings for Robert M. Gates, disclosed that as early as January 1990 he and other officials at the CIA began to consider the possibility that Iraq might engage in an all out attack against Kuwait. Allen noted that "there were economic indicators that developed prior to the military mobilization" (CIA Official's Testimony 1991). These early warnings did not reach senior officials in the administration.

27. Minutes of meeting in Department of Agriculture (Baguet, 1992a). On August 4, 1989, officials of the FBI and the Federal Reserve Bank seized documents from the Banca Nazionale del Lavoro in Atlanta. Investigators from the Department of Agriculture charged that Iraq was using the bank to divert funds granted by the Commodity Credit Corporation to third parties in exchange for military hardware and sensitive military technology. Officials confronted high-ranking members of Iraq's governments with the accusations in October 1989. Georgia's Attorney General Robert L. Barr, Jr., proposed returning an immediate indictment, but the Justice Department intervened to delay charges. Minutes of the meeting in the Department of Agriculture that listed the charges were released by the House Committee on Banking, Finance, and Urban Affairs (Baquet 1992a, 1992b; Gelb 1992).

28. The editorial broadcast by the Voice of America was entitled "No More Secret Police." It began with the comment: "Next, an editorial reflecting the views of the U.S. government: A successful tyranny requires a strong, ruthless secret police force. A successful democracy requires the abolition of such a force." The editorial then celebrated the defeat of tyranny in Eastern Europe and concluded: "Secret police are also entrenched in other countries, such as China, North Korea, Iran, Iraq, Syria, Libya, Cuba, and Albania. The rulers of these countries hold power by force and fear, not by the consent of the governed. But as East Europeans demonstrated so dramatically in 1989, the tide of history is against such rulers. The 1990s should belong not to the dictators and secret police, but to the people" (Voice of America 1990).

29. The Glaspie cable was obtained by *New York Times* columnist William Safire under the Freedom of Information Act.

30. Author's interview with Egyptian Ambassador-at-large Tahseen Bashir, Los Angeles, August 15, 1990.

31. On April 5, Saddam asked Prince Bandar of Saudi Arabia to assure Britain and the United States that he did not intend to attack Israel but that he wanted assurances that Israel would not attack. He explained to Bandar that, since Israel and the West were plotting against him, he had made his statement

to mobilize Iraqi opinion against the threat from the "imperialist Zionist" plan to destroy Iraq. See Seib (1990a, A10) and Oberdorfer (1991, 23, 36).

32. In October 1989, after the charges by the Department of Agriculture, President Bush issued National Security Directive 26 mandating the United States to "improve and expand our relationship with Iraq" (Gelb 1992).

33. Deterrence and reassurance address different dimensions of an adversary's incentives to use force. Although both may be necessary, each can undermine the effect of the other.

34. The concept of the United States as an imperialist oppressor, conspiring against the Arab people, had figured prominently in the thinking of President Gamal Abdel Nasser of Egypt; it is an image widely held by Arab leaders who appeal to populist sentiments against established governments.

35. For an analysis of the importance of "framing effects" on strategic choices, see Stein and Pauly (forthcoming).

36. See al-Khalil (1989) for an analysis of the obsessive fabrication of enemies that characterized Saddam's perpetual war against the adversaries of Arabism.

37. For a detailed examination of these dynamics, see Lebow and Stein (forthcoming).

38. Author's interview with a senior Iraqi official Geneva, April 1991.

39. During a visit by King Hussein of Jordan to the emir in Kuwait City, the Kuwaiti foreign minister told his Jordanian counterpart, "If the Iraqis attack us, we would call the Americans" Miller (1990).

40. Yevgenni Primakov, the Soviet official who visited Baghdad twice in October to mediate a peaceful resolution to the crisis, reported that Saddam was surprised by the Saudi reaction to the invasion. Saddam did not believe that King Fahd would allow American troops into the kingdom (1991b).

41. It is only Tariq Aziz who argues that it made no difference whether Iraq occupied all or part of Kuwait because, as he said, "We expected an American military retaliation from the very beginning." Other Iraqi officials claim that Saddam was persuaded that Washington wanted to undermine his regime through economic warfare and covert action but was uncertain in August about the likely scope of American retaliation. Author's interview with a senior Iraqi official, Geneva, April 1991.

42. The Joint Chiefs of staff would have vigorously opposed such a deployment. Author's interview with a senior Pentagon official, Washington, D.C., September 1991.

43. In a tense meeting with King Fahd, Secretary Cheney warned: "We will defend you, but we will not liberate you. You have a very short time to make your choice." Author's interview with a member of the National Security Council staff, Washington, D.C., August 1991. Saudi Arabia earlier had refused to join the joint exercises of the United States and United Arab Emirates. See Oberdorfer (1991, 38).

44. Saddam linked Baghdad's withdrawal from Kuwait to the immediate and unconditional withdrawal of Israel from the occupied Arab territories in Palestine, Syria, and Lebanon; Syria's withdrawal from Lebanon; and a mutual withdrawal by Iraq and Iran from each other's territory captured during the war. Saddam also demanded that U.S. forces leave Saudi Arabia and be replaced by

Arab forces under UN authority. Finally, he insisted that all sanctions against Iraq be lifted upon its withdrawal from Kuwait (1990d).

45. Author's interview with Tahseen Bashir, August 15, 1990.

46. Author's interview with a senior member of the National Security Council staff, Washington, D.C., May 1991. See also Woodward (1991, 290–96) for a discussion of "preventive war" scenarios.

47. In September 1990, King Hussein of Jordan, King Hassan of Morocco, and President Benjedid of Algeria proposed a compromise: Iraq would withdraw from Kuwait, but the two would have a special relationship similar to that of Syria and Lebanon; Kuwait would cede the islands of Bubiyan and Warbah and the Rumaila oil fields, and a free vote would be held in Kuwait for a successor government; the Iraqi withdrawal would be tightly coupled to a fixed date for the withdrawal of foreign forces from Saudi Arabia and to a discussion of the Palestinian problem ("Arab Initiative" 1990, 1–2). On September 24 President Mitterrand of France proposed to the United Nations a four-stage process of settlement. Iraq would declare its intention to withdraw from Kuwait, and the Kuwaiti people would exercise their "democratic will." An international conference would then address the Arab-Israel conflict and the future of Lebanon. Finally, the states in the Middle East would consider arms control agreements and arrangements (Lewis 1990). Yevgenni Primakov, President Gorbachev's personal envoy, traveled to Baghdad twice in October and proposed connecting Iraq's withdrawal from Kuwait to Israel's agreement to attend an international conference to resolve the Palestinian problem (Primakov 1991a).

48. Saddam insisted that talks could not occur while U.S. forces threatened Iraq and that the Arab-Israel conflict had to be on the agenda; in response, Presidents Mubarak and Asad rejected the proposal. The three Arab mediators accepted most of the terms laid out by Saddam in his speech on August 12 but insisted that Iraq must abide by UN Resolution 660 that called on Iraq to withdraw unconditionally from Kuwait; again, Saddam offered no concessions on Kuwait (Benjedid 1990).

49. Herrmann (forthcoming) makes a compelling case for the proposition that Saddam was given several honorable exits and that he was not trapped into war. For a competing interpretation, cogently argued, see Smith (1992).

50. Herrmann (forthcoming) argues persuasively that this decision is comprehensible only if Saddam expected to forestall an attack.

51. See, for example, Pape (1990, 1a), who concludes: "Air power alone cannot compel Saddam Hussein to retreat from Kuwait. If the embargo fails and the US remains determined to force him out, we must be prepared to commit immense ground forces as well as air forces for a protracted campaign, and be ready to pay a high price in blood and treasure."

52. In December 1990, General Norman Schwarzkopf was given the order "to accept losses no greater than the equivalent of three companies per coalition brigade." The order translated into casualties of approximately 10 percent among allied ground forces, or 10,000 allied soldiers. It is unusual that President Bush, Secretary of Defense Cheney, and General Colin Powell, chairman of the Joint Chiefs of Staff, would impose an upper limit on casualties as the date of military operations drew closer. The order is included in U.S. Department of Defense (1991), submitted to the Congress on April 10. See Cushman (1992).

53. Former head of the Bureau of Near Eastern and South Asian Affairs Nicholas Veliotes expressed concern that through war "you could set in train a series of actions to destabilize current governments" Seib (1990b, 10).

54. Author's interview with a senior member of the National Security Council staff, Washington, D.C., May 1991. See also Welch (forthcoming).

55. The proposition that deterrence is easier than compellence is widely accepted. See Schelling (1966). For an analysis of cases of "immediate" deterrence and compellence that challenges this proposition, see Lebow and Stein (1990a).

56. Yevgenni Primakov describes Saddam's thinking as consistent with a "Masada complex" (Primakov 1991a). *Masada* refers to the embattled stand made by Judean defenders against Roman legionnaires for three years after the decisive military battle in 70 A.D., with full knowledge that they were doomed. The defenders at Masada ultimately committed suicide rather than surrender to Roman forces. Primakov either misunderstands the analogy of Masada or misapplies it to Saddam, who expected to survive and win a political victory in the face of military defeat. The better analogy would have been to Egypt's Nasser in 1956: although Nasser's forces were defeated by Israel, Britain, and France, he won an enormous political victory by resisting.

57. Iraq's Ambassador to Washington Mohammed al-Mashat subsequently explained that "we had information that some authorities in the United States were working to destabilize Iraq" by sending emissaries to the Gulf states and "planting fear of Iraq in the heads of the sheikhs." Oberdorfer (1991, 21). Al-Mashat may have been referring to the periodic briefings given by the U.S. Central Command that identified Iraq as a potential threat in the region.

58. The intense emotional reaction to Kuwait's unwillingness to make concessions was part of a personality profile described as "defiant, grandiose, resting on the well-fortified foundation of a siege mentality." The impact of Saddam's personality on his behavior is analyzed in Post (1991a, 1991b).

59. This analysis does not suggest that Saddam Hussein was unstoppable under all conditions. In complying with UN resolutions after the war, Iraq acknowledged that it had thirty untested chemical warheads for its al-Husayn missile that it used against Israel's cities. Despite Saddam's overwhelming interest in provoking an Israeli retaliation, he did not arm the missiles with chemical warheads, even at the end of the ground war, when his army faced catastrophic defeat. That he did not use the chemical warheads may have been the result of successful Israeli deterrence. Alternatively, the untested warheads may not have been operational. See Welch (forthcoming) and Steinberg (1991).

REFERENCES

Apple, R. W., Jr. 1990. "U.S. 'Nightmare Scenario': Being Finessed by Iraq." *New York Times*, December 19.

"Arab Initiative Outlined." *FBIS Daily Report*. FBIS-NES-90-183, 1–2.

Baquet, Dean. 1992a. "Documents Charge Prewar Iraq Swap: U.S. Food for Arms." *New York Times*, April 27.

——— . 1992b. "Investigators Say U.S. Shielded Iraqis from Bank Inquiry." *New York Times*, March 20.

Benjedid, Chadli. 1990. "Press Statement by President Chadli Benjedid." *FBIS Daily Report*. FBIS-NES-90-240, 32–33.

Boustany, Nora, and Patrick E. Tyler. 1990. "Iraq Expands Forces Near Kuwait Border." *Washington Post*, July 31.

Broad, William J. 1991. "U.N. Says Iraq Was Building H-Bomb and Bigger A-Bomb." *New York Times*, October 15.

CIA Official's Testimony on Nomination of Gates as Director. 1991. Excerpts from transcript. *New York Times*, September 25.

Cockburn, Alexander. 1990. "West Vacationed While Saddam Burned." *Wall Street Journal*, September 6.

Cooley, John K. 1991. "Pre-War Gulf Diplomacy." *Survival* 33: 125–39.

Cowell, Alan. 1990. "Iraq Chief, Boasting of Poison Gas, Warns of Disaster if Israelis Strike." *New York Times*, April 3.

Cushman, John H., Jr. 1992. "Pentagon Report on the Persian Gulf War: A Few Surprises and Some Silences." *New York Times*, April 11.

Friedman, Thomas L. 1991. "Envoy to Iraq Faulted in Crisis, Says She Warned Hussein Seriously." *New York Times*, March 21.

Gelb, Leslie H. 1991. "Mr. Bush's Fateful Blunder." *New York Times*, July 17.

———. 1992. "Bush's Iraqi Blunder." *New York Times*, May 4.

George, Alexander L. 1991. *Forceful Persuasion: An Alternative to War*. Washington, D.C.: United States Institute of Peace.

———. Forthcoming. *The Limits of Coercive Diplomacy*, rev. ed.

George, Alexander L., David K. Hall, and William Simons. 1971. *The Limits of Coercive Diplomacy*. Boston: Little, Brown.

George, Alexander L., and Richard Smoke. 1974. *Deterrence in American Foreign Policy*. New York: Columbia University Press.

Gordon, Michael R. 1990a. "U.S. Deploys Air and Sea Forces After Iraq Threatens Two Neighbors." *New York Times*, July 25.

———. 1990b. "U.S. Says Troops Won't Be Rotated Until Crisis Is Over." *New York Times*, November 10.

Hassan, King. 1990. "Speech by King Hassan II of Morocco." *FBIS Daily Report*. FBIS-NES-90-219, 17–18.

Herrmann, Richard. Forthcoming. "Coercive Diplomacy and the Crisis Over Kuwait: 1990–1991." In *The Limits of Coercive Diplomacy*, rev. ed., ed. Alexander L. George.

Hoffman, David, and Helen Dewar. 1991. "State Department, Panel, Spar Over Envoy." *Washington Post*, July 13.

Hussein, Saddam. 1990a. "Speech to the Arab Cooperation Council Summit." *FBIS Daily Report*. FBIS-NES-90-039, 1–5.

———. 1990b. "Speech to the Arab Summit in Baghdad." *FBIS Daily Report*. FBIS-NES-90-103, 2–7.

———. 1990c. "Speech on Revolution Day." *FBIS Daily Report*. FBIS-NES-90-137, 20–23.

———. 1990d. "Initiative on Developments in the Region." *FBIS Daily Report*. FBIS-NES-90-156, 48–49.

———. 1990e. "Message to the Iraqi People, Faithful Arabs, and Muslims Everywhere." *FBIS Daily Report*. FBIS-NES-90-173, 27–29.

————. 1990f. "Address on the Al-Aqsa Incident." *FBIS Daily Report.* FBIS-NES-90-196, 22–23.

————. 1990g. "Interview with Saddam Hussein." *FBIS Daily Report.* FBIS-NES-90-219, 26–31.

————. 1990h. "Address to the Islamic Delegation." *FBIS Daily Report.* FBIS-NES-90-242, 14–17.

————. 1990i. "Address to the Jordanian National Democratic Alliance." *FBIS Daily Report.* FBIS-NES-90-249, 24–30.

————. 1991a. "Speech to the Islamic Conference." *FBIS Daily Report.* FBIS-NES-91-009, 2–4.

————. 1991b. "Interview with Saddam Hussein by Peter Arnett." *FBIS Daily Report.* FBIS-NES-91-021, 20–24.

International Institute for Strategic Studies. 1990. *The Military Balance, 1989–1990.* London: IISS.

Iraqi Transcript of the Meeting Between President Saddam Hussein and U.S. Ambassador April Glaspie. *New York Times,* September 23.

Jervis, Robert, Richard Ned Lebow, and Janice Gross Stein. 1985. *Psychology and Deterrence.* Baltimore: Johns Hopkins University Press.

al-Khalil, Samir. 1989. *Republic of Fear.* New York: Pantheon.

Lebow, Richard Ned, and Janice Gross Stein. 1990a. "Deterrence: The Elusive Dependent Variable." *World Politics* 62 (April): 336–69.

Lebow, Richard Ned, and Janice Gross Stein. 1990b. *When Does Deterrence Succeed and How Do We Know?* Ottawa: Canadian Institute for International Peace and Security.

Lebow, Richard Ned, and Janice Gross Stein. Forthcoming. *We All Lost the Cold War.* Princeton: Princeton University Press.

Lewis, Paul. 1990. "Mitterand Says Iraq Withdrawal Could Help End Mideast Disputes." *New York Times,* September 25.

————. 1992. "Iraq's A-Bomb Capability Overrated, U.N. Now Says." *New York Times,* May 20.

Matar, L. Fuad. 1981. *Saddam Hussein: The Man, the Cause, and the Future.* London: Third World Center.

Miller, Judith. 1990. "King Hussein on Kuwait and Dashed Hope." *New York Times,* October 16.

Oberdorfer, Don. 1991. "Missed Signals in the Middle East." *Washington Post Magazine,* March 17, 19–41.

Pape, Robert A. 1990. "Airpower Can't Dislodge Iraq." *Christian Science Monitor,* October 15, 19.

Post, Jerrold M. 1991a. "Saddam Hussein of Iraq: A Political Psychology Profile." *Political Psychology* 12 (Spring): 279–89.

————. 1991b. "Afterword." *Political Psychology* 12 (December): 723–25.

Primakov, Yevgenni. 1991a. "The Inside Story of Moscow's Quest for a Deal." *Time,* March 4, 40–48.

————. 1991b. "Interview with Yevgenni Primakov." *FBIS Daily Report.* FBIS-NES-91-021, 11.

Schelling, Thomas. 1966. *The Strategy of Conflict.* New Haven: Yale University Press.

Sciolino, Elaine, with Michael R. Gordon. 1990. "U.S. Gave Iraq Little Reason Not to Mount Kuwait Assault." *New York Times,* September 23.

Seib, Gerald F. 1990a. "Saddam Hussein Takes Pains to Spin Conspiracy Tales." *Wall Street Journal,* October 22.

———. 1990b. "A Strike by U.S. Could Unleash Flood of Enmity." *Wall Street Journal,* November 5.

Smith, Jean Edward. 1992. *George Bush's War.* New York: Holt.

Stein, Janice Gross. 1991. "Deterrence and Reassurance." In *Behavior, Society, and Nuclear War,* vol. 2, ed. Philip E. Tetlock et al. New York: Oxford University Press, 8–72.

Stein, Janice Gross, and Louis Pauly, eds. Forthcoming. *Choosing to Cooperate: How States Avoid Loss.* Baltimore: Johns Hopkins University Press.

Steinberg, Gerald M. 1991. "The Iraq-Israel Deterrence Relationship: Lessons from 'The Mother of All Wars.' " Prepared for the U.S. Institute for Peace Conference on Peace, Deterrence, and Regional Security, Washington, D.C., June 17–20.

Theodoulou, Michael. 1990. "Kuwait Fears Invasion Over Iraqi Demands." *Times* (London), August 2.

U.S. Department of Defense, 1991. *Report on the Gulf War.* 3 vols. Washington, D.C.: Government Printing Office.

U.S. transcript of Ambassador Glaspie's cable of July 25, 1990. *New York Times,* July 31.

Viorst, Milton. 1990. "Report from Baghdad." *New Yorker,* September 24, 89–97.

———. 1991a. "After the Liberation." *New Yorker,* September 30, 37–72.

———. 1991b. "Report from Baghdad." *New Yorker,* June 24, 55–73.

Voice of America Public Affairs. 1990. Voice of America editorial 9-93982. Washington, D.C., February 15.

Welch, David A. Forthcoming. "The Politics and Psychology of Restraint: Israeli Decision-Making in the Gulf War." In *Choosing to Cooperate: How States Avoid Loss.* Baltimore: Johns Hopkins University Press.

Woodward, Bob. 1991. *The Commanders.* New York: Simon and Schuster.

6

The War of Images: Strategic Communication in the Gulf Conflict

■

Jarol B. Manheim

One dimension of power can be construed as the ability to have one's account become the perceived reality of others.

—*H. Molotch and M. Lester*

We disseminated information in a void as a basis for Americans to form opinions.

—*Frank Manckiewicz*

EACH OF US can undoubtedly call to mind a repertoire of Gulf conflict images: Saddam Hussein petting a small boy who was a "guest" in Iraq; Ambassador April Glaspie under de facto house arrest in the State Department; George Bush trying to redefine the Gulf crisis as a *golf* crisis; the rockets' red glare over Baghdad and Peter Arnett hanging out the hotel window to describe it; the "baby formula" factory and the command bunker; bombs that were almost cartoonlike in their ability to select targets; protective gear for chemical warfare; Adolf Hitler. There were, as well, some missing images: the 80 percent collateral damage from less-than-smart bombing; individual stories of individual hostages and their families; body bags being unloaded for burial in the United States; the Kuwaiti emir rushing home to the embrace of a grateful people; an official U.S. estimate of the Iraqi death toll.

As the art of managing conflict evolves so, too, does the art of managing the images of that conflict that are conveyed to the populations of the principals and, increasingly, to a larger world audience. The motivations for image management during conflict are manifold, and they are not, for the most part, new. They include, among others, the mobilization of support among one's own population and the demobilization of support in the opposition camp, the legitimation of one's own objectives and the delegitimation of the opposition's, the empowerment of one's own forces and the disempowerment of those on the other side, the contrast of the potency of one's own forces with the impotence of those arrayed in opposition, and the very definition of the circumstances and objectives of the conflict on terms most favorable to one's own needs.

What *is* relatively new is the array of technological, institutional, and psychological tools available to the contemporary image manager and, importantly, the growth of expertise in a field now coming to be known as strategic political communication. The technology of image management is that of modern electronic communication generally: highly mobile field packs, two-way satellite transmission, instantaneous worldwide distribution, and the like. The institutional tools include, in addition to outright censorship, the creation and management of media pools, the selective provision of access to sources and events, the selective granting of media credentials, appeals to the patriotism of journalists and news organizations, briefings, and other devices intended to govern who is able to report what to whom, under what circumstances and, most important, at whose discretion. And the psychological tools are those typically found in the workbox of the professional persuader. They are, essentially, those devices by which public opinion can be created, shaped, sustained, manipulated, and directed toward defined objectives. The purpose of the present essay is to focus on the strategies that determined the specific use of these management tools in the Gulf conflict. To that end, it seems appropriate to offer a framework for understanding the role of strategic communication in the policy process.

The Conceptual Framework

Political communication encompasses the creation, distribution, control, use, processing, and effects of information as a political resource, whether by governments, organizations, or individuals. *Strategic* political communication is the subset of these activities in which the communicator employs sophisticated knowledge of such attributes of human behavior as attitude and preference structures, cultural tendencies, and media use patterns to shape and target messages so that their desired effect is maximized and their collateral effects minimized. In the present context, it involves the use of such devices as media management, grassroots organizing, image control, and lobbying for the purpose of either influencing, implementing, or mobilizing support for particular Gulf-related objectives. Strategic political communication differs from other forms of public diplomacy in the degree to which it is applied systematically and selectively in the pursuit of foreign policy aims, from psychological warfare to its focus on the regular behaviors of

policy-making institutions. For both of these it relies on essentially political processes in the target country.

From this it follows that no single model of image management defines strategic communication. Rather, the first step in deriving a strategy must be to gain an understanding of the model that operates within
the target country. In the instance of the Gulf conflict, there were several direct national and international participants and at least that number of distinctive targets. These included Iraq, Saudi Arabia, and the
other Gulf states; what was then the Soviet Union; traditional U.S. allies
in Western Europe; Japan; China; other members of the UN Security
Council; and, of course, the United States. It is not possible, given either the brevity of this essay or the limits on my expertise, to examine
each of these in turn. We can, however, begin from a model that is of
demonstrated utility for examining the internal political process of one
of these participants, the United States. This model may have other applications, and we can use it to frame a discussion of communication
strategies directed by and toward the United States throughout the period of the crisis.

I have offered what I term a model of agenda dynamics to illustrate
the relationship between the agenda-*setting* function of the media in the
United States and the agenda *building* that takes place more generally in
the political process (Manheim 1987). This model is presented in figure
6.1. The model portrays three distinct agendas—those of the media, the
public, and the policy makers—and suggests two key points about
them. First, and most obvious, there is a bidirectional, though not necessarily a balanced, flow of information and influence between each
pair of agendas. Second, and less obvious, there is an internal dynamic
within each agenda whose product derives from, and contributes to, the
exchange of information and influence with the other two. Thus, for example, newsroom decision making, which produces the media agenda,
incorporates responses to such matters as audience demographics, audience preferences, and political pressures. Public opinion, which helps
to define the context for policy making, is shaped by underlying attitudes and perceptions and also by salience cues and alternatives offered
by both media and policy makers. And so forth. In the present context, the most important outcome of this set of exchanges is the expansion or contraction of the freedom of action available to foreign policy
decision makers as they shape responses to events such as the invasion
of Kuwait.

Traditionally, studies of agenda-related processes in both communication studies and political science have assumed that the environment
in which such exchanges occur is benign, or at least ineffective, insofar
as it might influence these relationships. But the validity of that assumption is placed in doubt, at least in the arena of foreign affairs, by a

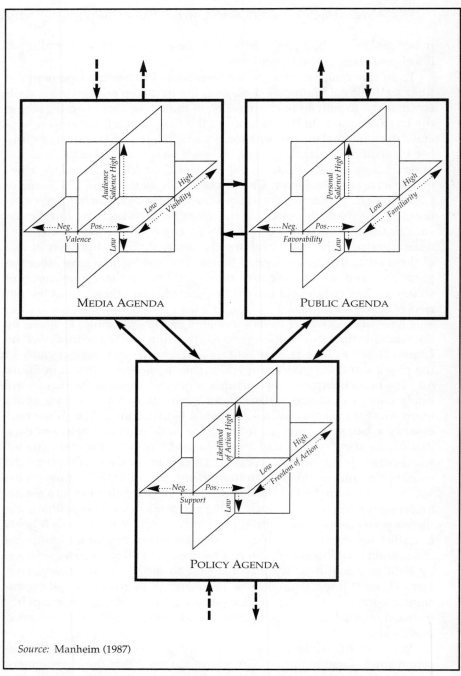

Source: Manheim (1987)

FIGURE 6.1 MODEL OF AGENDA DYNAMICS *Source:* Manheim (1987).

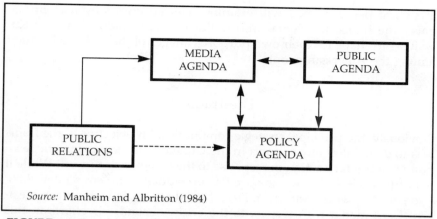

Source: Manheim and Albritton (1984)

FIGURE 6.2 THE AGENDA-SETTING SYSTEM *Source:* Manheim and Albritton (1984).

series of recent studies (Andersen 1989; Choate 1990; Davis 1977; Manheim 1990, 1991a, 1991b; Manheim and Albritton 1984, 1986, 1987; and Merritt 1980) indicating that efforts by the government of one country to manipulate policy processes internal to a second, may, in fact, have substantial effect. These studies show that countries as diverse as Nigeria, Japan, South Korea, Pakistan, and the Philippines have worked, sometimes with considerable success, to alter their portrayals by the U.S. media and the perception of them among leading U.S. pundits and policy makers, often leading to some noteworthy advance toward their respective objectives for U.S. foreign policy making. A prime example is provided by Pakistan, whose U.S.-targeted strategic communication effort in 1990 (Manheim 1990) produced a substantial increase in foreign aid, an armada of war planes, and U.S. approval for enriching nuclear stocks for the government of Prime Minister Benazir Bhutto. Figure 6.2 illustrates the process as it applies to foreign policy decision making in the United States. External actors, here labeled Public Relations but incorporating a diversity of informational and direct influence efforts, are portrayed as working through news management activities and through direct lobbying—but in each instance through the established domestic political process of the United States as represented by the elements of the agenda dynamics model—to influence U.S. foreign policy to their advantage.

Together, these figures provide the framework for the present analysis, one in which policy is determined in a political context that is defined by a repertoire of prevailing images and in which those images are the objects of substantial attention by the several national and quasi-national actors with the greatest stakes in the outcome. Employing this

analytical perspective, I will examine selected efforts by four principals—the Iraqis, the Pentagon, the Bush administration, and the Kuwaitis—to shape for their own purposes images of the Gulf crisis extant
among the American people.

The Iraqis

Obviously, the principal strategic communication objective of the Iraqis
was to demobilize any support in the United States for diplomatic, economic, or military action in response to the takeover of Kuwait. While it
is not possible to know the specifics of Saddam Hussein's intentions,
two general points seem clear. First, he did set out to manage the Western (U.S.) media with respect to the crisis. Second, his efforts in this
regard were generally counterproductive.

At the time of the Kuwaiti invasion, the Iraqis had a recent history
of efforts at media manipulation, but one not notable for its success.
One incident tells the story. In the fall of 1988, immediately upon the
conclusion of the war with Iran, the Iraqi army began an offensive
against the Kurds in northern Iraq. The Kurds claimed that their villages were being attacked by chemical weapons, weapons that the Iraqis
were known to have used against Iranian forces. In an attempt to dis-
prove these charges, the Ministry of Information arranged for foreign
journalists to visit the remote outpost of Zakhu, where they would be
able to interview Kurds returning to Iraq from camps in Turkey, to
which they had fled. Several dozen reporters were flown by helicopter
to Zakhu, only to discover that no Kurds were returning. The government promptly canceled the "photo opportunity" and prepared to fly
the journalists back to Baghdad. On the way back, the helicopters
landed for refueling at a military base, where reporters observed troop
transports, loaded with Iraqi soldiers wearing gas masks, driving toward the Kurdish region. In the end, the government confiscated
dozens of videocassettes from the foreign journalists to review them for
footage of burned-out villages over which the helicopters had flown
(Tyler 1988). The result was rather less than the intended public relations coup.

Saddam Hussein set out from the beginning to manage news portrayals of the Gulf conflict. His principal instruments at first were censorship and the taking of hostages, each designed in its own way to
manage a flow of information that was meant to continue. Later, when
the conflict deepened and the information flow proved largely unman-
ageable or when, at the very least, the objectives of news management
were not obtained, he evicted most foreign journalists. The hostage
story is perhaps the most revealing of the cynicism, and ultimately the

failure of understanding, that guided Iraqi propaganda efforts. Recall that several hundred thousand foreigners became unwilling "guests" of the Iraqi regime. Among them were large populations of laborers, principally from the countries of Southwest Asia, but also numerous skilled technicians and managers from the West, including the United States.

The model here was, rather clearly, that provided by the seizure of American hostages in Teheran during the Iranian revolution. In that instance, the Iranians were able to use their captives to take one additional, de facto, hostage, the president of the United States, who was overwhelmingly concerned with, and was politically overwhelmed by, their fate. More to the present point, it is clear that the Iranian government systematically stage-managed the hostage incident to great advantage. The slogans on the walls of the U.S. embassy compound and on many of the signs carried by demonstrators were written in English, not Farsi. Major government ministries had next-day delivery of the *New York Times* as well as critiques of individual reporters and their work sent by observers in the United States. Direct-dial telephone service with the United States provided the government with immediate reports on television coverage of the scene, complete with network-by-network and journalist-by-journalist assessments (Curtis 1983a, 134; Curtis 1983b). And Iranian "students"—an interesting construct in itself—provided daily advance assistance to American camera crews in identifying the most propitious locations and camera angles for each day's "spontaneous" events (Manheim 1991a; 172).

Saddam may well have intended to go the Iranians one better. For example, he did not need to rely on indirect observers of media coverage. He had CNN and his very own correspondent, Peter Arnett, whose efforts he could monitor with an immediacy denied even the Iranians. And he had, not a few dozen hostages, but enough to populate a small country. It must have been a rosy prospect. As matters developed, we did see similarities in the two cases. Media events were staged to emphasize the presence and vulnerability of Westerners held in Iraq, as they had been in Iran. A willingness to appear brutal was manifested in Iraq—though only with respect to captured pilots rather than detained civilians—as it had been in Iran. And even the signs in Iraq—as at the famous baby formula factory—were in English, hardly the language of daily discourse.

But what Saddam failed to understand about the Iranian success was that it was the smallness of scale, not its greatness, that was its key. The Iranian hostages were kept in one central and highly visible place and had names, faces, and families. They were grist for the mill of news media conditioned by more than a decade of pressure to shape programming to maximize audience appeal—to focus on drama and personalization, rather than on ideas, in conveying the content and import of world events (Bennett 1988). The human scale of the roster of hostages, and the simple imagery of the bevy of yellow ribbons, were central to the potency of the Iranian effort. But by inviting so many guests to remain in his native land, Saddam Hussein turned the story from one of people to one of numbers and lost an opportunity, for a linchpin of almost any media-based strategy of image management is the personalization of the story, providing the media with the human-interest content that serves one's purpose. And this Saddam failed to do. His especially awkward efforts to redress the loss—which, among other consequences, gave him the appearance to Western eyes of a pederast when he petted a small boy on television in an effort to appear to care about the welfare of his detainees, a gesture that did not translate well across cultures—served merely to undermine further his control of the story line. In the end, he was left only with the most intrusive and least sophisticated of all news management options: extensive censorship and the exclusion of journalists.

Saddam Hussein may also have had a second vulnerability in comparison with the Iranian hostage taking, for it was a central tenet of the Iranian revolution to expel all Westerners from the country. To Ayatollah Khomeini, their lives and safety were literally of no real value or concern except as they could be used to wring concessions from the United States. Saddam Hussein, however, had no intention of isolating himself from Western support or expertise and knew that in the long term his economy would require outside labor. In this situation, not only would threats against the hostages lack credibility, but they might render unwilling to return to Iraq classes of foreigners upon whom the country was in some measure dependent. This, it would seem, accounts as well for Saddam's eventual decision to permit his guests to depart.

The Pentagon

Much of the Pentagon's role in news management was explicit and visible. The faces of press spokesmen Pete Williams and Generals Thomas Kelly and Norman Schwartzkopf became as familiar to audiences around the world as the cross hairs on the monitors of the laser-guided Smart bombs that locked onto the doors and windows of so many Iraqi targets. But behind the public relations there lay a clear element of strategic communication. One aspect of this is evident in the "Hometown News Program," discussed below, one of whose objectives was to provide human interest news that would fill the media and, potentially, divert attention from other issues. Even C-SPAN got into the act here, with approximately twelve hours of original programming devoted to the transporting of one reserve military police unit to the Gulf and its daily life in Saudi Arabia. But there was more.

Even before the Gulf conflict developed, a small staff group called the CAIG (pronounced "cage")—an acronym derived from Chief of Staff of the Army Assessments and Initiatives Group—had been formed within the service that would bear the brunt of any ground combat in such circumstances. The group, composed of hand-picked uniformed personnel whose collective expertise covered the full range of army activity, was designed to provide quick, quiet, nonbureaucratic management of public perceptions of military action. Its purpose was, in part, to protect the army from the political consequences of what it saw as the potential for erroneous or unrealistic reporting. Two members of the CAIG had served with the National Security Council, and about half a dozen held doctorates. Members of the group were in regular contact with journalists throughout the Gulf conflict, contacts that required neither advanced clearance nor subsequent reporting to superiors. The CAIG employed a systematic strategy developed within an issue management framework, and—in the words of Lieutenant Colonel James Fetig, special assistant for public affairs to the chief of staff of the army and the group's communication coordinator—"This was not a loose cannon operation" (author's interview with James Fetig, Washington, January 1992).

At Fetig's initiative, the CAIG adopted a variant of the immunization strategy of persuasion. The notion of immunizing a target audience against messages that might undermine the position of a given persuader was first developed by social psychologist William J. McGuire, principally in the 1960s (see, for example, McGuire 1964). The essential idea is that one can induce resistance to persuasion through the use of refutational pretreatments. As characterized by Michael Pfau and Henry Kenski (1990, 75) in their book on the use of inoculation strategies in domestic political campaigns, these pretreatments "raise the specter of potentially damaging content to the receiver's attitude while simultaneously providing direct refutation of that content in the presence of a supporting environment, threaten the individual, triggering the motivation to bolster arguments supporting the receiver's attitudes, thereby conferring resistance." Pfau and Kenski go on to argue that the central element in such a strategy, and the one that sets it apart from simple preemptive refutation, is the use of threat as a motivating factor.

The principal communication objectives of the CAIG were (1) to keep snafus in perspective, (2) to preserve the army's credibility, (3) to prevent surprises, (4) to create the "right" first impression and to prevent false impressions, and (5) to "keep everybody sober." Specifically, with such precedents in mind as the Chinese entry into the Korean War, the Tet offensive in Vietnam, and the Beirut massacre, the group was charged with anticipating and averting potential media-public-political relations problems. To that end, the CAIG adopted an approach to its task that was grounded in an inoculation strategy. This was evidenced in at least three distinct areas: logistics, causalities, and chemical warfare.

With respect to logistics, the army knew that the scope of the undertaking, moving vast numbers of personnel and amounts of materiel halfway around the globe, would be laden with seeming delays and inefficiencies—and knew, too, that the media and the public would, if left to their own devices (not to mention the human interest stories encouraged by the "Hometown News Program"), focus on gripes from the lower echelons. Accordingly, the CAIG set out to downplay the level of expectations with respect to mobility and preparation. Members emphasized the limitations on the use of force, citing the example of the invasion of Panama, where war did not accomplish political change. Similarly, with respect to casualties, the CAIG set out to ensure that people would know that, as Fetig put it, "If we fought, we would bleed." No estimates of casualties were ever put forward, partly because the military planners were so optimistic in this regard that their estimates (ranging as low as 2,000 U.S. deaths) might have set the army up for a resurgence of the Vietnam syndrome of doubt and distrust. In each instance, the element of threat derived from lingering popular uncertainty over the quality of military leadership, personnel, and equipment, an uncertainty to which the military planners were extraordinarily sensitive.

But perhaps the clearest example of the application of an inoculation strategy by the CAIG came in the area of chemical warfare. The army knew that Iraq had chemical weapons, that it had demonstrated a willingness to employ them, and that, were these weapons employed, they would result in substantial casualties. This was regarded as a real possibility, one that might undermine the willingness of the American people to sustain any war effort. Rather than ignore or understate the danger, the CAIG initiated a dialogue with dozens of reporters, in which its members brought up and discussed the issue in what they regarded as realistic terms in order to get it on the agenda early and get people accustomed to the threat. For example, when members of the press were deployed to Saudi Arabia, CAIG members selected a small number of prominent journalists and briefed them on what to expect with regard to chemical warfare and on basic information about what the chemicals were. They made clear the army's expectation that it would suffer casualties if these weapons were used. Even the C-SPAN series included a briefing on protection against chemical agents. In this instance, the threat was explicit and one that every American could understand. It was raised early and often by the army so as to mitigate as far as possible any negative consequences for the conduct of the war—and for the army's long-term credibility—should use of the weapons be initiated (author's interview with James Fetig).

The Bush Administration

The Bush administration came to the Gulf crisis with its own lessons, experiences, and concerns. From Vietnam, the administration knew that it would not be possible to prosecute a war in the Gulf without the acquiescence, if not the support, of the American people. From Grenada—the invasion of which, you will recall, came less than a week after the massacre of U.S. marines in Lebanon—it was clear that the government could deflect concerns and opposition with a quick, decisive, and highly publicized victory (see Deaver 1987, 147 *passim*). And from the incursion into Panama, which was aggressively shielded from the prying eyes of journalists until virtually all of the action had been concluded and where it was only much after the fact that we began to learn of the hundreds of civilian victims buried in mass graves, the administration learned that it could maximize its freedom of action in such matters to the extent that it could hide that action from press and public view.

More than that, George Bush came to office as the clear beneficiary of the use of strategic communication in domestic politics. His presidency was the product of a partisan communication juggernaut that had rolled over one Democrat after another, both in electoral competition and in contests over policy and legislation. This is not the appropriate forum for a full discussion of the Reagan-Bush communication strategy, but it is important to consider some aspects of that larger strategy because so many elements of the domestic effort found their way into the strategic management of images in the Gulf conflict. The Reagan-Bush media advisors had, for example, considerable experience in limiting access to events by national journalists. Ronald Reagan met them principally in the blade wash of his helicopter. Candidate Dan Quayle confronted them in a press conference held, not in a quiet meeting room, but at a giant rally in his hometown. "Stormin'" Norman Schwartzkopf met them in a tent, where the only video available was what he showed on his own VCR. Lesson learned.

But rather than merely restricting journalists' access—a practice that might lend credibility to charges of their unresponsiveness—the Reagan-Bush media advisors had developed an alternative strategy, one that, like some of them, traced its origins to the Nixon administration. Having observed that local reporters were both less skilled and more easily overawed by access to the president and other key policy actors, that local media would give especially prominent play to national stories gathered by their own staffers, that local media increasingly have the technological capacity to cover national and world stories, and that public cynicism regarding national journalists generally did not extend to local media personalities, Republican operatives have developed techniques for granting access to local journalists at the expense of their national colleagues (Smith 1988; 402–12). The former are more easily managed, and objections from the latter can readily be portrayed as products of professional jealousy. This strategy was employed in the Gulf through the military's "Hometown News Program," a large-scale effort to bring local journalists into the Kuwaiti Theater of Operations (KTO) for the purpose, not merely of coopting grateful journalists who received free transportation to the area (DeParle 1991) but, more important, of creating a clutter of uninformed and repetitive questions that would give the military forces both the excuse to limit access to the front and an opportunity to appear patient and open at the same time that it minimized the likelihood that control over the story might be lost. Approximately 1,500 journalists passed through the KTO during the conflict.

Most interesting of all in this context, however, was the handling of the "blood for oil" issue. This was a major point of prospective danger for the president in this particular conflict and one to which he and his advisors were especially sensitive. In 1986, when Bush was preparing his candidacy for the presidency, his advisor Robert Teeter, through Market Opinion Research, conducted a review of Bush's image and came to the conclusion that his negatives were potentially quite high, especially since he was linked in the public mind with two negative cues: Arabs and oil. The decision was made and implemented to remove Bush from the public eye until the latest possible moment in order to give the public the opportunity to forget about this linkage. Bush dropped from sight for many months, a factor that contributed to his wimp image and even to the characterization of him in the Doonesbury cartoon strip as the invisible man. But if wimpdom was a cost of the strategy, it was not without evident benefits. For when Bush reemerged for the primaries, the linkage to Arabs and oil had all but disappeared. Evidence of this is provided by the news coverage of the *Exxon Valdez* disaster in Alaska, where slow federal action and a reluctance to penalize Exxon were actual policy outcomes but where little mention appears of the president's ties to Texas oil interests (Manheim 1991a).

Clearly, blood versus oil—especially in Kuwait—was a definition of events that Bush could not tolerate, especially if, as Steven Wayne notes in his essay in this volume, his was the first American company to have drilled wells in Kuwait. To his good fortune, though the theme surfaced from time to time, it generally did so without reference to his own ties to the oil industry. When one particularly threatening front-page story in the *New York Times* referred to "this oily war," Bush responded immediately by staging a rally in the parking lot of the Pentagon, at which he delineated the many objectives of American policy in the Gulf—none of which, not surprisingly, had to do with oil (Gitlin 1991).

One final component of the administration's strategy of information control in the Gulf conflict is noteworthy less for its substance than for its longevity. Throughout the period of the war and its aftermath, U.S. spokespersons declined all invitations to issue causality counts for Iraqi military or civilian personnel. The reasons can only be a matter of speculation. It may be, for instance, that the Bush administration could tolerate the ambiguity of being associated with an unknown number of deaths but not the specificity of association with an established count, was unwilling to admit to significant civilian casualties, or merely saw death as more tolerable to the American people when left as an abstract concept. It is clear, however, that it was established administration policy to avoid casualty counts. So long lasting was this aversion, and so all encompassing, that when Beth Osborne Daponte, a demographer with the U.S. Census Bureau charged with updating the bureau's population estimate for Iraq, following established bureau procedures, released to a reporter upon request her estimate of war-related deaths—86,194 men, 39,612 women, and 32,195 children—she was removed from the project, her files disappeared from her desk, and she was advised that she would be fired for having demonstrated "untrustworthiness or unreliability" (Gellman 1992).

Image management in the Gulf crisis, then, followed a script with a familiar plot line. Indeed, in the end, it was yet another device from the domestic sphere that ultimately controlled public images of the Gulf conflict. Willie Horton, meet Adolf Hitler. Before we can fully appreciate the strategic use of the demonization of Saddam Hussein among the media and public in the United States, however, and we must bring into our analysis one more set of actors.

The Kuwaitis

Of the four parties whose actions are under review here, the Kuwaitis and their agents are perhaps the most revealing of all, because they had no real power to influence events. They had only money, and their objective was to use it to create whatever leverage they could on U.S. policy. In effect, this meant that they needed to mobilize American support for their cause and to channel it into military action, which represented their only hope of regaining their homeland.

To this end, the Kuwaitis enlisted the assistance of Hill and Knowlton Public Affairs Worldwide, one of a number of so-called strategic communication firms that provide advice to foreign governments and corporations as to how best to pursue their policy objectives in the United States. This was accomplished through what amounted to a front organization, called Citizens for a Free Kuwait (CFK), which included Kuwaiti businessmen, political exiles, students, and even Kuwaiti tourists stranded in the United States at the time of the invasion. CFK spent some $11.5 million in the United States between August 22, 1990, and March 25, 1991, most, if not all, of it provided by the Kuwaiti government in exile. Of this, $10.8 million went to Hill and Knowlton ("Citizens for Free Kuwait" 1991).

Hill and Knowlton did little direct lobbying for the Kuwaitis, though the firm did help to structure the witness lists for congressional and UN hearings (see below) and organized Americans for a Free Kuwait, a group set up to lobby state and local officials. Most of Hill and Knowlton's direct efforts, however, centered on training their clients to deal with the U.S. media, drafting speeches and scheduling speaking tours, monitoring and analyzing legislative initiatives, and distributing video and other materials. The firm established a television crew in Saudi Arabia and served as the sole source for video footage from the Kuwaiti underground. It also arranged for a feature on events in Kuwait to be incorporated into the Thanksgiving Day National Football League telecast (Manheim 1991b).

According to sources at Amnesty International (which later publicly dissociated itself from the story to which it had given currency), Hill and Knowlton gave them the infamous story of Iraqi soldiers pulling Kuwaiti newborns from their incubators so that they could be taken to Iraq. The story made an appearance on Capitol Hill, where a young woman identified only as Nayirah told the House of Representatives Human Rights Subcommittee chaired by Representative Tom Lantos that she had witnessed this event firsthand. After John R. MacArthur, publisher of *Harper's Magazine*, revealed in a *New York Times* op-ed piece the fact that Nayirah was, in fact, the daughter of the Kuwaiti ambassador to the United States, it was also disclosed that Hill and Knowlton had helped to prepare her testimony, which she had rehearsed before video cameras in the firm's Washington headquarters. According to Kuwaiti doctors and other witnesses interviewed by Middle East Watch, a human rights group, the incident never occurred, a position that was rejected by the U.S. embassy in Kuwait (Cushman 1992; Priest 1992). True or not, this story clearly affected George Bush, as evidenced by the frequency with which he cited it, including his turn-of-the-year interview with David Frost. Similar testimony was presented before the UN

Security Council by a woman identified only as a Kuwaiti refugee, but who later turned out to be Fatima Fahed, wife of the Kuwaiti minister of planning and a prominent Kuwaiti television personality (Manheim 1991b; Strong 1992).

The most interesting image management activity undertaken for the Kuwaitis, however, was subcontracted by Hill and Knowlton to the Wirthlin Group, a Washington, D.C., area polling organization with strong ties to the administration. Wirthlin conducted a series of focus groups and tracking polls (the procedures are detailed in Manheim 1991b) to test the effectiveness of some fifty prospective messages, including the Kuwait-as-liberal-democracy theme that characterized much of the earliest Hill and Knowlton effort. The tracking polls, measuring such items as the mood of the country, support for the president and his Gulf policy, and the standing of various world leaders, were administered to some 200 respondents daily over a period of several weeks. Approximately eight focus groups were conducted to add texture to the data.

The results, some of which are reported in Wilcox, Ferrara, and Allsop (1991), show very clearly that Americans resonated, not to positive portrayals of Kuwait, but to images of Saddam Hussein as an enemy. Of particular importance was a group of some three dozen subjects who met in September 1990, roughly a month after the Hill and Knowlton contract was initiated, and were monitored electronically as they viewed video presentations of the various themes under consideration. Just as a similar focus group session had led to the emphasis on Willie Horton and Michael Dukakis's other negative attributes in the 1988 campaign, their clear reaction to the enemy theme grabbed the attention of the consultants. As a direct result of this finding, the theme of the public relations effort was immediately redefined to emphasize Saddam Hussein's negatives.

Themes demonizing Saddam Hussein—like those to which the focus group members so notably resonated—emerged early in the crisis. The Hitler analogy, for example, was employed early by Charles Krauthammer (August 3) and first used, at least indirectly, by President Bush on August 8. Between August 2 and January 15, the analogy was invoked 107 times in stories, editorials, or commentaries in the *New York Times* and 121 times in the *Washington Post* (Dorman and Livingston 1992). The Wirthlin focus group in effect tested its utility. It has not been possible to date to establish a firm linkage between research conducted for the Kuwaitis and rhetorical themes employed by the president and his administration. In this regard, however, it is tantalizing to note that, in addition to the strong ties of the Wirthlin organization to many in the administration, tracing back to the days when Richard Wirthlin served as Ronald Reagan's pollster, the head of Hill and Knowlton throughout this period was Craig Fuller, whose previous position had been as chief of staff to Vice-President George Bush.

Conclusion

From this analysis, two things seem clear. First, there is both conceptual grounding and practical evidence to suggest that strategic communication plays a significant role in framing, influencing, and implementing foreign policy, at least within the U.S. political system. Second, the Iraqis, the Kuwaitis, the Pentagon, and the Bush administration themselves all engaged in large-scale efforts to employ strategic communication toward the goal of creating or modifying the context within which the American response to the Iraqi invasion of Kuwait would be determined, albeit with differential success. The Iraqis were ineffective, the army surprisingly aggressive, and the administration predictable. But it may be the Kuwaitis who were the most successful of all. They did not come off looking like the democrats of the Gulf region—an image to which they did aspire—but they were able to identify and provide images that facilitated the movement toward armed conflict. And in doing so, they were quite evidently the beneficiaries of social engineering derived from the practice of strategic political communication.

REFERENCES

Andersen, Robin. 1989. "The Reagan Administration and Nicaragua: The Use of Public Diplomacy to Influence Media Coverage and Public Opinion." Paper prepared for the Annual Meeting of the Speech Communication Association, San Francisco.

Bennett, W. Lance. 1988. *News: The Politics of Illusion,* 2d ed. White Plains: Longman.

Choate, Pat. 1990. *Agents of Influence.* New York: Knopf.

"Citizens for Free Kuwait Files with FARA After Nine-Month Lag." 1991. *O'Dwyer's FARA Report* 1 (October): 1–2.

Curtis, Bill. 1983a. *On Assignment with Bill Curtis.* Chicago: Rand McNally.

———. 1983b. Interview on "Morning Edition," National Public Radio, December 13.

Cushman, John H., Jr. 1992. "U.S. Offers Proof of Iraqi Atrocity." *New York Times,* February 6.

Davis, Morris. 1977. *Interpreters for Nigeria: The Third World and International Public Relations.* Urbana: University of Illinois Press.

Deaver, Michael K. 1987. *Behind the Scenes.* New York: Morrow.

DeParle, Jason. 1991. "Long Series of Military Decisions Led to Gulf War News Censorship." *New York Times,* May 5.

Dorman, William A., and Steven Livingston. 1992. "Historical Content and the News: Policy Consequences for the 1990–91 Persian Gulf Crisis." Paper prepared for the annual meeting of the International Communication Association, Miami.

Gellman, Barton. 1992. "Census Worker Who Calculated '91 Iraqi Death Toll Is Told She Will Be Fired." *Washington Post,* March 6.

Gitlin, Todd. 1991. Commentary at the Social Science Research Council Conference on Media and Foreign Policy, Seattle.

McGuire, William J. 1964. "Inducing Resistance to Persuasion: Some Contemporary Approaches." In *Advances in Experimental Social Psychology,* vol 1, ed. L. Berkowitz. New York: Academic.

Manheim, Jarol B. 1987. "A Model of Agenda Dynamics." In *Communication Yearbook 10, ed.* Margaret L. McLaughlin. Beverly Hills: Sage.

———. 1990. "'Democracy' as International Public Relations." Presented at the annual meeting of the American Political Science Association, San Francisco.

———. 1991a. *All of the People, All the Time: Strategic Communication and American Politics.* Armonk: M. E. Sharpe.

———. 1991b. "All for a Good Cause: Managing Kuwait's Image During the Gulf Conflict." Presented at the Social Science Research Council Conference on Media and Foreign Policy, Seattle.

Manheim, Jarol B., and Robert B. Albritton. 1984. "Changing National Images: International Public Relations and Media Agenda Setting." *American Political Science Review* 78:641–54.

Manheim, Jarol B., and Robert B. Albritton. 1986. "Public Relations in the Public Eye: Two Case Studies of the Failure of Public Information Campaigns." *Political Communication and Persuasion* 3:265–91.

Manheim, Jarol B., and Robert B. Albritton. 1987. "Insurgent Violence Versus Image Management: The Struggle for National Images in Southern Africa." *British Journal of Political Science* 17:201–18.

Merritt, Richard L. 1980. "Transforming International Communications Strategies." *Political Communication and Persuasion* 1:5–42.

Pfau, MIchael, and Henry C. Kenski. 1990. *Attack Politics: Strategy and Defense.* New York: Praeger.

Priest, Dana. 1992. "Kuwait Baby-Killing Report Disputed." *Washington Post,* February 7.

Smith, Hedrick. 1988. *The Power Game.* New York: Random House.

Strong, Morgan. 1992. "Portions of the Gulf War Were Brought to You by the Folks at Hill and Knowlton." *TV Guide,* February 22, 11–13.

Tyler, Patrick E. 1988. "Kurds Disappoint Iraqi PR Effort." *Washington Post,* September 18.

Wilcox, Clyde, Joe Ferrara, and Dee Allsop. 1991. "Before the Rally: The Dynamics of Attitudes Toward the Gulf Crisis Before the War." Paper prepared for the annual meeting of the American Political Science Association, Washington, D.C.

COMMENTARY ON PART III
Images and the Gulf War

■

Robert Jervis

AS JANICE STEIN points out, the evidence available about the Gulf War is sharply restricted, thereby limiting the confidence with which we can advance our favorite explanations. I would go a step further and argue that we will never get good evidence about many crucial aspects of this case. Here, as in many other recent cases, records are likely to be incomplete and misleading. Even if all documents are preserved and opened for public inspection, we should not expect too much from them. There is little reason to think that they fully and accurately reveal the motives, calculations, beliefs, and goals of the actors. Many decisions were made under great pressure, and in few countries will the foreign policy organizational procedures have required a full explication of the relevant positions and considerations. The job of decision makers, after all, is to make decisions, not to lay out a record for future scholars.

Even if good position papers had been written, they would not tell us what people said—let along thought—in the rooms in which the decisions were made. I would be very surprised if adequate records of these deliberations exist. Occasionally, we are fortunate enough to have a statesman who surreptitiously tape-records meetings, as Kennedy did during the Cuban missile crisis. A few other leaders, particularly Eisenhower, saw that very complete notes were made at many—but not all—crucial meetings. But one cannot expect too much.

Excellent communications systems may work to the disadvantage of scholars. People know that anything they put down on paper can be photocopied and leaked. Furthermore, secure phones and rapid air transportation mean that less needs to be written. Habits have changed as well. In the nineteenth and early twentieth centuries statesmen kept diaries for purposes other than writing their memoirs. They also maintained extensive correspondence: members of the British cabinet were writing to their wives and mistresses during the crucial days when they were deciding whether to enter World War I. Such sources are not likely to emerge in this case.

An elusive but vital question that I suspect we will be arguing about for the indefinite future is which of these events were determined and which were contingent. Stein argues, by and large persuasively, that even excellent diplomacy could not have deflected Saddam Hussein, at least not after early 1990. But two points are in order. First, we often see history as highly determined and even overdetermined (Fischoff 1975; Fischoff and Beyth 1975). Once an event has occurred, it is relatively easy for us to think of all the reasons why it should have occurred as we recall all the forces that pushed in that direction. Possible turning points tend to be obscured, and considerations that led away from the decision that was taken get blotted out of our memories. Second, the American decisions do not seem to have been determined by broad factors in existence before the invasion. Things could easily have gone the other way. While one could predict an American policy of deterring an attack on Saudi Arabia on the basis of general American policy and interests, pushing Iraq out of Kuwait was more contingent, depending as it did on Bush's preferences if not personality and on the unprecedented decisions of other countries. Thus Saddam Hussein's decisions were not totally foolish. As Stein notes, it was crucial for the way events unfolded that Saudi Arabia permitted American troops into that country in order both to deter and attack. Furthermore, this might not have occurred had Saddam Hussein not deployed his troops in an offensive formation on the Kuwaiti-Saudi border.

Even with this, all else did not follow easily. Maintaining the domestic and international coalition was a stunning feat. In addition, I do not think it was foreordained that the American buildup would go as swiftly and smoothly as it did and that by December the U.S. commanders would be able to assure the president that the war could be fought with extremely low American casualties. Finally, the Bush administration's ability to fend off Soviet and French diplomatic initiatives before the war began and immediately before the ground defensive was launched could not have been predicted on the basis of broad general considerations, depending as it did on skillful diplomacy on the American part and a series of Iraqi blunders. The ease of the military victory should not mislead us into thinking that this was the inevitable or even the most likely outcome of the confrontation.

The chapters by Jarol Manheim and Stein demonstrate the importance of images and beliefs, and this will be the subject of the rest of my comment. We cannot begin to explain what happened without understanding how the various countries and statesmen saw one another. Analyses that assume that perceptions are accurate or that all people see the facts and events in the same way have very limited utility here—and in most other cases as well. States and statesmen are not interchangeable; they have particular beliefs and perceptions that shape their behavior. Generalizations are not impossible, and I will draw on them below. But there is significant room for differences at the individual and social level. Modes of analysis that seek to borrow from the discipline of economics and build parsimonious models on the basis of shared and accurate information are not a good place to start.[1] Neither can we assume that the outcomes represent any sort of equilibrium or that states succeeded in maximizing their expected utilities.

As Manheim's chapter reminds us, when we deal with images and beliefs we cannot assume that actors believe what they are saying. We need to understand what Alexander George (1959) in his analysis of German propaganda in World War II called the actors' "communication strategies." States seek to project desired images as part of the effort to get others to do what they want. Sometimes these images are accurate—but one should not assume that it is easier to convince others of things that are true than it is to deceive them; sometimes they are not—deception is central to strategic interaction, especially international politics (Jervis 1989). Even when more complete records are available, it will be difficult for us to determine whether statements were deceptive. Even after the fact, political leaders want their desired version of events accepted. Thus many Iraqi spokesmen probably think it is in their personal or national interest to have the world believe that Iraq attacked Kuwait because their leaders believed the United States was encircling it.

In a further twist, however, we should also realize that statements originally intended as deceptive can come to be believed by those who propound them. Only a few people are cynical enough to prevent their own views from being clouded by what they say, not only in public but also to their subordinates (whom they often want to deceive as well). Daryl Bem (1972) argues that people often infer their own beliefs from their behavior.[2] They also may be influenced by their own statements of belief. Decision makers who say they feel encircled not only often act in a way to make this prophecy self-fulfilling, they often come to believe that the evidence supports this view.

Misperception and differing national if not personal perspectives are the rule, not the exception. In the Gulf War, as in many other cases, *Rashamon* provides the model; the world that one actor sees is likely to be very different from the one in someone else's mind. This is true within a state as well as between them. Roger Hilsman (1967, 502) reports that when two special fact-finding envoys returned from South Vietnam and gave their report to a meeting of the National Security Council, their accounts were so different that President Kennedy said, "You two did visit the same country, didn't you?" In a real sense, they did not: they visited their own minds, which were filled by different beliefs, expectations, and concerns.

This is not all: actors rarely appreciate the extent to which others' views are wildly discrepant from theirs. Empathy is extremely difficult.[3] Statesmen realize that others have different goals and values than they do but usually fail to realize that others see the world very differently. Even when they do understand that their perceptions are not shared, they almost never succeed in recreating the other's general worldview and specific images, especially images of them. Decision makers, like people in general, are strongly invested in their self-images, which rarely correspond to the images held by others. Indeed, I cannot think of a single international conflict in which both sides have been able to grasp the perceptions of the other. Cultural differences and high conflict magnify these difficulties, as was true in the Gulf War. But they can occur between allies who have similar interests, speak the same language, and have multiple channels of communication. Those who need convincing should consult Richard Neustadt's (1970) marvelous and discouraging study of Anglo-American misunderstandings surrounding the Suez and Skybolt crises.

Beliefs and images of other actors are highly resistant to discrepant information (Holsti 1976; Jervis 1976; 143–216). Images can be most influenced when they are most malleable, which usually is early in the interaction process. But for a state seeking to project a desired image or correct a misleading one, this knowledge is not particularly helpful: early in the process they are not likely to realize that they have a problem on their hands. Thus by the time the United States realized that Iraq was a menace, it probably was too late to have much influence.

Because preexisting beliefs are so powerful, attempts to influence or manipulate what others believe require the actor to know what they already think. Thus the British ability to deceive Nazi Germany throughout most of World War II depended in significant measure on code breaking, which gave them access to German cognitive predispositions and allowed them to see how information was being interpreted. Similarly, focus groups can tell political leaders what messages will best resonate: we owe the Willie Horton advertising campaign in part to the knowledge and tools of social science. As Manheim shows, Kuwaiti and administration leaders understood these general principles well and skillfully employed focus groups to reveal which appeals to the American people would be most successful. The acceptance of the claim that Saddam Hussein resembled Hitler, furthermore, can be understood in terms of other principles of psychology: thanks to World War II, the Cold War, and the images of the Soviet Union that were widely held during it, the general concept or schema of a Hitler was familiar, psychologically readily accessible, and easily invoked. While Americans no longer see Russian-American relations in terms of an overriding threat and a pressing need for deterrence, these concepts still shape most

Americans' general views of international politics and can be quite readily applied to interactions with other countries.[4]

American policy before and during the Gulf War was complicated because the message the United States tried to convey pulled in two directions: the United States sought not only to deter Iraq from expanding but also to reassure it that the United States would not menace it if Iraq limited its ambitions. Either deterrence or reassurance is difficult enough in insolation. But here as in many other cases neither message by itself would have produced the desired effect. Deterrence alone could have led Saddam to believe that he would be attacked even if he did not challenge the status quo; reassurance by itself could have led him to conclude that the United States would not threaten Iraq even if he was aggressive. Communicating both a contingent promise and a contingent threat was particularly difficult, however. Statements and actions that showed resolve tended to undercut reassurance; those that might have convinced Iraq that the United States harbored no untoward intentions neutralized messages that the United States would block or fight Iraq if that became necessary. The United States had to make credible both threats and promises. Before the war, its leaders never paid enough attention to the problem to realize that this needed to be done, and even if they had understood the dilemma, I doubt if they could have solved it.

Earlier I noted how difficult empathy is. In this case an additional obstacle was that to have grasped the Iraqi worldview would have been to acknowledge bizarre interpretations and to understand that others saw us in a way that we found incredible and distasteful. The idea that we were out to destroy Iraq would have seemed ludicrous. Policy makers knew they had no such designs; they would not have taken seriously the proposition that others saw disconnected events as being masterminded by the United States. We knew the "truth"; others could not be so misguided as to believe their own propaganda or to see us as scheming and duplicitious.

This case is not unusual. To take a different example, one reason why the United States was surprised by the Tet offensive was that we knew that such a move would fail badly. American intelligence showed that there would be no general uprising, and so the United States assumed that the North Vietnamese, who were well informed about the mood of the peasants, would also know this and react accordingly. What the United States did not know was that North Vietnamese leaders were out of touch with reality and in fact expected that the offensive would trigger a general revolt (Wirtz 1991).

Another complication was that Saddam Hussein knew little about the outside world, and upsetting analyses were not likely to reach him. Democracies have many defects, but they are relatively open to information. Brutal dictatorships are at an enormous disadvantage because those who convey messages that their masters dislike will be lucky to escape with their lives. Such regimes are likely to destroy themselves unless their leaders' intuitions happen to be correct. They will also bring grave harm to others before painful reality makes itself known.

As Janice Stein shows, Saddam's perceptions of Saudi Arabia were crucial: he never thought that regime would dare invite American troops. In this he was not far wrong; the Saudi decision was not an easy one. But this crucial link in the chain of circumstances apparently never occurred to American decision makers. They never thought—and most of us would not have thought—that to deter Iraq the United States needed to convince Saddam Hussein that the Saudis would cooperate with the United States. As is often the case, the Americans concentrated on simpler bilateral matters.

Differences in national perspectives and a lack of empathy also played a large role in the fall and winter of 1990–1991. Americans found it difficult to grasp Saddam's view that he might win the war politically even though he would lose it militarily: crucial to him was the expected anti-Americanism among Arab mass opinion. The United States often is concerned with such sentiments, but in this case they seemed irrelevant, and so Americans could not see that others might focus on them. For the American public—and I suspect for most decision makers as well—the United States was operating in the interests of weak and threatened states around the globe; nothing could be further from the truth than to see our actions as defending American privileges, let alone American dominance. But Saddam had a different perspective and believed that an American-led attack would turn the Third World in general and Arab countries in particular against the United States. Furthermore, the worse Iraq fared militarily, the more the United States would look like an oppressor. Indeed, it is not clear that Saddam was wrong. Although the reaction has been muted so far, this may not be the end of the story. It may yet be that by bombing another nonwhite, non-Christian country, the United States will have produced an image of itself not as a defender of international law and human rights, but as an imperialist bully.

NOTES

1. Recent work in game theory deals with situations in which the players are uncertain or have conflicting information. But it has not explored how actors come to form and maintain the beliefs that are crucial to their behavior.
2. For an excellent application, see Larson (1985).
3. For an interesting discussion, see White (1990); also see White (1991).

4. This is shown by the results of an elite survey conducted by Cheryl Koopman, Jack Snyder, and Robert Jervis.

REFERENCES

Bem, Daryl. 1972. "Self-Perception Theory." In *Advances in Experimental Social Psychology*, vol. 6, ed. Leonard Berkowitz. New York: Academic Press.

Fischoff, Baruch. 1975. "Hindsight ≠ Foresight: The Effect of Outcome Knowledge on Judgment Under Uncertainty." *Journal of Experimental Psychology: Human Perception and Performance* 1 (August): 288–89.

Fischoff, Baruch, and Ruth Beyth. 1975. " 'I Knew It Would Happen'—Remembered Probabilities of Once-Future Things." *Organizational Behavior and Human Performance* 13 (February): 1–16.

George, Alexander. 1959. *Propaganda Analysis*. Evanston: Row, Peterson.

Hilsman, Roger. 1967. *To Move a Nation*. Garden City: Doubleday.

Holsti, Ole. 1976. "Cognitive Dynamics and Images of the Enemy: Dulles and Russia." In *Enemies in Politics*, ed. David Finley, Ole Holsti, and Richard Fagen. Chicago: Rand McNally.

Jervis, Robert. 1976. *Perception and Misperception in International Relations*. Princeton: Princeton University Press.

———. 1989. *The Logic of Images in International Relations*, ed. ed. New York: Columbia University Press.

Larson, Deborah, 1985. *Origins of Containment*. Princeton: Princeton University Press.

Neustadt, Richard, 1970. *Alliance Politics*. New York: Columbia University Press.

White, Ralph. 1990. "Why Aggressors Lose." Political Psychology 11 (June): 227–42.

———. "Empathizing with Saddam Hussein." *Political Psychology* 12 (June): 291–308.

Wirtz, James. 1991. *The Tet Offensive: Intelligence in War*. Ithaca: Cornell University Press.

PART IV

■

MASS PUBLICS

7

Arab Public Opinion and the Gulf War

■

Shibley Telhami

■ WHILE IT IS generally assumed that public opinion matters little in authoritarian polities, I argue in this chapter that, on issues of foreign policy, Arab public opinion has a discernible impact on the foreign policies of Arab states; moreover, in the conduct of the Persian Gulf War, Arab public opinion was a key element in the strategies of the central parties. I also argue that the absence of the predicted upheavals in the Middle East following the smashing of Iraq was partly due to the success of members of the alliance in controlling some of the variables that help shape Arab public opinion, partly to the failure of Saddam to deliver what he promised, and partly to the fact that the allies took seriously the predictions of public upheaval.

Methodology

My assessment of Arab public opinion is based on, first, extensive interviews in May–June 1990, December 1990, and July 1991. My travels in the region included visits to Egypt, Syria, Iraq, Jordan, Tunisia, Israel, and the West Bank. During those visits, I interviewed policy makers, academics, journalists, middle- and working-class families, and Egyptian workers returning from Iraq. Second, my assessment is based on extensive coverage of the Arab press; during the Gulf crisis, while on the staff of the United States' delegation to the United Nations, I read daily reports in most Arab publications, including the opposition press.

My interviews were not limited to elite views, although much of my assessment is based on those views and on Arab leaders' analyses of mass public opinion. However, it should be noted that while there are differences between elite and mass public opinion, the discrepancy works in favor of my argument in this chapter: to the extent that my assessment centers on strong Arab resentment of U.S. policy and on

Arab views about the Palestinian question, it is generally accepted that mass public opinion is more radical on those issues than elite and official positions. Contrasting the costs of Israeli concessions to Arab concessions, Syria's foreign minister, Farouq Sharaa, noted that the views expressed by Arab governments are already much more moderate than public opinion on the Arab-Israeli question, whereas views of the Israeli government are more radical than public opinion (Sharaa 1991). Yet the argument presented here documents even radical views among elites and government officials in Arab states with strong ties to the United States. Similiarly, while it is clear that the FBIS coverage of Arab press to which I refer is selective, the bias in this case also works in favor of my argument.

The Relevance of Public Opinion

Is Arab public opinion relevant to the conduct of Arab foreign policy? Even in democracies, where the public is assumed to have more influence on state policy, some students of public opinion rule out a causal connection.[1] A few argue, for example, that public opinion is primarily shaped by policy makers (Mueller 1973; Brody and Shapiro 1987; Ostrom and Simon 1985; Kohut 1988). Others hold that public opinion and public policy are causally unrelated, that neither influences the other (Caspary 1970; Leigh 1976). If this could be the case in democracies, where instruments of information are not in the hands of rulers, what could be said of authoritarian polities?

Indeed, during the Camp David negotiations, when Egypt's President Anwar Sadat argued that Egyptian public opinion would prevent him from making concessions, Israel's Prime Minister Menachem Begin countered that "the people of Egypt could be easily manipulated by Sadat, and their beliefs and attitudes could be shaped by their leader." Begin went on to cite Sadat's ability to convince his people that the Soviets were their best friends only to later cast them as their worst enemy. So heated was the exchange that the two men had to be separated for much of the Camp David negotiations (Carter 1982). Arab alignments following the Iraqi invasion of Kuwait in 1990 and the ability of several Arab governments to join the American-led coalition against Iraq, despite the reported unpopularity of this move, appear to reinforce doubts about the relevance of public opinion to the policies of Middle East states.

Yet Arab leaders act as though Arab public opinion matters. This judgment is historically valid, as witnessed by the popular revolution against an entrenched shah in Iran; the popular uprisings across the

Middle East in the 1950s that helped to topple several Arab governments; massive food riots in Egypt, Jordan, and Tunisia, all of which were followed by consequential policy shifts; and the apparent increase in the political power of social and religious movements. The concern of Arab leaders is not irrational.

Ironically, the importance of Arab public opinion to the foreign policies of Arab states derives from the very absence of electoral legitimacy (which is taken for granted in democratic polities) and the prevalence, instead, of transnational symbols of legitimacy. To be sure, governments in the Middle East, like others around the globe, are driven first and foremost by the interests of their nation-states. But since most political movements within each state profess broader Arab and Islamic objectives, any Arab government must present credentials on those issues: no matter what the governments of Egypt or Syria do in their own interests, these actions must also be in the interests of all Arabs or Muslims.

This common Arab need creates an uncomfortable interdependence, which alters the priorities of Arab governments. What happens in Arab and Islamic political movements outside a given Arab state affects political movements within that state. For this reason, many Arab governments continually engage in a competition for regional political leadership. The closer these states are in their ideology, and thus in their legitimacy, the fiercer the competition for leadership. Two examples tell much about the configuration of Arab alliances in the Gulf War.

One pertains to Syria and Iraq, the only two Baathist states in the world—an ideology centered on a single priority: Arab unity.[2] Yet Syria became the Arab world's only ally of non-Arab Iran during the eight years of the Iraq-Iran War. In the Gulf crisis of 1990–1991, Syria, one of the Arab states most critical of the United States, joined the United States to make sure that Saddam Hussein's influence in the Arab world did not rise at its expense.

The case of Egypt and Iraq in 1961 is even more telling: the regime of Abd al-Karim Qasim of Iraq had come to power in 1958, to the pleasure of Egypt, by overthrowing the pro-British anti-Egyptian monarchy. Qasim was as anti-British as Egypt's Gamel Abdel Nasser, advocating similar Pan-Arab ideals. But he was unwilling to subordinate himself to Nasser and quickly became Egypt's most targeted opponent. Nasser adamantly opposed Qasim's plan to control Kuwait following British withdrawal, a plan consistent with Nasser's Pan-Arab ideals. So sharp was Egypt's opposition to the Iraqi plan that it was willing to reconcile its differences with its ideological opponent, Saudi Arabia, and risk the dissolution of its union with Syria. More embarrassing, Egypt found itself unable to oppose the deployment of British troops in Kuwait to defend against potential Iraqi attacks.[3]

Given the transnational nature of symbols of legitimacy, the Arab publics look for external cues in assessing their own governments. And to the extent that governments can rarely hide their failures from their own people, Arab leaders championing transnational issues are often more popular outside their countries than within. The cases of Egypt's Nasser and Iraq's Saddam Hussein provide two examples. Indeed, in Nasser's case, the external Arab and Islamic legitimacy that he acquired following Suez preceded the increase in his popularity at home. Moreover, it is generally believed that he was less popular in Egypt than elsewhere.

While Arab governments are interdependent in their quest for legitimacy, there are few specific issues on which the competing ideological movements agree. Two issues stand out, both pertaining to the conduct of foreign policy. One is a general anticolonial sentiment and the other is the specific question of Palestine. To be sure, Arab states have abused this question for their own ends, with the Palestinians always paying the price. It is also true that the Palestinian issue is not high on the daily agenda of most Arabs. Still, for historical reasons, the Palestinian issue remains at the core of every major Arab, Islamic, and anti-Western political movement, providing the lens through which Arabs view the world. Its history is closely linked to the inception of Arab nationalism, anti-imperialism, and all those defining moments of Arab relations with the rest of the world. Palestine remains the subconscious cue that the Arab public employs in evaluating the behavior of the outside world toward the Middle East: a friend is he who supports the Palestinians; and an enemy is he who opposes them. Whenever the legitimacy of an Arab government comes into question, it will rush to wrap itself in the Palestinian flag.[4]

Arab governments have always understood that the regional influence that affects their legitimacy depends on the degree to which they offer advantages on the question of Palestine: in the 1950s and 1960s, Egypt's authority in the Arab world was predicated on its military leverage vis-à-vis Israel; when this leverage disappeared following the Camp David accords, Egyptian influence also disappeared. In the late 1980s, in the absence of any Arab military leverage, Egypt used its influence with the United States and Israel to bring about a satisfactory settlement of the Palestinian issue (with a successful dialogue between the PLO and the United States). By the spring of 1990, with the apparent failure of the first Baker-Shamir initiative despite perceived Arab concessions, Egypt's influence declined again in favor of Iraqi influence, as Iraq moved to project military leverage vis-à-vis Israel. It is this latter issue that must be explored in order to address the relationship between Arab public opinion and the recent Gulf War.

Arab Public Opinion
Before Iraq Invaded Kuwait

Whatever the sources of Saddam Hussein's ambitions toward Kuwait, his calculation of risk and his chances for success were linked to the prevailing mood in the region that afflicted the populace and the elites alike—a mood related to the end of the cold war and its perceived implications for the Arab-Israeli conflict. Most Arab leaders and elites did not see at the end of the cold war a victory of democracy over dictatorship, or the victory of consensus politics over power politics. Instead, to Arabs the end of the cold war, which signaled the decline of the Soviet Union as a major superpower, ushered in an era of American hegemony that also entailed Israel's regional hegemony.[5]

A common Arab view was summarized by Saddam Hussein in a speech to the Arab Cooperation Council in February 1990: "Given the relative erosion of the role of the Soviet Union as the key champion of the Arabs in the context of the Arab-Zionist conflict and globally, and given that the influence of the Zionist lobby on U.S. policies is as powerful as ever, the Arabs must take into account that there is a real possibility that Israel might embark on new stupidities within the five-year span I have mentioned. This might take place as a result of direct or tacit U.S. encouragement" (FBIS 1990a). If Saddam Hussein understood anything, it was his Arab colleagues' fear and apprehension about the new global political order.[6] Going beyond the typical interpretation of the end of the cold war as inaugurating an era of U.S. hegemony, and therefore Israeli hegemony, Saddam Hussein offered Arabs an alternative: if Arabs act jointly and consolidate their oil and financial resources, they will have to be taken seriously by the United States.

In pursuing his ambitious designs for Kuwait, Saddam had Arab public opinion behind him by early summer. At the end of the Arab summit conference held in May in Baghdad, anti-Americanism at the popular level was approaching the intensity of anti-British sentiment of the 1950s; Iraq had become the most influential Arab state; and Saddam Hussein's personal popularity had increased dramatically, despite his all too obvious shortcomings.[7] Driving Arab sentiment were the perception that the Arab-Israeli peace process was dead, the tilt to the right in Israeli politics, a U.S. veto of a UN Security Council resolution on protecting Palestinians, a congressional resolution declaring Jerusalem to be the united capital of Israel, and the immigration of Soviet Jews to Israel. The prevailing sentiment was concisely summarized by a former Egyptian ambassador to the United States: "Arabs are sick of their governments pathetically begging the U.S. to plead with Israel to please let them have peace."[8] The official spokesman of the Islamic deputies in the

Jordanian House of Representatives echoed the sentiment: "The U.S. hostility and arrogance must motivate our Arab and Islamic nation to put an end to the course of begging and capitulation that it is immersed in" (FBIS 1990b). By the end of June 1990, following the suspension of the U.S.-PLO dialogue, even Kuwaiti newspapers were calling on the Arabs "to adopt serious and objective stands against the US which persists in a position hostile to the Arab causes" (FBIS 1990f, 22). Egyptian President Husni Mubarak also warned that "the biased U.S. positions will certainly return the region to dependence on the military option" (FBIS 1990e, 10).

By flaunting his military capabilities, targeting Israel, and highlighting the Palestinian question, Saddam Hussein filled the gap of regional despair. The popular success of Iraq's leader in exploiting Arab desperation is best illustrated by the reaction of some Muslim fundamentalists, who earlier had targeted him as an atheist enemy of Islam for his eight years of squandering the resources of two Islamic nations—Iran and Iraq—instead of using them to liberate Jerusalem. By summer, some Muslim leaders had convinced themselves that Saddam now saw the light and that his calls for Islamic Jihad were real.

Indeed, if Saddam made any miscalculation in invading Kuwait, it concerned Arab, not American reactions. He had been saying for months that he expected the United States to have fewer constraints in advancing its interests now that the Soviets were out of the picture. But he believed that the United States could not succeed without Arab cooperation, and given the mood of despair and anti-Americanism in the region, he calculated, not unreasonably, that Arab governments would be reluctant to accept the deployment of American troops to attack an Arab state. Even in Washington, D.C., as the possibility of an Iraqi invasion of Kuwait was considered at the end of July 1990, Arab public opinion was considered the primary obstacle to countering a potential Iraqi invasion militarily.[9] What Saddam seemed to forget, however, is that the very competition that initially concerned Arab governments with the Palestinian question would prevent Syria and Egypt from allowing Saddam Hussein to seize the reins of Arab leadership.

Capitalizing on Arab frustrations, and exploiting the issue of massive Soviet Jewish immigration to Israel as a symbol of the dangers that would follow the end of the cold war, Saddam Hussein hosted a successful Arab summit in Baghdad in May 1990. This summit, which Saddam Hussein chaired and dominated, was telecast live in most Arab states, making Saddam even more popular.[10] Yasser Arafat concluded, "The most important thing to be said is that the latest Arab summit conference under the chairmanship of brother President Saddam Hussein has given a new Pan-Arab resurgence to our Arab nation through Iraqi ability" (FBIS 1990g). Arab speeches at the Baghdad summit and extensive interviews with elites and government officials in several Arab nations indicate relative unanimity on the negative consequences of the end of the cold war and on the extent of frustration with American policy toward the Arab-Israeli conflict. But there were two significant areas of difference.

The first issue on which Arab leaders did not have unanimous agreement concerned what tactics they could use to counter what was perceived to be a difficult global environment. In particular, most believed in 1990 that the world was entering an era of U.S. dominance that would last several years. They also believed that American policy in the Middle East was primarily determined by "the Zionist lobby in Washington" and that American preeminence thus entailed Israel's regional dominance. How the Arabs could overcome these strategic drawbacks was a disputed issue. The Egyptians and the Syrians, even without mutual cooperation, believed that these disadvantages could not be reversed and that the Arabs should try to make the best of a bad situation. In essence, the argument centered on the assumption that this was no time to get on the wrong side of the United States. While the Arabs could not reverse American policy in the Middle East, they could cooperate with the United States to prevent possible disaster and to buy time until a new global political order emerged.[11]

In contrast to Egypt and Syria, the Iraqis argued that the Arabs possessed sufficient economic and military resources to enable them, if they acted collectively, to either compel American cooperation or to help in the formation of a counterweight to the United States.

The third view, held by the Jordanians and the Palestinians, was one of impending disaster that could not be prevented. To begin with, the Palestinians and Jordanians perceived the United States to be in "collusion with Israel." Yasser Arafat believed that the political initiatives of the Bush administration were motivated by a desire to get more and more from the Palestinians, to buy time, and to kill the Intifada, without any serious intent to work toward Israeli compromise.[12] The Jordanians shared this assessment. In addition, both Palestinians and Jordanians believed that Israel was about to embark on a war to implement the Sharon plan to turn Jordan into Palestine. Arafat was anticipating that unless Arabs took serious countermeasures, Israel would launch an attack against Jordan within months, leading to the expulsion of Palestinians from the occupied territories. He was unconvinced by the argument that the Israeli public would not support such an incursion, especially given the lessons that Israelis had learned from their adventure in Lebanon. To his Arab colleagues, Arafat chanted: "Brother Arabs: The Israelis are beating the drum of war. They are beating the drum of war" (FBIS 1990c). In short, for Arafat, disaster was imminent.

A similar sentiment was expressed by Jordanian elites and leaders about the imminent danger to the Arab nation.[13] So desperate was King Hussein at the Baghdad summit, so tragic was the manner of his televised speech, that some of his most loyal citizens felt humiliated by the king's tone. The king, a man with legendary talent for the game of survival, ended his speech with the following warning to Arab leaders: "I have talked about my country with such candor and bitterness in the hope that the day will never come in which I and my people in Jordan—men, women, children, and young men—have nothing to repeat on every lip but that painful cry by the Arab poet: 'They have lost me, and what a brave man they have lost, for he would have defended their frontiers on the evil day.' Peace be upon you" (FBIS 1990d).

The unusually harmonious views of Arafat and Hussein further consolidated a relationship already strengthened by the Jordanian riots of April 1989 protesting against tough economic measures. Jordanian analysts argue that, besides the economic factor, Jordanians were inspired by the Palestinian uprising and the perceived heroics of the people in south Lebanon.[14] The demonstrations were especially threatening to the king since they took place almost exclusively in Jordanian, not Palestinian, communities. There was a sense that, had the PLO not advised its supporters in Jordan against joining the demonstrations, King Hussein would have been in serious trouble.[15] Expecting more difficult economic times ahead, complicated by fears caused by Soviet Jewish immigration to Israel, the king sought to defuse the situation and spread the blame by holding elections. The PLO, on the other hand, had every incentive to help the Jordanian monarch survive, lest instability in Jordan give Israel an opportunity to implement the option of turning Jordan into a Palestinian state. While these evaluations of Arab positions were made before Iraq invaded Kuwait, it is striking that the eventual lineup of alliances over the Kuwait-Iraq conflict matched these earlier groupings.

The second important issue on which Arab rivalry showed itself even before Iraq invaded Kuwait was the question of leadership. On this question, both Syria and Egypt were uneasy about Iraq's new preeminence in Arab politics. Syria, Iraq's primary rival, was the only Arab state absent from the Baghdad summit, even though the Syrians, like the Jordanians and Palestinians, were calling on the Arabs to prepare themselves to face a war that Israel intended to launch (Al Ba'th 1990). During the Baghdad summit, Syrian officials privately expressed fear of "excessive" Iraqi influence in Arab affairs.[16] Similarly, Egyptian officials were concerned with the new Iraqi role. Egyptian presidential advisor Usama Al-Baz expressed concern, symbolically, that Yasser Arafat was spending too much of his time in Baghdad (thus acquiescing in the notion that Saddam Hussein was the new Pan-Arab champ). Al-Baz argued that Arafat should be persuaded to spend more time in Cairo, instead.[17]

In contrast to Egypt and Syria, the Jordanians, the Palestinians, the Yemenis, and some North Africans appeared enthusiastic about Iraq's new role. The wealthy Gulf Arabs seemed uncertain. These divisions among Arabs on the question of Iraqi leadership were eventually reflected in the various Arab coalitions that emerged following Iraq's invasion of Kuwait.

Arab Public Opinion After
the Iraqi Invasion of Kuwait

While scholars continue to disagree about the relevance of public opinion to public behavior and state policy, several studies indicate that the causal links are affected by one important criterion: how the public ranks a given issue among its priorities. In the United States, for example, it has been shown that how an issue is ranked among public priorities affects how people contribute to campaign funds and how they vote. Those who rank an issue highest in their priorities (what Converse 1964 calls the "issue public") are more likely to act on the basis of that sentiment and are more likely to affect policy on that issue (Krosnick and Telhami 1990). Issue importance can explain some of the discrepancy between opinion and behavior. While most Middle East experts were correct in their estimations of the public sentiments in the Middle East during the Gulf crisis, many were wrong about public behavior. Assessing issue importance for each Arab country can be a helpful measure.

While voting behavior is hardly a useful indicator in Middle East politics, there are ways of measuring the impact of opinion on public behavior. For example, in the case of the Gulf War, one can look at public demonstrations as one indicator of the extent to which the public cared about the issue. While demonstrations in many Arab states are illegal and therefore risky, the pattern of demonstrations can be telling.

It is important to keep in mind that Iraq's invasion of Kuwait brought out several issues of contention for Arab public opinion. The first issue was the promise of deliverance from an unacceptable status quo, which was blamed on corrupt governments and foreign imperialism. The second question pertained to the principle of state sovereignty, clearly violated by Iraq. A third issue was the promise of economic redistribution in the Arab world. Fourth was the idea of a powerful Arab

state finally able to stand up to Israel and Western powers and to liberate Palestine. The fifth issue pertained to foreign intervention on Arab
soil. While all these issues were present in the calculations of most
Arabs, the relative weight of each issue varied across the Arab world.

To assess Arab popular behavior and the impact of that behavior on
the policies of Arab states, it is especially helpful to rank these issues in
light of the priorities of each Arab community. The fact that Arabs disagreed on the ranking of these issues—or disagreed on one issue, such
as the danger inherent in one Arab state invading another—did not indicate fundamental disagreement on others. For example, most Arabs
(with the possible exception of the Kuwaitis) were uneasy about the
presence of foreign troops on Arab soil, and most hoped that the crisis
could be exploited to resolve the Arab-Israeli conflict.

Clearly, the Jordanians and Palestinians, the two parties most vulnerable to possible Israeli threats, cared most about Iraq's potential in
standing up to Israel and the United States, especially given their expectations of impending disaster prior to Iraq's invasion of Kuwait. The
North Africans, the Yemenis, and the Sudanese—poor nations who en-
vied the Gulf Arabs and were frustrated by what appeared to be imperial designs for Palestine—were lured by the possibility of economic
redistribution and the resurgence of Arab pride. For wealthy Gulf
Arabs, immediately threatened by Iraqi aggression, confronting Iraq
was their primary objective.

As for the Syrians and Egyptians, the popular soul was more divided, although opinion tipped toward confronting Iraq only by strong
government decisions. First, both Syria and Egypt feared Iraq's regional
dominance; second, neither thought Iraq could stand up to the United
States, and both thought they would be on the losing side if they did not
confront Iraq. Third, extensive U.S. lobbying played an important role
in shaping opinion.

Public Demonstrations in the Arab World

The patterns of reported demonstrations in the Arab world support
the view that public behavior reflected the public ranking of issues.[18] In
the months preceding Iraq's invasion of Kuwait, most reported protests
took place in Jordan and Algeria: nine were reported in Jordan in April
and May, and seven demonstrations were reported in Algeria during
the same period.

The demonstrations held in Jordan were primarily related to the
Arab-Israeli conflict. The protests were over Soviet Jewish immigration,
the killing of several Palestinians by a lone Israeli in Reshon Lizion, and
American policy toward the Arab-Israeli conflict. It is not surprising,
therefore, that in the two months following the Iraqi invasion of Kuwait

more demonstrations were reported in Jordan than anywhere else in the Arab world, with the linkage between the Arab-Israeli conflict and the Gulf crisis emphasized.

In Algeria, demonstrations prior to the Gulf War focused primarily on domestic political and economic problems, with some favoring political reform, others protesting price rises. The Gulf crisis gave opposition groups in Algeria additional tools for mobilizing the masses and challenging the status quo.

No demonstrations were reported in the Gulf states, and only one was reported in Egypt during the crisis. In Sudan and Yemen, where only one demonstration was reported in the four months before the crisis, fourteen protests were reported in August, with the primary issue apparently being opposition to foreign intervention.

Still, despite differences in priorities, most Arabs, including Egyptians and Syrians (but probably not including the Arabs of the Gulf) felt that the defeat of Iraq would not be good for the Arabs, believed that the alliance against Iraq was an American hegemonic design, and once Iraqi forces came under attack, hoped for an Iraqi victory. Yet, beyond the few popular demonstrations in several Arab states, there seemed little threat to Arab governments that joined the U.S.-led alliance against Iraq. Even more puzzling is the relatively muted popular reaction following the apparent destruction of Iraq's military force and much of its industrial base, not to mention tens of thousands of Iraqi citizens. How is this possible, if Arab public opinion fits the picture described earlier?

Between Public Opinion,
Public Behavior, and State Policy

There are three primary variables linking events, opinions about them, and consequent policy. The first is the sources of public information about a given issue; second is the ranking of that issue in public priorities; and third is the assessment of the future outcome.

As for the first issue, Saddam Hussein must have made an erroneous connection between his reading of public sentiment on the Arab-Israeli conflict and the U.S. role in it, on the one hand, and his ability to feed that public his own version of events, on the other. Members of the alliance against Iraq understood from the beginning that Saddam's biggest leverage in the crisis rested on his ability to mobilize public opinion. His opponents among Arab governments were not about to make it easy for him.

Once Egypt, Syria, and Saudi Arabia decided to join a U.S.-led alliance against Iraq, they could no longer pretend they had misgivings about the United States' efforts, and they had every incentive to make a public case against the Iraqi invasion. Divided soul or not, they had to act as though the choice was utterly clear. A coordinated information campaign portrayed a uniform picture of events. In contrast to the 1950s, the substantially enhanced capacities of these states made the task easier. More important, the appearance of a collective position among the three primary Arab actors presented an important cue for Arabs looking for external signals by which to evaluate Arab and Islamic interests. It is not surprising that Syria and Egypt, like Iraq, explained their policies in terms of Arab and Islamic interests and the cause of the Palestinians.

The information campaign deprived Saddam Hussein of extensive access to the masses he sought to mobilize. One glaring exception was the case of Jordan: Jordanian television and radio, which are monitored in the West Bank and Syria, gave people access to Iraqi views. The impact of Jordanian television on Syrian public opinion may have been critical to the formation of what many scholars and journalists believed to be a pro-Syrian sentiment. It was probably this issue more than any other that brought Jordan under extensive criticism from the United States and its Arab allies.

Still, public opinion does not automatically affect either public behavior or state policy—issue importance is a key indicator. The patterns of public and state behavior in the Arab world indicate that two measures are useful in this regard. The first is the priority rankings of the issues among the Arab governments, informed by strategic calculations; the second is the priority rankings of the issues among the Arab publics informed by the proximity of a given Arab polity to one of two conflicts—the Arab-Israeli conflict and the Persian Gulf conflict. The further removed from the Gulf an Arab polity was, the less bothered it was by the violation of Kuwaiti sovereignty; the closer it was to the Arab-Israeli conflict, the more supportive it was of Iraq, in the hope of linkage.

Indeed, one interesting feature in the evolution of Arab public opinion is that, once the war was over and international intrusions into Iraq increased, Arab public opinion in states like Egypt, where pro-Iraqi sentiment was muted before the war, became more sympathetic to Iraq. The liberation of Kuwait removed the primary justification for opposing Iraq but left all the elements that had brought Iraq sympathy even among its opponents.

The opposite is true among those who were the strongest supporters of Iraq (Palestinians, Jordanians, North Africans): the devastating defeat of Iraq, while it remains a serious source of resentment, stifled public opposition. Two factors account for this: the new image of Saddam Hussein as a leader who let them down and the movement toward an Arab-Israeli peace.

American and Arab policy makers understood that part of Saddam's popularity in the Arab world stemmed from his promise to deliver militarily what his colleagues could not do through diplomacy: justice for Palestinians and Arab independence from foreign influence. But they believed that support based on such a promise would dissipate when it appeared to have been a hoax; people generally don't support losers. Saddam's failure, despite what now appears to have been real military potential, led many to blame him for the failure.

The United States' active role since the war in seeking a settlement to the Arab-Israeli conflict has raised hopes for a peaceful settlement of the very conflict that Saddam used to rally support. Adding to the relative quiet of the Arab public is the fact that key Arab states appear to be coordinating their policy and going along with this process; the external cue for most Arabs is the collective Arab position—an element that also contributed to the relative public quiet during the war (since Syria, Egypt, and Saudi Arabia were all on the same side).

If the Arab coalition falls apart and the Arab-Israeli peace process fails, the Arab public is likely to be roused again. And disagreements over the Gulf War (hidden feelings of guilt and resentment) are likely to surface. It is a mistake to conclude that the worst repercussions of the Gulf War have already come to pass—the most serious public consequences of the Suez crisis in the 1950s took several years to be revealed.

NOTES

1. For a summary of the literature on the links between public opinion and foreign policy, see Russett and Graham 1989.

2. Baathists also advocate freedom and socialism, which, together with unity, complete the Baathist trilogy.

3. For an interesting discussion of the Iraqi-Egyptian competition, see Kerr 1971.

4. It is not surprising that Arab governments that opposed Iraq in the Gulf crisis, and were frustrated by the PLO positions, argued that their strategy was the better one for serving Palestinian interests. For example, on November 1, 1990, a Syrian editorial argued that Israel is synonymous with U.S. interests in the Middle East and, given absolute U.S. support for Israel, the Arabs would do well not to take the risks inherent in backing Iraq (FBIS 1990h).

5. The speeches by Arab leaders meeting at the Baghdad summit at the end of May 1990 is a good indicator of official views on this question. These views were also consistent among Arab elites and leaders in Egypt, Syria, Iraq, Jordan, and the West Bank in May–June 1990. This assessment is based on dozens of interviews I conducted in the region during that period in preparing a report for Rep. Lee H. Hamilton, chairman of the House Subcommittee on Europe and the Middle East.

6. For an assessment of the Arab interpretation of the end of the cold war, see Telhami 1991.

7. The *Economist* quoted an Iraqi passer-by: "Nasser made promises, but could not deliver. But when Saddam speaks, he acts." A lot of Arabs, including millions beyond Iraq, seem inclined to agree." The article concluded that "by meeting in Baghdad, Iraq's capital, the Arabs hope to show the world that they stand fully behind their newest hero, with his mysterious new monster gun and his promise to destroy "half of Israel" if Israel dares to attack him" (Economist 1990). This picture corresponded well to my own conclusions during my visit to the region in May–June 1990.

8. Author's interview, Cairo, June 1990.

9. This was the assessment of several congressional aides and Middle East experts meeting in Washington, D.C., a few days before the Iraqi invasion of Kuwait.

10. In my report to the chairman of the House Subcommittee on Europe and the Middle East, I concluded that Saddam Hussein had emerged as the most popular Arab leader.

11. Author's interviews with Syrian and Egyptian officials, June 1990.

12. Author's interview with Yasser Arafat, Baghdad, June 1990.

13. Author's interviews, Amman, June 1990.

14. Author's interview with Jordanian political scientist (current foreign minister) Kamal Abu Jaber, Amman, June 1990.

15. This view was expressed by Yasser Arafat during our interview on June 5, 1990, as well as by several Jordanian analysts.

16. Author's interview, Damascus, May 30, 1990.

17. Author's interview, Cairo, 1990.

18. This account is based on a survey of the daily reports from the Arab world as published by the Foreign Broadcast Information Service. It should be noted that these reports are by no means comprehensive, because they reflect mostly official and local press accounts, which could not be entirely reliable given the strict information control campaigns during the Gulf crisis. Nonetheless, this survey is useful as a limited indicator in conjunction with the analytical and first-hand accounts.

REFERENCES

Al-Ba'th (Syria). 1990.

Brody, R. A., and C. R. Shapiro. 1987. "Policy Failure and Public Support: Reykjavik, Iran, and Public Assessments of President Reagan." Presented at the annual meeting of the American Political Science Association, Chicago.

Carter, Jimmy. 1982. *Keeping Faith: Memoirs of a President*. New York: Bantam, 1982.

Caspary, W. 1970. "The 'Mood Theory': A Study of Public Opinion and Foreign Policy." *American Political Science Review* 64: 536–47.

Converse, Philip E. 1964. "The Nature of Belief Systems in Mass Publics." In *Ideology and Discontent*, ed. David E. Apter. New York: Free Press.

Economist. 1990. "An anti-Zionist ink-blot," June 2, 44.

FBIS (Foreign Broadcast Information Service). 1990a. Saddam Hussein's speech to the Arab Cooperation Council. *FBIS Daily Report.* FBIS-NES-90. February 27.

——— . 1990b. Statement by official spokesman of the Islamic deputies in the Jordanian House of Representatives, *FBIS Daily Report.* FBIS-NES-90, May 10.

——— . 1990c. Statement by Yasser Arafat. *FBIS Daily Report.* FBIS-NES-90, May 29.

——— . 1990d. Statement by King Hussein. *FBIS Daily Report.* FBIS-NES-90, May 30.

——— . 1990e. Statement by Husni Mubarak. *FBIS Daily Report.* FBIS-NES-90-108, June 5.

——— . 1990f. Reports in Kuwaiti newspapers. *FBIS Daily Report.* FBIS-NES-90-122, June 25.

——— . 1990g. OLD1990e. Statement by Yasser Arafat at May 1990 Arab summit. *FBIS Daily Report.* FBIS-NES-90, July 11.

——— . 1990h. OLDH1990f. *FBIS Daily Report.* FBIS-NES-90, November 1.

Kerr, Malcolm. 1971. *The Arab Cold War: Gamal Abl-Nasir and His Rivals, 1958–1970.* London: Oxford University Press.

Kohut, A. 1988. "What Americans Want." *American Foreign Policy* 70: 150–65.

Krosnick, Jon, and Shibley Telhami. 1990. "Public Attitudes and American Policy Toward Israel." Unpublished.

Leigh, M. 1976. *Mobilizing Consent: Public Opinion and American Foreign Policy, 1937–1947.* Westport: Greenwood.

Mueller, J. E. 1973. *War, Presidents, and Public Opinions.* New York: Wiley.

Ostrom, C. W., and D. Simon. 1985. "Promise and Performance: A Dynamic Model of Presidential Popularity." *American Political Science Review* 79: 175–90.

Russet, B., and J. W. Graham. 1989. "Public Opinion and Natural Security Policy: Relationships and Impacts." In *Handbook of War Studies,* ed. M. Midlarsky. London: Allen and Unwin.

Sharaa, Farouq. 1991. *New York Times,* November 4, 1991.

Telhami, Shibley. 1991. "Middle East Politics in the Post Cold War Era." In *Beyond the Cold War,* ed. George W. Breslauer, Harry Kreisler, and Benjamin Ward. Berkeley: Institute for International Studies, University of California, Berkeley.

8

American Public Opinion
and the Gulf War

■

John Mueller

■ WHEN THE CRISIS in the Persian Gulf erupted with Iraq's invasion of Kuwait on August 2, 1990, American public opinion became a major consideration. President George Bush needed public backing as he attempted to deal with the crisis and as he led his country into war against what many feared might prove to be a formidable enemy. Those who opposed his war policies also appealed to public opinion, and like Bush, they sought to manipulate it in their favor. On the other side of the world, Iraq's president, Saddam Hussein, tried several times to influence the American public (with singularly counterproductive results), and he seems to have hoped that if war were to break out, popular support in the United States would quickly fade as his forces inflicted substantial causalities on American forces, leading to effective demands to end the conflict on terms congenial to Iraq. As he put it to U.S. Ambassador April Glaspie before the war: "Yours is a society that cannot accept 10,000 dead in one battle" (Friedrich 1991, 20).

The importance of public opinion in the crisis was fully apparent, of course, to the polling agencies and to the newspapers and television networks that sponsor them. Accordingly, during the crisis the agencies blew their budgets on telephone surveys asking hundreds of questions seeking to assess the reaction of the American public to events relating to the Persian Gulf.

This chapter is a preliminary report on what this mass of public opinion data seems to suggest. It begins with a prologue arguing that public opinion data are incapable of telling us with any precision how many people feel one way or the other about anything and are most likely to be revealing only if they are used comparatively.

The rest is archaeology—an effort to sort through and discern patterns in the shards and artifacts left behind by the polling agencies. I assess opinion on the Gulf crisis in three chronological chunks: the first deals with public opinion in the period up to the beginning of the war on January 16, 1991, the second evaluates public opinion during the war itself, and the third considers public opinion in the aftermath of the war. In all cases, an effort is made to put the data in broader political and military context and, where appropriate, to compare the Gulf episode to such earlier war experiences as Panama, Vietnam, and Korea.

Prologue: What Public
Opinion Polls Measure

In the opinion polling process, respondents, more or less randomly selected, are asked a series of questions that usually ranges over a variety of issues. Some people refuse to respond, but most oblige, and many find it a pleasant, even flattering, experience, as their every utterance is faithfully recorded.

Many people do not want to seem unprepared at this important moment, and they may find themselves pontificating in an authoritative manner on issues to which they have never given much thought. Polling agencies usually encourage this; they do not particularly like to have high "no opinion" or "don't know" percentages. They also try to make the opinion-uttering process easy by formulating uncluttered and direct questions. In the process, however, the issue at hand often gets severely simplified, and to facilitate analysis, the responses are usually forced into a few very rigid categories.

The interview situation, then, is best seen as primitive stimulus-response situation in which quick and often ill-considered answers are casually fitted to a set of simplistic questions. The data so gathered can be valuable in understanding popular attitudes, but they must be handled with care.

In particular, it is essential to pay close attention to the precise nature of the question-stimulus because on many issues seemingly minor changes in the wording of the question can notably alter the response. Respondents often seem to react as much to the tone or context of the question, or to key words in it, as they do to its objective content. For example, a set of questions asked in mid-November 1990 roughly suggests that 28 percent of the population was willing to initiate war in the Gulf, 38 percent was willing to go to war, 46 percent was willing to engage in combat, and 65 percent was willing to use military force.

Such results also suggest that it is impossible to say reliably what the public's opinion about anything actually *is*—although that is what the polling agencies are usually expected to do. During the Gulf crisis the polls were often asked to determine what percentage of the population favored war or sanctions or compromise or approved this or that decision or personality. Although they can sometimes give a rough feel for where the public stood on such issues (and they will occasionally be used in this way in the analysis that follows), polls are simply incapable of doing so with anything resembling precision.[1]

Poll data are more useful, however, if they are used in a comparative manner. The form of comparison principally applied in this chapter is trend analysis: comparing responses to the same question asked at various times over the course of the Gulf crisis. This can work because, whatever problems there may be in the way a question is worded, these remain constant, and, usually, one can reasonably discuss any changes over time in the response percentages. The main problem with trend analysis is that the polling agencies frequently "improve" questions, thus rendering trend comparison dubious or impossible, or else they drop key questions entirely as their interests turn to other issues or to new aspects of the old one.

One can also validly compare how different subgroups of the population respond to the same question: men versus women, for example, or blacks versus whites, or old versus young. A limited discussion of this sort will be found in this chapter.

Finally, one can compare differently worded questions that happen to have been asked at the same time to see what words, cues, and images affected the response. There is a lot of opportunity for this kind of analysis in the poll data from the Gulf crisis, because different polling agencies frequently asked questions about the same issues, thus creating a set of experiments that can be analyzed.[2]

The Runup to War:
August 2, 1990, to January 16, 1991

After its invasion of Kuwait on August 2, 1990, almost all countries of the world joined a severe economic blockade of Iraq, and several nations, especially the United States, moved protecting troops to Saudi Arabia. In response, Iraq detained westerners in Iraq and Kuwait as hostages to an attack. In October, the public's attention was shifted somewhat to disapproving resentment as Congress and the president engaged in a noisy battle over the budget, which was eventually resolved in a compromise.

Shortly after the November congressional elections (in which virtually all incumbents were returned), President George Bush announced a change of policy: troop levels in the Middle East would be substantially increased in order to attain an "offensive military option." Bush's policies in the Gulf had received wide bipartisan support, but this policy change was strongly questioned by many Democrats. At the end of the month, Bush was able to get the United Nations to authorize the use of force unless Iraq left Kuwait by January 15, 1991. This threat, it was hoped, would encourage Iraq to withdraw. Meanwhile, the American economy was entering a recession, and consumer confidence was dropping.

In December, Hussein released all the hostages, but apparently because neither side was sufficiently interested in compromising, various efforts at talks failed. A debate was held in Congress over whether force should be used after January 15 or whether sanctions would continue to be relied upon. On January 12, in a vote that substantially followed party lines and that was rather close in the Senate, Congress authorized the president to use force. (Although the Constitution requires that an ordinary treaty must be ratified by a two-thirds majority, a declaration of war—or in this case a functional equivalent thereof—apparently requires only a simple majority.) Unleashed, George Bush began the war on the moonless night of January 16, a few days before huge antiwar demonstrations were scheduled to take place in Washington, D.C.

Public Opinion Trends

Politically, the runup to the Gulf War became particularly contentious, characterized by an extensive public debate, which began in November and became notably partisan. The most remarkable aspect of public opinion during this period is that, despite (or perhaps because of) the pointed, dramatic, and noisy debate, most public attitudes on the issue changed little.

Early on, between August and October, there was one notable change: a substantial increase in the number of people who thought involvement in the Gulf was a mistake and a similar decline in the number who supported Bush's policy there. However, after that, as the debate over policy escalated, there was little further change in these measures. Apparently, as the initial heady urgency of the issue faded, fair weather supporters dropped out and support was maintained by a harder core.

Meanwhile, questions dealing more specifically with policy options—support or opposition for war or for continued reliance on sanctions—generally changed very little from the onset of the crisis in August to the initiation of war in January. It is possible to argue from some data that there was movement toward greater hawkishness, but other data indicate something of a movement toward dovishness, and considerable data suggest that there was no change at all. It is possible, of course, that quite a few people were changing their minds, but if so, movement from one side to the other was canceled out by people moving in the opposite direction. Thus, altogether the president was leading the country into war, he was not notably successful at generating increased support for war, nor were his opponents able to sway public opinion to their side.[3]

During this period there were very few official voices calling for compromise. Bush adamantly and repeatedly rejected any deals or negotiations that might seem to reward Iraq for its aggression. He was unwilling even to agree to something as mild as a postwithdrawal Mideast conference—which would be unlikely to result in anything other than empty atmospherics. His political opponents mainly favored continued reliance on sanctions as a functional equivalent of war, and they were not much more open than Bush to cutting deals with Hussein. Although no political leader made much of a play for compromise, there was considerable potential for leadership on this issue. Even on the eve of armed conflict, in January—as Congress was voting for war—most people said they were willing to give Iraq a piece of Kuwait to end the crisis if the Kuwaitis agreed, which presumably is the only way it could have happened. Thus it seems that the public would have bought a reasonable, properly packaged compromise as an alternative to war.

The public clearly responded differently to different arguments. The public, like the president, was greatly concerned about Iraq's chemical and nuclear capacity and about Iraqi atrocities in Kuwait; the notion of turning back aggression also enjoyed substantial support. On the other hand, the public was notably less moved by the notion that it was important to fight for Middle East oil (though it saw that as a major reason the United States had become involved in the crisis) and by sympathy for the Kuwaiti government. Those who opposed war used the slogan No Blood for Oil and heaped contempt upon the Kuwaiti government. However, it was possible for people to agree about oil and about the Kuwaiti government and still support war for other reasons. War advocates soon found that out.

In the course of the debate over the war, Bush repeatedly characterized Saddam Hussein as Satan: he was worse than Hitler, Bush suggested. Within the United States, Bush was preaching to the choir: from the start of the crisis, Hussein's mean rating on a scale from 0 to 100 was less than 10, and it held at that abysmal level for the rest of the year (in most polls, his median rating was 0) with a very slight (and very temporary) improvement after he released the hostages in December (Wilcox, Ferrarra, and Allsop 1991). Hussein was surely George Bush's secret weapon in bringing about the war. Indeed, as far as American public opinion was concerned Hussein's only accomplishment during the whole crisis period was his consummate portrayal of a demon. One of his early efforts to gain favor with the Western public was to appear on television with a group of extremely uncomfortable hostages. The event was singularly counterproductive.

Overwhelmingly, the American public (presumably including most of those who opposed war) expected the United States to emerge victorious from a war. Responses to questions about how long the war might last and about how many casualties Americans were likely to suffer suggest that few people had in mind the Vietnam War—which lasted several years and resulted in hundreds of thousands of U.S. casualties. Apparently, the realities of the situation, combined with Bush's repeated insistence that a war in the Gulf would not be a long, drawn-out conflict like Vietnam, got through. Nonetheless, there seems to have been considerable concern that the war could last months and cost thousands of casualties. There are causal problems in assessing the meaning of these data, however. Many people may have opposed war because it might be long and costly, but those who opposed war on principle were probably sympathetic to the supportive notion that the war would be long and costly.[4] And many who favored war may have been inclined to dismiss its costs.

There was notable change of opinion in two areas during the crisis period. Because of uncertainty and fear of war, consumer and business confidence dropped considerably. In addition, as the debate wore on and as the United States and Iraq battered each other with invective and jockeyed for position, the public came to view war as likely, even inevitable.

Sources for Support and Opposition to War

Various groups related differently to the Gulf issue. Women supported war notably less than men. This is not new: women were also less supportive of the Vietnam and Korean wars—and for that matter, of World War II (see Mueller 1973, 146–47). In some respects the persistence of this gender gap is surprising. After Vietnam, women entered the male work world in great numbers, and they have become more like men in the degree to which they smoke, commit crime, use foul language, and suffer from heart disease. But, interestingly, their attitudes toward war do not seem to have become more like those of men: women seem to have become liberated without losing their femininity in this respect.

Polls also show blacks to be more dovish than whites. This difference was also found during the Vietnam War. Some conclude that this attitude was inspired by the antiwar stance of Martin Luther King, Jr., and the civil rights movement of the 1960s, but the data strongly suggest that their attitude goes much deeper into the black experience; it is found in polls during both the Korean War and World War II (ibid., 147–48).

One particularly important group difference has to do with party. Because the wars in Korean and Vietnam were begun under Democratic administrations, Democrats tended to support them more than Republicans did. The Gulf situation was begun and engineered by a Republican president, and Republicans are thus much more supportive of his war-anticipating policies than are Democrats. The party difference is far wider than the difference between self-identified liberals and conservatives, and it increased after Bush's controversial escalation announcement in November.

Comparisons with Vietnam

The 1990–1991 debate over war in the Gulf has some similarities with the debate that preceded the escalation of war in Vietnam in 1965. The differences, however, seem far greater. For one thing, the enemy in the Gulf War was less significant. In Vietnam the enemy was seen by the administration, Congress, and the public to be part of a massive international communist threat that had as its ultimate goal the destruction of the United States. Saddam Hussein may have threatened American Middle East interests, and the man himself was eminently demonizable, but it was difficult to see him as that sort of menace.

More important, when American troops were sent to Vietnam there seemed to be only two alternatives: either the troops went in or the enemy would win. In the Gulf, by contrast, there was another potentially viable option for dealing with the enemy: economic sanctions.

Finally, there was an important difference in partisan support. Although Democratic leaders represent the party of such war presidents as Wilson, Roosevelt, Truman, and Johnson, still they are probably ideologically more reluctant to use international force than are Republican leaders. After all, it was from within the Democratic party, not from the opposition Republican party, that opposition to the Vietnam policy grew; and when a Republican, Richard Nixon, took over the presidency and the war in 1969, the Democrats swung substantially to an antiwar position (see ibid., 116–21).

Thus in the Gulf case, unlike Vietnam, there was a substantial debate over what Democrats saw as the rush to war, and the war vote was deeply split along party lines, with the Democrats supporting the middle-course sanctions policy. When a vote was taken in 1964 to authorize the president to take "all necessary steps including the use of armed force" in Vietnam, there were only two dissenting votes in the Senate and none in the House. Curiously, the military often claims that a central lesson from the Vietnam experience is that forces should not be committed to war unless they go in with solid public backing in advance. The troops had that backing in Vietnam, but not in the Gulf War.

Fatalism, Casualties, and the
Timing of the Gulf War

Public opinion about starting a war against Iraq changed little during the debate over Gulf policy. Bush was able to pull off his war, it seems not because he convinced a growing number of Americans of the wisdom of war, but because of his position as foreign policy leader, because he enjoyed, it seems, a fair amount of trust at the time with respect to this matter, and because of the anticipation that the war would resolve a pressing and important issue and would be comparatively quick and low in casualties. The opinion dynamic that probably helped him most, however, was a growing fatalism about war—as time went by, the public became increasingly convinced that war was inevitable. In that sense, the public was willing to be led to war: for many the attitude was, "Let's get it over with."

The anticipation of a low-cost war was reflected in official thinking as well. Military planners concluded that a war against Hussein's forces could easily be won, or as Bush put it, "we're going to kick his ass out" (Barnes 1991, 9; Drew 1991, 83).[5] Worst-case projections were for 20,000 American casualties, including 7,000 dead, but some senior officers were confident that no more than 1,000 Americans would die (Woodward 1991, 349, 376). An influential supporter of war, House Armed Services Committee Chairman Les Aspin, a Democrat, publicly concluded that "prospects are high for a rapid victory" and suggested that American casualty rates would be between 3,000 and 5,000, with 500 to 1,000 dead (Moore 1991).[6] Although Bush did not get into the numbers game, he continually insisted that a war with Iraq would not be long and drawn out like Vietnam—that it would, consequently, be short and decisive. And in a television interview a few weeks before the war, he expresses the hope that the war "would be over in a matter of days" (PBS 1991a).

Also reflected at the top was the public's growing sense of fatalism— a feeling that the United States simply couldn't back down from the expensive and heightened troop commitment that had been unilaterally instituted by the president two months earlier. On a television news show a day after the congressional vote, conservative commentator George Will, after noting "how wrong it was for the president to misdefine this interest as vital, to run up the deployment after November 8 to the point where the deployment itself became the policy," said he supported the resolution even though he thought a war would be "disastrous." Then newsman Sam Donaldson said he would have voted the same way even though he did not believe "we ought to have a war for this purpose," and moderator David Brinkley, who felt "this is not a war we should be in," said he supported the resolution because "we have been on the scene and we can't vote to undercut them" (ABC News 1991).

Asked in December about Hussein's next move, Bush told some reporters, "My gut says he will get out of there" (Woodward 1991, 351). But Bush, who became obsessed by the crisis and increasingly emotional over it (see Drew 1991; Woodward 1991; PBS 1991a), insisted that there could be no deals. In his view, Hussein must withdraw unconditionally and ignominiously, suffering maximum humiliation for his aggression: "There can be no face-saving" (Smith 1992, 222). Hussein, Bush's chief ally in bringing about the war, was unwilling to undergo that humiliation, and he apparently also became increasingly convinced that war was inevitable.[7] He called Bush's bluff and did not move his occupying troops. It was war by mutual self-entrapment.

However, despite such curious fatalism in the United States, there were strong forces in opposition, and war was not inevitable. The public was by no means averse to war-avoiding deals, and it could have as readily been led away from war as into it. In the past, it had often followed presidents who had decided to back down from overextended positions: when Ronald Reagan withdrew policing U.S. troops from Lebanon in 1983 after hundreds of them had been killed by a terrorist, few objected; and the public greeted the collapse of American policy in Vietnam in 1975 with remarkable equanimity (see Mueller 1984).

Moreover, unlike the situation in 1964–1965 in Vietnam, a substantial public antiwar movement had been launched in the fall of 1990. Encouraged by antiwar Democrats, it put together protest demonstrations, culminating in marches in Washington in January that were larger than most marches of the Vietnam era. The problem here was mostly one of timing—which in politics, as in comedy, can be everything. Essentially, Bush was able to pull off his war before the protesters could really get organized.

In debating the vote for war in the United Nations, the Bush administration sought to impose a deadline of January 1 for Iraqi withdrawal from Kuwait. The less impatient Soviets, however, suggested January 31, and a compromise of January 15 eventually was reached. Coming in the midst of a vacation period for colleges (which is where most protesters come from), a January 1 deadline would have been hopeless for the protest movement. January 15 was only slightly better—and when the big protests, planned weeks earlier, took place in Washington on January 19 and 26, the war was already on.[8] If the Soviet date had been accepted, the congressional debate might have been later, and the protests would have been more organized and effective.

It seems to me that much of the antiwar protest over Vietnam, particularly in the first three years of the war, was ineffective, even counterproductive (see Mueller 1973, 164–65; Mueller 1984; 1991b). A January 1991 protest on the Gulf, however, would have been more like the Vietnam protest after 1968 when the antiwar movement achieved enhanced impact and respectability because it was now championed by a major party. Furthermore, any protest before the war began could not as readily (and as effectively) be charged with undercutting the troops. It seems quite possible that this combination of factors could have turned enough votes—mainly Democratic ones—in Congress to tip the vote against war. Thus, the UN debate about the deadline was perhaps doubly significant.

Bush might have gone to war even without a favorable vote in Congress. However, it was the view before the war of his top security advisor, Brent Scowcroft, that "it would be a disaster to go to Congress and lose" (Woodward 1991, 325). At the very least, a negative vote in Congress would have unleashed a substantial constitutional crisis and would have massively increased the opposition to war.

War: January 16 to February 28, 1991

In military terms, George Bush's war was spectacularly successful. The technology, strategy, and training of the forces led by the United States proved far superior to the Iraqi defenders, who seemed to have little stomach for fighting. Saddam Hussein had promised to fight "the mother of all battles," but his troops delivered instead the mother of all bug-outs.

Several weeks of aerial bombardment of Iraq and of Iraqi positions within Kuwait led, on February 23, to a ground assault that lasted only a few days and that forced Iraq out of Kuwait and out of positions in southern Iraq. At that point, declaring the contest won and not wishing to risk any more American casualties, Bush announced a cease-fire. American losses were lower than anybody dared hope: total battlefield deaths were 148 (many from friendly fire), and 467 were wounded in action. Iraqi military deaths in the brief war were never counted carefully and have been placed anywhere from 8,000 to 200,000 (U.S. News and World Report 1992, 408: Freedman and Karsh 1991, 37n).

Public Opinion: Measures of Support

Predictably, the beginning of the air war on January 16 brought on a substantial increase in support—a phenomenon I have dubbed the rally-round-the-flag effect (Mueller 1973, 208). Those thinking we had made a mistake sending troops to Saudi Arabia dropped 13 percentage points, those approving Bush's handling of the Persian Gulf situation rose 19 points, those approving his handling of Iraq's invasion of Kuwait rose 24 points, those approving the way he was handling the Iraq situation rose 28 points, those approving the job he was doing as president rose 18 points, those thinking the situation in the Mideast worth going to war over rose 25 points, those favoring going to war rose 16 or 24 points, those thinking we should wait for sanctions to work dropped 26 points, and those satisfied with the way things were going in the country or thought the country was on the right track rose 30 points. These indexes generally remained at high levels throughout the war, and Bush's popularity took another bolt upward—to a phenomenal 89 percent—at the time of victory. Nothing in the five and a half months of debate over war changed opinion anything like the way war itself did.

The Public's Tolerance for U.S. Casualties

In Korea and Vietnam, popular support, variously measured, followed the same trend: high at first, then declining. It seems clear that it was U.S. casualty rates, not the length of the war, that determined the decline in these wars. Intensive casualties were suffered in the early months of the Korean War, and support for the venture dropped rather quickly. In Vietnam, on the other hand, casualties rose gradually, and support for the war accordingly declined slowly. Yet in each case, support followed the same logarithmic pattern—it dropped some 15 percentage points whenever the casualties increased tenfold (for example, from 1,000 to 10,000 or from 10,000 to 100,000; Mueller 1973, 42–157). Essentially, therefore, the wars quickly lost the support of those who were only lukewarm supporters; hard-core supporters did not become disaffected until casualty rates rose considerably higher. Although Vietnam is often thought of as America's most unpopular war, it became more unpopular than Korea only after casualty rates had far surpassed those suffered in the earlier war.[9]

When the Vietnam War began in 1965, a can-do military force anticipated—or hoped—that the enemy ("a raggedy-ass third rate country," according to Lyndon Johnson) would break after suffering punishment for some two or three years, about the duration of the Korean War. The public and Congress seem to have accepted that estimate, and they generally supported the war for that long: had victory been achieved by 1967 or 1968, the war would probably have been accepted as a success.[10]

In attempting to sell the Gulf War, the military, the president, and people like Representative Aspin let on that a low-casualty war of a few weeks, maybe even a few days, could be expected. Following such declarations, the public and Congress seem to have envisioned and were prepared to tolerate a war with casualty rates more like those suffered in Bush's 1989 invasion of Panama than in Vietnam. Some data from late December—less than three weeks before the war began—are helpful for getting a feel for the potential impact of U.S. casualties on American public opinion. Those who favored a military attack on Iraq were asked if they would still support such military action if various levels of casualties might be suffered. As with Korea and Vietnam, support dropped off as a logarithmic function of U.S. casualties: support for war was more than cut in half if it was posited that 1,000 U.S. soldiers would be killed or wounded, to less than a third if 10,000 might become casualties, and to less than a quarter if 30,000 casualties were anticipated.[11] Other polls found a less dramatic falling off of war support when casualty estimates were incorporated into the question, but the same basic pattern of decline is still there.

This low tolerance for casualties was, of course, never put to the test. But to inspire a decline in war support, the Iraqis did not need to win battles. They only needed to maintain a dedicated fighting force (no easy task) that would be able to push American casualties beyond tolerable levels—and those levels were probably far lower than they were in Vietnam or Korea.[12] Bush successfully led the country into war, but if American losses had become significant, public support for the war—Bush's war, it would surely have been called—would have swiftly eroded. In fact, there is evidence to suggest that there was some erosion of war support during the course of the Gulf War even with its amazingly low U.S. casualties: the percentage calling U.S. involvement in the conflict a mistake grew by 5 to 7 percentage points between the beginning of the air war on January 16 and early February. This erosion, however, was undone by a rally effect when the ground war was initiated on February 23 and by the military triumph that quickly followed.

A sustained decline of war support would have been enhanced by two political elements that were not found in Korea or in the early years of Vietnam. The opposition party in the Gulf case had mostly voted against war, and if the war had begun to go awry opponents were certain to become highly critical and to point out that they had supported a viable nonviolent option, an option the trigger-happy Bush had rejected. In addition, a large antiwar movement had already been mobilized at the time of the war's outbreak. It largely fizzled as the United States met success in the war, but if American casualties had mounted, the movement, led by responsible Democrats, would surely have been rejuvenated and might have had an impact.

Contrary to Saddam Hussein's ardent hopes, a drop in public support might not have led to effective demands to get out of the war. Once troops are engaged, as discovered in such unpopular armed conflicts as the War of 1812 and Vietnam, it is difficult to generate the political will to back away. But a loss of support could have forced the president to compromise embarrassingly and, as happened to his predecessors in Korea and Vietnam, it could have ruined his presidency even if the war had eventually been won.

The Effects of Public Reaction on the Media

War, as pacifist William James once remarked, is "supremely thrilling excitement" and "the supreme theater of human strenuousness" (1911, 282, 288). It has a way, as has often been noted, of bringing people together and of cutting away petty differences. It also tends to bring out an intolerance of disagreement and dissent. In the Gulf crisis, the media very quickly grasped two lessons about the desires of their customers: they wanted a great deal of information about the exciting war, and they did not want to hear anything critical. The media complied.

This is hardly new. Although one myth about Vietnam is that the press was critical from the start, in fact, the first years it largely parroted the official Washington line and was rarely critical even by implication.[13] Under the intense drama of the brief and hugely successful Gulf War, the media generally reacted with predictable boosterism, even sycophancy. For example, ABC television had managed to purchase satellite pictures of the war zone from the Soviets. These suggested that Iraqi forces were far smaller than American military authorities were claiming. ABC decided not to use the pictures because, they said, they thought maybe the ingenious Iraqis had hidden a lot of their forces and because the satellite images had missed a fifteen-kilometer band in which perhaps the stupendously clever Iraqis had stored great amounts of war materiel. One suspects that ABC did not use the story because it could have been taken as critical of the U.S. military forces.

The *Wall Street Journal* had a fully developed story about sex in the military during the war and during the five-month period of buildup, when American military personnel were cooped up on ships and in isolated camps in the Saudi desert. It turned out that units had established informal areas for sex, and a remarkably large percentage of the female personnel became pregnant. Indeed, it is quite possible that far more Americans were conceived during the Gulf affair than were killed in it—one report puts the number of pregnancies at over 1,200 (Dunnigan and Bay 1992, 386.) The newspaper decided not to run the story because, it said, it doesn't do stories about sex. Regular readers will be somewhat surprised at that claim, and anyway, the story is not really about sex but about an obvious development (or problem) in a sexually integrated military. One might, then, suspect that the story was suppressed because it could be taken to be critical of the men and women in the military service. Editors at the *Los Angeles Times* war desk, noting from polls that the public supported the war 80 to 20, decided that it made sense for their coverage to be similarly balanced.

Had the war gone badly, the media might have become critical—though, as in the Vietnam experience, it would probably have followed rather than led the public discontent. With the war's success, the press remained frozen in advocacy.

Although the media, and particularly television, supplied some pictures of the war, events, not pictures, primarily determined the reaction. To insist on the importance of pictures is to suggest that people are so unimaginative that they react only when they see something in graphic form. Yet, there was great sympathy for tortured and murdered Kuwaitis even though there were no pictures of the atrocities. Similarly, Americans were outraged at the Pearl Harbor attack weeks—or even months—before they saw pictures of the event. In the Gulf War, the message (and the customer) dominated, even intimidated, the medium.

The War's Aftermath

Press sycophancy, it appears, lingered into the postwar era. Few stories retrospectively examined the war carefully or even sought to explain why the Iraqis, previously so highly rated, were routed so astoundingly.[14] The U.S. military essentially refused to consider how many enemy soldiers it killed.[15] Perhaps this is because the number cannot come out right: if it is high, the episode would seem more like a massacre than a war; if it is low, people could legitimately question why Iraqi strength was so severely overestimated.[16] Thus no one tried to fill in the missing data so crucial for an objective evaluation of the war (see Tucker 1991).

Even more impressive (and very related) was the impact of the war on the Democrats. For months, it froze them into almost total catatonia on foreign policy. When they did occasionally show signs of life, it was over domestic issues.

As it turned out, the aftermath of victory in the Middle East was rather messy. Egged on by Bush and by U.S. propaganda, groups opposing Saddam Hussein within Iraq—Kurds in the north, Shiites in the south—seized the opportunity and rebelled. Then, even while triumphantly proclaiming the Vietnam syndrome to be a thing of the past, Bush proceeded to wallow in it: after blasting the pathetic Iraqi defenders out of their bunkers, he refused to send troops into Iraq to get Saddam or to help the rebels because he did not want them to become involved in a Vietnam-style quagmire. As the United States stood watching from the sidelines, the remnants of Hussein's army put the rebellions down, and a massive and well-publicized exodus of pathetic, fleeing Kurds occurred. It seems likely that far more Iraqis died from these rebellions and from the breakdowns in hygiene and in health facilities that followed the war (see Tyler 1991) than died in the war itself.

Most important, contrary to the confident assumptions by the Bush administration of his early demise (Rosenthal 1991), the demonized Saddam Hussein remained defiantly in control of Iraq. As it happened, then, the Gulf War resulted in the deaths of tens, possibly hundreds, of thousands of Iraqis, none of whom was the archfiend. If all Bush wanted was to drive Iraq out of Kuwait and not to topple Saddam, that could have been accomplished at vastly lower human cost, it could be argued, by the judicious sanctions policy advocated by the Democrats, Chairman of the Joint Chiefs Colin Powell (Woodward 1991, 300), and much of the American public.

Meanwhile, the old order—authoritarian, feudal, and essentially incompetent—was reestablished in Kuwait, and the rescued Saudi Arabia showed little interest in helping out American Middle East policy even as Bush and his secretary of state, James Baker, sought to fashion a set of conferences to settle Arab-Israeli issues.

Retrospective Views of the War

Current events can often change or cloud the way one looks at, and remembers, the past. The intensely dramatic Gulf War, not surprisingly, provides a case in point. In December 1990, respondents had split about 50-50 on a question asking whether they preferred sanctions or military action. Asked after the war how they had felt beforehand, those inclined to remember they had supported military action outnumbered those recalling their support for sanctions by nearly 4 to 1. Before the war many people said they thought Bush was too quick to get American military forces involved in the Middle East, but after the war began far fewer said he had been too eager to wage war. And although many people before the war had said they believed sanctions could drive Iraq out of Kuwait, few were of that view at the war's end.

People also changed their attitudes toward what the conflict was all about. When asked in December whether the United States was chiefly motivated by a need to keep oil flowing or by the moral principle that invasions could not be allowed, most people picked the oil motivation. When the same question was asked again after the war, however, people had come overwhelmingly to prefer morality to oil. Relatedly, when asked after the war to select reasons for going to war against Iraq, respondents liked every reason offered to them more than they had before the war; the oil argument, however, gained only slightly in attractiveness.

By some measures, retrospective support for the war declined somewhat in the months after its end. The percentage thinking it had been a
mistake to get involved in the Gulf or in the war increased by 5 to 9
points between the end of the war and the summer of 1991. Larger
declines—14 and 19 points—were tapped by two questions asking
whether the war had been worth it or not, while another found a drop
of 6 points by summer and a further decline of 5 points by fall. On the
other hand, there was no decline by the summer of 1991 in the percentage who approved the decision to go to war, nor does there appear to
have been a decline in the percentage who felt the American attack had
been right. Thus, rather illogically, while the public became somewhat
more inclined to view the war as a mistake and quite a bit more inclined
to believe the war hadn't been worth the cost and effort, there was no
diminution in the numbers who favored the decision to go to war in the
first place.

Initial Assessments of Bush

If the war had gone badly, it would very likely have ruined Bush's
presidency, since he was the war's principal author and salesman. The
war went well, however, and it put him on cloud nine, at least initially.
If one compares the numbers Bush achieved at a time of triumph,
March 1991, with those tapped the previous July, before crisis erupted
in the Gulf, it is clear that the war greatly increased—by 15 or 20 percentage points—the number of people who would apply to him such
words as *sincere, steady, intelligent, confident, strong, leader,* and *active.*
Moreover, his ratings for *warm, friendly* went up somewhat, even though
they already stood at 84 percent. One can only regret that Gallup neglected to inquire about *brave, clean,* and *reverent.*

In rating Bush's performance on various tasks, the public similarly
waxed enthusiastic in the immediate wake of the war. Compared to July
1990, many more people said they thought he was doing an excellent or
good job in making appointments, being an efficient manager of government, developing programs to address America's pressing problems, communicating his ideas to the public, following through on his
ideas, working with Congress, being a good representative or symbol of
the country, and being an inspirational leader. In all cases, it was clearly
the war, not the crisis more generally, that boosted Bush. His ratings in
midcrisis (November 1990) were the same as or a bit worse than they
had been in July.

A set of questions was also posed asking whether Bush was making
progress handling various problems facing the country. In October 1990
Bush had broken his "No new taxes" pledge, and in November the public, not unreasonably, gave him low marks for "making progress" at

"avoiding raising taxes." Bush's tax policy was unaffected by the war in the Gulf, but after it was over his ratings for "making progress" at avoiding a tax raise jumped upward by 22 percentage points. Also impressive: by going to war (and winning it), Bush increased his score for "making progress" at "keeping the nation out of war" by 27 percentage points from where it had stood in November.

Opinion on Saddam Hussein and the Iraqis

Even before the war, Americans seem to have come substantially to feel that getting Saddam should be a central war aim, and that attitude became, if anything, more firm once the war started. Even when the question specifically pointed out that the United Nations had authorized force only to remove Iraq from Kuwait, most people opted for continuing the fight until the demonic Saddam was removed, and most of these said they were willing to spend several thousand American lives to bring this about.

Early in the war most people were strongly inclined to say that the war could not be considered a victory if Hussein remained in power, but at the end of the war, to questions that seem comparable, people had substantially reversed themselves. Less than two months after the war, however, even as Americans began to welcome the troops home in various "victory" parades, the percentage willing to maintain that victory had been achieved dropped 20 percentage points. And, relatedly, the percentage thinking the war had been ended too soon rose dramatically.

Americans and their leader may have demonized Hussein, but some data suggest that, despite the depredations committed by the Iraqi army in Kuwait, little of this animosity rubbed off on the Iraqi people.[17] This does not mean, however, that there was a great deal of sympathy for civilian casualties caused by U.S. air attacks.

Lessons from the War

A few poll questions allow for an assessment of broader conclusions that the public might draw from the war. Although the war was clearly one against a dictatorship and although it was sometimes billed as a fight for democracy and freedom, easy success in the war did not boost support for further efforts to intervene to change dictatorships—if anything, the reverse was true. However, at least while it was still on, the war did substantially raise support for the notion that "wars are sometimes necessary to settle differences."

The war seems to have notably reduced the numbers of Americans who said they thought the United States was in decline as a world power. But it only marginally increased the number who said they thought the United States would be the top economic power in the next century—more people still picked Japan.

Satisfaction with the United States and its Economy

The Gulf War made Americans happy and proud, even euphoric, about themselves for a while. There was a lot of flag waving and innumerable editorials about a new surge of patriotism. That particular balloon, it seems, began to fizzle rather quickly. Although the war caused a jump of some 30 percentage points in the degree to which Americans registered satisfaction with the way things were going in the country, by April or May 1991—just a few weeks after the Gulf triumph—satisfaction had slumped to about the same level as in July 1990, before it all began.

Much of the problem seems to have been economic. The war may have buoyed spirits, but it didn't improve the economy—as the Democrats eventually pointed out. The war initially caused people to say they believed themselves to be better off financially than they had been a year ago. Within six weeks of the end of the war, this effect had worn off.

At the time of the Gulf War, lots of people said they were very proud to be Americans, but pride so measured was actually lower than it had been in 1986 and no higher than in 1981. On the other hand, the confidence of Americans in the ability of their country to deal wisely with world problems increased substantially compared to the mid-1980s. By contrast, even with triumph in the Gulf War, Americans were actually *less* likely to express confidence in the future of the country than they had been in the mid-1980s. And, quite astoundingly, they were even less confident in this respect than they had been in 1980 during the lengthy Iran hostage crisis, a phenomenon that they said had lowered their confidence substantially.

There did seem to be a surge in the urge to wave the American flag, but Americans were substantially (and perhaps fortunately) less willing than they had been in the distant 1950s to subscribe to the amazingly unclouded sentiment that "The United States is the greatest country in the world, better than all other countries in every possible way."

Long-term Effects on Opinion

At the time, the Gulf War was hailed by Secretary of State Baker as "a defining moment in history" (Atkinson 1991). The war hardly seems to have lived up to this advance billing.

Bush's Ratings.   Although Bush's successful war in Panama in December 1989 boosted his rating on his handling of the "situation in Central America" by 26 percentage points and his rating on handling the "drug problem" by 16 points, six months later his rating on Central America was back down to where it had been before that venture, as was his drug rating.

The Panama lesson may be general. By the summer of 1991, Bush's presidential popularity had declined from the stratospheric 89 percent at the Gulf War's end to levels he had attained in the early days of the crisis. More to the point are questions specifically asking how Bush was handling the Gulf "situation." His approval rating reached an astronomical high at the war's end, from which it declined 14 points in a month. A few months later—after all the victory and welcome home parades—it had plunged 20 to 30 points, quite as much as his Central America rating dropped after the successful invasion of Panama.

In the following months, other concerns—particularly the apparently perilous state of the economy—took over, and Bush's popularity ratings plummeted as he headed into the 1992 reelection campaign. One element in Bush's decline, clearly, was the public's increasing belief that the war, contrary to presidential hype at the time, did not appear to have made the Middle East more stable and secure, and there was rising disappointment with him because Saddam Hussein remained in charge in Iraq. The public had followed Bush in large part because it accepted, or fully agreed with, his demonization of Hussein. Then when, contrary to ardent hopes, the demon managed to linger on uncooperatively after the war to commit yet more outrages, the whole enterprise was soured for many.

Accordingly, postwar criticism came from two directions. One was to suggest that the war was simply not thought through—Bush failed to plan for what many people had come to think was the central problem. The other concerns Bush's precrisis Iraq which had sought to placate—or "coddle," as his postwar critics put it—the dictator in Iraq. Because of the demonization of Saddam Hussein, Bush left himself peculiarly vulnerable to problems on this score. If people come to accept Hussein not merely as an irritating minor thug but a world-class criminal—the image Bush helped him to develop in the runup to war—the administration's inability to comprehend his full villainy before the crisis leaves it open to very substantial criticism.

Electoral Consequences.   Initial punditry held that the Gulf War would redound in the Republicans' favor. It had been their war, after all—they had voted solidly for it in Congress, while the craven, wimpy, and now terrorized Democrats had mostly opposed it—and the war had turned out to be a towering success. Moreover, their standard bearer, George Bush, had risked all on the venture and had come out looking like a decisive leader and a certifiable (if "warm" and "friendly") hero. Surely his magic would rub off on the party in upcoming elections. The effects of the traumatic event might even permanently change the party balance by shifting party identification. As they vanished from sight, Democratic leaders could only mutter hopefully and unconvincingly that it was still a long time until the 1992 elections and that a lot could happen during that time. As it turned out, a lot did.

In general, even polls conducted shortly after the triumphant end of the war suggested that the war might not have all that much electoral impact. Although they voted against the war, the Democrats swung into line as soon as it started, and shortly after the war people seem to have been inclined to see the parties as being equally supportive of the war. Moreover, half the population at that time was unable to recall how their representative or senator had voted on the war, and of those who could remember, the overwhelming majority recalled a vote in favor of war.

Party identification levels were not notably changed by the war. And when a set of questions dealing with the parties' comparative ability to handle various jobs was asked in the immediate aftermath of the war, little change was found from a year earlier, when hardly anybody had even heard of Saddam Hussein (see also Yang 1991).

The electoral impact of the war proved to be modest, however, not because the issue was so complicated with so many pluses and minuses to balance out, but because voters simply neglected it as they turned to other, more immediate concerns, particularly domestic ones. There are historical precedents.

The Democrats have had bitter experience with wars and elections. Under popular presidents, they led the country into two world wars, both of which were exhilarating and patriotic displays of the American can-do spirit and both of which ended in decisive victory over evil enemies. Yet in the elections of 1920 and 1946, held a year or two after the fighting stopped, the Democrats were clobbered as the public came to focus on things at home: in 1920 they lost the White House, fifty-nine seats in the House, and ten in the Senate; in the congressional elections of 1946 they lost fifty-five House seats and twelve in the Senate.

Another analogy is with the British election of 1945. The war against Germany had been won only a few months earlier, and the ruling Conservatives were led by an extraordinarily popular leader, Winston Churchill. Yet the electorate had already begun to focus on domestic issues, and it turned the Conservatives and Churchill out.

Then there is the brief 1982 war, costing a total of 800 lives, between Britain and Argentina over the Falkland Islands, a desolate piece of territory populated by fewer than 2,000 souls—an event an Argentine

writer has characterized as "two bald men fighting over a comb."[18] Like
the Gulf War for the Americans, the Falklands War was mesmerizing to
the British public, and they were elated when their side won handily
and at low cost. The ruling Conservative party gained considerably in
the election of 1983, although, since the economy improved at the same
time, there is a debate over how much of this gain can be credited to the
war (see Sanders, Ward, and Marsh 1987; Clarke, Mishler, and Whiteley
1990; Sanders, Marsh, and Ward 1990; Norpoth 1987a, 1987b).

However, even if this experience is taken to suggest that quick,
cheap, successful wars can lead to notable electoral gains, the Falklands
episode differs importantly from the Gulf War in its aftermath. When
the British won, the issue was settled, and the Argentines helpfully deposed the government that had led them into the war, replacing it with
a reasonably responsive democracy. After the Gulf War, by contrast,
there continued to be substantial bloodshed and turmoil, and Saddam
Hussein emerged in the rather exquisite position of being able to inflict
maximum psychic pain on his archnemesis, George Bush, by simply remaining alive and in power—something he would want to do anyway.
As noted earlier, substantial numbers of Americans did not consider the
war won as long as Hussein continued to reign and to thumb his nose
at the putative victors. It seems likely that any positive electoral benefits
of the war would be severely undercut as long as Hussein continues to
hold sway in Iraq.

A comparison with another war may also be useful. The Vietnam
War came to an end in utter debacle in 1975. A year and a half later, a
presidential election was held in which the man who presided over
that event, Gerald Ford, ran for reelection. Although many people anticipated that a loss in Vietnam would lead to political turmoil in
the United States, Vietnam played scarcely any role at all in the election.
Indeed, far from engendering a debate over who lost Vietnam, the
debacle in Indochina, amazingly enough, was actually used by Ford
as a point in his *favor* in his reelection campaign. When he came into
office, he observed, "We were still deeply involved in the problems of
Vietnam"; but now "we are at peace. Not a single young American is
fighting or dying on any foreign soil" (Kraus 1979, 538–39). His challenger, Jimmy Carter, seems to have concluded that it was politically
disadvantageous to point out the essential absurdity of Ford's remarkable argument. Actually, foreign policy was the great nonissue of the
1976 campaign, which was dominated by domestic—particularly
economic—considerations (see Niemi, Mueller, and Smith 1989, 44;
Mueller 1977, 328; Mueller 1984, 1989, 189–90).

This experience (as well as those of the elections of 1920 and 1946)
suggests that Americans, like the British in 1945, are capable of turning
from foreign to domestic preoccupations with a truly impressive

virtuosity. As domestic concerns rise in comparative importance, the Gulf War may, like Vietnam, fade into memory and succumb to the American public's remarkable capacity for inattention. Thus despite Bush's claims, promises, and prophecies, the Gulf War, at least in that special sense, became "another Vietnam."[19]

The Gulf War as Spectator Sport.   During the war, commentators were often swept away by analogies and metaphors from sports, particularly football. General Norman Schwarzkopf led the charge, likening one of his most important military maneuvers to football's "Hail Mary" play (though it could probably more appropriately be compared to an end run). When discussing the enemy he noted, perhaps with some disappointment, "You know, a football game can be over very quickly if the other team decides not to play. And that's what you had in this case. When the kickoff came, okay, our team was there to play. Our team came to play ball. And they were not willing to fight" (PBS 1991b). As one writer put it a year later, "The Gulf War more resembled a Gulf Bowl. It was the biggest spectator sport of the year, and as euphoric as any playoff—a groundswell of giddy enthusiasm for Team America, like a homecoming game, with Stormin' Norman as Big Man on Campus" (Farwell 1992).

The analogy shouldn't be pushed too far, but there are quite a few similarities. Football, or at any rate tackle football, is indeed a spectator sport in the sense that, unlike other team sports, it is not commonly played in sandlots.[20] Thus viewers generally experience it, like war, vicariously—only a few actually participate. In both war and football, teamwork, team morale, and a sense of comradeship are extremely important (see Mueller 1991c). And in both cases, the fans cheer for their team to win and to be number one, experience a sort of catharsis when the event is over, and tend to overlook the long-range costs to the participants.[21]

For present purposes, the analogy with spectator sports carries with it one parallel that seems particularly instructive. At the time of breathless anticipation and then finally of violent consummation, the big game becomes thunderously, all-consumingly important. But once it is over, even the most ardent of fans, after perhaps a few hours or days of residual exhilaration and celebration (or depression and gloom), move on to other concerns and leave it all behind. One last poll result may be instructive in this regard. Conducted in December 1984, the poll asked people who said they were football fans which team had won the Super Bowl the previous January. Only 39 percent were able to recall (CBS Sports 1984).[22]

Something like this may be happening with the Gulf War. Those affected physically or personally by the event may never be able to forget it; those affected only psychically seem to be able to do so quite easily. Few of its American fans will forget who won, at least in the strict military sense. But like the Big Game, which always seems at the time to be so important, the Gulf War soon faded as a notable and motivating event. Thus when George Bush suggested as he launched the war that it would "chart the future of the world for the next hundred years" (1991, 314), he seems to have inflated its impact by a factor of 365. For some people the war may live on as a sort of glowing legend of manly achievement and American prowess. But for most people it may prove to have little lasting relevance.

NOTES

For generous assistance in supplying data, I would like to thank Michael R. Kagay of the *New York Times*, William C. Stratmann and John Palmerini of the Gordon S. Black Corporation, and especially Thomas W. Graham and the Institute on Global Conflict and Cooperation at the University of California, San Diego. I would also like to thank Marc Maynard of the Roper Center for his assistance.

1. Even some of the most careful analysts sometimes fall into this error. For example, one report concludes at one point that "Persian Gulf hawks currently outnumber doves by better than 2-to-1" but states that "depending on how questions are framed, support for a hard line can be depressed to the 40 to 50 percent range or increased to 70 or 80 percent" (Morin and Dionne 1990). As indicated, it was possible to generate an even wider range of responses. See also Mueller 1993.

2. For able, if unusual, journalistic discussions of the question-wording issue, see Morin (1991) and Brennan (1991). For classic analyses, see Payne (1951) and Schuman and Presser (1981).

3. Bush and others in his administration were apparently convinced that the "polls had finally turned around" by January, with clear public support for his Gulf policy and for the use of force (U.S. News and World Report 1992, 202; see also Smith 1992, 162). Similarly, some postwar analysts have argued that Bush was able to "lead, mobilize, and shape public opinion to support his actions; at every turn he was able to garner international support and then turn and use it to mobilize approval from Congress and from the general public" (Inman et al., 1992, 70–71; see also Gergen 1991/92, 9). The notion of the January "turnaround" may well be one of those myths about public opinion that will last.

4. In the many years of debate over nuclear policy, for example, there was a tendency for those who were most opposed to the bomb to emphasize, and to exaggerate, its destructiveness. Similarly, after World War I war opponents often anticipated that the next war would bring the end of civilization; see Mueller (1991a, 17–19).

5. White House press secretary Marlin Fitzwater, however, insisted that this "wasn't macho talk" (Barnes 1991, 9).

6. On the other hand, Defense Intelligence Agency analyst Walter Lang, who had been just about the only person to predict the Iraqi invasion in August, said he anticipated that a war with Iraq would be long and difficult (Woodward 1991, 216–17, 360).

7. For a discussion of the sense of fatalism about war that developed in Iraq, see Viorst (1991, 67–68); Karsh and Rautsi (1991, 67–68). On war fatalism before World War I, see Joll (1984).

8. According to police estimates, the January 19 protest (dominated by Left-wing groups) drew a crowd of 25,000, while that of January 26 (much more moderate in tone) drew 75,000—quite significant numbers, considering their anticlimactic timing. Held in the heady early days of a successful war, neither drew many establishment politicians as speakers. See Walsh and Valentine (1991).

9. From the perspective of the American public, Korea differed from Vietnam in two notable ways: there was no vocal antiwar movement, and television coverage was in its infancy. Since popular support declined for the Korean War in the same way and at the same level as it did for the Vietnam War, one is entitled to conclude that neither the antiwar movement nor television was vital to that decline. People need neither pictures of a war nor people screaming at them to determine that they don't like the costs. On this issue, see Mueller (1973, chap. 6; 1984, 1991b); Mandelbaum (1981); Lichty (1984); and Hallin (1986).

10. McGeorge Bundy's comment in 1968 is apt: "It is a miracle, in a way, that our people have stayed with the war as long as they have" (Hallin 1986, 211). On the issue of American war strategy and calculations in Vietnam, see Mueller (1980).

11. Unusually, the poll also asked about Iraqi casualties, and one might extrapolate from the comparative results that support for a war in which 100,000 (or more) Iraqis were killed or wounded was about the same as for one in which 5,000 Americans became casualties. That is, in the view of the U.S. public, one American life is worth at least twenty Iraqi lives.

12. There is little evidence, however, that the Iraqi leadership, such as it was, gave much coherent thought to how they might pull this off. One possibility that was at least technically within their means would have been to make an Alamo-like fortress of populated (and therefore hostage-filled) areas like Kuwait City and to take a stand there. Instead, they apparently put their faith on inflicting casualties in set piece battles in the desert. Since Iraqi forces were decidedly smaller in numbers (see note 16 below), and since, as was well known before the war, Iraqi equipment was vastly inferior to that of the opposing forces (Iraqi tanks had a firing range of perhaps 1,200 meters, while U.S. tanks had a range of over 2,000, for example), such a strategy was destined to fail even if the Iraqis fought bravely. Simple arithmetic, however, does not seem to be Saddam Hussein's strong suit.

13. See Hallin (1986, especially chap. 4). Although he eventually became known as a Vietnam War critic, journalist David Halberstam in 1965 called Vietnam a "strategic country in a key area, it is perhaps one of only five or six nations in the world that is truly vital to U.S. interests." And another future war critic, Neil Sheehan, concluded in 1964, "The fall of Southeast Asia to China or its denial to the West over the next decade because of the repercussions from an

American defeat in Vietnam would amount to a strategic disaster of the first magnitude" (see Mueller 1989, 169–70).

14. As a book published a full year after the war observes, "the complete story of why and how [the war] happened has gone largely untold" (U.S. News and World Report 1992, vii).

15. U.S. General Norman Schwarzkopf's sympathetic biographers note his "obstinate refusal to provide any figures on Iraqi casualties," and even they observe, "In a war where such precision was shown by U.S. forces in so many areas, and intelligence was generally sophisticated, this analysis was almost absurdly vague" (Cohen and Gatti 1991, 270).

16. The latter seems to be the case. Most evidence suggests that Iraqi troop levels were wildly overestimated. Prewar calculations by the military concluded that the Iraqi forces stood at 540,000 or even higher (compared to their opponents' 700,000). As an adulatory postwar book by the editors of *Time* points out, this estimate assumes Iraqi units were at full strength and notes that "many Iraqi commands were at less than two-thirds of their scheduled manning levels" (Friedrich 1991, 72)—though elsewhere the book casually accepts the 540,000 figure (ibid., 53). A later, more thorough, analysis suggests there were fewer than 250,000 Iraqi troops in the area when the ground war began (U.S. News and World Report 1992, 405–07), and another comes up with 183,000 while suggesting that that "number could easily be lower" (Aspin and Dickinson 1992, 33–34).

17. One reporter in postwar Iraq observes that this lack of people-to-people animosity is reciprocated: to his surprise, he found that "Iraqis expressed virtually no anti-American feeling" (Viorst 1991, 60).

18. Quoted in Norpoth (1987b, 957). However, the costs of the war, proportionate to the value of the stakes, could be taken to suggest it was one of the most brutal in history.

19. The War of 1812 may also hold some lessons. Like the Gulf War, it was a partisan affair, and as it dragged on, the opposition did well at the ballot box. However, after the war its partisan champions were able to fashion a helpful and appealing myth that the war had been a glorious triumph, and the opposition was often successfully stigmatized as a band of unpatriotic—even treasonous—obstructionists who had prolonged the war and undercut the gallant American fighting forces (see Hickey 1989). This experience could be taken to suggest that the Democrats might have gained substantially if the Gulf War had gone badly, quite probably destroying the presidency and the political career of George Bush in the process. But they might have found it difficult afterward to avoid appearing to have hampered a great, if perhaps misguided, patriotic effort.

20. However, football was commonly played by U.S. marines in the desert as they waited for the war to start. Although they were ordered to play only touch football, they disobeyed, and many injuries resulted. Overall in the Gulf venture, twice as many U.S. troops were hospitalized with sports injuries as with combat injuries (Dunnigan and Bay 1992, 396).

21. The gladiators of professional football average only four and a half seasons. Each season 80 percent are injured, and virtually all suffer later from spinal compression. Among the million or so men who play football at the high school, college, and professional level each year, there are nearly 500,000

injuries. Knee injuries account for 125,000, and 30,000 of these are severe enough to require surgery. There are no data for retired players, but a large percentage undergo multiple operations, and many are permanently disabled (HBO 1985).

22. Actually, in some respects this number is high. The winner of the previous Super Bowl had been the Los Angeles Raiders, but the poll accepted the erroneous response, Oakland Raiders, as correct even though the team had moved to Los Angeles two or three years earlier. The questions about who had won the Super Bowl came at the end of the survey, after several memory-jogging questions about favorite players and teams. The poll was based on a sample of 1,340 adults, of whom 744 were determined to be football fans.

REFERENCES

ABC (American Broadcasting Corporation) News. 1991. *This Week with David Brinkley.* January 13.

Aspin, Les, and William Dickinson. 1992. *Defense for a New Era: Lessons of the Persian Gulf War.* Washington, D.C.: Government Printing Office.

Atkinson, Rick. 1991. " 'A Defining Moment in History': As Midnight Deadline Approaches, Stakes for U.S. Are Enormous." *Washington Post*, January 15.

Barnes, Fred. 1991. "The Hawk Factor." *New Republic*, January 28, 8–9.

Brennan, John. 1991. "Key Words Influence Stands on Minorities." *Los Angeles Times*, August 21.

Bush, George. 1991. "The Liberation of Kuwait Has Begun." Speech of January 16, 1991. In *The Gulf War Reader: History, Documents, Opinions,* ed. Micah L. Sifry and Christopher Cerf. New York: Times Books/Random House.

CBS Sports/New York Times Poll. 1984. "The State of the NFL." Press release. December.

Clarke, Harold D., William Mishler, and Paul Whiteley. 1990. "Recapturing the Falklands: Models of Conservative Popularity, 1979–83." *British Journal of Political Science* 20 (January): 63–81.

Cohen, Roger, and Claudio Gatti. 1991. *In the Eye of the Storm: The Life of General H. Norman Schwarzkopf.* New York: Farrar, Straus, and Giroux.

Drew, Elizabeth. 1991. "Letter from Washington." *New Yorker*, February 4, 82–90.

Dunnigan, James F., and Austin Bay. 1992. *From Shield to Storm: High-Tech Weapons, Military Strategy, and Coalition Warfare in the Persian Gulf.* New York: Morrow.

Farwell, Rebecca. 1992. "Two Cents." *TDC*, January 4.

Freedman, Lawrence, and Efraim Karsh. 1991. "How Kuwait Was Won: Strategy in the Gulf War." *International Security* 16 (Fall): 5–41.

Friedrich, Otto, ed. 1991. *Desert Storm: The War in the Persian Gulf.* Boston: Little, Brown.

Gergen, David. 1991/92. "America's Missed Opportunities." *Foreign Affairs* 71: 1–19.

Hallin, Daniel C. 1986. *The "Uncensored War": The Media and Vietnam.* New York: Oxford University Press.

HBO (Home Box Office). 1985. *Disposable Heroes.* John Else, Bill Coutarie, and Bob Moore, writers.

Hickey, Donald R. 1989. *The War of 1812: A Forgotten Conflict.* Urbana and Chicago: University of Illinois Press.

Inman, Bobby, Joseph S. Nye, Jr., William J. Perry, and Roger K. Smith. 1992. "Lessons From the Gulf War." *Washington Quarterly,* Winter, 57–74.

James, William. 1911. *Memories and Studies.* New York: Longmans, Green.

Joll, James. 1984. *The Origins of the First World War.* New York: Longmans.

Karsh, Efraim, and Inari Rautsi. 1991. *Saddam Hussein: A Political Biography.* New York: Free Press.

Kraus, Sidney. 1979. *The Great Debates: Carter vs. Ford, 1976.* Bloomington: Indiana University Press.

Lichty, Lawrence W. 1984. "Comments on the Influence of Television on Public Opinion." In *Vietnam as History,* ed. Peter Braestrup. Lanham: University Press of America.

Mandelbaum, Michael. 1981. "Vietnam: The Television War." *Daedalus* (Fall): 157–69.

Moore, Molly. 1991. "Aspin: War Would Start with Air Strikes, Escalate to Ground Battles." *Washington Post,* January 9.

Morin, Richard. 1991. "2 Ways of Reading the Public's Lips on Gulf Policy: Differently Phrased Questions Seem at First Glance to Yield Contradictory Results." *Washington Post,* January 14.

Morin, Richard, and E. J. Dionne, Jr. 1990. "*Vox Populi:* Winds of War and Shifts of Opinion." *Washington Post,* 23 December.

Mueller, John. 1973. *War, Presidents and Public Opinion.* New York: Wiley. (Reprinted 1985 by University Press of America, Lanham, Md.).

———. 1977. "Changes in American Public Attitudes Toward International Involvement." In *The Limits of Military Intervention,* ed. Ellen Stern. Beverly Hills: Sage.

———. 1980. "The Search for the 'Breaking Point' in Vietnam: The Statistics of a Deadly Quarrel." *International Studies Quarterly* 24 (December): 497–519.

———. 1984. "Reflections on the Vietnam Protest Movement and on the Curious Calm at the War's End." In *Vietnam as History,* ed. Peter Braestrup. Lanham: University Press of America.

———. 1989. *Retreat from Doomsday: The Obsolescence of Major War.* New York: Basic.

———. 1991a. "Changing Attitudes Towards War: The Impact of the First World War." *British Journal of Political Science* 21 (January): 1–28.

———. 1991b. "Korea, Vietnam and the Gulf." *The Polling Report* 7 (18 February): 1, 7–8.

———. 1991c. "War: Natural, but Not Necessary." In *The Institution of War,* ed. Robert A. Hinde. London: Macmillan.

———. 1993. "American Public Opinion and the Gulf War." *Public Opinion Quarterly* 57 (Spring).

Niemi, Richard G., John Mueller, and Tom W. Smith. 1989. *Trends in Public Opinion: A Compendium of Survey Data.* Westport: Greenwood.

Norpoth, Helmut. 1987a. "The Falklands War and Government Popularity in Britain: Rally Without Consequence or Surge Without Decline?" *Electoral Studies* 6:3–16.

———. 1987b. "Guns and Butter and Government Popularity in Britain." *American Political Science Review* 81 (September): 949–59.

Payne, Stanley C. 1951. *The Art of Asking Questions.* Princeton: Princeton University Press.

PBS (Public Broadcasting Service). 1991a. *Talking with David Frost: An Interview with President and Mrs. Bush.* January 2 (taped December 28, 1990).

———. 1991b. *General Norman Schwarzkopf . . . Talking with David Frost.* March 22.

Rosenthal, Andrew. 1991. "U.S. Expecting Hussein to Be Out by Year's End." *New York Times,* March 18.

Sanders, David, Dave Marsh, and Hugh Ward. 1990. "A Reply to Clarke, Mishler and Whiteley." *British Journal of Political Science* 20 (January): 83–90.

Sanders, David, Hugh Ward, and David Marsh. 1987. "Government Popularity and the Falklands War: A Reassessment." *British Journal of Political Science* 17 (July): 281–313.

Schuman, Howard, and Stanley Presser. 1981. *Questions and Answers in Attitude Surveys.* New York: Academic.

Smith, Gene Edward. 1992. *George Bush's War.* New York: Holt.

Tucker, Robert. 1991. "Justice and the War." *National Interest* (Fall): 108–12.

Tyler, Patrick E. 1991. "Health Crisis Said to Grip Iraq in Wake of War's Destruction." *New York Times,* May 22.

U.S. News and World Report. 1992. *Triumph Without Victory: The Unreported History of the Persian Gulf War.* New York: Times Books/Random House.

Viorst, Milton. 1991. "Report from Baghdad." *New Yorker,* June 24, 55–73.

Walsh, Elsa, and Paul Valentine. 1991. "War Protest Draws Tens of Thousands Here." *Washington Post,* January 27.

Wilcox, Clyde, Joe Ferrarra, and Dee Allsop. 1991. "Before the Rally: The Dynamics of Attitudes Toward the Gulf Crisis Before the War." Paper prepared for the annual meeting of the American Political Science Association. Washington, D.C., September.

Woodward, Bob. 1991. *The Commanders.* New York: Simon and Schuster.

Yang, Frederick. 1991. "After the Storm: The Political Impact of the Gulf War." *The Polling Report* 7 (1 April): 1–3.

9

The Political and Psychological Impact of the Gulf War on the Israeli Public

■

Asher Arian and Carol Gordon

Go my people into your rooms, and close the doors behind you. Wait a short moment until the anger has passed.
> —*Isaiah 26:20*

I will send to Babylon strangers. They will smite it and rend that land asunder. And they will surround it on the day of wickedness. . . . Spare not its young men; completely destroy its army.
> —*Jeremiah 51:2–3*

ISRAELIS HAVE developed a large repertoire of reactions to crisis situations during their history of conflict and war. The Gulf War, Saddam Hussein, and his missiles and threats to destroy the country represented another chapter in the Israeli history of coping with challenges.

The intertwining of death and life, grief and joy, is an ever present fact with both existential and emotional consequences that, in Israel, perhaps more than in other countries, is impossible to avoid. Life and death come together in the culture, in the values, in the very ethos of the country. The intermingling of death and life is powerfully institutionalized in Israel by the sequencing of the days of mourning in memory of victims of the Holocaust and of Israel's fallen soldiers just before Independence Day—creating an emotional and vivid juxtaposition of mourning for loved ones and affirming life.

Fear of one's own death—as well as of the death of loved ones—is generally accepted to be a natural, normal human emotion.[1] During war, one is more consciously aware of this fear. Excessive preoccupation with the fear of death is considered pathological (see Feifel 1959; Templer 1972). While many, perhaps most, Israelis were afraid and anxious during the Gulf War, they nevertheless carried on with their lives and did not become preoccupied with death. In fact, one could almost say that, overall, pathology was down in the country. Mental health clinics and private therapists reported a dramatic decline in the

227

number of people who sought help. Psychologists were on duty at hospitals twenty-four hours a day—but almost no one came in. Israelis were busy coping.

On the other hand, there were unobtrusive measures of the stress Israelis were under. First, heart attack rates increased dramatically, with the greatest increase reported for the Tel Aviv area, somewhat lower rates of increase in Haifa, and even lower rates for areas that had not experienced SCUD attacks. Second, Israelis had more problems sleeping than before the war. In addition, incidents of domestic violence and rape were up, with shelters for battered women filled to overflowing after the war. In the six weeks of the war seven women were battered to death, compared with the usual *annual* rate of three to four (Avgar 1991).

The Gulf War was very difficult for Israelis—and with good cause. The missile attacks were designed to terrorize the civilian population and to involve Israel in the war. But the population was not terrorized. There was no collapse of civilian morale. And Israel did not get involved in the war.

In the forty-two days of the war, eighteen missile attacks were launched against Israel, for an average of one attack every two and one-half days. Forty missiles reached Israel: twenty-six fell in the Tel Aviv area, six in Haifa, five in the West Bank, and three in the south of the country. In two-thirds of the attacks (twelve of eighteen), a lone missile arrived; in the other six incidents, six SCUDs landed. In the largest single attack of the war against Israel, eight SCUD missiles arrived simultaneously. Once, six missiles were sent toward a single area in one attack.

It is notable how low the casualty rate was. As a direct result of the missiles, only one person was killed and 230 were wounded, only one critically.[2] Eleven additional people died indirectly from the missile attacks, four from heart attacks and seven from improper use of the gas masks that had been distributed to save lives. In addition, 226 people were injured by unnecessarily injecting themselves with Atropine, used to counteract the nerve gas that was not sent, and 539 cases of panic and anxiety were treated in hospitals. Only sixty people were actually hospitalized, and most of them only for a day or two.

While no damage was reported in ten of the eighteen attacks, on the whole property damage was relatively heavy, totaling several hundred million dollars. In Tel Aviv, 3,991 apartments were hit; 87 were destroyed, and 869 were badly damaged. More than 100 public buildings and business structures were also hit. A total of 1,647 people were evacuated to hotels. The damage in the Tel Aviv suburb of Ramat Gan was similar: 3,742 apartments hit, 105 destroyed, 600 badly damaged, and 100 public buildings and business structures hit. A total of 1,047 Ramat Gan residents were evacuated to hotels.

Israel was under attack, and even with all their experience, for Israelis this war was different. Israel was not part of the coalition that fought against Iraq; there was no battle front—only a home front. Israeli civilians instead of soldiers were the targets of missile attacks—and yet there was no military activity. This was a never-before-experienced event in Israel. The fear of chemical attack was ever present. The possibility of a gas attack prompted the authorities to institute a dramatic change in procedure. When the air raid sirens sounded, Israelis grabbed their gas masks and ran to sealed rooms in their apartments, as Isaiah had foreseen. The warning time was measured in seconds or a few minutes; the use of communal air raid shelters were not encouraged, partly because not enough had been prepared and partly because it would take too much time to collect people there. Accordingly, unlike other wars in Israel, there was no sharing of time with neighbors, no alternative social structures that emerged, no spontaneous leadership, no group solidarity, and no psychological and emotional support.

Most important, rather than being a nation at arms, Israel during the war was a nation at home. There was no general call-up, so most fathers, husbands, sons, and brothers were present with their families and as helpless as the other civilians usually thought of as weaker in war. Israelis living abroad did not return to join their army units, since most of these units were not called up. The physical existence of Israelis at home had never seemed so threatened. There had been shelling of civilians previously, but the symbolism of death by gas made this situation different. Even the decision to station patriot missiles with their American crews, while broadly supported, was a symbol of dependence and powerlessness. Day after day, as darkness approached and anxiety levels increased, Israelis came home and waited for attack. In Tel Aviv, the streets emptied by 4 P.M. Observers noted that while the history of the Jewish people had many examples of such behavior, the history of Israel did not. During the Gulf War, Israeli males were not warriors protecting their families but citizens as helpless as their children. In many families, roles were reversed. It was the children who, having been drilled for weeks in their schools, showed their parents how to put on gas masks and seal the room.

The Gulf War provides an especially good case for the study of changes in beliefs and attitudes, and there is clear evidence that the experience of the war influenced Israelis cognitively, emotionally, and behaviorally. Political attitudes, beliefs about God, and religious practice all show evidence of change in the wake of the war.[3]

In general, shifts in attitude are more likely to be gradual than sudden (see McGuire 1985). Dramatic events are capable of stimulating attitude change precisely because a new definition and understanding of the situation is in place after the event. Attitude change is especially

likely if the reinterpretation is echoed by opinion leaders, thus strengthening the new position and reinforcing the change.[4] But the evidence of
change is not likely to be distinct or immediate. Most people continue to
hold the attitudes they held, often using the event that just occurred to
provide further justification for the position they held before the event.

The elements of the Gulf War situation make it ideal to search for
attitude change. First, the time frame is very short. Although the crisis
began with the Iraqi invasion of Kuwait in August, for most Israelis the
real pressure began after the first missiles fell in the middle of January
1991. By the end of February it was over. Second, the concentration on
the war and its implications was almost total. The country closed down
for the first five days and then, for the next five weeks, concentrated
almost solely on the war each evening and night. Third, almost all
commentary reinforced the notion that this was a period of change. For
Saddam Hussein, it was "the mother of all wars," but George Bush was
equally flamboyant when he talked of "a new world order" and "a defining moment."

In Israel, it was clear that the Americans were calling the tune. Israel
was told not to retaliate, and it did not. Officials turned to Washington
for money to repair the economic damage done during the war. U.S. officials said very clearly that new patterns of behavior and relations
would be expected in the Middle East after the war, and Israelis had no
doubt that Americans included them in their expectations for creating a
new era.

We now turn to these changes, organized as follows: political attitude change, change over time, and psychological coping.

Political Attitude Change

There can be little doubt that the Gulf War had an impact on Israeli public opinion. Israelis said so quite clearly. When asked about it in the 1991
survey, 29 percent said that the war had changed their opinion regarding the security and political situations. Seventy-one percent indicated
that their political positions had not changed as a result of the war.

The *net* effect of the change, however, was not clear. Half of those
who reported that they changed (15 percent of the total sample) said
that they were more ready for compromise regarding the territories than
before the war, but the other half (14 percent) said that they were less
ready than before for compromise. To confound matters even more, 29
percent said that their attitude regarding the territories had changed
due to the war; of those who reported change, 17 percent said they now
thought that the territories were more important to Israel's security, and

TABLE 9.1. Polarization and Vote Choice, March 1991 (percent)

Did the Gulf War change or did it not change your opinion regarding the security and political situation? If it did, would you say you became more moderate or more militant?[a]

	Left (8%)	Labor (20%)	Likud (36%)	Right (10%)	Religious (7%)	Decision (20%)	Total Respondents
More moderate	18	22	15	11	3	14	15
No change	79	66	68	66	90	75	71
More militant	4	12	17	23	7	11	14

And what about the importance of the territories for the country's security? Did the missiles fired from Iraq change or did they not change your opinon regarding the importance of the territories for the country's security? If they did, did you think the territories had become more important for the country's security, or did you think that they had become less important for Israel's security?[b]

	Left	Labor	Likud	Right	Religious	Decision	Total
More important	5	10	23	24	18	16	17
No change	76	71	67	70	76	73	71
Less important	19	19	11	7	6	11	12

a. Effective N = 1,052.
b. Effective N = 1,049.

12 percent said they were convinced by the war that the territories were less important than they had thought before. These differences are not statistically significant; what is important is that changes occurred in both directions and tended to cancel out each other.

Further analysis of those who reported change underscores the polarization that characterized Israeli politics in the 1980s (Arian, Talmud, and Hermann 1988) and that was accelerated by the war. Evidence of this polarization is seen clearly when the voting intention of those who reported that their attitudes changed is examined (see table 9.1). The more extreme the party of choice, the more likely the respondent was to report change in the direction of the pole of the party. That is, those with a left-leaning orientation were more likely to report change in attitude as a result of the war, and that change was most likely to be in a conciliatory direction. Respondents on the right similarly changed, but to even more militant positions. There was much evidence that opinion was further polarized as a result of the war; there was little evidence that the war caused many to shift from one side to the other.

Some numbers will illustrate the point. For those who reported that the war changed their opinion and that they would vote for the left-of-center Citizens Rights Movement, the ratio of change to a more moderate position compared to a more militant position was 12 to 1. For every Moledet voter (a right-wing party) who reported change in a moderate direction in the wake of the war, two Moledet voters said that

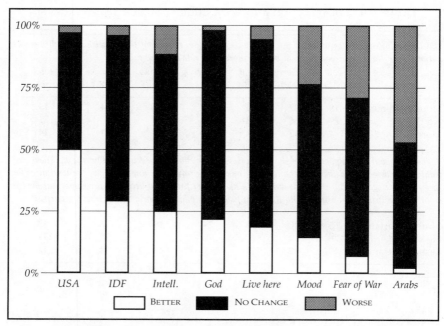

FIGURE 9.1. Effects of the Gulf War on Various Opinions

their attitudes were hardened on security and political matters as a result of the war. Labor voters who changed reported moving more in a
conciliatory direction at a rate of 2 to 1.

Two groups changed in a balanced manner; that is, those who reported that their attitudes became more conciliatory as a result of the
war were balanced in number by those who said that they became more
militant. The two groups were those who reported Likud as their voter
choice and the undecided. These are the two largest groups in the analysis (Likud 35 percent, undecided 20 percent). Their decisions and the
complexity of their patterns will likely have an important impact on the
future of Israeli politics.

When asked directly whether opinion had changed about other subjects, change was reported (see figure 9.1). The Israelis' opinion of the
United States improved dramatically after the war, with one of every
two respondents expressing an improved assessment. The image of the
Israel Defense Forces (IDF) and the intelligence community also improved in the public eye as a result of the war. Belief in God and the
desire to live in Israel also grew. Personal mood and the fear of war
changed for the worse; the evaluation of Arabs (Israeli citizens, territories residents, and Arabs in general) deteriorated in a striking manner.

Israel's deterrent capability was not damaged by the war, according to 72 percent of the sample. Sixty-four percent saw the IDF as the source of Israeli deterrence, 18 percent thought nuclear weapons, 11 percent the United States, 6 percent God, and 1 percent the United Nations. The vast majority of Israelis—85 percent—were satisfied or very satisfied with the government during the crisis.

Previous work has reported the strong connection between perceived threat and attitude and attitude change (Arian 1989). During the Gulf War, people reported feeling threatened by what was happening. Those who reported feeling *very* threatened on assorted security and nonsecurity issues follow:

- Nonconventional weapons in the hands of the Arabs, 76 percent.
- A nondemocratic regime in Israel, 66 percent.
- An equal number of Arabs and Jews in the country, 58 percent.
- Another war with the Arabs, 55 percent.
- A Palestinian state, 51 percent.
- The cessation of U.S. aid, 49 percent.
- A state based on Jewish religious law, 43 percent.
- Returning the territories, 36 percent.
- Separating state and religion, 12 percent.
- Mass Jewish immigration from the Soviet Union, 8 percent.

A number of points are of interest in this list. First, the fear of nonconventional weapons is striking, as is the fear that Israeli democracy, with all its blemishes, will be taken away. Strong fears, but slightly less strong, were generated by the issues of the Arabs and the territories. It is important to note that religious tensions, always near the surface of conflict in Israeli domestic political life, seemed to be of lesser magnitude in comparison to the threats posed by security and the loss of democracy. Least threatening was the prospect of absorbing the immigrants from the Soviet Union.

The higher one's anxiety during the war, the more likely one was to feel threatened both by nonconventional weapons in the hands of the Arabs and by another war with them.[5] Anxiety was not related to any of the other issues. More interesting is the relationship between some of these issues and the strength of one's belief that peace was possible in the near future. The more likely one believed that peace was possible in the near future, the more threatened one was by a nondemocratic regime in Israel, another war with the Arabs, or the threat of nonconventional weapons in the hands of the Arabs[6] and less threatened by the thought of a Palestinian state ($r = -.15$, $p = .000$, N = 1,098) and returning the territories ($r = -.15$, $p = .000$, N = 1098).[7]

Threats and fears notwithstanding, Israelis were certain of their ability (see figure 9.2) to overcome a war with Syria, terror and uprisings of

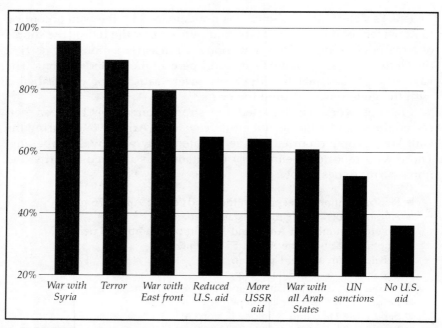

FIGURE 9.2. CONFIDENCE IN ISRAEL'S ABILITY TO OVERCOME CHALLENGES

Arabs under Israel's jurisdiction, and a war with the countries of the eastern front (Syria, Jordan, and Iraq). At a lower level, Israel could manage if the United States reduced aid, if the Soviet Union increased aid to its enemies, and if a war broke out with all Arab states. Half of the sample thought that Israel could overcome economic sanctions, even if supported by the United States; a third felt that Israel would get by if the United States stopped all aid.

Over the years, an important change has been observed: the specter of war with the entire Arab world has inspired decreasing confidence. In 1986 and 1987, three out of four Israelis were certain that the country could win such a war. In 1988, a year into the Intifada, the rate fell to 68 percent; by 1990 and 1991, it was down to 61 percent.

Change over Time

It is a truism that Israeli public life has been characterized since the 1970s by a near-even split between a more militant and a more conciliatory stand on the political and security issues related to the territories under Israel's control since the 1967 Six Days War (see Shamir 1986; Yishai 1987). But it is equally true that support for the more dovish positions has been growing over the past years. The Gulf War furthered this creeping conciliation.

The Israeli public is very sensitive to political developments, and the Gulf War affected public stances (Gutman 1978; Stone 1982). The issues we consider here are (1) war and peace, (2) the solutions regarding the future of the territories, (3) negotiations with the PLO and the establishment of a Palestinian state, (4) the use of nuclear weapons, and (5) the superpowers.[8]

War and Peace

In the period before the Gulf War, Israeli public opinion saw both the likelihood of war and the hope for peace (or the absence of war) grow as the years went by (see figure 9.3). After the war, the assessment that war was likely fell, as the chances of peace continued to grow. In 1987, 57 percent thought that war was probable or very probable between Israel and an Arab state in the following three years; by 1990, the rate had climbed to 68 percent; after the war, the corresponding number was only 54 percent. Peace, by contrast, was perceived as more likely as time went on. From 57 percent in 1986, the numbers rose dramatically until, after the war, more than three out of four respondents believed that peace was possible.[9]

If peace was increasingly possible, it was not because the perception of the aspirations of the Arabs moderated. The samples were asked about the aspirations of the Arabs toward Israel; in 1991, half the sample said they thought that ultimately the Arabs wanted to destroy Israel and kill Jews (see table 9.2). Yet, when forced to choose between initiating peace talks and strengthening military capacity, 74 percent in 1991 chose peace talks.

Solutions

There was a steady increase in the percentage of Israelis prepared to give up the territories for a peace treaty with appropriate security arrangements (see figure 9.3) (compare Katz 1989). The attitude about the future of the territories was measured by asking the respondents two questions. First, respondents were given a choice between exchanging land for peace, annexation of the territories, or "leaving things as they are." For those who would leave things as they are, a second question asked respondents to choose between returning and annexing. The forced-choice method is useful in ascertaining positions regarding very

TABLE 9.2. OPINIONS ON ASPIRATIONS OF THE ARABS AND
ISRAELI PREVENTION OF WAR, 1986–1991 (PERCENT)

What in your opinion are the aspirations of the Arabs in the final analysis?

	January 1986	December 1987	October 1988	March–October 1990	March 1991
To regain a part of the territories taken in the 1967 war	5	7	12	7	6
To regain all the territories taken in the 1967 war	22	23	27	21	21
To conquer Israel	36	31	29	28	23
To conquer Israel and to annihilate a large portion of the Jews in the country	37	39	33	45	49
Effective N	(1,145)	(1,094)	(854)	(1,228)	(1,105)
To prevent a war with the Arab countries, Israel should					
Try to initiate peace negotiations	64	68	64	64	74
Increase her military power	36	32	36	36	27
Effective N	(1,127)	(1,083)	(839)	(1,180)	(1,085)

complex issues; as we shall see below, however, we must not assume that respondents are consistent in their responses when faced with questions worded differently or asked in a very different political situation. Still, the constancy of the trend over time using identical wording clearly points to a process of moderation that applied to public opinion in Israel in the years studied. In 1986, before the Intifada, a little less than half of the population agreed to return the territories; by the end of the war, the number had risen to 58 percent. The population remained split, and the political system was unable to solve the problem decisively one way or the other, but the shift in public opinion was important, and it is likely that this gradual transformation will have an impact on policy and policy makers in the long run.

The PLO and a Palestinian State

One very emotional issue in Israeli politics has been the proposal to carry on negotiations with the Palestine Liberation Organization. Branded as a terrorist organization by the government, it was a crime for an Israeli citizen knowingly to have contact with a member of the organization. Still, there is strong evidence that the moderating trend in Israeli public opinion extends to this topic as well (see figure 9.3). The

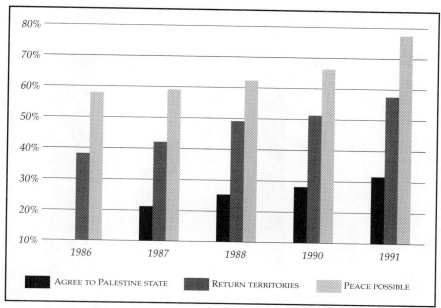

FIGURE 9.3. Expectations of War and Hopes for Peace

time series generated by Hanoch Smith shows that the acceptability of negotiations with the PLO, if it officially recognized Israel and ceased terrorist activity, moved from 43 percent in April 1987, through 53 percent in August 1988, to 58 percent in March 1989 (Brinkley 1989).

In 1991, after the war, the rate of support for negotiations with the PLO fell. This rate was below the pre-Intifada (before 1987) rate and is not surprising, considering that the PLO openly sided with Saddam Hussein and Iraq in the war. When confronted with a series of conditions in 1991, about half of the sample agreed to negotiations with the PLO; 51 percent persisted in their opposition regardless of the conditions described. Eight percent were willing to enter negotiations with the PLO if it recognized Israel, an additional 8 percent if it recognized Israel and renounced terror. For 13 percent more, the PLO would have to recognize Israel, renounce terror, and stop the Intifada. Twenty percent were willing to face the PLO in negotiations if it would recognize Israel, renounce terror, stop the Intifada, and rescind the PLO charter.

If the Palestine Liberation Organization had its support lowered as a result of the war, support for a major goal of the organization—establishing a Palestinian state—gained in favor. The rate of support generated was much lower, but the growth was steady and uniform and was not interrupted by the war (see figure 9.3).

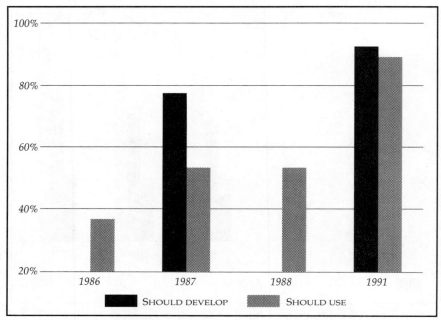

FIGURE 9.4. SUPPORT FOR NUCLEAR WEAPONS

In 1987, less than one in four respondents advanced the notion of a Palestinian state, while in 1991, the rate was one in three. It must be clearly stated that the large majority of Israelis rejected such a notion, with about half of the samples declaring that they *strongly* opposed the creation of a Palestinian state. Still, the increase in support was significant because the two large parties, the Likud and Labor, both spurned the idea.

Nuclear Weapons

The orientation of the public to the topic of nonconventional weapons and especially nuclear ones, was markedly affected by the war. There were three pieces of evidence of this shift: the change over time in the position of the public regarding the development and use of nuclear weapons, the attitudes expressed regarding arms control and limitation, and the perception of threat posed by such weapons. Support for developing nuclear capacity rose from 78 percent in 1987 to 91 percent in 1991. Tolerating use of nuclear arms went up dramatically: to 88 percent in 1991, from 53 percent in 1987 and 1988 and 36 percent in 1986 (see figure 9.4).

Most Israelis perceived the use of nuclear weapons to be appropriate as a tactic of last resort after an atomic attack by another country or following a chemical or biological attack. At a lower rate, about half the sample supported nuclear weapons use in a desperate situation or in order to save a large number of Israeli lives. At a much lower level was the support for using these weapons to save a small number of lives or in place of a conventional army. This order was the same as in 1986 and 1987, except that by 1991 the threshold of opposition to nuclear use had been lowered considerably. Israelis who experienced higher anxiety during the war were more likely to think that the use of nuclear weapons is never justified.[10]

Israelis like the idea of arms control regarding nonconventional weapons but felt much less so regarding conventional armies. They were willing to abandon all nonconventional weapons if the other countries of the region also did (75 percent). More (79 percent) were willing to give up chemical and biological nonconventional weapons (but not nuclear) if the other nations relinquished all of their nonconventional weapons (including nuclear ones).

On other arms control proposals, Israelis were less enthusiastic. Sixty-four percent supported preventing all outside arms supply to nations of the region. Sixty percent promoted enlarging demilitarized areas, but only 54 percent backed the plan to reduce the size of armies in the area.

The nuclear issue crystallized during the Gulf War. It represented the major threat identified by the public, and support for development and use grew. The conditions for use seemed to be clarified in the Israeli mind.

The Superpowers

As seen in figure 9.1, the way Israelis perceived the United States improved greatly in the wake of the war. Other indicators of that same trend were recorded by the following responses:

	1991	1990
Positive opinion of the United States	85%	73%
U.S.-Israel relations very good or good	82%	60%
U.S. security commitments reliable	64%	54%

The United States sees Israel as a strategic asset, and that is the main reason it supports Israel, according to 60 percent of the sample. An additional quarter attributed this to the shared values of democracy and freedom, while 13 percent attributed this support to the influence of American Jews. The new world order discussed by President Bush would work in Israel's favor, according to 39 percent.

The positions of Israeli Jews regarding American Jews were more mixed:

	1991	1990
American Jews would support Israel government policy very strongly or strongly	72%	58%
If there is a serious policy conflict, American Jews would side with Israel	59%	52%
American Jews can influence U.S. policy regarding the Arab-Israel conflict	50%	50%

By contrast, only 19 percent had a positive evaluation of the Soviet Union, although 75 percent thought there was a change for the better recently in that country's orientation toward the Arab-Israel conflict. A third thought the Soviet Union could have a major impact on the search for peace. According to 60 percent of the sample, the Soviet Union was active in the Arab-Israel conflict because it wanted to reestablish its influence in the Middle East, another 15 percent believed it was because the Soviets wanted to achieve peace, and 12 percent saw it as a way of cooperating with the United States.

Psychological Coping

Israelis understood that there were political, strategic, and tactical reasons for not entering the war. The sense of helplessness was nonetheless real as missiles rained down and foreigners were called upon for protection. The Gulf War was not long lasting, but the uncertainties of when the country would be attacked and whether Saddam could deliver chemical warheads were primary sources of fear.[11]

The connection between helplessness (of which uncertainty is a part) and stress has been thoroughly documented. Psychologists have demonstrated a consistent relationship between an increase in stress and an event as bland as uncertainty regarding the exact conditions under which a mild electric shock will be delivered. In addition to increased stress, a decrease in tolerance for mild pain was reported. While these feelings can be produced in minutes, they are also readily reversed. Of course, when the uncertainty is greater and sustained over long periods of time, and the threat of possible death is implied, the effects are greatly increased (see Seligman 1975; also see Garber and Seligman 1980).

While the Gulf War was relatively short, Israelis were certainly under stress. In a survey done during the war, two-thirds of those interviewed reported having more fear than before. Women, more than men, expressed high levels of fear and low morale, people with children expressed higher levels of fear, and, not surprisingly, residents of the Tel Aviv area expressed higher levels of fear than residents in the rest of the country. During the war, of those who said they felt "much more fear," 98 percent were women.[12] In a survey done four weeks after the war, 78 percent reported having felt personally endangered, and 70 percent reported having more anxiety than usual. Sixty-one percent of Israelis thought Saddam would use chemical weapons. And when asked if unconventional weapons in the hands of the Arab states represented a threat to them, three-quarters of Israelis responded "to a great extent" and another 20 percent responded "to a certain extent."

In addition, reported behavior during the war was indicative of a group that felt very threatened. When asked if they went into their sealed rooms and wore their gas masks during the missile attacks, 65 percent said they always did and another 30 percent said they sometimes did.

Saddam kept insisting that he would destroy Israel. Did Israelis believe that he meant what he said? The great majority did. A month after the end of the war, Israelis reported that when the missiles started falling they believed that Saddam was out to get them. Two-thirds agreed "to a great extent" that Saddam was out to get them "as a Jew," and three-quarters believed both that he was out to get them "as an Israeli," and as "the Jewish people." Only a very small percentage did not think Saddam was out to get them as a Jew (11 percent), as an Israeli (5 percent), or as the Jewish people (6 percent).

More important, when asked to what extent they thought Saddam was out to get "you personally," 30 percent agreed "to a great extent," another 31 percent agreed—although with less intensity—and 38 percent responded "not at all." The "you personally" question generated a very different distribution from the others; considering the extreme nature of the question, this is a dramatic finding (see figure 9.5). In addition, because it was distributed across the entire spectrum of Israeli society—men and women, religious and nonreligious, married and single, those living in Tel Aviv and those living elsewhere—it is even more noteworthy.[13] The response to this question gives a strong sense of the stress Israelis were under during the Gulf War.

What helped Israelis cope? Did they change their attitudes, behavior, or beliefs in order to be able to deal with their fears and anxieties during the Gulf War? Were there differences between the ways in which men and women, religious and nonreligious, young and old coped.

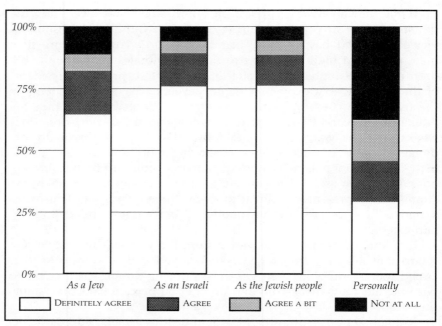

FIGURE 9.5. To What Extent Is Saddam Out to Get You?

There is little doubt that the extraordinarily low casualty rate helped Israelis cope with the situation—and paved the way for some Israelis to turn to religion in one form or another. It was an event that was very difficult to explain logically or on the basis of past experience. When missiles fall, people die. But in Israel that sequence did not hold. In Israel, missiles fell, there was extensive destruction, people's homes collapsed on them and around them—but almost no one died.

How did the Israelis explain this to themselves? Two weeks after the war, when asked to what extent they agreed that the low rate of casualties was a miracle, 38 percent "certainly agreed" and another 32 percent "agreed."[14] When asked if "as a result of what you went through you became more believing or more religious," 10 percent said they became much more religious, and another 17 percent said they became a little more religious. When asked about their belief in God, 22 percent reported that it became stronger. Six weeks after the war, in answer to the same question, the results were almost the same, with 19 percent reporting that belief in God became stronger as a result of the crisis.

For religious respondents, the low rate of casualties was strongly associated with a miraculous event. When asked to what extent they agreed with the statement that the low rate of casualties was a miracle, 90 percent of religious Jews responded that they agreed (65 percent "definitely agreed" and 25 percent "agreed").

In an attempt to define some of the boundaries that Israelis place on the relationship between the sacred and the profane, a series of questions that included both concepts was asked. Not surprisingly, for the religious there was a relationship between the extent to which one agreed that the low rate of casualties was a miracle and the extent to which one agreed that "God will take care of us, if we are worthy, even if we are not prepared for the next war," that "Israel is, and will continue to be, a nation dwelling alone," and that "the guardian of Israel will neither slumber nor sleep."[15] And yet when asked who was the guardian of Israel, only half of the religious responded that it was God. Thirty-three percent of the religious responded that the Israel Defense Forces (IDF) was the guardian of Israel. While it seems that the more observant religions relied heavily on God for protection, it is also the case that for the religious in Israel there was an important mix between the miraculous and the mundane.

That mix, with somewhat different proportions, was evident for the secular as well. When nonreligious Jews were asked to what extent they agreed that the low rate of casualties was a miracle, 65 percent agreed (27 percent definitely agreed, and 35 percent agreed). And, like the religious, there was also a relationship between the extent to which one agreed that the low rate of casualties was a miracle and the extent to which one agreed that "God will take care of us, if we are worthy, even if we are not prepared for the next war" and that "Israel is, and will continue to be, a nation dwelling alone."[16]

But regarding hard-core reality, the miraculous lost ground with the nonreligious. When the nonreligious were asked who is the guardian of Israel, only 12 percent responded God. Sixty-five percent of the secular responded that the IDF was the guardian of Israel. A breakdown of the entire sample by amount of observance makes the relationship even clearer. The more observant one was, the more likely one was to name God as the guardian of Israel, and vice versa for the IDF.

Seventy percent of those who reported that they observed religious tradition completely said that God is the guardian of Israel; the same percentage of those who did not observe the tradition at all said that the IDF was the guardian of Israel. The general pattern persisted with some small changes; all groups generated an increase in the percentage who chose God and a decrease in those who chose the IDF (see figure 9.6).

The decrease in the percentage of those who selected the IDF may be due to the Intifada and the trouble the army had in coping with it, but can we say that the increase in the percentage of those who selected God was due to the war in the Gulf? While the high percentage of secular who believed that the low rate of casualties was a miracle provides some support for this interpretation, there were other indicators as well.

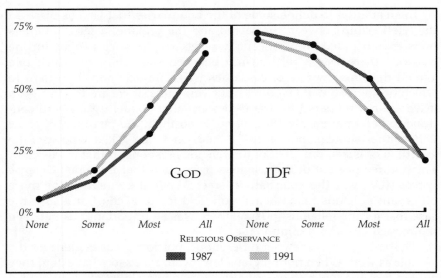

FIGURE 9.6. Who Is the Guardian of Israel?

Five weeks into the war, Israelis were asked whether they said more private prayers that day than before the war. Thirty-five percent of all respondents replied yes—itself an impressive finding. Half of the religious reported an increase in private prayer, but what is far more interesting is the fact that one-third of the nonreligious also reported an increase in private prayer. Breaking the sample down by gender, 37 percent of women and 30 percent of men reported an increase. Having children did not make a difference. Thirty-six percent of those who had children and 34 percent of those without reported an increase. Nor did living in Tel Aviv or Haifa or elsewhere make much of a difference. Thirty-six percent of those living in the Tel Aviv area, 34 percent of those living in Haifa, and 34 percent of those living elsewhere reported an increase in private prayer.

Israelis were also asked whether, during the time of the crisis, they observed more of the tradition. Were they, for example, lighting candles or blessing the wine before the Sabbath? Eighteen percent of the sample replied that they were. When broken down, we find that 39 percent of the religious and 15 percent of the secular said they observed more of the tradition during the crisis, 22 percent of females and 12 percent of males, 19 percent of those with children and 17 percent of those without, and 18 percent of those living in the Tel Aviv area, 11 percent of those living in Haifa, and 21 percent of those living in the rest of the country replied that they were observing more of the tradition.

Not all of those who reported an increase in observance also reported an increase in private prayer. Over a third of those who reported an increase in religious observance did not report an increase in their private prayers. Combining the results of both questions, 42 percent of the sample reported an increase either in private prayer or traditional observance or both. And breaking that figure down, two-thirds of the religious and a bit more than one-third of the secular reported some form of increase.

One possible reason why Israelis are very good at living with clear danger is their ability to push away fear and anxiety. Data from the three war surveys provide strong demonstration of this ability. In the survey done during the war, 12 percent reported having much more fear. In the survey done two weeks after the war, 22 percent reported having had much more anxiety. In the survey done six weeks after the war, 33 percent reported having had much more anxiety. While it is important to note that the question used during the war asked about "fear" and the question in the two other surveys asked about "anxiety," nevertheless the results are striking. Even if we consider only the results of the two surveys after the war, which used the identical question, the increase was substantial and provided an important contrast to the consistency of the results over time regarding the question of increase in belief. During the crisis it was most important to have as positive an attitude as possible and to go on with life as normally as possible. This notion is an important norm into which children in Israel are socialized at an early age; in addition, it is usually good psychological advice. Keeping busy gives one less time to concentrate on feelings.

Behaving as normally as possible helps one feel as normal as possible—instead of feeling afraid. The mayor of Tel Aviv who "ordered" the people in his city to stay put and to go to work and get on with their lives was undoubtedly articulating this norm. But when the crisis ended and life returned to normal, with more and more distance from the event Israelis allowed themselves to acknowledge how they really felt during the war.

When missiles started falling on the Tel Aviv and Haifa areas, some in these areas left their homes. This was facilitated by the government's decision to close the schools and most of the economy. Estimates of the numbers of people who actually left vary widely, but based on our survey, less than one in five of those who were in dangerous areas reported that they left those areas, at least occasionally, because of the attacks. A public uproar ensued when some, and especially Tel Aviv Mayor Shlomo ("Chich") Lahat, declared that those who left town during the missile attacks were "deserters." Later he hedged by exempting families with young children from that epithet. But the question of whether this judgmental standard should be applied to a civilian population under attack became a major topic of discussion for a population that had little else to do than wait for the next attack. In fact, the large majority of Israelis rejected the position. Seven out of ten Israelis strongly disagreed with calling those who left endangered areas "deserters," and another 12 percent disagreed to a certain extent. Only one in five agreed or strongly agreed with the term.

The notion that many people turn to God in moments of extreme anxiety is an old one, well documented in anecdotes, in literature, and by social scientists. We know, for example, that there is a relationship between secure feelings of attachment—a strong permanent bond—between oneself and another and the diminishment of the fear of one's death. People who are secure, as opposed to those who are insecure, tend to be less fearful of danger because they do not feel alone in the existential reality of smallness, finitude, and helplessness.[17] It is not difficult to extend this argument to the relationship between humans and God.

We found a consistent, although not very strong, relationship between the level of fear or anxiety and religious behavior. During the war, of those who reported having much more fear, 50 percent reported an increase in private prayer and almost a third an increase in religious behavior. Of those who reported feeling no fear, a third reported an increase in private prayer and 12 percent an increase in religious behavior. Four weeks after the war, of those who felt "much more anxiety," 36 percent reported that they became more religious; of those who felt "more anxiety," 28 percent became more religious; and of those who reported "no change" in anxiety, only 16 percent became more religious. Those who agreed that the low number of casualties was a miracle went up as the level of anxiety went up (see figure 9.7).

Six weeks after the war, of those who felt personally endangered "to a great degree," one quarter reported stronger belief in God; of those who felt in danger "to a certain degree," 19 percent reported stronger belief; and of those who did not feel in personal danger at all only 10 percent reported an increase in belief. Although the percentages varied from question to question, the relationship between higher levels of fear or anxiety and an increase in belief or religious behavior was clear.

Interestingly, while the level of anxiety was not related to one's belief that Saddam was out to get you as a Jew, as an Israeli, or as the Jewish people, it was related to the belief that Saddam was out to get you *personally*. Of those who "agreed to a great degree" that Saddam was out to get them personally, almost half had much more anxiety, one-third had more anxiety, and only one-fifth of the sample reported no change in anxiety (see figure 9.7).

Saddam's repeated threats to destroy Israel were seen as part of a harsh reality, and therefore responses to the statements that Saddam

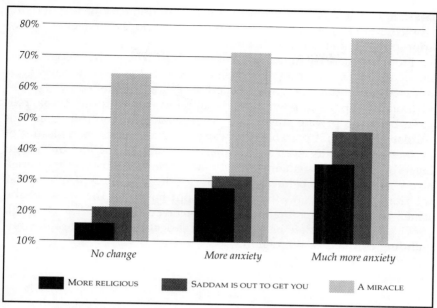

FIGURE 9.7. LEVEL OF ANXIETY AND RELIGIOUS ATTITUDES

was out to get you as an Israeli, as a Jew, or as the Jewish people apparently had a rational, rather than an emotional, basis and were not related to anxiety. On the other hand, agreement with the statement that Saddam was out to get you personally, an obviously irrational and profoundly emotional statement, was related to one's level of anxiety.

Conclusion

The Gulf War, Saddam Hussein, and his missiles and threats to destroy the country were another chapter in Israel's history of coping with challenges. This crisis was especially intense, but the mechanisms discussed here have long been in the repertoire of Israeli reactions.

No political solution sprang from the war, and evidence of further polarization of attitudes was documented. On the other hand, the slow motion of aggregate opinion in a conciliatory direction may well be a factor that will have an impact on Israeli politics in the long run.

Peace was considered possible by an overwhelming fraction of Israelis, and this, in the long-term perspective, is a dramatic change. The reality of nonconventional weapons entered the public consciousness as a result of the war, both in terms of high levels of anxiety regarding their possible use against Israel and in the striking increase of respondents who could imagine that the use of nuclear weapons by Israel would be appropriate under certain conditions.

From the increase in the number of Israelis who acknowledged feeling more anxiety during the crisis, powerful forces may have been released. Level of anxiety was related to feeling threatened by nonconventional weapons in enemy hands, another war with the Arabs, religious behavior, private prayer, and personalizing the confrontation with Saddam Hussein; if possible, the war and its aftermath made issues of politics and security even more salient in Israeli public life. Such high levels of perceived threat and anxiety may express themselves in aggressive and belligerent behavior; but considering the present monopolar international world and the creeping conciliation of the views of the Israeli public, perhaps high levels of perceived threat and anxiety will provide the appropriate background for peaceful settlement of the outstanding conflicts of the region.

NOTES

1. For a discussion of these issues, see Kastenbaum and Aisenberg (1972) and Zilboorg (1943).

2. The planning of the Israel Defense Forces anticipated an average of three to five deaths for each conventional missile. See Ben-Meir (1991).

3. Surveys reported in this chapter questioned representative samples of the adult Jewish population of Israel, not including individuals from kibbutzim or from the territories taken by Israel in the 1967 Six Days War. Sample sizes were 1,172 in 1986; 1,116 in 1987; 873 in 1988; 1,251 in 1990; 426 on February 20–21, 1991, during the war; 1,131 on March 14–21, 1991, two weeks after the cessation of hostilities; and 405 on March 26–27, 1991, a month after the cessation of hostilities.

The 1986, 1987, 1988, 1990, and March 14–21, 1991, surveys were prepared and conducted by the National Security and Public Opinion Project of the Jaffee Center for Strategic Studies at Tel Aviv University, directed by Asher Arian. The February 20–21, 1991, survey was designed by Mina Zemach, and the March 26–27, 1991, survey was authored by Carol Gordon. The fieldwork for all surveys was done by the Dahaf Research Institute, headed by Dr. Mina Zemach.

4. See Mueller (1973); for an example from the Israeli literature, see Keis (1975).

5. The correlations were .11 and .17, respectively. For both, $p = .000$, $N = 1,089$.

6. The correlations were .14, .11, and .11, respectively. For all, $p = .000$, $N = 1,089$.

7. The correlations were both $-.15$, $p = .000$, $N = 1,098$.

8. The pattern of incremental growth of responses that can be considered moderate was constant and has also been found based on analysis of panel data. See Arian, Shamir, and Ventura (1992).

9. For a comparison with European countries, see Rabier, Riffault, and Inglehart (1986).

10. The relevant statistics were $t = 1.95$, $p = .05$.

11. Dr. Reuven Gal of the Israel Institute for Military Studies reports that the results of a survey done during the war show that the primary source of fear for 40 to 50 percent of the population was uncertainty and the second was gas. Quoted in Ashkenazy (1991).

12. Statistical analyses between men and women, those with and without children, and those who live in Tel Aviv compared with those who live elsewhere show that, overall, women, those with children, and those who live in Tel Aviv had significantly higher fear. On a scale from 1 to 4, with 1 being greatest fear, the average for women was 2.5 and for men was 3.4. A t-test of differences between means resulted in a t score of 9.52. The difference between those with children (mean = 2.6) and those without (mean = 2.9) was smaller ($t = 2.6$, $p = .01$) but still significant. There was also a significant difference ($t = 3.4$, $p = .001$) between those who live in Tel Aviv (mean = 2.6) and those who live elsewhere (mean = 3.0).

In the psychological literature of fear of death it has been shown that women tend to have significantly higher fear than men. See for example, Ungar, Florian, and Zernitsky-Shurka (1990).

13. In each survey the following question was asked: To what extent do you keep the religious tradition? Possible answers were (1) every detail, (2) to a great extent, (3) a little bit, and (4) not at all. In the following analyses, *religious* is the combination of those who responded 1 and 2 and *nonreligious* is the combination of those who responded 3 and 4.

14. The Pearson correlation for the entire sample, between level of observance and agreement with the statement that the low rate of casualties was a miracle, indicates a strong relationship ($r = .41$, $p = .000$, $N = 1,092$).

15. The correlations were .30, .23, and .26, respectively. For all, $p = .000$, $N = 300$. These questions are discussed more completely in Arian (1989).

16. The correlations were .32 and .19, respectively. For both, $p = .000$; the N was 775 for the former, 300 for the latter.

17. This discussion is based on Mikulincer, Florian, and Tolmacz (1990).

REFERENCES

Arian, Asher, 1989. "A People Apart: Coping with National Security Problems in Israel. *Journal of Conflict Resolution* 33: 605–31.

Arian, Asher, Michael Shamir, and Raphael Ventura. 1992. "Public Opinion and Political Change: Israel and the Intifada." *Comparative Politics* 24 (3): 317–34.

Arian, Asher, Ilan Talmud, and Tamar Hermann. 1988. *National Security and Public Opinion in Israel.* Boulder: Westview.

Ashkenazy, Daniella. 1991. "All Quiet on the Home Front." *Jerusalem Post,* March 3.

Avgar, A. 1991. "Lessons from the Gulf War: What Price Did Women Pay?" *Na'amat Woman* (September): 29.

Beu-Meir, Yehuda. 1991. "The Effect of the War on the Home Front." In *The Strategic Implications for Israel of the Gulf War*, ed. Yosef Alpher. Tel Aviv: Am Oved. In Hebrew.

Brinkley, Joel. 1989. "Majority in Israel Oppose P.L.O. Talks Now, a Poll Shows." *New York Times*, April 2.

Feifel, H. 1959. *The Meaning of Death*. New York: McGraw-Hill.

Garber, Judy, and Martin Seligman, eds. 1980. *Human Helplessness: Theory and Applications*. New York: Academic Press.

Gutman, Louis, 1978. *The Israeli Public, Peace and Territory: The Impact of the Sadat Initiative*. Jerusalem: Jerusalem Institute for Federal Studies.

Kastenbaum, A., and R. Aisenberg. 1972. *The Psychology of Death*. New York: Springer.

Katz, Elihu. 1989. "Majority Hawkish, but Dovish Trend Seen." *Jerusalem Post International Edition*, February 18.

Keis, Naomi. 1975. "The Influence of Public Policy on Public Opinion—Israel 1967–1974." *State, Government and International Relations* 8: 36–53.

McGuire, W. J. 1985. "Attitudes and Attitude Change." In *Handbook of Social Psychology*, ed. G. Lindzey and E. Aronson. New York: Random House.

Mikulincer, Mario, Victor Florian, and Rami Tolmacz. 1990. "Attachment Styles and Fear of Personal Death: A Case Study of Affect Regulation." *Journal of Personality and Social Psychology* 58: 273–80.

Mueller, J. E. 1973. *War, Presidents, and Public Opinion*. New York: Wiley.

Rabier, Jacques, M. Riffault, and Ronald Inglehart. 1986. *Euro-Barometer 24*. Ann Arbor: Inter-University Consortium for Political and Social Research.

Seligman, Martin. 1975. *Helplessness: On Depression, Development, and Death*. San Francisco: W. H. Freeman.

Shamir, Michael, 1986. "Realignment in the Israeli Party System." In *The Elections in Israel—1984*, ed. Asher Arian and Michael Shamir. New Brunswick: Transaction Books.

Stone, Russell A. 1982. *Social Change in Israel: Attitudes and Events 1967–1979*. New York: Praeger.

Templer, D. 1982. "Death Anxiety: Extroversion, Neuroticism, and Cigarette Smoking." *Omega* 3: 53–56.

Ungar, Lea, Victor Florian, and Esther Zernitsky-Shurka. 1990. "Aspects of Fear of Personal Death, Levels of Awareness, and Professional Affiliation Among Dialysis Unit Staff Members." *Omega* 21: 52–67.

Yishai, Yael. 1987. *Land or Peace: Whither Israel?* Stanford: Hoover Institution.

Zilboorg, G. 1943. "Fear of Death." *Psychoanalytic Quarterly* 12: 465–75.

COMMENTARY ON PART IV

The Reaction of Mass Publics
to the Gulf War

■

Herbert C. Kelman

THE GULF WAR was a landmark event for all three of the publics discussed in the preceding three chapters. For Americans, it was the first
war in the post–cold war era: the first time since the end of World War
II that the United States engaged in a war that reflected the new role of
the country in the global system. For Israelis, it was the first war in
which their country did not attack or counterattack but—for political
reasons—essentially had to remain passive in the face of the aerial attacks against its population centers. For Arabs, while it was not the first
time that Arab states confronted each other militarily (that had already
happened in Yemen), it was the first time that major Arab states joined
forces with the United States and other Western powers to fight another
Arab state.

Yet, from the evidence presented in these three chapters, it appears
that the war did not produce major shifts in public opinion—at least as
recorded by opinion polls in the United States and Israel or as manifested by public demonstrations in the Arab world. There is no question
that the war had a powerful impact on all three of these publics, but this
did not seem to translate into measurable and observable changes in relevant political attitudes. The absence of such a shift is a central feature
of John Mueller's message. Asher Arian and Carol Gordon do not explicitly make this point, but the findings they present show mostly a
continuation of earlier trends, rather than major shifts in attitude. Finally, Shibley Telhami emphasizes that the widely predicted upheavals
in the Middle East following the defeat of Iraq did not materialize—at
least not thus far.

The lack of evidence for major shifts in public opinion does not
necessarily mean that the Gulf War had no significant impact on collective attitudes. It may well be that changes have occurred, but that they
cannot be readily picked up by the methods used in the present
analyses. For example, comparative analysis of poll data over time may

251

fail to reveal changes that involve the development of new assumptive frameworks. It may be that such changes can be captured only by asking new kinds of questions, since the questions repeated from past polls are derived from the old assumptive frameworks. Such a phenomenon would be consistent with the way in which changes in ideologically rooted attitudes and beliefs generally manifest themselves: they do not necessarily lead to a rapid abandonment of the old attitudes and beliefs but to the gradual development of new ones alongside of the old. If this is what is happening, then the old questions may continue to elicit the old answers, and it would take new questions to provide evidence of change.

When public opinion is assessed by public behavior—such as mass demonstrations—rather than by opinion polls, as in Telhami's analysis of public opinion in the Arab countries, there are other reasons why changes in public thinking may not be reflected in the evidence examined. There is, as Telhami points out, a complex relationship between public opinion, public behavior, and state policy. State policy and regional events have an impact on the shaping of public opinion and particularly on the translation of such opinion into public behavior, such as mass demonstrations. Thus, important changes in public sentiments may be brewing without being fully articulated and certainly without manifesting themselves in collective actions.

There is another reason, apart from methodological considerations, why the lack of evidence for major shifts in public opinion does not necessarily suggest that the war had no significant impact on public thinking. It is quite possible that changes produced by landmark events, such as the Gulf War was for the three populations under consideration here, take some time to crystallize into coherent new attitudes. Thus, it may be too early for these new attitudes to be observed in poll data or in collective actions.

My own speculation is that the Gulf War did have a significant impact on public thinking in the United States, Israel, and the Arab world. For all three of the populations, the war has thrown into question some of the old assumptions about the world in which they live. It will take some time before a new set of assumptions fully evolves and reshapes public opinion about the range of issues relating to war and peace and to the global and regional roles of each society.

The three chapters provide useful insights into the assumptions that the Gulf War has thrown into question within each of the three societies and into the new directions that each public opinion may take—depending, of course, on state policies and regional events. To highlight some of these issues, let me comment on each of the chapters in order.

American Public Opinion

In reacting to John Mueller's analysis, I raise and partly address three questions: What does the analysis tell us about the U.S. public's support for the war? What do the poll data suggest about the lessons the public learned from the war? And, can public opinion data help us sort out some of the ambiguities in American policy?

Public Support for the War

My reading of the data reviewed by John Mueller supports my earlier impression that, until January 16, 1991, American public support for the Gulf War was fairly thin. My informal impression was based on such observations as the reactions of military families to the call-up of troops. One could hear on the media many public expressions of concern about the comfort and safety of the men and women who were being sent to Saudi Arabia. This is not the kind of reaction that one would expect to hear—at least in a public forum—when a military action is clearly seen as essential to the well-being of the nation.

Various poll data, marshaled by Mueller, suggest that the public was almost evenly divided about the war. The public division reflected a division in Congress and expressed itself in the early mobilization of an antiwar movement—quite in contrast to what happened in the early days of the Vietnam War. A number of indicators show that, after an initial rise in August, there was a steady decline in public support for the war during the fall of 1990. The percentages supporting the war depended quite a bit on the particular wording of the question. Questions that asked about American casualties suggest clearly that support for the war would decline rapidly as casualties rose.

I found particularly interesting the attitude toward compromise expressed by the public. In light of the administration's equation of negotiation with compromise and of compromise with appeasement and surrender, it is not surprising that the majority of Americans in different polls opposed compromise or negotiations. But, despite that negative image of compromise and negotiations, the public turned out to be quite selective in its responses. For example, in a poll conducted in November 1990, when people were presented with the choice of compromise with Saddam Hussein or starting a war, 58 percent of the respondents chose compromise. In a December poll, when people were presented with a choice between military force and an agreement with some concessions to Iraq on the control of the disputed oil fields (in other words, an agreement that was probably perceived as a "reasonable" compromise), a majority favored such an agreement. In a poll conducted January 11–13, 1991, a plurality considered it acceptable to end the crisis if Kuwait offered to trade a piece of its territory in return for Iraq's withdrawal from the rest of Kuwait (see chapter 8, note 4). In short, despite President Bush's consistent rejection of the very idea of concession, compromise, or negotiation, the public seemed willing to accept a negotiated agreement if (1) the cost of the alternative was seen as too high, and (2) the concessions did not seem to violate important principles.

It is evident from Mueller's analysis that the public was not driving the country to war but rather was being led to it. Furthermore, the media played a major role in leading the public to war. The media were not catering to public preferences but were essentially serving the administration in advocating the war. Mueller concludes that, if the war had gone badly, the media would probably have become critical—but, as in the Vietnam War, they would probably have followed, rather than led, the public discontent.

All of these indicators of a divided and halfhearted public are based on polls prior to January 16, 1991. At that point, there was a major shift in public opinion toward strong support for the war effort. This response can almost certainly be explained in terms of the phenomenon of rallying around the flag—of supporting the president and the troops—once the war was begun (and had not yet gone sour). An important part of this process was a tendency to suppress or discredit dissenting views. Here again, the media played an important role, as evidenced by their choice of commentators and by their tendency to ignore antiwar protest and underreport major demonstrations.

A second significant shift in public opinion came with the coalition victory. At that point, the war became highly popular—which suggests that the American public may not particularly like war, but it does like victory. As time went on, however, positive attitudes toward the war began to decline, since the victory was clearly not as glorious as it originally appeared to be. Saddam Hussein is still in power; he has crushed the rebellions against his regime; he continues to oppress his population; and the only people in Iraq who are not suffering are the very ones against whom the war was directed. Thus, the euphoria experienced at the moment of victory has given way to disappointment, reflected in a decline in retrospective support for the war.

Lessons Learned from the War

Some positive lessons may have been learned from this war, such as the need for collective security arrangements and international response to aggression. I am more impressed, however, with the danger that the war may have taught the U.S. public, as well as other publics, some wrong and humanly harmful lessons. Let me mention a few such potential lessons and ask whether existing or future public opinion data can inform us about the extent to which they have in fact been drawn by the American public in response to the Gulf War.

First Lesson: The use of superior military force, rather than negotiation, diplomacy, and conflict resolution, is the way to deal with international crises. From the data reported by Mueller, I conclude that the public has not fully bought this view, even though it was vigorously promoted by the Bush administration in response to the Gulf crisis.

Second Lesson: Politicians make themselves more vulnerable by opposing a war than by supporting it. In the first few months after the war, the behavior of Democratic politicians who had opposed the war suggested that this was precisely the lesson they had learned. A year later, as memory of the victory began to fade and the negative consequences and inconclusive outcome of the war became increasingly clear, early opposition to the war seemed to become fairly irrelevant. Nevertheless, it is important to know whether the public has tended to discredit politicians who had opposed the war and to subject them to electoral punishment.

Third Lesson: The human costs on the enemy side count for very little in the determination of the cost-benefit ratio for engaging in war. The data reviewed by Mueller indicate that, while the cost of American lives was a major deterrent to the support of war, cost of Iraqi lives was not. (Mueller concludes that, in the view of the U.S. public, one American life is worth at least twenty Iraqi lives.) It would be useful to assess public thinking on this issue in the aftermath of the war. The cost in enemy lives remains one of the big untold stories of the war, and the continuing secrecy has helped to suppress public debate about the issue.

Fourth Lesson: The United States can achieve glory, regain its self-respect, overcome the Vietnam syndrome, and once again feel pride by successfully launching a high-technology war against a Third World country, with a kill ratio of almost 1,000 to 1. The issue of glorifying the war is independent of the question of whether the war was justified or necessary; one can consider the war justified and necessary and yet deeply regret its human cost. There are indications that the sense of pride and self-glorification has evaporated, but we need to learn much more about the long-run effects of this lesson.

Fifth Lesson: The United States can establish its world leadership in the post–cold war era through its status as the only remaining superpower, the supreme military force, and the only country with the massive, high-technology military capability that was so conspicuously displayed in Iraq. What is implied here is the advocacy of a new world order based on American hegemony. It will be important to find out whether this concept appeals to wide segments of the American public or only to a narrow band of our political elite.

Ambiguities in American Policy

I approach the discussion of American public opinion toward the war from the perspective of a basically unreconstructed opponent of the war. My opposition to the war was not based on the feeling that the cause was unjust; indeed, I believed from the beginning that it was important to respond vigorously to Saddam Hussein's aggression. But I believed that the decision to go to war was flawed because (1) it did not take account of the full array of the costs of military intervention, and (2) it gave no serious consideration to alternatives short of military action, particularly to the possibilities of negotiating an agreement.

Little has happened to change my view that the decision to go to war in January 1991 was flawed. Yet the arguments are not all on one side of the ledger. A number of ambiguities about the costs and benefits of American policy need to be addressed in our retrospective analysis of the war and the decision-making process that led up to it. Public opinion data cannot settle any of the issues, but they can provide some useful inputs into the debate.

Since a major source of my criticism of American policy in the Gulf crisis is that we did not give negotiations a chance, I have to confront the question of whether negotiations could have worked. I cannot say with great conviction that negotiations would have succeeded, particularly as I look at Saddam Hussein's behavior in defeat—for example, his intransigence in response to United Nations efforts to ferret out his nuclear capacities and plans. But the fact remains that negotiations were not tried, and so we cannot say with any degree of certainty that they would *not* have succeeded.

I definitely reject the a fortiori argument that some analysts present in this connection: since military force did not persuade Saddam Hussein to react reasonably, sanctions or negotiations certainly could not have done so. This argument assumes a unidimensionality of political effectiveness, with military force at the top of the scale. This is precisely the assumption that I challenge. Negotiations have their own dynamic, and we cannot dismiss out of hand the possibility that creative diplomacy could have achieved an Iraqi withdrawal from Kuwait—which is, after all, the point at which President Bush ended the military action. Thus, as Mueller suggests, Iraqi withdrawal from Kuwait could have been accomplished at a much lower human cost, whether through sanctions, through negotiations, or, as I believe, through a combination of the two. I find very heartening in this connection the public opinion data already cited that indicate a willingness to consider a reasonable compromise that does not violate fundamental principles. What is particularly remarkable here is that the public did not reject the option of a negotiated compromise despite the president's concerted effort to equate negotiation and compromise with appeasement and surrender.

While it is quite possible that negotiations could have achieved an Iraqi withdrawal from Kuwait, they could not have achieved Saddam Hussein's removal from power. But, as we now know, military action did not achieve that end either. Saddam Hussein's oppressive regime remains in power and continues to stifle all opposition and sacrifice the welfare of the Iraqi population to the cause of its own survival. The failure to topple Hussein and to support the rebellion raises another kind of ambiguity. Could it be argued perhaps that the war was stopped too soon? Even some initial opponents of military action have felt that, once we started the war, we should have seen it to completion—at least to the point of safeguarding the uprisings that we had encouraged. I cannot accept this view, particularly when I contemplate the likely consequences of an American march on Baghdad and occupation of Iraq. Instead, I share the ambivalence about the endgame of this war that is displayed in the public opinion data: frustration about the state of affairs imposed on Iraq with the ending of the war, but no inclination to argue that we should have continued and expanded the military operation. There are no satisfactory answers to the ambiguities created by the way the war was ended, but these ambiguities illustrate the administration's failure to consider the costs and limitations of the military option before embracing it over all other alternatives.

While the war has not so far loosened Saddam Hussein's domestic control, it has clearly weakened him as a regional actor and as a military threat to neighboring states. It is unclear how effective negotiations would have been in this regard—whether, for example, they would have led to the dismantling of Iraq's nuclear capacity that is now taking place under UN pressure. I am not prepared to say that negotiations were completely incapable of achieving a comparable outcome at a far smaller cost, but I have to concede that the containment of Iraq's buildup of conventional and nonconventional weapons represents a positive contribution of the Gulf War. At the same time, some of the negative regional consequences that opponents of the war had feared have not so far materialized. Thus, there have been no major popular upheavals in the Arab states that joined the anti-Iraq coalition and no indication that the regimes have been destabilized as a result of the war. Telhami discusses some of the possible reasons for this state of affairs and also reminds us that the verdict is not yet entirely in. Similarly, there is no evidence that the standing of the United States in the Middle East or its ability to broker an Arab-Israeli peace agreement has been

impaired. Indeed, the new status that the United States has achieved in
the aftermath of the Gulf War seems to have increased the administration's incentive and capacity to push the Arab-Israeli peace process forward. American public opinion gives the administration high points for
its peacemaking efforts—and, despite some reservations, I share this
assessment. How successful this effort will ultimately be depends in
part on Israeli and Arab public opinion in the wake of the Gulf War.

Israeli Public Opinion

The starting point for Arian and Gordon's analysis of the impact of the
Gulf War on the Israeli public is the question of how this war differed
from Israel's prior wars in the eyes of the population. Three major differences emerge. First, this was the first war in which Israeli population
centers were seriously threatened. In fact, as Arian and Gordon note,
there was no battle front—only a home front. Second, the potential of
gas attacks—concretized by the gas masks and sealed rooms—had a
powerful symbolic meaning in a society in which the memory of the
Nazi gas ovens is still very much alive. The symbolic effect was, of
course, greatly enhanced by the very real danger of escalation into a
nonconventional war with chemical and nuclear weapons. In this connection, some of the opinion data reported by Arian and Gordon are
particularly noteworthy. The issue cited most frequently by Israelis during the Gulf War as a source of significant threat was nonconventional
weapons in the hands of the Arabs; and public support for the use
of nuclear weapons under extreme circumstances rose sharply during
that period.

The third way in which this war differed from Israel's other wars was
the country's inability—primarily for political reasons—to defend itself
from attack. This predicament brought out a number of psychological
reactions, well described by Arian and Gordon: a sense of helplessness
and vulnerability, which is a central element of negative identity for Israelis, particularly when coupled with the symbolism of gas attacks; an
unwelcome sense of dependence on others (e.g., on coalition air strikes
or U.S. Patriot missiles) for national defense; and a concern about the
weakening of Israel's deterrent posture, which had always called for an
unambiguous message that every act of aggression would invariably
produce retaliation.

This special character of the war in Israeli eyes, taken together with
the end of the cold war and the current military supremacy of the
United States in the Middle East and the world, has several implications
that have no doubt filtered down to the level of public opinion:

1. The Gulf War underscored the change in Israel's strategic relationship with the United States, brought on by the end of the cold war. Israel's status as a strategic asset to the United States has declined. The United States did not need Israel in the Gulf War and, in fact, saw its relationship to Israel as something of an obstacle. Clearly, the United States gave priority to its strategic relationships with several of the Arab states.

2. There has been some erosion of U.S. support for Israel and the unique relationship that Israel has enjoyed with the United States. In my opinion, the closeness of the relationship in the past has been somewhat exaggerated; it has always depended on a perceived congruence between Israeli and American interests. Now that the constellation of American interests is changing, one can expect a change in the U.S.-Israeli relationship. Moreover, the change is not just due to the particular attitudes of President Bush and Secretary Baker. A different administration may differ in its style of relating to Israel, but it would probably impose similar conditions on its continuing support for Israeli policies.

3. Along with the perception in Israel of a weakening relationship to the United States, there is a sense of increasing dependence on the United States. This dependence was symbolized by the spectacle of U.S. military personnel setting up and deploying Patriot missiles in Israel in defense against Iraqi SCUD missiles. For Israelis, it has always been important to know that they could rely on their own human and technical resources to defend their country.

4. All of these changes are taking place within a changing political context. U.S. power in the Middle East and its willingness to use that power have increased. Corresponding to that greater power, there has been a greater readiness on the part of Arab states to accommodate U.S. interests and to respond with increasing flexibility to American demands.

The Israeli Public's Readiness for Negotiation

Have these experiences during the Gulf War and their implications affected the political attitudes of the Israeli public? In particular, have they increased or decreased the public's readiness for Israeli-Palestinian negotiations?

The first set of data presented by Arian and Gordon refers to perceived changes in attitudes. In other words, these are data on attitude change based on self-reports, which are inevitably subject to a certain degree of ambiguity. These data show that a sizeable proportion of the Israeli public reported that the Gulf War led to changes in their opinions regarding security and political matters. The changes, however, went in both directions. Some reported that the war had made them more ready for compromise and had persuaded them that the continued Israeli occupation of the West Bank and Gaza was less important than they had believed before. Others reported just the opposite effect. Thus, it seems that the war further contributed to the polarization in Israeli public opinion that had been taking place since the Intifada.

When these reports are broken down by party preference, we find that those who plan to vote for left-of-center parties moved further in the direction of moderation; while those who plan to vote for right-wing parties moved further in the direction of militancy. (Interestingly, Likud voters and undecideds showed movement in both directions, which suggests that a significant segment of the Israeli public can move either way, depending on changing realities and their leadership's interpretation thereof.) Assuming that the voting preferences themselves are fairly stable (i.e., that they were not themselves affected by the war), what we seem to find here essentially is a *bolstering* effect: the war confirmed and strengthened certain realities that had been apparent for some time. The pronegotiation forces and the antinegotiation forces had been responding to these realities in different ways, and new events gave each group additional reasons and arguments for doing so.

When we examine actual opinion changes over time, as revealed by repeated poll questions, we find that the postwar data (obtained in the early spring of 1991) more often than not show change in the direction of moderation. Perhaps the most dramatic shift occurred on the question of whether Israel should try to initiate peace negotiations. The affirmative response to that question rose from 64 percent in 1990 to 74 percent in March 1991. On other questions, the data basically revealed a continuation of trends that had been observed since the Intifada. Thus, to the question of whether peace was possible, affirmative responses rose from 57 percent in 1986 to 76 percent in 1991. Willingness to return territories rose steadily from less than 40 percent in 1986 to 58 percent in 1991. The number of Israelis accepting the idea of a Palestinian state has also risen steadily since 1987 and continued to do so through the Gulf War, but still, as of the spring of 1991, only about one-third of the population subscribed to that view. It seems likely, on the basis of other poll data, that a larger proportion of the Israeli public would accept a Palestinian state if the idea were presented in a fuller context: for example, as a state to be established after a transitional period of autonomy and confidence building and to be confederated with Jordan—both positions that are now accepted by the Palestinian leadership.

In sum, the poll data indicate that the Gulf War at least failed to interrupt the trends toward greater moderation in Israeli political attitudes. Beyond that, the war seems to have led to an increase in the readiness to negotiate, probably for a combination of reasons, such as recognition of the new strategic situation in the Middle East and a desire to put an end to the continuing violence and threat of war.

Negotiating with the PLO

There is one exception to the finding that the war accelerated or did not interrupt the trend toward greater moderation: the issue of negotiations with the Palestine Liberation Organization. By March 1989, 58 percent of the Israeli population (up from 43 percent in April 1987) indicated a willingness to negotiate with the PLO, if it officially recognized Israel and ceased terrorist activity. To be sure, a much smaller percentage of the population believed that the PLO had actually met these conditions, but the principle of negotiating with the PLO had gained increasing acceptance. The war seemed to produce a major opinion shift on this issue. After the war, only 16 percent expressed a willingness to negotiate with the PLO if it met these two conditions, although a total of 49 percent were willing to negotiate if the PLO met two additional conditions: stopping the Intifada and repealing the PLO charter. This shift is probably due to a combination of at least two factors: a reaction to the PLO's support for Saddam Hussein during the Gulf crisis and the feeling that the PLO has become marginalized in the Arab world and increasingly irrelevant.

The feeling that the PLO has become irrelevant may have been reinforced by the exclusion of the PLO from official participation in the current peace negotiations. In Israel and elsewhere there is some tendency now to assume that the Palestinian leadership has shifted from the PLO, based in Tunis, to the West Bank and Gaza residents who officially represent the Palestinians in the negotiations. I do not know what, if anything, recent Israeli public opinion polls show on this issue, but I think it would be a mistake to underestimate the continuing role of the PLO and to draw too sharp a distinction between the "inside" and "outside" Palestinian leaders.

There are, of course, some differences in interests and experiences between the Palestinians in the territories and those in the diaspora. The local leadership is more familiar with the problems of the West Bank and Gaza and more experienced in dealing with the Israelis at various levels. Moreover, since the Intifada, the vanguard of the Palestinian movement has shifted to the occupied territories. For all of these reasons, there are some inevitable conflicts between the two leadership elements. Nevertheless, the inside Palestinians see themselves as part of the Palestinian national movement, which was sparked by the PLO and is symbolized by it. The unity of the Palestinian people is central to their claim for national identity and self-determination. They cannot separate themselves from the outside Palestinians—to whom, in any event, they are tied through kinship bonds. They cannot seek a solution for the West Bank and Gaza while ignoring the problems of the diaspora Palestinians, particularly the refugee population. All of this also means that they must work within the framework of the PLO. The idea that support for the PLO in the occupied territories is merely lip service produced by physical threats represents a distortion of the reality.

It is also a mistake to assume that the inside Palestinians are more accommodating than the outside Palestinians. There are similar divisions in both communities. The mainstream elements of both, however, have worked together in pursuing the Palestinian peace initiative that began in 1988 as well as in the current negotiations. The Palestinian participation in the negotiations would not have been possible without approval of the Palestine National Council, and Chairman Arafat himself played a central role in engineering that approval. Since that time, it is widely known that the PLO—though officially excluded—has played an active role in the negotiating process. On a number of occasions, the outside leadership has been more willing to compromise on the procedural issues that have arisen in the negotiations than the inside leadership, which is more directly constrained by the frustration and skepticism about the process in West Bank and Gaza public opinion.

In short, the reversal of the trend in Israeli public opinion toward accepting the PLO as a negotiating partner is a barrier to negotiations, even though in other respects the Gulf War seems to have increased or at least not decreased the Israeli public's willingness to negotiate. Ultimately, a satisfactory solution will have to address the situation of the Palestinian nation, which includes both its inside and outside constituencies. Israel, of course, will have to pursue its own interests in the course of the negotiations, but it will have to let the Palestinians define their own national identity and choose their own leadership. It appears that the Gulf War has contributed to obscuring this issue, but a serious commitment to negotiations should help to clarify it.

Arab Public Opinion

Shibley Telhami's chapter begins with a useful discussion of the role of public opinion in Arab states. Since most Arab regimes are authoritarian, to a greater or lesser extent, it is often assumed that public opinion is irrelevant to their leaders. In fact, however, public support is a major source of legitimacy for these regimes. Of course, they can rule for long periods without legitimacy, by relying on their coercive power and internal security agencies. Lack of legitimacy, however, makes them vulnerable, not only to direct popular rebellion but also to military coups. Paradoxically, public opinion may be more important to the legitimacy of such autocratic regimes, at least in the short run, than is the case for democratic regimes. Since their legitimacy does not rest on such procedural criteria as elections, it is more dependent on performance— including performance at the regional and international levels.

As Telhami suggests, Arab regimes require and maintain legitimacy, both domestically and internationally, by the power and influence they wield within the region. Thus, regional leadership is actively and competitively pursued by the major Arab states. This in turn requires adherence to transnational symbols of legitimacy, providing evidence that the state is championing the larger Arab and Islamic cause. It is in this context that the Palestinian issue has gained such significance over the years. The question of Palestine has become the touchstone for assessing the genuineness of the Arab and Islamic loyalty and commitment of leaders and states in the region. Needless to say, Arab leaders have been willing to exploit and manipulate the Palestinian cause for their own ends and to sacrifice Palestinian interests if they conflicted with their own perceived state interests. Nevertheless, they have all tried to present themselves as the most reliable advocates for Palestinian interests and have all competed for ownership of the Palestinian cause. In particular, as Telhami says, whenever the legitimacy of an Arab government comes into question, it will rush to wrap itself in a Palestinian flag.

By the spring of 1990, Saddam Hussein had managed to become a highly popular figure among the Arab masses and a top contender for Arab leadership through the skillful use of the Palestinian issue and associated Arab sentiments. Among those sentiments, as described by Telhami, was growing anti-Americanism, based on the perception that the United States was using its undisputed power in the post–cold war era to give unlimited support to Israel's hegemonic ambitions; fear that the massive immigration of Soviet Jews to Israel would inevitably encourage Israeli annexationism and expansionism; and despair about the possibility of an acceptable solution to the Arab-Israeli conflict, particularly in light of the increasing power of the Right in Israel and the apparent unwillingness of the United States to set limits. By presenting himself as a leader who was willing to stand up to the United States, and who had his own plan for the region and the military capacity to put it into effect, he generated enthusiastic support in large segments of Arab public opinion.

A considerable degree of popular support continued even after Iraq's invasion of Kuwait. It is interesting that some of the most vocal support for Saddam Hussein was expressed in those Arab states that had moved furthest in the direction of democratization—perhaps simply because those states are more prepared to tolerate public demonstrations. Egypt was an exception here; large segments of the Egyptian public may have turned against Saddam Hussein because of the severe mistreatment of Egyptian workers in Iraq, which touched many Egyptian families and was widely reported in Egypt. Even so, there were public expressions of pro-Iraqi sentiment in Egypt and even in Syria. Those Arab leaders who joined the coalition against Iraq had to do so in the face of considerable public sympathy for Saddam Hussein. Of course, as Telhami points out, the increasing popularity of Saddam Hussein, on which he rested his claims for Arab leadership, was precisely one of the main reasons for forming an Arab coalition against him. Jordan and the PLO did not join that coalition, partly because the popular sentiment in favor of Saddam Hussein among their constituencies was too strong to overcome. In addition, the Jordanian and Palestinian leaderships derived their own benefits from their alliance with Iraq, which were only gradually outweighed by the costs of that alliance.

The public support for Saddam Hussein—the degree to which he seemed to have captured the imagination of the Arab masses and almost stepped into the shoes of Gamal Abdel Nasser—led many analysts to predict that his defeat would create serious upheavals in the Arab world, resulting in destabilization of the Arab regimes that joined the coalition against Iraq. These predictions have, at least so far, not been borne out. It may well be that the public reaction was muted because the campaign ended when it did, with the expulsion of Iraqi forces from Kuwait, and the United States and its allies did not go on to destroy Baghdad and occupy Iraq. Yet, even by that point, Iraq had been devastated, its social and economic structures shattered, many thousands of its citizens and soldiers killed, and its leadership humiliated. How, then, can one account for the low-key public response?

The prediction of continuing public support for Saddam Hussein was based on the assumption that, even as a loser, he would be perceived as a winner in the Arab context (just as Nasser had been, despite his military defeats). He would be seen as having championed the Arab cause, fought for the Palestinians, and stood up to the West. He would be given credit for resisting for as long as he did and finally succumbing only to vastly superior force. As it happened, however, he was seen not as a winner but as an ignominious loser. The Arab members of the coalition, as Telhami points out, were apparently successful in conveying their interpretation of the events to the Arab publics. In the eyes of much of the public, it seems, Saddam Hussein did not live up to his promise in any respect. After blatant attempts to exploit the Palestinian issue to his advantage, he quickly abandoned the Palestinian cause. He demonstrated no capacity to promote a new economic order in the Middle East. In the final analysis, he turned out to be concerned only about maintaining his own power. Even granting the vastly superior forces of the U.S.-led coalition, he did not use his own military capacities effectively. The military incompetence of his forces became increasingly evident. All in all, it seemed that he was wrong in his analysis of the new realities in the world and the region and that he had engaged in a reckless challenge to American power, for which his own people and his allies had to pay a heavy price.

The disenchantment with Saddam Hussein was probably linked to a recognition—based on highly visible evidence—of U.S. power and of its increasingly significant role in the Middle East. Major segments of public opinion may have become persuaded that the Saudi, Egyptian, and Syrian leaderships were more accurate and effective in their assessment of the U.S. role than Saddam Hussein had been. The recognition of U.S. power is obviously a source of great ambivalence in Arab public opinion. What may have helped to reduce the negative reaction—to give the United States some of the benefit of the doubt—is the active involvement of the administration in promoting an Arab-Israeli peace process in a relatively evenhanded way. Thus, there may be some hope that perhaps the United States will now become—in Arab eyes—part of the solution rather than part of the problem. How Arab public opinion in response to the Gulf War finally plays itself out will therefore depend to a considerable degree on the continuing role of the United States in the peace process.

PART V

■

THE CONSEQUENCES
OF CONFLICT

10

Leaders and Publics in the Middle East: Shattering the Organizing Myths of Arab Society

■

Marvin Zonis

■ IN WHAT IS probably Nietzsche's best-known aphorism, a madman, carrying a glowing lantern in the morning sun, runs through the marketplace crying, "I seek God!" Taunted by the many unbelievers, he turns to them and cries:

> "Whither is God? . . . I shall tell you. We have killed him—you and I. All of us are his murderers. But how have we done this? How were we able to drink up the entire sea? Who gave us the sponge to wipe away the entire horizon? What did we do when we unchained this earth from its sun? Whither is it moving now? Whither are we moving now? Away from all suns? Are we not plunging continually? Backward, sideward, forward, in all directions? Is there any up or down left? Are we not straying as through an infinite nothing? Do we not feel the breath of empty space? Has it not become colder? Is not night and more night coming on all the while? Must not lanterns be lit in the morning? . . . God is dead. God remains dead. And we have killed him. How shall we, the murderers of all murderers, comfort ourselves? . . . What festivals of atonement, what sacred games shall we have to invent?"
>
> Here the madman fell silent and looked again at his listeners; and they too were silent and stared at him in astonishment. At last he threw his lantern on the ground, and it broke and went out. "I come too early," he said then; "my time has not come yet. This tremendous event is still on its way, still wandering—it has not yet reached the ears of man. . . . This deed is still more distant from them than the most distant stars—and yet they have done it themselves."

I have related this story from Nietzsche (1954, 95) for two reasons. First, and most important, it touches on what this chapter is and what it is not. It is not a description or analysis of the Arab world in the wake of the Gulf War. It is, rather, an attempt to discern and interpret events that have either not yet happened or not yet come to light. It is thus

269

impressionistic rather than rigorously empirical, interpretive rather than descriptive. It is an analysis of an aspect of the present Arab political culture.

Second, the event that Nietzsche, through his madman, was announcing can be thought of as one example of a more general kind of catastrophe—the death, destruction, or loss of what I will call *organizing myths*. An organizing myth is a cultural belief that makes sense of some aspect of the world for the people committed to that myth by offering an explanation of why this aspect is as it is. The organizing myth may or may not have empirical veracity. But the belief of those who share in it lends it a sense of utter facticity. The existence of God and his death, as Nietzsche labeled the phenomenon, is here considered one among many organizing myths, one with immense consequences for the human condition as a whole, but an organizing myth nonetheless.

In this chapter I claim that the shattering of key organizing myths has constituted the principal historical dynamic of the Arab world in this century. More important, the Iraqi invasion of Kuwait and the war to oust the Iraqi invaders by the international coalition led by the United States will come to be understood as another great catastrophe—another myth-shattering event—in the Arab twentieth century.

The Palestinians refer to the establishment of the state of Israel as the *nakba*, or catastrophe. The invasion of Kuwait by Iraq and the Gulf War will eventually come to be seen as another Arab catastrophe. For those complex events will have served to fatally weaken a number of central symbols and myths by means of which the inhabitants of the Arab Muslim world have organized their lives and given meaning to their existence.

The aphorism from Nietzsche, as I have already mentioned, suggests the magnitude of the consequences of the shattering of myths. As the madman says, the chaos that follows such a catastrophe is near total in the domain that was previously governed by the myth.

And, as Nietzsche points out, even a conceptual disaster of this magnitude is not readily recognized by its perpetrators or, more to the point, even by those for whom the organizing myth fulfilled such crucial functions. Long periods of time may follow before the consequences of the destruction of an organizing myth are understood.

Finally, while I end this chapter by suggesting some areas from which new and revitalizing organizing myths might come, prognostications of this kind are more like weather forecasts than scientific predictions. As those lonely Arab intellectuals who have tried to make Marxism meaningful to their compatriots have found, organizing myths grow out of the structure of a society and culture as a whole and cannot easily be implanted either by indigenous or foreign rulers or intellectuals.

A number of processes are set in motion as a result of the shattering of an organizing myth. In the absence of recognition that the myth has been destroyed, there is frequently an enhanced commitment to the traditional explanations of why the world is as it is. But the commitment takes the form of ritual adherence, and the myth, having been shattered, becomes increasingly dysfunctional. The ritualistic nature of the commitment reveals the hollowness at the root of the society. The compulsive ritualism suggests the inappropriateness of the behaviors based on the shattered myth to the demands of the world as it has changed rather than as it was explained by the shattered organizing myth.

What is called for is not more assiduous ritual adherence to, but the clearing away of, the wreckage of the shattered myth and the construction and adoption of new and more functional organizing myths.

This chapter attempts to clarify these points in the following manner. First, I review some key statistics relating to various dimensions of well-being in the Arab Muslim Middle East. These statistics, presented as tables, clearly indicate that there is something wrong in the Arab world. For those dimensions of well-being generally accepted in the Arab world as elsewhere, Arab states rank appallingly low in comparison to many other countries. The low ranking is especially shocking in light of the stupendous wealth that many Arab countries have earned from oil sales in this century and especially since the quadrupling of oil prices in 1973 and their doubling again in 1979.

The billions of dollars earned from the sale of petroleum could have been used to transform the social conditions of the oil-exporting countries and still left sufficient extra revenues to do the same for the non–oil-exporting Arab states. The result would have been a far different world ranking for the Arab states than contemporary data indicate. The low ranking, it is claimed here, is an indication of the degrading effects of shattered organizing myths. (On many of the measures, I average oil-producing states with non–oil-producing ones. Though this might appear questionable, I argue in a later section that Arab unity and brotherhood form a central organizing myth of Arab Muslim political culture, and one measure of the actual level of inter-Arab brotherly feeling is willingness to share resources, especially financial ones. The poorer Arab and Islamic nations have themselves given expression to this expectation, which also has deep roots in Islam. I argue, then, that the evident failure of the richest Arab countries to spread the wealth is indicative of the falsity of many assertions of Arab unity.)

I then examine more closely the concept of the organizing myth, with particular attention to a useful text by Clifford Geertz and discuss a few of the key organizing myths of Arab Muslim culture. Next, I review an argument I have previously made (Zonis 1984) regarding what I term a *sense-making crisis*, and relate it to the present argument to give

TABLE 10.1. Road Network, 1988 (kilometers)

Region	Total	Motorways	Main Roads	Density (km/km²)
OECD states[a]	12,650,384	123,684	992,411	.41
Sub-Saharan Africa	1,211,329	2,109	272,438	.06
Middle East[b]	564,062	2,978	125,794	.06

Source: The Economist Book of World Statistics.
a. Organization for Economic Cooperation and Development.
b. Algeria, Cyprus, Egypt, Iran, Iraq, Israel, Jordan, Kuwait, Lebanon, Morocco, Saudi Arabia, Syria, Tunisia, and North Yemen.

some idea of the psychodynamics and consequences of the loss of organizing myths and of self-objects more generally. I then discuss some of the social and political turmoil that has ensued in the wake of the Gulf War and attempt to place it in the context of the shattering of organizing myths and of sense-making crises. Finally, I identify and briefly describe some of the directions from which new, regenerative organizing myths might emerge for the Arab Muslim Middle East.

Arab Well-Being

Available statistics—usually supplied by individual Arab governments—demonstrate that Arab countries generally lag behind many others on a number of commonly recognized dimensions of economic, social, and physical well-being (see tables 10.1–10.9). This generalization does not, of course, apply to all Arab states in all dimensions. Almost all statistics from Arab states reveal more developed societies than those of almost all African states. Indeed, on some measures, Arab states rank among the most advanced societies in the world. Statistics from Saudi Arabia on the availability of medical care, for example, show that nation to have one of the most progressive health care systems in the world. However, when taken together, the countries of the Middle East, while generally ranking high above the sub-Saharan African countries, also generally rank much below European countries, even on measures of such basic items as medical care and poverty.

The statistics in these tables reveal a serious general level of backwardness in the Arab world. Considering that Arab societies have been in the vanguard of the development of high civilization and that many Arab societies in modern times have been able to boast seemingly limitless wealth in the form of oil revenues, the developmental level of Arab societies is startlingly low. These statistics reveal that there is something wrong in Arab societies.

TABLE 10.2. Vehicle Ownership, 1988

Region	Total (1,000s)	Cars (1,000s)	Buses/Coaches	Trucks/Vans (1,000s)
OECD states	388,219.8	304,499.1	1,506,670	79,613.3
Sub-Saharan Africa	8,537.9	5,636.9	68,680	1,609.5
Middle East[a]	14,303.9	9,981.8	161,834	3,510.8

Source: See table 10.1.
a. Algeria, Bahrain, Cyprus, Egypt, Iran, Iraq, Jordan, Kuwait, Lebanon, Libya, Morocco, Oman, Qatar, Saudi Arabia, Syria, Tunisia, United Arab Emirates, North Yemen, and South Yemen.

TABLE 10.3. Post and Telecommunications, 1988

Region	Permanent Post Offices	Letters per Capita (Average)	Percentage of Homes with Mail Delivery (Average)
OECD states	222,819	249.79	88.89
Sub-Saharan Africa	13,911	4.65	20.8
Middle East[a]	14,167	14.48	59.05

Source: See table 10.1.
a. Algeria, Bahrain, Cyprus, Egypt, Iran, Iraq, Jordan, Kuwait, Libya, Malta, Morocco, Oman, Qatar, Saudi Arabia, Syria, Tunisia, United Arab Emirates, North Yemen, and South Yemen.

Organizing Myths

The cognitive revolution in the empirical and philosophical study of humanity established meaning as the core concept of the human sciences. As a result, the social sciences have seen a resurgence of interest in issues of text and interpretation. The most fruitful area of this meaning-centered view of human nature has been the study of the symbolic modes of human existence and activity.

This study of meaning has occasionally been disrupted by competing definitions of the notion of *symbol*, especially from field to field. In this chapter, following Geertz (1973, 91), I define a symbol as "any object, act, event, quality, or relation which serves as a vehicle for a conception—the conception is the symbol's 'meaning.' "

The concept of symbol has itself become a powerful organizing tool in the social and philosophical sciences because of its utility for understanding the constitution of the world of an individual or of a group. It has been immensely heuristic for understanding life not so much as

TABLE 10.4. Newspapers, Radio, and Television, 1988

Region	Daily Newspapers		Radios per 1,000 Inhabitants	Television Sets per 1,000 Inhabitants
	Number	Circulation per 1,000 Inhabitants		
OECD states	142.79	318.68	769.63	377.54
Sub-Saharan Africa	3.67	13.5	127.58	15.86
Middle East[a]	8.1	70.13	316.86	184.57

Source: See table 10.1.
a. Algeria, Bahrain, Cyprus, Egypt, Iran, Iraq, Jordan, Kuwait, Lebanon, Libya, Malta, Morocco, Oman, Qatar, Saudi Arabia, Syria, Tunisia, United Arab Emirates, North Yemen, and South Yemen.

TABLE 10.5. Illiteracy, 1988

Region	Percentage of Illiteracy
OECD states	5.11
Sub-Saharan Africa	57.16
Middle East[a]	37.33

Source: See table 10.1.
a. Algeria, Bahrain, Egypt, Iran, Iraq, Jordan, Kuwait, Lebanon, Libya, Malta, Morocco, Oman, Qatar, Saudi Arabia, South Yemen, Syria, and Tunisia.

TABLE 10.6. Childbirths, per Woman, 1988

Region	Children	Children Dying Before Five Years of Age
OECD states	1.8	.02
Sub-Saharan Africa	6.5	1.18
Middle East	5.6	.99

Source: See table 10.1.

reflected in symbols or patterns of symbols but as *patterned by* those symbols. Symbol systems are understood to be so fundamentally constitutive of human life that their abrupt loss of meaning produces profound consequences. Geertz (ibid., 99) notes that "man depends upon

TABLE 10.7. LIFE EXPECTANCY AND INFANT MORTALITY, 1988

	Life Expectancy		Mortality		
Region	Male	Female	Maternal (per 100,000 Live Births)	Infant (per 1,000 Live Births)	Low-Birth-Weight Babies (percent)
OECD states	72	78	10	9	3.9
Sub-Saharan Africa	49	52	733	109	15.6
Middle East[a]	62	64	213	71	6.4

Source: See table 10.1
a. Algeria, Bahrain, Cyprus, Egypt, Iran, Iraq, Jordan, Kuwait, Lebanon, Libya, Malta, Morocco, Oman, Qatar, Saudi Arabia, Syria, Tunisia, United Arab Emirates, North Yemen, South Yemen.

TABLE 10.8. HEALTH CARE PROVISION, 1988

Region	Doctors per Million Inhabitants	Hospital Beds per Thousand Inhabitants
OECD states	2,199.5	8.0
Sub-Saharan Africa	70.7	1.5
Middle East[a]	472.4	1.8

Source: See table 10.1.
a. Algeria, Bahrain, Cyprus, Egypt, Iran, Iraq, Jordan, Kuwait, Lebanon, Libya, Malta, Morocco, Oman, Qatar, Saudi Arabia, Syria, Tunisia, United Arab Emirates, North Yemen, South Yemen.

TABLE 10.9. POPULATION BELOW POVERTY LINE, 1988 (PERCENT)

Region	Urban	Rural
OECD states	0	0
Sub-Saharan Africa	35.29	57.86
Middle East[a]	20.6	24.40

Source: See table 10.1.
a. Algeria, Egypt, Jordan, Morocco, Syria, Tunisia, South Yemen.

symbols and symbol systems with a dependence so great as to be decisive for his creatural viability and, as a result, his sensitivity to even the remotest indication that they may prove unable to cope with one or another aspect of experience raises within him the gravest sort of anxiety."

The profound power and consequences of these organizing myths or paradigms, however, does not mean that they cannot be somewhat circumscribed in their influence. Individuals and groups, as Geertz notes, can step out of and reenter symbolic forms as expansive and encompassing as religion. People and peoples, not infrequently, leap from the domain of one symbol system to that of another. Different and not necessarily compatible meaning systems, such as symbol systems, myths, or paradigms, may organize the religion, eschatology, politics, economics, and social consciousness of a single people.

Now, the loss of meaning that follows from the failure of a symbolic system may be at least partially compensated for by reinforcing commitment to an alternative symbolic system. Some of the ways people reconstruct disturbed or shattered symbolic systems are discussed below. Here it is worth mentioning that these techniques can be either healthy or unhealthy. As regards the latter, the ubiquitous need to experience the world in an orderly way is at the root of many mental illnesses at the personal level, in that such illnesses—paranoia, for example—are largely the expression of the need to impose some order—any order—upon a world that has become frightening and unfamiliar. At the social level, there are analogous processes at work. The collapse of an organizing myth—for example, the myth that the USSR is the evil empire—triggers a search for new myths—in this case, perhaps a new external enemy for the United States. In the process, emotional well-being may be preserved. But all too often, that is accomplished at the expense of other social goals—for example, economic well-being, intellectual and cultural vitality, or political power. Something very much like this process appears to have been occurring in the Middle East during the twentieth century.

The Organizing Myths of the
Arab Middle East

None of this is meant to suggest that one can neatly separate these domains—religion from politics or economics from social issues. In fact, much of the power of symbol systems to constitute our lives is in their interconnectedness. Resilient and vital societies are characterized by a high degree of overlap in the meaning systems that constitute their different domains. The vitality of the society is enhanced when the constitutive dimensions of the economy, for example, are enhanced and invigorated, even empowered by the meaning systems of religion and society. But one negative consequence of that interconnectedness is the more general unraveling that follows upon the loss of meaning of any one of the constitutive symbol systems. When one system is shaken, other interconnected systems are weakened as well.

While this chapter is specifically concerned with politics, examples of Arab Muslim organizing myths will be drawn from other domains because their meanings spill over into the political realm. Although the myths are discussed separately, it will become clear that they are interconnected, reflecting the power of Arab Muslim society and culture.

Umma, Hajj, and Wihda

The single most important organizing symbolic system of Muslim culture, and the best known to both Muslims and non-Muslims, is *Umma*, the community of Islam. The first mention of the concept is in the Koran, and Muhammad frequently invoked the concept and explicated its meanings. *Umma* has been a focal point of Islamic jurisprudence, history, social thought, and literature to the present day. Islam is suffused with vehicles for the articulation of this notion of community. In the realm of language, Arabic is the language of revelation and the sacred tongue of the faith. In the realm of ritual, *hajj* (pilgrimage to Mecca) serves to congregate Muslims from all corners of the world to reinvigorate the meaning of *umma* while simultaneously devaluing cultural, social, and national diversity. The idea of the *umma* has been a familiar theme in Arab and Muslim political theory.

One of the most important contemporary concepts informed by *umma* is that of *wihda*, unity. Hisham Sharabi makes the link explicit. The concept of *wihda*, he suggests,

> involves political unity, but also the aspiration for a more profound unity transcending the merely political or economic. This has deep psychological roots that must be sought in the idea of the Muslim community advanced by Muhammad's early teachings and embodied in the community of his first followers. Arabism posits the indivisibility of the Arab nation; the longing for *wihda* reflects the will to restore to wholeness what has been violated by history, adversity, and accident. (Sharabi 1966, 97)

With the Iraqi invasion of Kuwait and the subsequent split in the Arab world between those who celebrated that invasion and those who fought to repel it, even by inviting infidel forces onto Islamic lands, Arab *umma* and *wihda* have been decisively split.

Perhaps the most powerful articulator of Arab unity, who did more than any other contemporary leader to realize that dream, was the late Egyptian leader Gamal Abdel Nasser. Much of his political life was devoted to realizing the dream of Arab political, economic, and social union, and he took a significant step in that direction by forging the United Arab Republic in the 1960s. However, only Syria responded to his call, and in the end regional intrigue and power struggles split what there was of the UAR. The final blow to Nasser's dream, because his death followed only days afterward, was the bloody struggle in September 1970 between Palestinian guerrillas and the Jordanian authorities in the civil war known as Black September. Since Nasser's demise, there has been little practical content to the idea of Arab unity at any level.

But from time to time, Arab states act as if they seek to realize the myth. Before the Gulf crisis, the Arab League had been resuscitated and reincorporated Egypt as a member in good standing. Its headquarters had even been moved to Cairo. The Iran-Iraq War was over, and the deviation of Syria's supporting a non-Arab state against a fellow Arab state was brought to a close. An increasing number of cooperation agreements were being forged among regional Arab states. And, to a greater extent than ever before, individual Arabs were working in Arab states other than those in which they claimed nationality and sending home remittances to support their families. This had been the case for decades for Palestinians; but now, all the population-rich Arab states were sending their laborers to the petrodollar states.

Of course, this state of affairs represented only a modest beginning of any real kind of Arab unity. And this fledgling renewal of the myth of Arab unity was shattered by the Gulf crisis—through the dparture of Egypt, Syria, and Saudi Arabia from the Arab camp to the side of the international coalition and the rapid transformation of Iraq to international pariah status.

Enemies

A persistent organizing theme of Arab Muslim political and social consciousness has been an intense sense of domination and opposition by external enemies. Even before the establishment of the state of Israel in 1948, this theme of oppression at the hands of foreign "enemies" was pervasive.

Of course, the Arabs have had many foreign enemies, and those enemies were powerful and usually dominating. For centuries, virtually the entire Arab world was ruled by the Ottoman Empire. With the fall of those foreign rulers during World War I, Arab independence was achieved. But a new set of masters—the British and the French—received the legitimacy of the League of Nations to dominate the Arab world. In the minds of many Arabs, the state of Israel was but another device by which foreigners could determine the destiny of the Arab people, a more clever stratagem surely, but a stratagem nonetheless. The foreign colonialists withdrew formally, this interpretation has it, but left behind a European outpost in the heart of Arab territory through which they could continue to exercise at least indirect domination.

Few other beliefs have exercised such sway over the minds of Arabs as this one. From this point of view, all Arab problems can be attributed to the presence of Israel or to the machinations of the superpowers, the new foreign enemies of the Arab people. To be sure, external enemies have existed and, perhaps, still do exist. The state of Israel was established by the colonial powers on land in the heart of the Arab world. There have been wars between Israel and the Arab states. Israel also continues to occupy the Arab lands it occupied in war, land on which live millions of Arabs. Moreover, Israel is not alone. Iran has also fought a lengthy and painful war against Arab Iraq and sought the overthrow of Arab governments and their replacement by Islamic fundamentalist regimes friendly, if not loyal, to Iran. Nevertheless, the fact that Arab states and peoples have had a long experience with oppression and enmity does not mean that the concept of enemies is uninteresting for the student of Arab political culture. Although the experience of oppression and enmity is almost ubiquitous, not every people has created a category like *enemy* and infused it with such importance as have the Arabs.

The paradigm of foreign domination is reinforced by the image of the Arab world as a homogeneous whole constituting one *watan* (Arab fatherland). The role of the valiant Arab states in defending that *watan* has been dramatized and enhanced by Arab rulers largely in pursuit of a mechanism for maintaining their own political legitimacy while rationalizing their failings. Insofar as the Arabs or a particular Arab regime can be shown to have been singled out for special malevolent treatment by powerful foreigners, that regime must be doing something hostile to the interests of those foreigners. It must, in short, be seeking to resist foreign domination of the Arab world while maintaining the independence of Arab political and economic action. In the process, the legitimacy of the regime is enhanced by the belief that it has become the target of foreign powers only because it is so obviously a truly national regime.

It is also the case, in virtually all circumstances, that the Arab regime cannot hope to triumph against the foreigners. For, after all, those foreign regimes—the Ottomans, then the British and the French, then the United States and, for a period, the USSR, and (endlessly for the Arabs) the state of Israel—are inarguably more powerful than the Arabs. The Arabs, in short, are victims.

If the indigenous Arab regime has mobilized its resources for the struggle against the foreigner, then the failure of the regime to solve the problems of the Arabs can be excused. For, so the myth goes, it is the foreigners who seek to impose backwardness on the Arabs and maintain the Arabs as pliable tools of the foreign, usually Western conspiracy. After all, how can an Arab regime be blamed for failure as long as it has made its best effort to resist the encroachment of external enemies?

In addition to the conveniences this particular myth provides for Arab regimes and elites, it also has real visceral import for the people to whom the regimes must justify themselves. That is, the concept of *enemy* is an attractive one for all kinds of people. What I am interested in here is the way in which the category is given political, cultural, or some other supraindividual content by political and intellectual leaders. This phenomenon can be called conspiracy thinking. Conspiracy thinking's appeal derives in part from the need to reorder a world that has become meaningless from the individual's point of view as a result of historical or political events over which he or she has no control. As stoic as we moderns are required to be about evils, including poverty, racial division, earthquakes, and so on, faceless evils are in fact intolerable, and people will act in various ways to put faces on the evils that surround them. Conspiracy thinking as a form of political discourse, just like paranoia as a form of individual psychopathology, performs this function well. A world peopled largely by powerful enemies may be scary, but at least it is comprehensible, and the individual is thus spared greater anxieties.

This paradigm of the enemies of the Arab people has organized Arab political consciousness and action in powerful ways. That non-Arab states, principally located in East and Southeast Asia, have successfully challenged the supremacy of the West appears to have provided no inspiration to the Arabs. To the contrary, their success serves only as evidence to many Arabs that the West has concentrated its resources in maintaining its control over the Arab states.

Whatever the significance of the myth, it is now clear that the Arabs have enemies within the Arab camp. The enemies do not seek, necessarily, to sustain Western imperialism. (There are some in the Arab world who manage nonetheless to interpret the Iraqi invasion in precisely that way thus demonstrating the power of the myth. To this small group of interpreters, secular, socialist Iraq was acting as an agent for Western imperialism by attempting to destroy Kuwait and, ultimately, Islamic Saudi Arabia.) It is no longer possible for the vast majority of Arabs to divide the world into enemies (non-Arabs) and friends (Arabs).

Palestine

The idea of Palestine has acquired a hold on Arab consciousness that approaches an organizing myth. As with the other organizing myths, this is not meant to imply that either Palestine or Palestinian rights to statehood are mythical, only that the concept of Palestine has assumed significance as an organizer of Arab consciousness. As suggested above, political legitimacy in the Arab world is marked by resistance to supposed external enemies. No greater measure of legitimacy has been fostered by Arab regimes than resistance to the state of Israel in order to defend the rights of the Palestinians.

An Arab regime denouncing Israel and proclaiming its fidelity to the Palestinians manages to generate legitimacy. Its actual service to advancing the Palestinian cause appears less central to its legitimacy than its steadfastness in maintaining the intensity of its hostility to Israel and the West. In this, the Arab states have been profoundly influenced by the leadership of the Palestinians themselves. Palestinian leaders, particularly the PLO, have—until being excluded from the most recent Middle East peace talks—been committed more to maintaining their domination over Palestinian politics and the unity of the Palestinian people than to advancing toward a settlement of the issues outstanding with Israel.

While Arab regimes maintain their steadfastness to generate legitimacy, the Palestinians themselves have understood for some time that many of their Arab brothers had long since ceased all but lip service to the cause of Palestine. In a certain sense, the cause of the Palestinians in the minds of the Arabs has become too significant to leave to the Palestinians themselves. The legitimacy of Arab states has depended, at least until the invasion of Kuwait by the Iraqis and the initiation of the recent peace talks, on the Palestinian cause. The basis of that legitimacy—maintaining commitment to the Palestinian cause—could not safely be left to the Palestinians. Instead, it had to be in the hands of the most powerful Arab states.

The Iraqi invasion has transformed the power of this myth as well. Iraq conclusively demonstrated that its commitment to Palestine was incidental to its pursuit of its national interests.

Kuwait and Saudi Arabia responded in kind, as did Syria and Egypt. All the Arab states demonstrated that their legitimacy derived, in the first instance, not from the pursuit of the cause of Palestine but from the defense of their national interests, defined quite conventionally as enhancing the power of the state. This will ultimately have beneficial effects for the Palestinians. They will be freed from the control of other Arabs to make the deals with Israel they define to be in their own national interests. But in the interim, the organizing myth of devotion to the cause of Palestine and the derivation of state legitimacy from that devotion has largely been buried.

Mahdism and Charismatic Leadership

Another pervasive organizing myth of Arab Muslims has been the fantasy of the power of a charismatic leader. That leader, the Mahdi, is divinely inspired or merely possessed of superhuman quantities of courage, strength, and cunning. It is widely believed he will emerge to lead the Arabs out of decadence, repel the invaders, and restore Islam and the Arabs to their rightful, august place among the peoples and cultures of the world.

There have, of course, been especially powerful and successful charismatic leaders throughout Islamic history. According to the believers but also according to historical scholarship, the Prophet Muhammad and his son-in-law, Ali, the Shiite Mahdi, were both magnificent leaders and magnificently charismatic. In recent history, Gamal Abdel Nasser, Libya's Muammar Qaddafi, and Imam Musa al-Sadr of Lebanon (see Ajami 1986) have been marked as charismatic.

Psychoanalytic commentators on charisma (see Winer 1989; Winer, Jobe, and Ferrono 1985) have hypothesized that charismatic leaders are accorded magical power by their followers on account of their presenting solutions to the psychically burdensome problems of their followers. In particular, Winer and his colleagues argue, sometimes in their lives charismatic leaders adopt an active stance that allows them to overcome a passively endured trauma in their past. Through their personal histories, they offer their followers the promise of escaping or overcoming their own passively endured traumas.

The escape from passivity that leaders offer their followers may, of course, take the form of substitute, symbolic solutions rather than solutions to the passively endured trauma that were actually endured. In the context of Middle Eastern politics, this activity may be any kind of opposition to Israel and the superpowers, or, on a less purely reactive level—as in Khomeini's Iran and Nasser's Egypt—a "return," in the form of a contemporary reconstruction, to the golden age of Islam and the Arabs.

The Iraqi invasion of Kuwait demonstrated that the Arabs would not be saved by the arrival of a charismatic leader who would use his magic to restore the greatness of the Arabs. To the contrary, the Arabs were saved by the arrival of 500,000 U.S. troops and high-technology weapons, the fruits of the West. Nor, of course, has a charismatic leader emerged to save Palestine for the Arabs or to deal with any other challenge in a victorious fashion. The belief in the magic of the Mahdi has been severely weakened.

Salaf

Another of the major contributions that Islam has made to the political psychology of the Arab Muslim world has been the notion of *salaf*, or the time of the Prophet. This concept is intertwined with that of *umma* and relates to the formation of the Islamic community by the Prophet in Mecca and Medina. That era in the history of the Muslim peoples is widely perceived to be the most pure, from a religious point of view, with the followers of the Prophet more nearly fulfilling God's wishes for his people than at any other time. The extraordinary successes of the early Muslims in spreading the faith is seen as tangible proof of that purity. The startlingly rapid expansion of *umma* under the early followers of the Prophet is God's tangible proof of the purity of *salaf*. Never since, perhaps, has *umma* been as successful as in those early years. As a result, that period is widely seen as the golden age. In that sense, Islamic history is seen as being fulfilled through regression: insofar as the Muslim peoples can fulfill the conditions that pertained in seventh-century Arabia, they will more nearly approach the perfection of early *umma*. As a consequence, there is a powerful pull to the past in the contemporary Arab world. This pull is most powerfully manifested in the calls of Islamic fundamentalists to return to the ways of life at the time of the Prophet.

But the war in the Gulf also contributed to shattering the myth of *salaf*. The most strident calls for support of Saddam came from Islamic fundamentalist groups throughout the Islamic world. Although they knew Saddam to be a ruthless secularist, they supported his invasion of Kuwait as a blow to the greater evil—the immoral and wealthy ruling families of the Persian Gulf. That support, ultimately, came to have the greatest effect on the Saud family. The members of this family had fashioned themselves as the foremost supporters of Islam in the Arab world—yet here were the very groups they had financed celebrating the invasion of Kuwait. Slowly, the Saudis came to see those fundamentalist groups as their enemy and by early 1992 had moved to end their funding.

Salaf may still have been the golden age but there would be no return to it, at least not one financed by the oil-exporting states of the Gulf.

Catastrophe and Myth Shattering

Organizing myths are a subset of a larger psychosocial category that has been most systematically and thoroughly treated by psychoanalytic self-psychology as "self-objects."[1] In his first major theoretical statement, the psychoanalyst Heinz Kohut (1971) defines self-objects as "objects . . . which are either used in the service of the self and of the maintenance of its instinctual investment or objects which are themselves experienced as part of the self." He also notes that "some of the most intense narcissistic experiences relate to [these] objects" (xiv).

Self-Objects—Part of the Self

To readers familiar with classic Freudian psychoanalysis, this concept may be reminiscent of the idea of cathexis, and self-psychologists, as the followers of Kohut style themselves, consider self-objects to be highly cathected. But to restrict the meaning of self-objects to cathected external phenomena would obscure the fact that self-objects are not purely external objects for the individual but become, in fact, part of the self. Thus while one might mourn the loss of a treasured object that is not a self-object, the loss of, or a disruption of the relationship with, a self-object has different and potentially much more serious psychic consequences. The loss of a self-object threatens the very integrity of one's self and, thus, one's psychological existence.

For Kohut, the relations in earliest childhood between one's self and one's self-objects are the crucial raw materials from which psychic structure is created. The psychic structure, in turn, provides the child and later the adult with a wholesome sense of self-esteem. According to Kohut, psychic structure is created through the child's progressively dealing with the failings of the parents. If the child's myth of the parents' omnipotence is gradually and not abruptly or traumatically shattered, the child's own narcissistic energies will be transformed into his or her psychic structure. The creation of psychic structure, in Kohut's model of psychological development, is the most important achievement of childhood and its most important developmental task.

In the absence of adequate psychic structure, Kohut argues, the child will have a "defect in the self," as he puts it in his later work (Kohut 1977), or a "narcissistic personality disorder," as he has it in his earlier formulation (1971). However conceptualized, the result is an adult who needs to use other persons and objects to provide a sustaining sense of self-worth, that is, as substitutes for his missing psychic structure.

But Kohut also argues that not merely people with inadequate psychic structures—neurotics and psychotics, to use an earlier terminology—have a need for self-objects. A secure "matrix" (Kohut's word) of self-objects is essential to everyone's psychological health. Kohut likens the psychological need for self-objects to the physiological need for oxygen. The distinction between adequate and inadequate psychic structure is revealed not by the presence of self-objects but by the intensity of the individual's need of them to maintain well-being. Kohut argues that irrespective of psychic structure, trauma produces a flight to self-objects. When one's narcissistic equilibrium is threatened by a traumatic external event, both healthy and narcissistically vulnerable individuals will intensify their use of self-objects to restore that equilibrium.

Other theorists posit the conditions under which the flight to self-objects will fail to sustain the individual's psychic integrity.

Self-objects, objects experienced as part of the self, according to H. Hartmann (1950), serve to maintain the individual's "self-representation." The notion of self-representation was later defined by R. Stolorow as "the unconscious, preconscious, and conscious endopsychic representations of the bodily and mental self" (1975, 180). Building on the work of Kohut and of others, Stolorow argues that in terms of its narcissistic aspects, self-representation has three main components: its unity and coherence, its continuity over time, and its valence. The "functional definition" of narcissism that Stolorow proposes suggests that "mental activity is narcissistic to the degree that its function is to maintain the structural cohesiveness, temporal stability, and positive affective coloring of the self-representation" (ibid., 179).

Self-objects clearly play a role in maintaining all three of these components of the self-representation. To the extent that an object functions as a self-object and to the extent that the object is positively valued, the individual will find it easier to maintain the idealization of his or her self-objects. As a result, one's narcissistic well-being will be enhanced. To the extent that there is an interruption in one's relations with one's self-objects—in self–self-object relations—one's well-being will be lost. A principal source of a break in self–self-object relations is a massive degradation in one's self-objects. If an individual's self-objects have been disesteemed, the individual's well-being will be shattered. The enhanced narcissism supplied by the positive valence of one's self-objects would be lost as the esteem in which those self-objects are held decreases. One's sense of cohesiveness, stability, and self-esteem will fail, and incoherence, instability, and self-disesteem, all characteristics of acute narcissistic imbalance, will characterize one's psychic condition.

Sense-Making Crisis in the Arab World

An individual's self-objects may be so degraded that the result is a sense-making crisis, an occasion when an individual can no longer give meaning to his psychic world because of the change in the value of his or her self-objects (Zonis 1984). Rapid or catastrophic social change, such as occurred in the Arab world, can trigger a sense-making crisis even in persons with firm psychic structures. The self-objects that are components of that psychic structure—organizing myths on a personal level—can be shattered by the rapidity of social change. A degradation of the individual's self-objects occurs. The familiar and esteemed values, goals, political symbols, and institutions of a culture—aspects of which have become part of the individual's self-representation—may lose their social utility with rapid change. As they become devalued, so will the sense of self that used them as self-objects.[2]

Clinical data reveal that the experience of the disintegration of the self and of the resultant disintegration anxiety are among the most terrifying and disorganizing of psychological phenomena. Devalued self-objects have the power to trigger that disintegration. The argument here is not that people of the Arab Muslim Middle East can usefully be characterized as having experienced the crisis of disintegration. The point rather is that rapid transformations in one's object world—either of the content of that world or of the social evaluation of those objects—can have profoundly disturbing psychological consequences.

There are numerous individual responses to a sense-making crisis. But a sense-making crisis may trigger the overload of a feedback loop that can lead eventually, after traveling the loop with increasing intensity, to political revolution. Social change may foment a sense-making crisis, producing widespread discontent. Political leaders may articulate that discontent and articulate it in terms of political demands. Those demands may foment inappropriate regime responses, contributing to political instability that induces deeper sense-making crises and, finally, revolution (Zonis 1984, 268). Precisely that feedback loop appears to explain the Iranian revolution, which seems to have been the culmination of an economic crisis induced by the overheating of the Iranian economy due to massive increases in oil revenues and combined with the effects of the Pahlavis' aggressive program of modernization. This Westernization had as a principal component the attempt to suppress Islam as a political and social force.

Rage and Revolution

Revolution is an omnipresent threat from sense-making crises because the devaluation of self-objects always produces rage. When the cohesiveness, stability, or positive valuation of the self-representation is threatened or diminished, the reaction is rage and aggression directed at the perceived source of the narcissistic injury (see, e.g., Kohut 1971). This rage can serve as the driving force for revolution or, less dramatically, for other political movements when political leaders understand how to tap into and channel the immense energies of the rage generated by a sense-making crisis.

The potential for mobilizing narcissistically enraged followers appears to facilitate the emergence of a charismatic leader. Traditionally, charismatic leadership has been studied by sociologists, especially Weber (1968) and by Shils (1965, 1968). More recent psychoanalytically based formulations have been offered by Camic and by Winer and colleagues. Psychoanalytic theory on charisma focuses on the relationship of the leader to the follower and on the psychosocial factors that predispose followers to seek charismatic leadership (Camic 1980; Winer, Jobe, and Ferrono 1985; Winer 1989).

According to Winer, the charismatic leader uses unconscious ideation that results in the followers attributing great power to him. The attribution stems from each follower's conviction that only supernatural or at least special gifts can account for the leader's capacity to read his mind, which is how the experience of being empathically understood is interpreted. Because of the immense power exercised by the charismatic leader over his followers, he may contribute to their building lasting psychic structures. The charismatic relationship can also be used regressively as a soothing substitute for the absent psychic structure (Zonis 1984, 281).

Conspiracy Thinking

Another possible response to sense-making crises appears especially prevalent in the Arab Middle East—a propensity to explain the world in terms of plots and the machinations of enemies through an alleged conspiracy. The popularity of conspiracy thinking in reasoning about political and other affairs has long been recognized by students of the Middle East, as Hishan Sharabi notes:

> The Arab political climate is heavy with conspiracies and plots, for political opposition is mostly underground and secretiveness is the normal condition of political life. Thus the whispering campaign is as effective as radio broadcasts, and news is not so much reporting as reading meaning into developments and events. Just as the obvious is never taken at face value, so the hidden motive is always the object of examination and questioning. The line separating credulity from cynicism is often too thin even from the standpoint of those who are engaged in political action. The mystery permeating this atmosphere induces suspicion and mistrust. The ordinary man sees a plot behind every shift in policy, every decision or development, whether within the army, by a foreign power, or by a political group. There is an oil conspiracy, a Communist conspiracy, and an imperialist conspiracy. (1966, 101)

Conspiracy thinking proliferates during times of severe political, economic, and conceptual crisis. Eastern Europe and the successor states of the Soviet Union, for example, have experienced a surge in conspiracy thinking.[3] My principal argument on conspiracy thinking is based on psychoanalytic and psychiatric theories of paranoia. The most persuasive theories of the paranoid process emphasize that paranoia is the product of a failed attempt to reconstitute a meaningful social world, however painful that meaning may be, after a period of regression and disintegration.[4] Paranoia, then—and by extension conspiracy thinking—can be seen as a means for individuals in the throes of a sense-making crisis to construct a meaningful world after a profound disturbance in self–self-object relationships.

Social Change Since the Gulf War

Since the military expulsion of Iraq from Kuwait, the Arab world appears to be characterized by the same low level of social and political turmoil that has marked its recent history. In one sense, this outcome contradicts the fundamental premise upon which the United States fought the Gulf War. This premise has it that the defeat of Saddam would strengthen the hand of the moderates and enhance stability in the entire Middle East (Rodman 1991). But if my analysis is correct, the Iraqi invasion will unleash powerful forces that will weaken the organizing myths of the Arab and Muslim peoples of the region.

The most dramatic developments since the end of the Gulf War have concerned Iraq itself and its immediate surroundings. The uprisings of the Kurds and the Shiites were suppressed with characteristic brutality, but the unrest continues unabated, spreading to neighboring Turkey and threatening periodically to reenvelop Iraq. Algeria has gone to the brink of an Islamic uprising as Islamic fundamentalists, organized as the Islamic Salvation Front, threatened to win electoral control of the government—a prospect sufficiently horrifying to the military to lead them to seize power in a coup d'état. The Sudan has been brought under the control of a military government apparently dominated by an Islamic fundamentalist leader. The result has been renewed fighting in the south between animist and Christian forces on the one hand and the Islamic military on the other. Saudi Arabia has not seen turmoil because of a preemptive strike by the king. The ruler has instituted a Consultative Council and a Bill of Rights, both to head off criticism from the ardent modernizers and to control the more fundamentalist clerics. The Palestinians have entered peace talks with the Israelis after excluding the leadership of the PLO from the negotiating team and selecting a group from the West Bank as Palestinian negotiators.

These events appear to presage a redirection of the Arab Middle East. The Saudis have effectively stood with the Algerian military to take a stand against Islamic fundamentalism. Yet no powerful vision of any alternative future has yet been articulated.

Arab Myth Making and the Regeneration of Arab Society

If the foregoing argument is correct, the Arab Muslim Middle East is in a state of psychological, as well as social, political, and economic, disarray. What, to borrow from Lenin, is to be done? What is clearly necessary, to remain within the theoretical frame of this argument, is to replace the lost or shattered Arab organizing myths or self-objects with substitutes that work for the Arab people and allow them to make sense of their world in a functional way. Those myths, it would seem, would allow the Arab world to integrate into the social, political, and economic spheres of the West while preserving what Binder, borrowing from Heidegger, refers to as Arab authenticity. The challenge, of course, is to modernize and Westernize while remaining Arab and Muslim in a profound way. Abdallah Laroui would seem to argue that the Arabs cannot, in fact, have it both ways—they cannot achieve both goals simultaneously. Binder also notes that the notion of modernity may be more germane for Western that Eastern authenticity. But some form of accommodation with the West and especially with Western forms of economic life seems to be essential for the Arab world in order to deliver to its members the economic well-being they demand.

The Arab world seems to possess a large array of intellectual systems from which the components of such an accommodation—new and regenerating organizing myths—might be forged. Islamic liberalism (expressed and described in Rahman 1982, Binder 1988, Laroui 1976) is a powerful wellspring of possible forms of accommodation while preserving authenticity. The challenge seems to be for the Islamic world to regain access to *salaf*, the period of greatest closeness between God and the Muslims, while simultaneously adopting key Western ideas.

Sharabi (1966) notes the divergences between the myth of *umma*, or the brotherhood of Arabs, and the practices of the Arab states and Arab peoples. The diversity of religious beliefs and practices subsumed under Islam, the diverse Arabic dialects, and the utter abandonment of Arab unity in the interest of consolidating national territorial control with the ending of colonialism are all instances of those divergences. Sharabi also draws attention to the exclusive emphasis in Islam, including the Koran, on external signs of piety (evinced in prayer and other behaviors) as opposed to concern with the believer's inner life. As a result, Sharabi notes, introspection has been slow to develop among Arabs, with concomitant difficulties of formulating new and more useful self-objects and organizing myths. But, though many forms of Islamic fundamentalism are basically reactionary, Islam has the potential to be a vital, progressive force, even when it attempts to move forward by first moving back to regain and consolidate the virtues of *salaf*. Rahman was in the forefront of those arguing that a judicious interpretation of the principles and scriptures of Islam would produce an active and energetic social and political philosophy.

The time for a comprehensive formulation of the ideas that Rahman adumbrated and their consequences for Arab political life is now. The organizing myths and self-objects of the Arab world have been dealt a decisive and perhaps fatal blow as a result of the Iraqi invasion of

Kuwait. That invasion violated many of the basic principles of the Islamic and Arab peoples. The traditional rationalizations by which many of those peoples had been able to preserve their myths will fail in the aftermath of the war. It is unlikely to prove satisfying to explain the invasion of Kuwait with its wanton destructiveness and gratuitous environmental degradation in terms of the machinations of the Zionists or the imperialists. Those explanations and others will, of course, be used initially to deal with the immediate assault to the self-objects of the peoples of the Middle East, but they will ultimately prove unsatisfactory. By then, those myths and self-objects will have been abandoned.

In the process, the social turmoil in the Middle East will be greater than ever before. But the way will be opened for creative formulations— both by Muslims and outsiders—that will integrate the Arab Islamic world into the market-oriented economies of the West while preserving the authenticity of the peoples of the Middle East.

NOTES

I wish to thank Stanley Renshon for helpful comments and other assistance in the development of this chapter, and Craig Joseph, a graduate student at the University of Chicago, for his assistance.

1. Self-psychology is a flourishing branch of psychoanalysis that was founded by Heinz Kohut (1971, 1977, 1985). Kohut, beginning from Freud's observations on narcissism, postulated on the basis of his clinical experience an independent line of development for narcissism. On the basis of this observation, Kohut developed a highly useful set of psychological and developmental concepts, including a typology of "narcissistic transferences" and "narcissistic personality disorders." In addition to having a strong following in clinical psychoanalysis, Kohut's work has been warmly received among psychoanalytically inclined social scientists and humanities scholars, both because of his explicit interests in history and literature and because of the amenability of his theory to historical and social scientific explanation. The concept of the self-object has been especially fruitful as a bridge between traditionally individualistic psychoanalysis and the study of social phenomena.

2. The particular kinds of events that can threaten narcissistic equilibrium, the individual's reaction to them, and their consequences depend on the particular content and structure of the individual's self-object world. Self-objects may have primarily private meanings or, as in the case of the subject of this chapter, may be shared by members of a culture or other group. Some people become depressed when "their" team loses, and most people would be severely wounded if laughed at in public—particularly at a professional forum or other venue that implicates their self-representation. This chapter, of course, concerns the consequences of narcissistic injury caused by the loss and destruction of deeply important cultural symbols, or organizing myths.

3. Similarly, many of the critiques of Oliver Stone's recent film *JFK* have suggested that its appeal, and the readiness of people to believe the convoluted conspiracy theory propagated in the movie, derives from a crisis of confidence in American governmental and social institutions.

4. See, for example, Norman Cameron's classic articles on the paranoid pseudo-community (1943, 1959).

REFERENCES

Ajami, F. 1986. *The Vanished Imam: Musa al-Sadr and the Shia of Lebanon*. Ithaca: Cornell University Press.

Binder, Leonard. 1980. *Islamic Liberalism: A Critique of Development Ideologies*. Chicago: University of Chicago Press.

Cameron, N. 1943. "The Paranoid Pseudo-Community." *American Journal of Sociology* 49 (July): 32–38.

——— . 1959. "The Paranoid Pseudo-Community Revisited." *American Journal of Sociology* 65 (July): 52–58.

Camic, Charles. 1980. "Charisma: Its Varieties, Preconditions, and Consequences." *Sociological Inquiry* 50 (1): 5–23.

The Economist Book of Vital World Statistics. 1990. New York: New York Times Books/Random House.

Geertz, C. 1973. *The Interpretation of Cultures*. New York: Basic Books.

Hartmann, H. 1950. "Comments on the Psychoanalytic Theory of the Ego. *Psychoanalytic Study of the Child* 5: 17.

Kohut, H. 1971. *The Analysis of the Self: A Systematic Approach to the Psychoanalytic Treatment of Narcissistic Personality Disorders*. Psychoanalytic Study of the Child 4. New York: International Universities Press.

——— . 1977. *The Restoration of the Self*. New York: International Universities Press.

——— . 1985. "On Leadership." In *Self-Psychology and the Humanities: Reflections on a New Psychoanalytic Approach*, ed. C. Strozier. New York: W.W. Norton.

Laroui, Abdallah. 1976. *The Crisis of the Arab Intellectual: Traditionalism or Historicism?* Trans. Diarmid Cammel. Berkeley: University of California Press.

Nietzsche, F. 1954. *The Portable Nietzsche*, ed. W. Kaufmann. New York: Viking.

Rahman, Fazlur. 1982. *Islam and Modernity: Transformation of an Intellectual Tradition*. Chicago: University of Chicago Press.

Rodman, P. W. 1991. "Middle East Diplomacy After the Gulf War." *Foreign Affairs* (Spring): 1–18.

Quandt, William. 1991. "The Middle East in 1990." *Foreign Affairs* 70 (1): 49–69.

Sharabi, H. B. 1966. *Nationalism and Revolution in the Arab World*. New Perspectives in Political Science. Princeton: Van Nostrand.

Shils, Edward. 1965. "Charisma, Order, and Status." *American Sociological Review* 30: 199–213.

——— . 1968. "Charisma." in *International Encyclopedia of the Social Sciences*, ed. D. Sills. New York: Crowell.

Stolorow, R. 1975. "Toward a Functional Definition of Narcissism." *International Journal of Psychoanalysis* 56: 179–85.

Winer, J. A. 1989. "Charismatic Followership as Illustrated in George Eliot's *Romola." Annual of Psychoanalysis* 17: 129–43.

Winter, J. A., T. Jobe, and C. Ferrono. 1985. "Toward a Psychoanalytic Theory of the Charismatic Relationship." *Annual of Psychoanalysis* 12/13: 155–75.

Zonis, M. 1984. "Self-objects, Self-representation, and Sense-making Crises: Political Instability in the 1980s." *Political Psychology* 5 (2): 267–85.

11

The Gulf War's Possible Impact on the International System

■

Alexander L. George

■ ASSESSING THE political-psychological consequences of the Gulf War and their possible impact on the international system is a daunting task. The assessment offered here is necessarily selective and speculative. Before I proceed, two central factors must be identified that were in all likelihood necessary conditions for both the response to Iraq's aggression against Kuwait and its success. First, the Bush administration's motivation to take the lead in a vigorous effort to thwart Saddam Hussein was especially strong because it combined the logic and imperatives of U.S. national self-interest with the ideal of collective security.

Second, President Bush's decision to act in so determined a manner, his remarkable success in forging an international coalition, and the equally remarkable endorsement of the effort by the UN Security Council could take place only because the Gulf crisis was preceded by the end of the cold war. And as the abortive coup of late August 1991 in Moscow reminds us, much of the impact the Gulf War may come to have on the international system depends upon a continuation of the possibilities for change set into motion by the end of the cold war and the more recent disintegration of the Soviet Union. Indeed, one may go so far as to say that these developments have implications for the development of the international system that are more important than those stemming from the Gulf War. I will consider first some implications of these changes in the global strategic environment for regional conflicts.

The New Strategic Environment of Regional Conflicts

It is evident that the end of the cold war has created a new strategic environment that may affect the incidence, the management, and the resolution of regional conflicts. Inspired by his "new thinking,"

Gorbachev's effort to *deideologize, degeopoliticize,* and *demilitarize* Soviet foreign policy—terms employed by Gorbachev and his closest advisors—succeeded in decreasing superpower rivalry and competition in the Third World virtually to the vanishing point. In its place, we witnessed the emergence of a remarkable cooperation between the superpowers to liquidate their involvements in many outstanding regional conflicts and to use their influence instead to bring about a compromise settlement of internal conflicts between rivals whom they had so long supported. The very fact of their support for one side or the other in past regional conflicts gave them the important leverage needed for inducing their clients to move toward resolution of the long-lasting, bitter, inconclusive struggles in such countries as Angola, Afghanistan, Nicaragua, El Salvador, to some extent Namibia, and perhaps eventually also Cambodia.

We must expect that the United States and the republics in what was formerly the Soviet Union, no longer driven by acute geopolitical rivalry, will have less incentive to be concerned about the incidence and outcome of regional disputes in which their important national interests are not at stake and when secondary or minor interests in a particular country are no longer vastly inflated by the dynamics of the cold war. Now that the game of geopolitics that characterized the cold war has subsided, the United States as well as the Russian Republic will find it much easier to limit investment and involvement in those parts of the world in which they do not have anything approximating vital interests. Both states can be expected to apply narrower or at least different conceptions of their interests in regional affairs than during the cold war. They will have to redefine their objectives in those areas and adjust the means employed to achieve them. This requires a major readjustment in conceptualization of foreign policy, a task recognized several years ago by leading Soviet new thinkers and officials in the Foreign Ministry who were engaged in reviving the concept of national interest and considering how it might be utilized as a new basis for Soviet foreign policy. Whatever progress they made in this direction, however, will now have to be reconsidered in the light of the breakup of the Soviet Union. Both the internal process for making foreign policy decisions and the meaning of *national interest* will be affected by the type of federal or confederal structure, if any, that eventually replaces the strongly centralized system of the old Soviet Union.

The possibility must be recognized that an authoritarian regime may emerge in the Russian Republic, that it may attempt to absorb other republics, and that it may eventually attempt to reestablish itself as a great power with regional and global foreign policy objectives. Such a development, although not marking a return to the cold war, would once again alter the strategic environment and reintroduce regional competition with the United States. While taking note of this possibility, the present analysis proceeds on the assumption that the emergence of the Russian Republic as a global superpower that rivals the United States as did the Soviet Union is not likely in the foreseeable future.

Declining interest and involvement in regional affairs, more pronounced in the case of the former Soviet Union than for the United States, is likely to have somewhat contradictory impacts on regional actors. To be sure, it deprives some former regional clients of the support of their superpower patrons; but it also tends to free regional actors from the influence and control that the superpower patron exerted in the past. The consequences of the loosening or breaking of patron-client relations can be expected to vary, but in all cases it requires important adaptations or changes in the former client's policies. Some former clients, deprived of the protection provided by a superpower patron, must find a new basis for their security. This may lead to realignment in their relations with other regional actors or, as in the case of Syria, prompt a tactical move toward greater cooperation with the United States. Other former clients, freed of the constraining, at times moderating, hand of a former superpower patron, may use their new freedom to consider more daring policies in regional disputes. As for Israel, the collapse of the Soviet position in the Middle East weakens Israel's strategic importance to U.S. policy in the region. Although America's moral commitment to the security of Israel remains undiminished, there are already indications that this will not prevent Washington from increasing pressure on Israel to show more flexibility on some regional issues.

We are faced, therefore, with the possibility that unless regional actors behave with uncommon prudence and restraint in their disputes with each other, and unless regional organizations and the United Nations can play an effective role in mediating conflicts, the future may see considerable regional instability and conflict. This leads to a consideration of what role the United States, the United Nations, and regional organizations can be expected to play in reshaping the international system. To focus on their role in this chapter is not to ignore the important role that other members of the international community will continue to play.

What Role Will the United States Play?

This analysis argues that the impact of the Gulf War on the international system will depend in good part on how the United States will define its role in the post–cold war, post-Gulf era. Having emerged from the prolonged bipolar era of the cold war as the only superpower in a novel, complex, multipolar world and having gained new assets and opportunities from its role in the Gulf crisis, the United States is in a unique position to help shape the contours of a new international system, or at least important parts of it. But this leaves unanswered the critical question of the kind of role the United States will define for itself, how acceptable it will be to other states, and how well the United States will be able to implement its chosen role.

In his address to the United Nations on September 23, 1991, President Bush assured his audience that "the United States has no intention of striving for a Pax Americana. However, we will remain engaged. We will not retreat and pull back into isolationism. We will offer friendship and leadership and, in short, we seek a Pax Universalis, built upon shared responsibilities and aspirations." Implicit in the president's statement is a sobering lesson drawn from the Gulf War, namely that important American foreign policy interests cannot always be safeguarded by unilateral U.S. actions but will require multilateral, cooperative arrangements with other states. But what a Pax Universalis implies more concretely for U.S. policy and how much reliance can be placed on multilateral as against unilateral policies for protecting U.S. interests are neither self-evident nor easily predicted. Very likely what role the United States should play in world affairs will remain a controversial issue among opinion leaders and the public.

Indeed, substantial disagreement on this fundamental question exists within the Bush administration itself and was not resolved, if indeed it can be resolved once and for all, at the time this chapter was written. Thus, for example, in early March 1992 the draft "Defense Planning Guidance for the Fiscal Years 1994–1999," released to the press by an unnamed official in order to stimulate public discussion, made the case that the United States should strive to create a world order dominated by one superpower, the United States, which should attempt to perpetuate its leadership position by a combination of constructive behavior and sufficient military might to deter any nation or group of nations from challenging American primacy ("Defense Planning Guidance" 1992). Much more specific than the concept of a new world order outlined by President Bush, the defense planning document's concept resembled a version of Pax Americana much more than it did the Pax Universalis mentioned by the president in his UN address.

Conspicuously, the document reflected a traditional realist concept of security based on the logic of balance of power rather than the logic of collective security. Thus, it stated that the United States should "endeavor to prevent any hostile power from dominating a region whose resources would, under consolidated control, be sufficient to generate global power. . . . We must maintain the mechanisms for deterring potential competitors from even aspiring to a larger regional or global role." Deterrence, however, would be coupled with constructive policies that would attempt to remove or neutralize incentives other states might have for challenging the dominant position of the United States. This would require leadership on the part of the United States "to establish and protect a new order that holds the promise of convincing potential competitors that they need not aspire to a greater role or pursue a more aggressive posture to protect their legitimate interests. . . . In the non-defense areas, we must account sufficiently for the interests of the advanced industrial nations to discourage them from challenging our leadership or seeking to overturn the established political and economic order."

Addressing the possibility of regional conflicts, the Pentagon document was, as the *New York Times* notes, "conspicuously devoid of references to collective action through the United Nations." Instead, the "Defense Planning Guidance" stated that "while the U.S. cannot become the world's 'policeman' by assuming responsibility for righting every wrong, we will retain the pre-eminent responsibility for addressing selectively those wrongs which threaten not only our interests, but those of our allies or friends, or which could seriously unsettle international relations." Hence, "the United States should be postured to act independently when collective action cannot be orchestrated" or in a crisis that demands quick response ("Defense Planning Guidance" 1992).

After sharp criticism, the "Defense Planning Guidance" document was revised by the Pentagon to eliminate passages that conveyed that the United States would pursue the aim of maintaining itself as the only superpower (Tyler 1992). It remains to be seen whether the Bush administration or its eventual successor will be able to develop a new national consensus in support of any kind of ambitious global foreign policy. One can hardly be sanguine about this, given the fact that quite divergent views are being expressed by opinion leaders as to how the United States should orient itself to the rest of the world. At one extreme the country is urged to seize the historic opportunity to finally establish a robust Pax Americana by means of assertive politics and a willingness to employ military capabilities whenever necessary and useful to achieve this grand design. At the other extreme there are variants of a quasi-isolationist stance, which share in common a preference for significantly reducing our overseas commitments and involvements but which differ significantly along conservative and liberal lines as to the domestic agenda to be pursued after "coming home to America."

In between these two extremes there are many distinct shades and varieties of opinion and much groping for a new conceptual approach. Not all those who emphasize giving priority to urgent tasks of domestic renewal veer toward isolationism. Some see putting our society into better order as essential if the United States is to project a model of an effective democratic system and to retain the resources and motivation needed to play a constructive leadership role in reshaping the international system.

Moreover, internationalists who believe the United States should continue active involvement in world affairs subscribe to quite different philosophical approaches to international politics, which, in turn, have diverse implications both for the conceptual design of a more stable and peaceful international system and for the policies needed to move toward that goal. Some internationalists, understandably exhilarated by the role of the United Nations in the Gulf crisis, believe that this compelling example of collective action should now be generalized and institutionalized. For them the Gulf War success has revived and inspirited the old Wilsonian ideal of a world system based on international law and a robust United Nations. However, this liberal internationalist perspective differs strikingly from that of internationalists of the realist persuasion. For the latter a stable, peaceful international system requires above all sophisticated management of the global and regional balances of power.[1] To be sure, the realists concede, the United Nations can sometimes be induced to assist in this endeavor, but it cannot be regarded as the main vehicle; and there will be many occasions in the future, as in the past, when one or more of the great powers will need to bypass the United Nations. It is not impossible to get agreement among liberal and realist internationalists on how to deal with specific security issues on occasion, but the tension between these two perspectives is fundamental and cannot be eliminated.

Just as internationalists are divided along familiar liberal and realist lines that cannot be easily synthesized, so too adherents of the realist school are not fully in tune with each other. As in the past, realists can be expected to disagree among themselves as to whether the national interest is sufficiently engaged in certain situations to warrant U.S. action; and the familiar question as to whether the United States is overcommitted is likely to emerge in debates among realists.

Given the diversity of foreign policy perspectives among influential Americans it will not be easy either for the Bush administration or a successor to it to develop a broad, stable consensus on behalf of a comprehensive and well-defined role in the post–cold war, post–Gulf War era. This does not exclude useful progress toward a better international system, but Washington's efforts are likely to take the form of ad hoc measures and "building blocks" that are not part of a larger, more ambitious conceptual design to which the administration, Congress, and the public are committed.

One of the building blocks that the United States has pursued for a number of years is likely to be reinforced by the Gulf War experience. Americans have traditionally subscribed to the view that totalitarian regimes pose a greater threat to the peace than democratic states. Saddam's aggression has no doubt confirmed this view and is likely to strengthen the existing U.S. determination to promote democracy abroad. Other foreign policy objectives the Bush administration has set for itself include the encouragement of free markets, trade, and human rights; the peaceful resolution of disputes; preventing the spread of weapons of mass destruction; and the curbing of international terrorism. All but the last of these objectives were mentioned in the president's address to the United Nations. In his brief reference to the quest for a new world order the president described it, as on previous occasions, as "an order characterized by the rule of law rather than the resort to force." It is precisely with respect to this particular aspiration for replacing resort to force with the rule of law that ambiguities and difficult questions remain, to which we turn later in this chapter.

Will the United States React to Blatant Aggression in the Future as It Did in the Gulf Crisis?

It is argued here that the initiative and leadership role the United States took in organizing a coalition and obtaining action by the Security Council to oppose Iraq in the Gulf crisis occurred under special circumstances and that such action by the United States in future instances of aggression cannot be counted on. As numerous observers have noted, the response by the United States in the Gulf crisis—as its response to the North Korean aggression against South Korea in June 1950—was motivated as much, if not more, by considerations of U.S. national interest as by principled adherence to the ideal of collective security. President Bush had the good sense to forgo unilateral action against Iraq and decided instead to work through the UN Security Council. Similarly, he had the good sense not to advocate that the Security Council authorize the use of military force at the outset. Rather, he realized that other nations and the American people would support use of force only as a last resort, after coercive diplomacy backed by economic sanctions had been tried.

Working through the Security Council recommended itself to the president not merely out of a desire to implement the principle of collective security but also as a way of dealing with a number of otherwise quite difficult diplomatic and political constraints on U.S. intervention.[2]

Particularly in retrospect we can see that the president exhibited rare political and diplomatic skill in seizing the opportunity—indeed, perhaps the necessity—to marry the logic and imperatives of realpolitik with the logic and modalities of UN-based collective action. Further, it needs to be noted that appealing to the principle of collective security did not suffice to activate Security Council action; Bush was obliged to make use of a variety of potent inducements and pressures to cajole and persuade other states to participate in the coalition against Iraq and to obtain the requisite Security Council resolutions. Finally, as Alvin Rubinstein observes, "It was Washington's leverage, not the authority of the United Nations, that pried loose the funds from countries allied to the United States" that were needed to finance the war against Iraq (1991, 59).

In sum, it is unrealistic to expect the United States to undertake the same kind of strong, determined leadership on behalf of collective security it mounted in opposing the North Korean aggression in 1950 and Iraq's aggression in 1990 in cases when it does not perceive very important national interests of its own to be at stake.

However, this need not prevent the United States from exerting leadership in shaping elements of a new world order in other respects, and for this it can draw upon some important newly acquired assets. Its military and diplomatic supremacy in the post–cold war, post–Gulf War era is understood and often openly acknowledged by other states. It has achieved greater international credibility and respect, however grudging that may be in some cases. Its ability to use its military forces so effectively in meeting a difficult challenge in the Gulf seems to answer questions of will and capability. Its effective leadership of the international community in the Gulf crisis has restored the confidence of some states and their leaders in U.S. leadership in world affairs.

In addition, the victory of American arms in the Gulf has compensated, at least for the time being, for the bad memory and legacy of Vietnam. An overwhelming majority in one public opinion survey favored using combat forces again if confronted with a dictator like Saddam Hussein who sponsors international terrorism, acquires chemical, nuclear, and biological weapons, threatens neighbors, and violates fundamental human rights.[3] However, the labile nature of public views on matters of this kind is well known to specialists in polling. Thus in another survey a majority (51 percent) opposed the United States taking "the lead military role where there are problems in the world requiring a military response," and an overwhelming majority (78 percent) believed "we can't afford to defend so many nations" (Oberdorfer 1991).

It would be a mistake to assume that the Vietnam syndrome is no longer present to serve as a major constraint on U.S. military interventions. In fact, concern over becoming bogged down in a new quagmire in Iraq—one of the lessons of Vietnam—was among the reasons the administration decided to halt military operations in Iraq when it did. Success in the Gulf War has not dimmed responsible Washington policy makers' understanding of the ever-present domestic constraints on interventions abroad and other lessons of the Vietnam experience. In a speech several months after the end of the Gulf War, Robert Gates said that the greatest constraint on the use of military forces abroad is "a lesson learned from Vietnam—every American politician thinks twice about getting into a military conflict with American ground troops where you can't see your way through to the end of it, with high assurance there is only one possible outcome and within a reasonable time frame. . . . I think the constraints on a major overseas use of American power are as strong today as they would have been ten years ago" (ibid.).

Finally, we should take note of another potential limiting factor on the role the United States will want to play in regional conflicts: the possibility that pervasive disenchantment with the military success in the Gulf War will set in if Saddam Hussein survives. Disillusionment in that event could be severely compounded if the administration's Middle East diplomacy proves to be ineffectual and it is forced to admit failure in its efforts to produce progress toward a regional peace settlement.

Does the Success of UN Collective Security in the Gulf Crisis Constitute a Precedent for Dealing with Aggression in the Future?

Certainly the defeat and punishment of a ruler who engaged in naked military aggression is salutary and gratifying, and it also adds something to the deterrence of would-be aggressors in the future. But there are several reasons for doubting that this strikingly successful example of collective security approved by the UN Security Council can be institutionalized and employed to curb the variety of assertive efforts by discontented, ambitious states to change the status quo to be expected in the future.[4]

In the first place, Saddam Hussein's action against Kuwait was one of the most extreme and blatant types of aggression imaginable: a large military force was sent across an established border in an all-out effort to overrun and conquer an independent state whose sovereignty was recognized by the international community and which was a member of the United Nations. But can UN-sanctioned military intervention be expected in response to lesser forms of aggression? Consider, for example, whether the response of the United States and the United Nations would have been the same had Saddam limited his aggression to seizure of a small border area and the Bubiyan or Warbah islands or had Saddam occupied some Kuwait territory as a bargaining chip to extract concessions that Kuwait had refused him in their earlier negotiations. In that contingency it seems hardly likely that the United States would have attempted to deploy a deterrent force in the Gulf, that Saudi Arabia would have accepted such a force on its territory, or that the United Nations would have delivered more than a slap on the wrist or imposed a weak form of sanctions on Saddam.

Neither can the UN role in the Gulf experience become a protypical response to other types of hostile actions—in particular, various types of indirect or covert aggression, even when these have far-reaching objectives such as the overthrow of an existing regime. Still other conflicts that strain the ability of the UN to invoke the principle of collective security are intrastate ethnic and religious conflicts. The rising incidence of such civil conflicts in the post–cold war era, some of which threaten to spill across existing borders, is likely to pose a greater challenge to the international community. As its members struggle to create a new world order they are confronted with the new world disorder. It will not be easy to extend the concept of *aggression* and apply it to such internal conflicts. Thus, for example, one heard very little discussion of who, if anyone, was the aggressor in the internal Yugoslav convulsion of 1991, and the United States was unwilling to exert leadership in dealing with that conflict.

Finally, one cannot expect that the triumph of collective security in the Gulf crisis will enable members of the United Nations finally to agree, after many past failures, on a more comprehensive, inclusive definition of aggression that will then serve as a basis for implementation of collective security.

An Enhanced Role for the United Nations in Maintaining Security?

Qualified optimism coupled with important cautions seems appropriate in assessing whether and in what ways the Gulf War success will contribute to an enhanced role in security matters for the United Nations.[5] *Peace enforcement*, a term used to characterize the UN's role in the Gulf crisis, is perhaps the most difficult contribution to security to expect from that body. However edifying the demonstration that the Security Council can work the way it was supposed to in the face of flagrant aggression, for reasons already suggested in discussing the special character of the U.S. motivation, the United Nations is likely to be able to do so only under very special conditions that are not likely to be present in many other cases. The ad hoc improvisation in the Gulf crisis of a military coalition that fielded very large forces cannot be easily replicated in future cases of aggression. Since other states have only a very limited power projection capability it would be difficult for the United Nations to mount effective action of any substantial size without the participation of U.S. military forces to provide the necessary logistical support. Moreover, it will continue to be very difficult for the United Nations to establish a permanent standing military force of any substantial capability that can be deployed to defend a victim of aggression. Even more problematical is the possibility that the dormant Military Staff Committee of the United Nations can be activated, as the Soviets urged for several years, possibly to plan for and conduct substantial military operations against an aggressor state. On the other hand, the Military Staff Committee might play a role were the Security Council to authorize a small peace enforcement operation.

In contrast to peace enforcement, the peacekeeping and mediation activities of the United Nations had already been significantly enhanced before the Gulf crisis. Since 1988 the United Nations has been called upon to mount eight new peacekeeping operations, compared to thirteen in its previous forty-three years of existence. This development can be expected to continue, particularly if the considerable practical difficulties and financial costs of such operations are addressed (see Rikhye forthcoming). Also promising is the possibility that the United Nations may be able to develop a small rapid deployment force that could respond to a request from a member state that feared attack and that would serve not as a war-fighting force but rather as a trip wire deterrent and as a step toward moving the dispute into negotiation and mediation.[6] At a Security Council meeting of heads of government on January 31, 1992, the secretary-general was asked to present his recommendations by July 1 for strengthening the capacity of the United Nations for preventive diplomacy, peace making, and peacekeeping (missing was any reference to a peace enforcement role for the United Nations.)

In assessing whether the UN role in defeating aggression by Iraq can be generalized to a broader set of cases it must be recognized that by virtue of their veto power in the Security Council the five permanent members of that body will continue to be shielded from its condemnation and punitive action. In this connection an intriguing question arises: will the fact that the five major powers did cooperate to enable the United Nations to take action against Saddam Hussein, thereby identifying themselves with the general norm against aggression, make it more difficult for them in the future to resort to unilateral military interventions in pursuit of their national interests? It would be predictable that much of the rest of the international community would denounce such actions. More concretely with respect to the United States, will the leadership role it performed so effectively against Iraq's aggression and will President Bush's call for a new international order based on the rule of law constrain it in the future from unilateral military actions such as those it took in Grenada and Panama? In this connection, Adam Roberts asks whether the United States "while upholding international law in general . . . will continue to apply it in a limited and partial way" (1991, 523). The more fundamental point to be made is that the corpus of international law and indeed the UN Charter are capable, through selection and interpretation, of providing justification for the unilateral resort to force to protect one's interests against perceived threats.

The fact that the five permanent members of the UN Security Council cooperated in dealing with Iraq's aggression, and the increased cooperation of the superpowers generally in dealing with regional conflicts since the end of the cold war, has provided evidence that the Security Council can become an increasingly important force for stability and order in the international system. But it should be noted that this possibility will not necessarily be viewed with complete equanimity by some smaller countries that fear that cooperation among the five permanent members might lead to the transformation of the Security Council into a potent directorate of the big powers that would attempt to impose its will on smaller powers in security matters of great concern to them.[7] Similar concerns were expressed at various times in the past, it may be recalled, when improved relations between the superpowers and the possibility of their cooperation in dealing with regional security problems raised the specter of a superpower condominium.

Increased Prospects for Intervention for Humanitarian Purposes?

As noted earlier, the end of the cold war has contributed indirectly to the rising incidence of intrastate ethnic and religious conflicts. This development poses a new challenge and a difficult dilemma for the United Nations and members of the international community. Immediately after the end of the Gulf War, Saddam's efforts to suppress the Kurds and the flight of many of them to Turkey and Iran raised the question of outside intervention in Iraq to enable the masses of Kurdish refugees to return in safety. The problem was compounded by similarly repressive measures taken by Iraqi forces against the Shiites in southern Iraq. Not surprisingly, the UN secretary-general took the traditional position that the UN could not intervene in the internal affairs of a sovereign country without its prior consent. Absent that consent, not only UN intervention to mediate a civil war or to engage in peacekeeping but even a humanitarian mission would be excluded. The UN, therefore, limited its activities on behalf of the Kurds and the Shiites to those acceptable to the Iraqi government, and these included some humanitarian activities on behalf of the Shiites in southern Iraq and efforts to facilitate an agreement between the Iraqi government and Kurdish leaders on the question of the scope and character of autonomy for the Kurdish minority in northern Iraq. On the other hand, the United States and several other members of the victorious coalition interpreted their responsibility more broadly than did the UN. They responded to the exigencies of the situation in northern Iraq by putting diplomatic pressure on the Iraqi government to withdraw its forces from the Kurdish homeland area and, without Baghdad's consent, sent a small military force into northern Iraq to establish a safe haven zone to which the Kurdish refugees in Turkey could return. The Bush administration based this action on an interpretation of Security Council Resolution 688 (April 5, 1991), which called on all member states to contribute to humanitarian efforts on behalf of the plight of the Kurdish minority.

These responses to the Kurdish and Shiite difficulties raise the possibility that in the future members of the international community may assert a new norm demanding the right to intervene for humanitarian purposes in the internal affairs of a regime engaged in repression of minorities.[8]

The possibility of outside intervention in an internal conflict arose again under different circumstances when the efforts of Slovenia and particularly those of Croatia to declare independence of the Yugoslav state led to large-scale, prolonged military clashes between Croatian forces and the substantial Serbian minority in Croatia backed by the Yugoslav armed forces. In this chaotic situation during the summer of 1991 the role of the United Nations was conspicuous by its absence, until finally, in late September, it voted an arms embargo on participants in the internal Yugoslav war. The earlier effort of the Conference on Security and Cooperation in Europe (CSCE) and its newly constituted Crisis Prevention Center to fill the vacuum proved quickly to be abortive. The strong reluctance of a number of its member states to create a precedent for its intervention in situations of intrastate ethnic or religious conflicts quickly came to the surface, and coupled with the requirement of unanimity of its member states, this blocked any action. In consequence, the CSCE abandoned thoughts of playing a constructive role in the Yugoslav crisis. Even less was heard about the possibility of a NATO role. Instead, members of the European Community made concerted but futile efforts to persuade Croatia, Serbia, and the Yugoslav governments to agree to a cease-fire and to mediate the dispute. The European

Community threatened economic sanctions to induce the central Yugoslav government to rely on diplomacy rather than force in dealing with
Croatia, and it also sent a small number of peace monitors and offered
to introduce a peacekeeping force once a stable cease-fire was achieved.
Repeated breakdown of the cease-fire agreements it had helped to ar-
range finally led foreign ministers of the European community in September to consider introducing a military force that would have the
more ambitious peace enforcement objective rather than merely a peacekeeping mission, but they held off doing so when several members
warned that so risky a step could draw their own forces into substantial,
prolonged fighting. Indeed, members of the European Community
found it difficult to agree on how to respond collectively on many aspects of the Yugoslav crisis. One-quarter of Croatia was taken over by
Serbia, triggering a mass of Croatian refugees.

Finally, in early November the European Community placed broad
economic sanctions on Yugoslavia and urged the UN Security Council
to order an oil embargo in the hope that this would lead to a curtailment
of military operations. The members of the European Community decided to seek an oil embargo through the UN because Serbia's main
suppliers are the Soviet Union and Libya, countries that would not be
affected by an embargo ordered by the community. President Bush then
announced that the United States would join in the sanctions and
would support the call for a UN oil embargo.

With the European Community unable to bring about a cease-fire,
the United Nations finally joined the effort. Former U.S. Secretary of
State Cyrus Vance was designated as special envoy and after repeated
trips to Yugoslavia finally secured the agreement of the warring parties
to a formula that would send 14,000 members of a peacekeeping force to
Yugoslavia to monitor a cease-fire and to protect Croatia's Serbian minority. After March 1992, Serbian forces occupied a large part of Bosnia
and undertook massive "ethnic cleansing" of non-Serbs. The United
Nations intervened in an effort to provide humanitarian assistance to
the beleaguered population of Sarajevo.

Whatever the final outcome of European Community and UN efforts
to end the internal Yugoslav conflict, the case illustrates the need to give
more attention to strengthening the mediation and peacekeeping capabilities of regional organizations. Their past record may not be encouraging in this respect, but it does include some successes. The Economic
Community of West African States, for example, deployed a military
force in Liberia in August 1990 to help end the civil war in that country.
And, more recently, the Organization of American States (OAS) intervened in Haiti, although thus far unsuccessfully, in an effort to restore
its deposed, democratically elected president.

Will Efforts to Curb Proliferation of Weapons of Mass Destruction and to Limit Conventional Arms Transfers Be Successful?

The Gulf War heightened concern over the proliferation of weapons of mass destruction and has given additional impetus to efforts to curb this development. The revelation that Iraq had been secretly at work developing atomic weapons was not unexpected by specialists who were aware of the loopholes in the inspection procedures of the International Atomic Energy Agency. But the magnitude of the violations perpetrated by Iraq, which became better known after the end of the war, jolted members of the IAEA to consider ways of strengthening its monitoring and inspection procedures under the safeguards agreement in the Nuclear Non-Proliferation Treaty. Discussions are under way to create a special unit of the agency that would receive national intelligence information from permanent members of the UN Security Council on possible violations of the nonproliferation accord. Also under consideration is a proposal for special inspections to ferret out covert nuclear weapons programs. This idea, generally supported by the European Community and Moscow, however, is said to have created unease among Argentina, Brazil, and other countries (Devroy, 1991; Lewis 1991a, 1991b, 1991c). Under this plan the IAEA would assert its right to demand "challenge" inspections that, if refused, would lead to the matter being placed before the Security Council.

In any case, it is possible, if the UN-supported coalition of states succeeds in its effort to ferret out all of Iraq's weapons of mass destruction, that the United States and other members of the international community will use this unusual action as a precedent to warn other states against acquiring similar weapons, particularly states perceived to be bent on pursuing aggressive aims. While unilateral action of the kind Israel undertook against Iraq's nuclear facilities in 1981 is always possible against other states, less likely is the establishment of a new international norm that would legitimate forceful action by one or a coalition of states in a peacetime situation to disarm the production facilities and weapons of mass destruction of a hostile state. The absence of such a norm, however, need not deter a state that felt threatened to invoke the UN Charter provision regarding the right of self-defense in order to undertake a preemptive strike against such targets.

The Gulf War has also given impetus to international efforts to regulate and control transfers of conventional arms by the major suppliers to the Middle East. Meeting in Paris in early July 1991 in response to an initiative by President Bush, the five permanent members of the Security Council agreed not only to seek exclusion of weapons of mass destruction from the Middle East but also to develop "rules of restraint" on conventional arms sales and to share information about weapons transfers to the Middle East. The five powers also agreed to support a British initiative to create an international arms registry at the United Nations and to expand their future discussions to address global weapons sales. (In December, the UN General Assembly voted overwhelmingly to establish such a register, which will initially apply only to sales of heavy arms that can be used to seize and hold territory.)

At their second meeting in London in mid-October, the five powers developed a list of general guidelines to regulate export of conventional weapons. They also agreed to inform each other about their transfer of weapons to the Middle East but, it should be noted, without prejudice to their existing commitments to governments in that region. Finally, they agreed to meet regularly at least once a year.

The five permanent members of the Security Council, it should be noted, account for approximately 85 percent of all arms exports. Serious questions may be raised as to whether the outcome of their deliberations is more than a paper agreement. In addition to important economic stakes in continuing the sale of weapons, some of the five powers will wish to continue arms transfers in order to contribute to the security of friendly states. The very general guidelines stated by the permanent five at their London meeting are not lacking in ambiguity and, certainly, legitimate questions can be raised as to whether they can be operationalized. It would be premature, however, to dismiss the guidelines as meaningless. The process established by the permanent five is at an early stage; a consultative mechanism has been set up that may lead to useful discussion of specific aspects of conventional arms transfers later on. Instead of undertaking the ambitious objective of using arms transfer controls to impose ceilings on the conventional forces of recipient states, a more realistic aim would be to focus selectively on certain classes of weapons, such as ground-to-ground missiles, that are particularly destabilizing. Indeed, one way of characterizing the general guidelines is that they boil down to a rule of thumb that suggests it is all right to export conventional arms when it contributes to stability in the Middle East or other regions but not when it would be destabilizing. Whether and to what extent the permanent five can agree on how this rule of thumb applies to specific weapons transfers remains to be seen.

The Middle East: Will There Be Progress Toward a Peace Settlement?

It is in the Middle East, not surprisingly, that the end of the cold war and the Gulf War have had their greatest political psychological impact.

It may be, as Marvin Zonis suggests in his chapter, that the Gulf War will lead to a questioning of old Arab myths and their gradual replacement; but it is also likely, as Carl Brown suggests in his chapter, that for many Arabs the experience of the Gulf War may reinforce existing beliefs and images. Perhaps what is to be expected is a greater polarization of Arab opinion between traditional and more pragmatic orientations. It remains to be seen what impact such changes will have on the policies of different Arab governments. Nor should one overlook the fact that the war produced enormous dislocation of peoples, created a stream of refugees, and disrupted local and regional economic patterns, all of which may contribute eventually to internal instability in some of the countries of the region and in relations among them.[9]

For the time being, however, the ends of the cold war and the Gulf War have created a new strategic environment that offers opportunities for greater stability in the region, though, paradoxically, greater stability does not necessarily provide momentum for a peace settlement. The United States has emerged as the predominant military power in the region and has acquired a position of unprecedented influence, which can be employed to reshape the basis for security and peace in the region. As Martin Indyk notes, "All the regional powers now recognize us as the preponderant power and seek our good graces. All our friends in the region have been strengthened by the war's outcome; all our enemies have been weakened" (1991, 33).

Among the many complex features of the Middle East that have contributed to its instability in the past, as Indyk notes, is the unusual character of the strategic game in this region. Diplomacy in the Middle East has been subject to not one but four balances of power! These balances concern the relationship between Israel and the Arab states, between moderate and radical Arab states, between the Arab states and Iran, and between the two superpowers. In the past the United States faced the challenging task of using its resources and influence to maintain favorable balances in all four of these axes and to manage the often intricate relationship between some of the balances. American policy was required to identify newly emerging threats to these balances and to shift its policies accordingly. However, Washington did not always succeed in doing so, the most recent and notable failure of its balance of power maneuvers being its failure to recognize the threat Iraq posed to its neighbors after the conclusion of its war with Iran.

Quite remarkably, all four balances are now stable and favorable at least for the maintenance of peace though, paradoxically, not for rapid movement to a settlement of the Arab-Israeli conflict. The end of the cold war had already alleviated the task of preventing the Soviet Union from extending its influence in the region and using it to the disadvantage of the U.S. position and the interests of Israel and pro-Western

Arab states. From the standpoint of the United States the outcome of the Gulf War had a very favorable impact on the other three balances. Iraq's effort to alter the balance between Arab states in order to move toward a hegemonic position was thwarted. Even if Saddam Hussein survives and attempts to recoup, the other Arab states backed by U.S. power are in a strong position to deter him or a successor who entertains similar aspirations and to deal with new transgressions. Currently, U.S. policy addresses this task by providing substantial arms assistance to Saudi Arabia and other Gulf states and by attempting to make individual arrangements with some of them for maintaining a U.S. military presence, the prepositioning of military equipment, and military cooperation. Efforts immediately after the Gulf War by Egypt, Syria, and Saudi Arabia to develop joint defensive security arrangements were stillborn. As for a possible Syrian threat to the balance between Arab states, that danger seems remote in the foreseeable future. Adjusting to the loss of his Soviet patron and to the dominant position of the United States in the region, President Assad has found it advisable for tactical reasons to move closer to the United States and to adopt a more accommodating diplomatic profile.

The balance between the Arab states and Iran also remains reassuring for the time being. Iran's preoccupation with internal problems since the end of the costly war with Iraq and its realistic assessment of its interests during and after the Gulf War have alleviated the anxiety of the other Gulf states that Iran might quickly move after the defeat of Iraq to establish a hegemonic position in the Gulf. Iran continues to move cautiously toward a rapprochement with the West. On the other hand, recent intelligence and news reports indicate a possible interest by Iran to develop a nuclear weapons capability and other strategic weapons. Whether and how soon Iran will reemerge as a threat to other Gulf states remains to be seen.

Finally, the war left Israel in an unusually favorable balance vis-à-vis potentially hostile Arab states. With Iraq defeated, the PLO and Jordan discredited for having sided with or tilted toward Iraq during the war, and Syria struggling to adjust to the loss of Soviet support and U.S. predominance, Israel emerged from the war with a marked improvement in its security position that seems likely to persist for a number of years. Not only did Israel manage to stay out of the Gulf War despite Iraq's provocative SCUD attacks, other Arab states opposing Iraq gave some indication during the conflict that they would accept Israel's right to retaliate should it choose to do so. Perhaps for the first time, moderate Arab states and Israel faced in common a severe threat from a radical Arab state.

Thus, it would appear that the altered strategic landscape in the Middle East created greater stability and reduced the likelihood of another war in the region. However, while there are opportunities also for reduction of tensions and the building of greater mutual trust, the situation did not appear ripe for mediation of a comprehensive peace settlement immediately after the end of the Gulf War. One must ask how strong were the incentives of the regional actors, in contrast to those of the United States, to move in this direction if they perceived that changes in the status quo might involve risks and costs that would not be compensated by significant gains. Perhaps not all the Arab states that participated in the coalition that defeated Iraq regarded the new strategic environment created by the Gulf War as so unsatisfactory as to require concessions that might be necessary for a peace settlement with Israel. Perhaps they did not view the postwar situation in the region as highly unstable or likely to spawn substantial new threats to their well-being. And, most likely, they did not see opportunities for making significant gains at Israel's expense through unilateral action or in concert with each other; for this, they realized they must rely on U.S. pressure on Israel.

The dominant position of the United States in the region has a quieting effect for the time being on whatever impulses for a more assertive policy Syria may nurture. Assad's priorities are to consolidate his position in Lebanon, find ways of continuing to develop his military power as best he can, and continue to improve relations with the United States without giving up anything of value in the hope that the United States can provide a protective buffer against Israel if the need arises. Finally, having actively cooperated with the United States in defeating Iraq, Syria believes that it is shielded from undue pressure from the United States to agree to security and arms control initiatives that it judges to be contrary to its interests—though it, too, can be expected to listen to the positive inducements the United States may offer in return for cooperation.

Of the various regional actors it is probably the Palestinians on the West Bank whose attitudes and policy preferences have been affected most by the Gulf War. Palestinian leaders who participated in the Munich Conference displayed a pragmatism that surprised most observers. That West Bank Palestinian leaders accepted the general concept of autonomy and achieved a more prominent position and greater influence vis-à-vis the PLO leadership appeared at first to augur well for serious discussions with Israel in their bilateral talks. However, when these talks occurred the two sides took sharply divergent positions on the type of autonomy that would be acceptable. Domestic political constraints on the Israeli government and pronounced differences among elements of the Palestinian leadership evidently will make it difficult to reach a mutually acceptable compromise. And from the beginning the PLO and the Palestinians on the West Bank and Gaza were apprehensive that, given their relatively weak bargaining position vis-à-vis Israel, they would be pressured at some point by the United States to accept arrangements for a form of limited autonomy that might well foreclose genuine self-determination and independence in the future. Such concerns could only be reinforced when, after another round of inconclusive talks in early March 1992, the United States sharply criticized the Palestinian delegation for foot-dragging and for holding out for elections and near total control over the occupied territories and urged the Palestinians to be more receptive to the limited form of autonomy the Israeli delegation had put forward (Friedman 1992).

As for Israel, it had little incentive to make more substantial concessions. Operating from what it considered to be an unusually favorable position of strength vis-à-vis the Palestinians and the Arabs, the Likud government envisaged that peace, if it was to come, should be essentially on its own terms. The chief problem Israel expected to have was with the United States, depending on how much pressure for important concessions it was subjected to by Washington. Before the Israeli elections in June 1992, the United States limited itself to pressing Israel to accept a moratorium on new settlements on the West Bank, perhaps on the assumption or in the hope that such a concession on Israel's part might suffice to induce the Palestinians to settle for a type of autonomy close to that offered by Israel. With the electoral victory of the Labor party and the emergence of Rabin as prime minister, a more flexible policy on settlements on the West Bank and the question of autonomy strengthened the possibility of an agreement.

If this characterization of the immediate postwar attitudes on regional actors is essentially correct, the Arab-Israeli conflict can hardly be said to be ripe for successful mediation. Several of William Zartman's conditions for ripeness of regional conflicts for mediation—a "hurting stalemate" and the expectation that one's position may soon deteriorate—were not present (1985). Nor was the U.S. effort to organize a Middle East conference based on the supposition that the regional conflict was ripe for mediation. It was for other reasons and with lesser objectives that the Bush administration worked indefatigably to bring the Arab states, Palestinian representatives, and Israel to the table. The sense of urgency displayed by Washington to organize the conference appears to have been stimulated by a number of considerations. Certainly it was important for the administration to honor the tacit commitment it made to its coalition partners during the war, to dissuade them from supporting linkage of terms for settling the conflict with Iraq with a Middle East conference and to organize such a meeting after the war.

But other considerations and hopes also drove Washington's effort to assemble a conference. Even though the new strategic situation in the region viewed from a balance of power perspective was favorable for the time being, the Bush administration may have drawn the lesson from its failure to anticipate and prevent Saddam Hussein's attack on Kuwait that it is hazardous to continue to rely on a policy of manipulating the various balances within the region. In addition, Washington may fear that new and unforeseen developments will sooner or later undermine moderate regimes in some of the Arab states and produce new instabilities and threats to the peace in the region. Similarly, the administration may be reluctant to settle for the kind of stability in the region that requires the prolonged presence of U.S. military forces. And it may be concerned lest threats to the peace arise that once again call for the deployment and possible use of large U.S. ground forces. Notwithstanding the success of U.S. arms against Iraq, Washington cannot view with equanimity the possible costs and risks of intervention against increasingly better armed regional actors. The administration may regard it as urgent to push for a movement toward peace also because it believes that U.S. influence in the region will never be greater, that the United States will not be able to maintain indefinitely the level of resources it devotes to safeguarding its interests in a volatile Middle East, and that delay in getting a serious peace process started may lead to a further hardening of positions in the Arab-Israeli conflict and stimulate efforts of some regional states to acquire weapons of mass destruction.

In sum, the end of the cold war and the end of the Gulf War have created greater fluidity in the international system, particularly in the Middle East, and have given greater impetus to efforts to control the proliferation of weapons of mass destruction and the traffic in conventional arms. It is possible to foresee a further strengthening, though no dramatic changes, in the role the United Nations plays in maintaining and restoring peace. And there may be the beginnings of some movement toward new international norms legitimating or at least tolerating humanitarian intervention in civil conflicts. However, much depends on what role the United States adopts in attempting to contribute to the emergence of a new world order, and as suggested in this chapter, there is considerable uncertainty as to the domestic support available within the United States for pursuing an ambitious internationalist foreign policy.

NOTES

I want to express appreciation to the United States Institute of Peace and for helpful comments on an early draft by Hugh DeSantis, Juliette L. George, James Goodby, Don Peretz, Samuel W. Lewis, Indar J. Rikhye (major general retired), Eugene Rostow, and Dankwart Rustow.

1. Arguing that the major challenge the United States will face after the end of the Gulf War will be "to preserve the new balance of power that will emerge from this conflict," Henry Kissinger dismisses the notion of " 'a new world order,' which would emerge from a set of legal arrangements and be safeguarded by collective security." The problem with such an approach, he says, is that "it assumes that every nation perceives every challenge to the international order in the same way, and is prepared to run the same risks to preserve it" (Kissinger 1991, 44).

2. For a detailed analysis, see Herrmann (forthcoming).

3. This survey was conducted by a bipartisan group, the America Talk Issues Foundation, using leading Republican and Democratic polling experts. The results of the poll were reported by Johnson (1991).

4. The term *collective security* is employed loosely here to encompass both an enforcement action against aggression undertaken and carried out by the UN Security Council and, as in the Gulf crisis, collective "self-defense" approved by the Security Council.

5. For a more detailed analysis, see Bennett and Lepgold (forthcoming).

6. In fact, just such a rapid deployment force to serve as a possible trip wire has been recommended by Urquhart (1991, 37).

7. For an illuminating and sobering discussion of various reservations regarding the way in which the UN Security Council operated during the Gulf crisis and the use of that body by the United States, see Fletcher Roundtable (1991).

8. For a useful discussion of the historical background and possible legal basis for intervention in the internal affairs of a state on behalf of humanitarian objectives, see Henrikson (1991). See also the forthcoming study by Inter-American Dialogue on changing norms regarding legitimate international action against states in flagrant violation of human rights.

9. For a detailed discussion, see Peretz (1991).

REFERENCES

Bennett, Andrew, and Joseph Lepgold. Forthcoming. "Reinventing Collective Security: Criteria and Prospects After the Cold War." *Political Science Quarterly*.

"Defense Planning Guidance for the Fiscal Years 1994–1999." Excerpts from transcript. 1992. *New York Times*, March 8.

Devroy, Ann. 1991. "Bush Advised to Set Arms Search Deadline." *Washington Post*, September 21.

Friedman, Thomas L. 1992. "Peace Talks: Israeli Elections Barges In." *New York Times*, March 8.

Henrikson, Alan K. 1991. "Defining a New World Order: A Discussion Paper." Prepared for the Fletcher Roundtable, May. Medford: Fletcher School of Law and Diplomacy, Tufts University.

Herrmann, Richard. Forthcoming. "Coercive Diplomacy and the Crisis over Kuwait: 1990–1991." In *The Limits of Coercive Diplomacy*, rev. ed., ed. Alexander L. George. Boston: Little, Brown.

Indyk, Martin. 1991. "The Post-War Balance of Power in the Middle East." Unpublished manuscript.

Inter-American Dialogue. Forthcoming. Study in progress. Washington, D.C.

Johnson, Haynes. 1991. "Oh, Those 'Splendid Little Wars.' " *Washington Post*, July 26.

Kissinger, Henry. 1991. "A Postwar Agenda." *Newsweek*, January 28, 24.

Lewis, Paul. 1991a. "Baghdad Detains 40 U.N. Inspectors Who Find A-Plans." *New York Times*, September 24.

———. 1991b. "U.N. Maps Plan to Nab Atomic Cheats." *New York Times*, October 11.

———. 1991c. "U.N.'s Nuclear Inquiry Exposes Treaties' Flaws." *New York Times*, November 10.

Oberdorfer, Don. 1991. "Strategy for Solo Superpower." *Washington Post*, May 19.

Peretz, Don. 1991. "The Impact of the Gulf War on Israeli and Palestinian Political Attitudes." *Journal of Palestine Studies* 21 (81): 17–35.

Rikhye, Indar J. Forthcoming. Study in progress. Washington, D.C.: United States Institute of Peace.

Roberts, Adam. 1991. "A New Age in International Relations?" *International Affairs* 67 (3).

Rubinstein, Alvin Z. 1991. "New World Order or Hollow Victory?" *Foreign Affairs* 70 (Fall): 59.

Tyler, Patrick. 1992. "Pentagon Drops Goal of Blocking New Superpowers." *New York Times*, May 24.

Urquhart, Brian. 1991. "Learning from the Gulf." *New York Review of Books* 38 (March 7).

Zartman, William. 1985. *Ripe for Resolution*. New York: Oxford University Press.

The Gulf War and the
Future Global (and Arab?) Order

■

Dankwart A. Rustow

THE GULF WAR of 1990–1991 raises major psychological and political questions, in both an inter-Arab and a global context. Many of these themes have been discussed from a variety of viewpoints in the preceding chapters by Marvin Zonis and Alexander L. George. In this commentary, I try to integrate these, as well as other, broader themes, within a single historical, psychological, and political perspective.

Among the specific questions this essay will address are: What was the peculiar background of international relations that made Iraq's brutal attack on Kuwait possible? What was the unusual conjuncture of attitudes and expectations among the leaders of outside powers that allowed them to become involved in the unprecedented diplomatic and military counteroffensive against Saddam Hussein's aggression? And, most crucially, what will be the likely impact of the Gulf War of 1990–1991 on the future of inter-Arab relations and as a precedent for a new world order? More specifically, as Marvin Zonis suggests, does the Gulf crisis indicate that the Palestinian issue is no longer the convenient basis for inter-Arab legitimacy or, as L. C. Brown puts it, a *"diabolus ex machina"*? More broadly, has the crisis brought about a basic shift so that, as Zonis puts it, "The defense of the state territory, not the Arab homeland, has become the most significant priority"?

Like Alexander George, I consider myself a cautious optimist, although I find myself more confident—at least within a medium time span of the next thirty to fifty years—about a new global order than about peaceful integration within the Arab world.

The Global Context

By way of background, it is essential to recall that the 1990–1991 Gulf War occurred in a unique context of intense international communication within the ever more closely knit global village. It was a televised war in which correspondents of CNN (Cable News Network) reported the latest events, hour by hour, from Kuwait, Washington, Baghdad, Tel Aviv, Moscow, and elsewhere to world audiences of unprecedented size. Two aspects of this new global communication seem particularly relevant to the questions raised initially: the worldwide movement toward democracy and the intensive global trade in such items as petroleum and advanced and conventional weapons.

The Gulf crisis erupted at a time when modern nations were moving toward liberal democracy at an unprecedented pace. Mikhail Gorbachev's policies of *glasnost* and *perestroika* that were spelling the end of communism and of the Soviet superpower were only the climax of a much broader movement that began in the 1970s with the exit of Europe's oldest dictatorships from Spain and Portugal. By 1990 elected governments had replaced military regimes from Chile to Haiti, and transitions toward democracy had been initiated in countries from Turkey, South Korea, and the Philippines to South Africa (see Rustow 1991).

There were, of course, some holdouts, such as Cuba, North Korea, and most notably China among the communist, and Thailand, Burma, and Singapore among the authoritarian or military regimes. There also have been recent relapses in countries such as Haiti, Algeria, and Peru. Above all, the collapse of the imperial Soviet Union and its arrogant attempt at a totally planned command economy has left an economic vacuum and many ethnic and political tangles in and among its fifteen successor states.

As Samuel P. Huntington points out, this was not the first tide of democracy to sweep across the world's continents (Huntington 1991; see also Rustow 1992). Still, in the periods after 1776–1789, 1828, 1918, or 1945, democracy found itself in active competition with hereditary monarchies or with Bonapartist, Leninist, or Fascist dictatorships. But now, the self-admitted failure of Leninism has left, for the first time in history, liberal democracy as the only alternative to which successor regimes from Bucharest and Warsaw to Moscow and Alma Ata must aspire—or at least pretend.

In this same final quarter of the twentieth century there has been an exponential increase in international trade and financial transactions, including interacting stock markets in New York, London, Frankfurt, Tokyo, and Singapore; financial havens for ill-gotten gains from Switzerland to the Cayman Islands; and a political transfer of cartel power over the world's petroleum from Western companies to Third World governments.

The unprecedented profits of OPEC countries in the 1970s and 1980s, in turn, largely flowed to banks in North America and Europe, whose lending spree caused the unprecedented debt crisis in Latin American and other developing countries in the 1980s. And the need to reschedule unpayable debts, in turn, undermined the prestige of militarist or authoritarian regimes and, conversely, strengthened the international role of such institutions as the International Monetary Fund and the World Bank. Those institutions, in turn, tended to have greater confidence in liberal-democratic rather than authoritarian regimes as offering better long-term prospects for growth and stability.

It is this currently unchallenged global stature of liberal democracy that has prompted the political philosopher Francis Fukuyama to depict our era as the end of history, or, more specifically, as the terminal point of the Hegelian or Marxian dialectic of human exploitation and integration that has been seen to direct human societies since the advent first of agriculture and then of industry (Fukuyama 1991).

The Gulf crisis (as George points out) presaged, for the first time in nearly half a century, the *possibility* of a new constructive global role for the United Nations and its Security Council. More broadly, it raised the question with which Woodrow Wilson vainly wrestled after 1918: how to institute a new order that would make "the world safe for democracy."[1]

My initial hypothesis is that events in the Gulf War reflected a major political dilemma—and its possible resolution. (1) Major wars have never broken out between two democracies—and yet democracies emerged as the unquestioned victors in two world wars initiated by hereditary monarchies in 1914–1918 and by a totalitarian dictatorship in 1939–1945. Yet to practice democracy safely at home, there must be a safe external environment. Thus, democracy does need the framework of an external—regional, or preferably global—order.

(2) But democratic governments *ex hypothesi* are fully subject only to domestic stimuli, since it is only the voters at home that have the right to install or depose those governments. Thus Wilson's dream of climaxing the victory of 1918 with American leadership toward a democratic world order thoroughly failed, as he lapsed into illness and American foreign policy withdrew into two decades of extreme isolationism.

(3) Nonetheless, sixty years later the Gulf crisis seemed to provide a resolution to this very dilemma by a strange, and hitherto unrecognized, dialectic that allowed leaders in Washington, Moscow, and Ankara to escape from insoluble political problems at home into brave international adventures in the name of human rights and global order.

In Washington, the administration had inherited—but largely ignored—intractable economic problems, including a trillion-dollar debt and a lingering recession. George Bush thus was only too glad to focus his own and the American public's attention on foreign events and on the magic power of America's high-tech aerial warfare. But to make that adventure politically acceptable at home and abroad, Secretary of State James Baker worked valiantly and brilliantly to obtain the endorsement of the UN Security Council—thus avoiding the implications of President Reagan's rash adventure into Lebanon, let alone those of the earlier Vietnam syndrome.

In Moscow, Mikhail Gorbachev had failed at initiating an orderly transition from planned to liberal economics and at transforming the remaining twelve Soviet republics into a true Commonwealth of Independent States. Soon, indeed, his own political career was ended in the wake of the August 1991 coup and Boris Yeltsin's successful resistance. In the meantime, however, Gorbachev was only too happy to try to reap more glory abroad by sending his friend Yevgeniy M. Primakov on a last-minute mediation mission to Baghdad and, after that mission's failure, by having his representatives actively cooperate with the Bush-Baker initiatives both in the Gulf crisis and toward Israeli-Palestinian peace talks.

In Ankara, there was a somewhat similar, though less publicized, escape act from domestic into foreign policy. Turgut Özal had managed to establish the only truly democratic party that rescued Turkey from the military regime imposed by its leading generals in 1980–1983. For the next six years (1983–1989), with his party's heavy parliamentary majority, Özal steered a boldly liberal, right-of-center economic course. Nonetheless, as Turkey's other democratic parties resurfaced in the mid-1980s and Özal's own government faced persistent problems of double-digit inflation and mounting unemployment, he used his party's continuing parliamentary majority to have himself elected president of the republic in November 1989. Earlier that year, however, the party's popularity, both in public opinion polls and in nationwide local elections, had dropped to an all-time low of 22 percent. His presidential election thus provoked such outrage that major opposition leaders decided to boycott his inauguration.[2]

But within less than two years, along came the Gulf crisis—giving Özal (with his parliamentary majority continuing until the fall of 1991) the opportunity to claim some of the disputed foreign policy powers of his military predecessor. Boldly, in response to the first Security Council resolution against Saddam's aggression, he ordered the closing of the pipeline through which Iraq via Turkey was exporting most of its oil. Subsequently, in a questionable interpretation of his country's commitments under NATO and other international agreements, he allowed U.S. planes to use the Incirlik airbase in southern Turkey for flights against northern Iraq—and meanwhile basked in the global publicity of long, personal phone calls from President Bush.

In sum, the widely televised savagery of Iraqi troops in Kuwait, along with the Security Council resolutions skillfully crafted under James Baker's aegis, provided the legitimation for a crucial shift by governments in Washington, Moscow, and Ankara from domestic political weakness to victorious foreign adventure.

Implications of the Gulf Crisis
for the Arab and World Futures

A major question for the future is whether the end of the cold war will alleviate the intraregional tensions that have prevailed and intensified in the Middle East in the last half century. Certainly the willingness of Syria to participate in the peace negotiations that began at Madrid might be interpreted as an optimistic sign. And yet, in view of Syria's performance at Madrid, where its representative recited all of Yitzhak Shamir's terrorist past in detail, it seems to me more accurate to say that we have proceeded so far only from a war of guns (and, for resident Palestinians, stones) to a war of words. Still, it would seem that it was the loss of its superpower sponsor in Moscow that persuaded the nimble Hafiz al-Assad to participate; that, indeed, the end of the cold war created a situation where no party concerned—Syria, resident Palestinians, Israelis, Jordanians, and Saudis—wanted to refuse James Baker's invitation and thus shoulder the blame for spoiling the peace process.

It seems likely, however, that the Israeli election of June 1992, with its clear shift toward parties in support of peace, and the negotiation stance announced by Yitzhaq Rabin's new government do signify a new start. Among the immediate responses was a visit of Rabin to Mubarak in Cairo; Mubarak's statement that he would visit Jerusalem in return; and, most remarkably, the announcement by Yasir Arafat that he, too, would be willing to meet with Rabin. If all this initial momentum is kept up, it may well be that, more than a decade after Camp David, 1992 will be the crucial turning point toward Israeli-Arab peace.

Still, I agree with Alexander George that continuing weapons supplies in earlier years gave the superpowers much leverage in helping to settle regional disputes from Nicaragua to Cambodia. I therefore would argue that the very best moment for settlement of these disputes was the brief Gorbachev interval, when the declining Soviet Union had both the will to settle such disputes and continuing leverage on its cold war clients in the Third World. By contrast, the irresolvable situation in Afghanistan would seem to show what chaos can ensue when both superpowers have withdrawn their support but leave massive amounts of weapons in the hands of a bitterly divided population.

Let us also keep in mind that many Middle Eastern countries are both rich and technologically clever enough to exploit the competition in the international arms market among countries such as France, Germany, China, North Korea, Brazil—and, not least, the United States itself.

The Middle Eastern arms race, as I note in my commentary on part 1, has been accelerated by the massive inflow of oil money. It is also worth noting that the specific direction of these arms flows has often been determined by the eagerness of both regional and outside powers to preserve existing boundaries and the regional balance of power. Thus Saudi Arabia and other Arab Gulf states formed the Gulf Cooperation Council at the time of Iraq's aggression against Iran in 1981, keeping at first a neutral stance (and presumably congratulating themselves that Saddam Hussein had picked Iran as his target). But then, as Iraq began to lose the war with Iran, the GCC members began to give support to Iraq—as, indeed, secretly did the United States.[3]

Indeed, I argue elsewhere that international relations in the Middle East tend to form a consistent and remarkably stable pattern in which each country tends to be enemies with most of its immediate neighbors, and friends with most of its neighbors once removed; and where, in any given conflict, regional and outside powers tend to support the weaker side (Rustow 1989).

By another of those dialectic twists of logic that we have encountered earlier in our argument, the very fact that many Middle Eastern borders are accidental or illogical tends to reinforce the prevalent desire of existing states in the region—and even of outside powers—to preserve those boundaries as they are. A vivid illustration of this is provided by Washington's sudden shift of policy in the midst of the Gulf War of 1990–1991. At first Saddam Hussein was declared the enemy and rhetorically compared to Adolf Hitler, and all opposition to him was encouraged. But when the opposition of Iraq's Shiite-Arab majority and its Kurdish minority gained credible proportions, Washington seemed to shift course and prefer a unified Iraq even under Saddam to a divided one. And the same attitude was shared by the government of Turkey—which, even though it has relaxed much of its repression against its own Kurdish minority, still retains a vivid fear of the breakup of its country as occurred during the Turkish-Kurdish civil war of 1925.

Nonetheless, along with these enduring patterns of rigid preservation of present boundaries and restoration of the existing regional balance, the Gulf War has also offered some unprecedented and notable developments. Most remarkably, although the United States helped with its Patriot missiles to protect Israel from the ravages of Iraqi missiles, the U.S.-led alliance did not allow Israel to engage in preemptive or retaliatory strikes against Iraq—presumably by not revealing the alliance's combat codes to the Israeli air force.

The anti-Iraq coalition also for the first time actively brought together Arab countries such as Syria and Egypt, which since the the days of Anwar al-Sadat had been on opposite sides in the cold war. Even though the military force against Iraq was almost entirely provided by the United States and several European allies, the Allied command was careful, as Iraqi forces withdrew from Kuwait, to have those forces replaced by Arab rather than Western units in the coalition.

And yet, it seems questionable whether such Arab cooperation against Iraq may be taken as a positive omen for future Arab regional cooperation. For one thing, the Gulf crisis occurred at a time when Syria's Hafiz al-Assad was quietly but effectively consolidating his own domination over Lebanon. Moreover, although there were pressures brought on by the Gulf War on both Kuwait and Saudi Arabia for more representative government, neither the Kuwaiti nor the Saudi rulers chose to yield to those pressures once the war was over. And the emir of Kuwait, far from making positive contact with those of his subjects who had led the resistance to the Iraqi occupation, refused to return to his capital until a new palace (complete with gold-plated toilet seats) had been built for him. The Gulf crisis thus posed a major dilemma for U.S. policy—it was an intervention in the name of human rights and global order that, at least in the short term, turned out to be a defense of the most traditional and least representative regimes in the Middle East or, indeed, the world.

And yet there were several coincidental developments that one might take as good omens for an Arab integration into a better world order of the future. Among these I would single out two major personnel decisions that happened to occur shortly before and after the Gulf crisis. The first of these concerned Jacques Attali, a French economist of Egyptian family background, who became a close advisor to President Mitterand. In May 1990 he was designated the president of the newly formed European Bank for Reconstruction and Development and since then has been developing the European Bank into a major vehicle for the peaceful conversion of Russia and other post-Soviet states toward capitalism. The second major personnel decision was the selection, effective on January 1, 1992, of the Egyptian diplomat and statesman Boutros Boutros Ghali as secretary-general of the United Nations.

Perhaps in the twenty-first century a new pattern of cooperation might develop between Arab countries, such as Egypt and Saudi Arabia, based on the western European model of economic integration and free migration since the 1950s. Indeed, this European example could serve not only as a model for closer cooperation among Arab countries but also in Latin America and tropical Africa and, above all, for the post-Soviet Commonwealth of Independent States. If, on the contrary, the efforts to reintegrate the remnants of the Soviet empire are to fail, there is much danger that the turbulence and militarization that developed in the Middle East between the 1940s and the 1980s might spread to all of the Caucasus and Central Asia.

The European Community itself faces the current dilemma of deepening its institutions (as provided by the plans drawn up by Jacques Delors and others for the years after 1992) and broadening its outreach by admitting new members. But, of course, such deepening and broadening could be combined—first by creating more representative and manageable institutions among the current twelve members and then by admitting successive groups of newcomers first as associate and eventually as full members. First in line for such admission would be the members of EFTA, the European Free Trade Association (Austria, Finland, Iceland, Norway, Sweden, and Switzerland) with the next group formed by former Eastern bloc countries that have ventured into a successful transition to liberal economies and democratic politics—perhaps including Poland, Hungary, the Czech Republic (or Czechoslovakia), and the three Baltic republics.

The most important lesson from Europe remains that regional integration, however slow at first, can become a self-sustaining and cumulative process. Thus Great Britain in the 1950s sternly opposed the European Common Market and founded the EFTA as a rival alternative—but by 1961 applied for admission to the market. By the 1970s, the European Community, with its impressive rate of growth and its strict insistence on democratic institutions in applicants for membership, became a crucial force in the conversion of Spain and Portugal toward democracy. By the early 1990s the further process of full economic integration had been so widely publicized by Delors and others that corporations in member states found it expedient to merge across borders within the twelve-member community, thus further adding to the pressures for full economic integration.

On a broader global basis, an informal process of economic integration among the United States, Europe, and Japan would appear to be under way, symbolized both by closer interaction among stock and commodities exchanges from New York to Frankfurt to Tokyo and also by Japan's massive investment in the bonds that finance America's gigantic debt. It is not unlikely that in the first part of the twenty-first century we will drift further along this rocky road of global triangulation, reinforcing the economic incentives for global integration and hence the heavy penalties on those countries that stay out—in short, setting off a dynamic, self-accelerating process.

To connect this global triangulation with peace and regional progress in the Middle East, the most urgent step would be an agreement, first between the United States and the European Community and then with states of the post–Soviet Union, to convert their arms exports to civilian uses—establishing, in effect, an updated New Deal for the United States and a new Marshall Plan for the post–Soviet Union, Eastern Europe, and other developing regions. If those three major arms-exporting groups could agree, other exporters such as China, Brazil, North Korea, and Israel could readily be brought into line by threatening arms exporting and importing countries with suspension from IMF and World Bank privileges. More immediately, the German and U.S. governments could be more stringent in enforcing their own rules against high-tech weapons exports to governments like Saddam Hussein's Iraq.

In sum, if this entire dynamic process of regional and global inter-dependence can continue and expand in developing regions such as Latin America, post-Soviet Eurasia, and the Middle East, and more broadly by economic triangulation among the United States, Japan, and the new Europe, then the Gulf War might indeed turn out to have been not the opening of, but a crucial turning point in zigzagging toward a new world order.

NOTES

1. The phrase was used in Wilson's speech of April 2, 1917, urging Congress to declare war on Germany.

2. On the circumstances of Özal's election to the presidency, see Heper (1992); on the earlier context of Turkish domestic politics see Rustow (1987), esp. pp. 57–83.

3. On the shocking details about U.S. arms supplied to Iraq shortly before the August 1990 Gulf conflict, see *New York Times*, April 27, 1992, pp. 1–8. As this book goes to press, evidence is accumulating that, during the last phase of the Iraq-Iran war, the United States secretly supported Iraq not only by facilitating its weapons purchases but even by outright military action.

REFERENCES

Fukuyama, Francis. 1992. *The End of History and the Last Man*. New York: Free Press.

Heper, Metin. 1992. "Consolidating Turkish Democracy." *Journal of Democracy* 3 (April): 105–17.

Huntington, Samuel P. 1991. *The Third Wave: Democratization in the Late Twentieth Century*. Norman: University of Oklahoma Press.

Rustow, Dankwart A. 1987. *Turkey: America's Forgotten Ally*. New York: Council of Foreign Relations. Rpt. 1989.

———. 1989. "Safety in Numbers: Reflections on the Middle Eastern Balance of Power." In *The Islamic World from Classical to Modern Times: Essays in Honor of Bernard Lewis*, ed. C. E. Bosworth, Charles Issawi, Roger Savory, and A. L. Udovitch. Princeton: Darwin Press.

———. 1991. "Democracy: A Global Revolution?" *Foreign Affairs* 69 (Fall): 75–91.

———. 1992. "The Surging Tide of Democracy" [Review of Huntington 1991]. *Journal of Democracy* 3 (January): 119–22.

PART VI

■

EPILOGUE

12

The Gulf War Revisited:
Consequences, Controversies,
and Interpretations

■

Stanley A. Renshon

Long after the war with Iraq is over, long into the future, people will be going over and over the story, trying to figure out how we got into this war, and whether it was necessary. The extent to which the latter question will be studied will depend on things that can't be known now—not only on how successful the war actually is, but also whether it is a political success.

—*Elizabeth Drew*

███ BECAUSE THE Gulf War was short, apparently successful, and minimally costly in American lives, newer concerns have engaged our attention. The war has receded from national consciousness yet has also left an unsettled feeling. Saddam Hussein is still in power and threatens to be a source of difficulty in the near future and possibly longer. The movement for an overall Middle East settlement proceeds slowly and will be long and difficult, if it succeeds at all. And the world scarcely seems to be a more secure place in spite of the performance of the anti-Iraq coalition.

These and other apparent anomalies have led to several sets of questions and, as is to be expected in the case of an event as serious as war, controversy. Some have concluded that the Persian Gulf conflict was a "just war" (Walzer 1992). Others are highly critical of the war's rationale and conduct (Graubard 1991; Smith 1992). This final chapter explores four areas of controversy in light of what is known at the present time. First is the background of the war and the United States' contribution to events. Second are the alternatives available to the parties, particularly the United States, before the war. Third is the conduct of the war. Finally, I examine some of the war's consequences.

Origins of the War

Two important sets of questions that have emerged in the war's after-math concern the prewar relationship of the United States and Iraq. One concerns whether the United States was not somehow responsible for creating the problem it ultimately faced, namely a powerful, well-armed, and aggressive Saddam Hussein. A second set concerns whether immediately before the invasion of Kuwait the United States gave Saddam Hussein conflicting messages about its concerns and likely response that encouraged a belief that it would not react strongly.

Phase One: The Pro-Iraqi Tilt During the Iran-Iraq War

The first questions have some validity. While the full dimensions of U.S. support for the Iraqi regime are not yet known, it is clear that in 1982–1988 period, the United States and its allies (probably with the direct or tacit support of the United States) supported Iraq in its war with Iran in a number of ways.[1] The United States supplied Iraq with intelligence information regarding Iranian forces during the war, supported the transfer of arms from allies to Iraq to aid in its war, and provided economic credit guarantees that allowed Iraq to divert more of its financial resources to the war against Iran.

Such support seemed clearly aimed at keeping Iran from defeating Iraq and emerging as the strategically dominant, radical, and commanding Arab power in the Middle East. Neither the United States' interests in the region nor those of conservative Arab states overtly or tacitly associated with the West would be served by the ascendance of a politically radical Iran.

That aim appears to have been realized. Both Iraq and Iran emerged from the war in August 1988 with substantial losses. Although Iraq apparently emerged from the war in a somewhat stronger military position than Iran, both countries needed significant aid to rebuild their damaged social and military infrastructure.[2] It is at this stage that a second prewar phase of Iraq-U.S. relations becomes evident.

Phase Two: The Attempt to Develop Better Relations with Iraq

The second phase is characterized by U.S. efforts to develop a relationship with Iraq that built on the military help provided during the previous phase and on the countries' mutual strategic interest in containing Iran. In October 1989 George Bush signed a then-secret policy directive (National Security Directive 26), that proposed "economic and political incentives for Iraq to moderate its behavior and to increase [U.S.] influence with Iraq" (Sciolino 1992c, 3). During that period, the United States approved new loan guarantees from the Department of Agriculture and helped secure more from the Export-Import Bank.[3]

The question of how Iraq came to be strong enough to invade Kuwait cannot be answered by focusing solely on the United States. Iraq obtained its weapons from a number of sources by following various complex strategies. Still, it seems clear that the Bush administration's policy was not to confront and weaken Saddam but to enlist him as a partner and in the process moderate his behavior. This controversial decision (A. Lewis 1992) had a legitimate and plausible strategic rationale but also entailed risks.

The Bush administration appears to have adapted a hedge-your-bets policy strategy. On the one hand, there were several reasons to think that the use of loan credits and guarantees might foster a working relationship. Economic inducements might have led to a further convergence of some U.S. and Iraqi interests, which might have led to a more stable regional structure. Iraq needed capital to finance rebuilding after the war. Indeed, this is one reason for Iraq's pressure on Kuwait.

The decision to provide Iraq with credits and loans was a direct response to Iraq's serious economic needs, but there were no doubt other considerations. The strategy of providing loans and machinery to finance and develop industrial infrastructure also might have encouraged domestic development rather than external adventures. And finally, the more Iraq developed, the more it had to lose, and thus the more moderate its policies vis-à-vis other Middle East countries might become.

This policy can also be viewed as reassuring Iraq about U.S. intentions. Reassurance is a primary tool for developing a new policy relationship and is also a cardinal component of deterrence. A U.S. decision not to provide bank credits or loans might well have had the opposite effect, heightening suspicions already held about U.S. intentions toward Iraq. Indeed, Janice Stein suggests that even given U.S. help in his war with Iran and loan guarantees, Saddam Hussein was still deeply distrustful of U.S. intentions.

One reason to believe that cooperation with the United States might have been attractive to Saddam Hussein is that it would have added to his stature and influence as a major player in the region, an outcome apparently compatible with his political and psychological goals. In phase two, U.S. policy clearly looked to the possibility of bringing Saddam into a regional framework and thus making him a substantial player. However, this may not have accorded with Saddam's more robust vision of his own place and that of Iraq in such an arrangement. The failure of this aspect of U.S. policy to satisfy Saddam's aspirations

undercuts the argument that an explicit regional role for him might have
helped avert the war or end it more quickly.[4]

There were of course risks connected with trying to moderate Saddam Hussein by aiding Iraq. Most serious was that the United States
might end by strengthening Saddam, without moderating him. There
is evidence that the Bush administration was aware of some of the
dangers associated with such a policy. In testimony before Congress,
Robert M. Gates, director of the Central Intelligence Agency, revealed
that a 1989 national intelligence assessment estimated that Iraq would
not attack any of its neighbors for two to three years (Sciolino 1992c).
This forecast proved to be mistaken in its timing but, interestingly, the
assessment clearly envisioned the possibility of such action. It both
frames a potential problem and provides an estimated time frame for
policies intended to forestall such an event.

It is within the context of its attempt to avoid this problem and its
associated costs that the Bush policy needs to be assessed. The attempt
failed. Bush briefly discussed his attempts to moderate Iraqi behavior
early in the crisis and noted that "we held no illusions" about the outcome of that attempt (Bush's Speech on Iraq Policy 1990). Indeed, National Security Directive 26 signed in October 1989 had stated the U.S.
intention to defend its interests and allies in the area, by force if necessary, from the Soviet Union or any regional power. As George Bush later
assessed this period in U.S.-Iraqi relationships, "We tried working with
him and changing [him] through contact . . . the lesson is clear in this
case . . . it didn't work" (Draper 1992b, 38). By the single criterion of
results, the policy can be considered flawed. But it was a plausible and
calculated policy risk, not a foolish one.[5]

One major policy of this period—U.S. policy toward Iraq's attempt to
develop nuclear weapons—did not involve a calculated risk. Since the
war it has become clear that part of Iraq's strategy was to emphasize its
development of peaceful nuclear technology while buying so-called
dual-use technologies, which can be used to develop both peaceful technology and nuclear weapons. They were provided by a number of countries, principally Germany but also Brazil and France and, to some
extent, the United States.[6] Bush administration officials were aware of
this problem: National Security Directive 26 indicates that economic
and political sanctions were part of the planned response should Iraq
use biological weapons or try to develop nuclear weapons. There is evidence that high government officials monitored the sales of technical
components to Iraq and intervened to keep sensitive equipment from
reaching the Iraqis. One piece of evidence comes from List of Strategic
Exports to Iraq (1992) drawn from Commerce Department export licens-
ing records. The list notes the sale of one item (computers to run ma-
chine tools capable of manufacturing atom bomb parts) as "stopped by

President order in June, 1990." Stein also notes in chapter 5 that in the spring of 1990 a shipment of devices that could serve as triggers for nuclear weapons was intercepted in London, presumably by agencies monitoring the development of Iraq's nuclear capacities.

These data suggest that high-level government officials were monitoring these shipments and making judgments about which ones were "safe" to export to Iraq. However, the extent of this monitoring and the thinking that informed general policies or specific decisions have never emerged clearly. What specific plans the administration evolved to counter Iraq's possible development of nuclear weapons is also unclear. The answers to these and similar questions are important to our understanding and evaluation of the administration's foreign policy judgments. Certainly, providing technology that could be used only for bomb construction would constitute a major strategic blunder. The question of dual-use technology is more complex.[7] But a more basic question concerns the political basis for strengthening Iraq's nuclear capacity in any way.

Phase Three: The Period
Immediately Before the Invasion

The third phase that has drawn critical attention immediately preceded the invasion of Kuwait. Did the United States in its communications with Iraq, and specifically with Saddam Hussein, convey the impression that Iraq could count on a mild U.S. response to any incursion into Kuwait? Much like the remark of Harry Truman, which some read as conveying the message that the United States would not defend South Korea, U.S. remarks on Iraq spurred discussion on whether the attack could have been deterred by speaking out clearly.

Many commentators have specifically cited Ambassador Glaspie's remark that the United States had "no opinion on the Arab-Arab conflicts, like [Iran's] border disagreement with Kuwait." These observers have suggested, and Saddam Hussein has claimed too, that this comment gave the impression that the United States would not intervene. True, one could put such an interpretation on this remark, but the full transcript reveals a more complex message.

As Janice Stein documents, the problem was not that the United States sent the wrong signal but that it sent mixed signals. An effective strategy of deterrence requires strong and consistent signals of intentions, but the United States gave Iraq several signals of varying intensity that could lend themselves to different interpretations and conclusions.

Responsibility for this does not necessarily rest solely with the United States. To mount a unified deterrent strategy, one must first appreciate that there is a specific event in the making that one wishes to deter. It is important that Saddam Hussein summoned Ambassador Glaspie, whom he had not chosen to meet with in her two years as U.S. ambassador. Possibly he did so only to understand the position of the United States better. But it is also quite possible that he had his own agenda. In that meeting Saddam Hussein gave contradictory signals regarding his willingness to assert his rights, but also promised not to resort to force. In the transcript of their talk, Saddam Hussein said of his problems with Kuwait, "A solution must be found within an Arab framework." He later said, "We want to find a just solution, that will give us our rights, but not deprive others of their rights." He reinforced this message, discussing in detail the agreement with Kuwait made at Jedda and the new round of talks that were scheduled to take place in the next week or so. Ambassador Glaspie then asked Saddam Hussein how he assessed the efforts of those Arabs who had offered their good offices to resolve the problems with Kuwait, and he responded positively.

Within this context, Ambassador Glaspie raised the issue of Saddam Hussein's troop buildup along the Kuwaiti border. She noted U.S. knowledge of Saddam's view that Kuwait was in effect waging war against his country and, noting the troop buildup along the border, said, "It would be reasonable for me to be concerned. And for this reason, I received an instruction to ask you . . . regarding your intentions. I simply describe the concern of my government" (ibid.). Saddam Hussein then reassured Ambassador Glaspie regarding the progress of the talks, a new round of which were scheduled for the following week.

The number of contradictory signals in this one talk suggest either Saddam's real and uncontrollable ambivalence or a calculated effort to preserve options and keep the United States off balance. He might have had several good reasons for doing so. Ambiguous messages might keep the United States from sending strong and unequivocal warnings, which once publicly stated it might feel compelled to enforce. Saddam Hussein may also have wished to keep the United States in doubt about his intentions and goals. Stein reports that in this he succeeded, since even after the invasion began neither the extent of his plans nor the extent of the U.S. response was clear to American policy makers.

The Question of Deterrence

Whether Iraq would have been deterred by a strong and unequivocal U.S. stance is a plausible but complex question. Consider first the question of the invasion's timing. According to Tariq Aziz, Saddam Hussein's decision to invade Kuwait "was made at the last minute, after the collapse of the final negotiating session between Iraq and Kuwait, on August 1st in Jedda" (Viorst 1991, 67). This is the Iraqi version of the last-straw theory. In this view—Iraq surrounded by enemies (the United States and its allies), economically strained to the point of collapse, and having tried desperately but unsuccessfully to negotiate a settlement that would have allowed it dignity and resources—began the invasion one day after all efforts had failed.

The view that the invasion was decided at the last minute also conflicts with what we understand of Saddam Hussein's psychology. The last-straw theory suggests an impulsive personality, but that does not fit with Jerrold Post's or my analysis, which suggests that Saddam Hussein is extremely shrewd, cunning, and calculating. It is difficult psychologically to be all these things and impulsive at the same time. Possibly the final decision to invade Kuwait was made at the last moment, but that doesn't mean that planning hadn't been going on for some time. Iraqi troops had massed on the border two days before the invasion, but certainly intense military preparations must have preceded this. No country masses troops for a possible invasion that will have enormous international repercussions, especially an anticipated military response from a hostile (according to the Iraqi view) superpower, without intense planning.

The theory that the invasion was a last-minute decision does not address the question of how detailed and for how long military planning had been in progress. Was planning for the invasion taking place at the same time that Saddam Hussein was warning the Arab Council (Speech to the Arab Cooperation Council 1990) about the hegemonic intentions of the United States? Were Saddam's warnings an attempt to set the stage and deflect attention from himself? At this point we can only ask, not answer, these questions. Information on these points is not likely to emerge from Iraqi archives for some time, if ever.

Stein suggests that deterrence may not have been possible, since Saddam Hussein believed that the United States and its allies had a general interest in exercising hegemony in the Middle East and a specific interest in neutralizing him. Certainly, Saddam Hussein voiced his suspicions regarding U.S. intentions in speeches before the war, but these views became much more pronounced in his postwar speeches.[8] This makes some sense, and one can argue that the war simply confirmed Saddam's suspicions. But it is also possible that his prewar speeches could have had other, not necessarily contradictory, motives. For example, Saddam Hussein's prewar complaints could have been meant to generate a more supportive response from the United States. At the same time, his remarks about U.S. hegemonic intentions in the Middle East were surely useful in solidifying his position among Arabs long suspicious of the United States and other Western powers.

Were his warnings about U.S. intentions an attempt to set the stage by justifying his own behavior? Perhaps. In one of his postwar speeches, he went so far as to suggest that his invasion of Kuwait was a matter of "legitimate deterrence" and "was one of the main gates for deterring the plot and for defending all Iraq from the plotters" (Hussein's Radio Speech 1991).

Just how the invasion of Kuwait could serve to deter the United States is unclear. If Saddam Hussein thought that the United States was out to get him, it is a curious logic that he must offer a flagrant and public reason for doing so. In an interview given after the war, Tariq Aziz commented, "We expected an American military retaliation from the very beginning" (Viorst 1991, 67). But if armed retaliation was expected from the beginning, and if Aziz's comment is not simply a post hoc explanation to cover a gross miscalculation, another question arises. Why would Saddam Hussein risk the large-scale destruction of his country's military and economic infrastructure to secure Kuwait? Alternatively, why risk such destruction when Iraq could have accomplished much of what it wanted by making only a limited incursion to the Rumaila oil fields and the islands of Bubiyan and Warbah? Tariq Aziz's explanation is that Saddam Hussein thought that whether he took all or part of Kuwait, the U.S. response would have been the same, namely to "crush Iraq."

This explanation, however, simply returns us to the question of why he would want to provide a pretext for his own destruction. In his next sentence Tariq Aziz seems to contradict himself, noting, "I have no conclusion about what might have happened if we had engaged in a limited incursion." Certainly it is hard to imagine a thirty-eight-member international coalition led by hundreds of thousands of U.S. troops being effectively mobilized and sustained to oust Iraq from a limited occupation of these disputed areas.

The Process of Conflict

The question of the degree of Western and U.S. complicity in the development of Iraq's military capacity and motivation is somewhat separate from what, if anything, should be done regarding the invasion. There seemed to be general consensus that the invasion represented a bold and strategically consequential move by Iraq, presenting Arab and Western states with stark and serious choices. Few argued that nothing should be done. The issue became not whether to respond but how. A major question then as now is whether a nonviolent alternative to a military response would have achieved the same or similar results. Clearly, avoiding conflict would have been preferable even to a successful conflict, especially if the same goals could have been accomplished.

Economic Embargo: An Alternative to War?

The question of the effectiveness of an economic embargo was raised at the outset of the conflict. One analysis notes that "the modern history of economic embargoes is checkered at best" (Lohr 1990, 1). Testimony before the Senate Armed Services Committee by Dick Cheney and Colin Powell on December 3, 1990, and by William Webster and James Baker on December 5, 1990, suggests that the embargo that began after the invasion was effective in cutting off Iraqi's imports and exports (Gulf Testimony 1990; Remarks by Webster and Baker 1990). Webster, director of the CIA, estimated that "more than 90 percent of imports and 97 percent of exports had been shut off." The question of whether Iraqi imports and exports were effectively being shut off, however, was preliminary to another, more central question: Would the embargo succeed in achieving the objective of forcing Saddam Hussein to withdraw from Kuwait? On this specific question almost all the senior administration officials who testified were pessimistic, while a number of former defense secretaries suggested that economic sanctions be given twelve to eighteen months to work.[9] Would the economic sanctions alone have been effective in forcing Saddam Hussein to withdraw? A definite answer to this question is not possible. But the postwar evidence suggests that the doubts about using sanctions alone had merit.[10]

Since the end of the war, the West has continued economic sanctions against Iraq in an attempt to induce it to pay reparations for the damage caused to Kuwait and continues to try to destroy Iraq's nuclear weapons research facilities. These in essence carry on prewar sanctions, with the exception of humanitarian food imports. Thus sanctions have been in effect for almost two years as of this writing, during which period Iraq has also suffered substantial damage to its economic and industrial base because of the war. Yet the pre- and postwar sanctions, as well as the effects of the war itself, have apparently been ineffective in bringing about Iraq's compliance with the terms of the cease-fire that went into effect on April 11, 1991.

One reason is that dictatorships can subject their citizens to economic deprivation without fear of being voted out of office. Paradoxically, an economic embargo may have the effect of strengthening a dictatorship's domestic position: by controlling the distribution of food, medicine, or other resources, the leader can both weaken those who oppose him, who are able to resist his rule, and strengthen his own position by distributing resources. Moreover, if he is willing to pay the economic costs, standing up to sanctions may be a relatively inexpensive way to demonstrate his determination and strength. The perception of continued strength after the damage incurred during the war undercuts the appearance of defeat.

The period between the doubling of coalition troop strength on November 8 and the onset of the war on January 17 provides more evidence that sanctions alone would not have worked. That period was one of coercive diplomacy, which George (1991, 5) defines as a generally defensive attempt to get an opponent to stop or give up an action already taken. Although defensive in nature, it can be accompanied by threats and even the judicious application of limited force.

There is no doubt that during this period the threat of war was a major component of U.S. strategy whose underlying rationale was an attempt to accomplish U.S. goals without resorting to force. This policy was based on two premises, one strategic, the other psychological. The strategic element involved the belief that the threat of force was better than its immediate use; the psychological element involved the view, supported by analyses like that of Jerrold Post, that Saddam was more likely to consider withdrawing from Kuwait if the United States assembled a credible force and the capacity to expel him. Yet in spite of the force assembled against him and the vulnerability of his industrial and military base given the emerging belief among coalition partners that Saddam's military capacities must be destroyed, he refused to withdraw. His defiant stance in the face of such enormous potential destruction weakens the argument that economic sanctions alone would have accomplished their purpose.

Last, there is the question of whether the coalition could have been maintained during a long embargo. At the time of the congressional hearings on the embargo, the administration raised the question of whether the coalition could continue to hold in the face of a long, difficult and nondecisive standoff.

The decision to invade Kuwait was bold, dramatic, and decisive. There was no ambiguity about it, except how far it would go. The Bush administration argued that it demanded a similarly bold, dramatic, and decisive response in return. The advantage of this kind of response was that it would galvanize further action and mobilize cohesion. The administration feared that drawing ambiguous lines, which could be constantly tested with yet another request for a dispensation or would need constant reinterpretation in light of the shifting views of many participants, was likely to result in emotional and political fatigue among coalition members.

How realistic were these concerns? Again, as with the case of the economic embargo, no definite answer can be given. But here again, we can make some assessments based on postwar events.

Consider for example the impasse that developed after Saddam Hussein's refusal to allow UN inspectors access to his nuclear facilities. Certainly there was general consensus among all the allies that allowing Saddam Hussein to develop nuclear weapons would lead to an extremely dangerous situation. Yet Saddam refused to allow inspections. In response, President Bush hinted at—and prepared contingency plans for—the bombing of such sites. One report notes that "a number of allies voiced reservations or even opposition" and that the Bush administration was "finding it more and more difficult to forge a consensus among its allies over steps to bring down President Saddam Hussein" (Tyler 1991).

This report quotes a senior Egyptian diplomat as saying that "public opinion in the Arab world has turned markedly sympathetic to the plight of the Iraqi people . . . who continue to suffer the effects of the international sanctions" and notes the suspicion of some Western officials that "Mr. Hussein is cynically promoting much of the suffering and shortages in Iraq to break support for the embargo." More recent evidence supports that suspicion (Aspin 1991, 14–16).

Eight months later, considering what to do about neutralizing Saddam Hussein's weapons of mass destruction, a report found that "the coalition of 30 countries that conducted or financed the military campaign has shrunk to the core nations that are most intent on driving Mr. Hussein from power" (Tyler 1992). That core did not include Russia, France, Turkey, Egypt, or Syria. The presidents of the last two "publicly pulled out of the old allied coalition on Wednesday by opposing any new military action" (ibid.).

Among the evidence that the economic sanctions would not have been effective are both the postwar difficulties of maintaining consensus and the prewar maneuvering. The multiple peace initiatives (described in detail by Herrmann, forthcoming) are important for several reasons. They reflect just how much effort went into finding a way to give Saddam what he said he wanted in his August 12 speech outlining his basis for a negotiated settlement. Peace plans were put forward by Russia, Morocco, Jordan, Syria, and the United Nations. What these efforts suggest in the context of this discussion is the vulnerability of the coalition's consensus. On the eve of the ground war, President Gorbachev called George Bush and argued that the coalition should give Saddam more time. It was, as General Scowcroft recalls, "a long, long conversation, very difficult conversation for the President" (American Enterprise Insititute 1992, program 3, 14).[11]

It seems fair to suggest that even after the decisive event of the invasion, a dramatic, unified collective response was by no means a certainty. The various peace plans that were offered can be read as an indication of how hard various countries struggled to give Saddam some of what he said he wanted while still getting him to withdraw. It is therefore not too tenuous to suggest that similar attempts to find some accommodation would also have been vigorously pursued during an extended economic blockade.[12]

As Jarol Manheim points out, Saddam was in some respects very shrewd in his calculation of what appeals would find resonance in the Arab world. As Shibley Telhami notes in his survey of Arab attitudes, there was much overt and covert sympathy for Saddam, the positions he espoused, and his views of the West and the United States in particular. Even within the United States, as John Mueller observes, after the initial rally effect, support for a strong stand was not uniform by any means.

Both during and after the war, Saddam continually raised the issue of the devastating impact of the economic blockade on Iraqi women and children. It does not take much imagination to envision the political impact on the Gulf region and elsewhere of pictures of such suffering. The dramatic images of deprivation and desperation among Kurdish refugees after the war stimulated enormous political pressure on the Bush administration to take some remedial steps for what many viewed as the direct consequences of its actions.

It seems clearer in retrospect that the coalition was a temporary association of somewhat, but not fully, like-minded partners. They were drawn together for somewhat different reasons and held differing views on the danger posed by Saddam and on what needed to be done about it. It was difficult to manage these differences during the relatively brief period of the conflict. It would have been even harder given an extended, day-by-day economic embargo accompanied by a steady stream of objections, requests for "humanitarian exceptions" accompanied by pictures and reports of suffering and mediation efforts spurred by sympathy but no sense of urgency.

Hussein's Decision to Stay in Kuwait: A Psychological Puzzle in Four Parts

The process that led to the war, as well as the process of the conflict itself, can be viewed as sequences of decisions taken by each side. At each point, choices were made and implemented that affected choice points yet to come. At at each of these choice points, there was another opportunity to move in a different direction and thus avoid the consequences of moving the conflict to the next stage toward war.

The major choice point (framing decision) for both sides was Saddam Hussein's decision to invade Kuwait (which is examined from different perspectives in the Post, Renshon, and Stein chapters), but once that was done, there were at least four critical periods: the first four months, which ran from the invasion on August 2, 1990, until November 8, when George Bush doubled the U.S. commitment to coalition forces; the second three months, from November 8 until the deadline of January 15, 1991, (3) the third, a one-day period from the January 15 deadline to the start of the coalition bombing on January 17; and the final period, from January 17 until the actual ground assault beginning on February 24, 1991.

Each of these periods offered Saddam Hussein options and opportunities. In the first two periods, especially, a number of opportunities were available to Saddam Hussein to make a tactical retreat and preserve his economic and military assets. Yet he chose not take advantage of the attempts by sympathetic Arab states (Jordan, Morocco, Algeria, Yemen) and Western countries (France and the Soviet Union) to help him extricate himself before the onset of war. These countries all had some empathy for Saddam Hussein's views and were united in trying to find a way out of the crisis, often responding favorably to some of the conditions for settlement outlined by Saddam in his August 12 speech (Proposals by Iraqi President 1990). Jerrold Post argues that Saddam would retreat from the confrontation with the United States only with power and honor intact. Yet the multiple peace plans advanced during the war gave Saddam the opportunity to do just that, and he spurned them. One of the largest psychological puzzles that emerged from the war is why Saddam failed to take advantage of these peace efforts.

During the first phase, before November 8, Saddam Hussein possibly perceived no need to negotiate away what he believed he could keep. Between November 8 and January 15, however, one wonders why Saddam did not use negotiation to achieve one of his purposes, namely splitting apart the coalition. A decision by Saddam Hussein to negotiate would have set political forces in motion toward a settlement that would have been difficult, if not impossible, for the Bush administration to reject. Saddam Hussein's intractability during these two periods contrasts dramatically with his flexibility at other times. At the outset of the Gulf War, for example, Saddam Hussein reached an agreement with his archenemy Iran that essentially undid all of Iraq's very costly gains during the Iran-Iraq War. Could that about-face have been more difficult than a partial withdrawal coupled with a pledge to negotiate?

Care must be exercised in considering why someone did not follow what the analyst believes was a more prudent and productive course. Explanations may run the risk of insensitivity to a calculus influenced by different political, historical, cultural, and psychological factors than those of the person making the analysis. Yet these factors, while arguably relevant, must be weighed in the context of the strong political and military realities that shape the situation.

Elaine Sciolino (1991) and Janice Stein (chapter 5) suggest a number of specific reasons why Saddam Hussein may have erred in his calculations, including a belief that he could outlast the United States in a ground war, that he could count on political divisiveness in the United States to extricate him, and that he would win politically even if not militarily. These explanations help us make sense of what otherwise seem to be remarkably poor decisions taken over a span of almost half a year. But they raise another question. How could someone viewed as so shrewd, so calculating, and so cunning be so out of touch for so long with the likely consequences of those decisions?

Particularly striking is a comparison of the settlement basis put forward by Saddam on August 12 with the proposal he put forward on February 15, 1992, after the bombing had been going on for almost a month (Iraqi Statement 1991; Proposals by Iraqi President 1990). The plan not only repeated past demands and conditions that had already been rejected, but added new ones that were certain to be rejected as well. These included canceling Iraq's debts to other Arab counties and the requirement that countries engaged in the war make "reparations to Baghdad." Saddam Hussein, in his peace proposal of February 15, 1991, acted as if the month-long destruction of his military and economic infrastructure had not taken place. One can acknowledge the bravado in such an act even while asking how such gross miscalculations could hold up in the face of substantial evidence that they were unproductive. By that time the bombing had destroyed much of what Saddam had built, the masses in opposing Arab states had not risen up to overthrow his opponents, and it was clear that the United States was wary of a frontal assault that would result in heavy causalities to its forces.

Saddam Hussein's Mistakes: Misperception and Miscalculation? Or Character and Poor Judgment?

While the focus on misperception and miscalculation offers plausible understandings of Saddam Hussein's behavior, it is not fully satisfactory. The large number of "misperceptions" and "miscalculations" displayed during these four post-invasion periods, and continuing through each stage of the conflict—from the original framing decision to invade Kuwait through the decision leading to a ground war—suggests a need for further psychological explanations. To put it another way, while Saddam Hussein's numerous misperceptions and miscalculations help to explain his behavior in one sense, these very elements themselves require explanation.

Weaving together the analyses by Post and Renshon, we can develop the following composite picture. Saddam Hussein is a leader of intense personal and political ambition whose rise to power has been facilitated by his well-honed and efficient use of violence. Violence has played an important role in Iraqi politics (as it has elsewhere) and has not been effectively inhibited by constitutional, legal, or political constraints. In this milieu, Saddam Hussein, the person and leader, developed both psychologically and politically.

Psychologically, the ability to use violence ruthlessly against any potential enemy means that one cannot form any lasting attachment to others. For such people, there are no relationships, only alliances of convenience. Such persons are not bound by conventional morality. The sadism and aggression in their character structures could not be acted upon if they were inhibited by guilt.

Aspirations to prominence (what Post refers to as dreams of glory) are part of an idealized view of the self. This idealized self-view tends to reinforce the belief that one is special and, by virtue of this specialness, entitled. Where does this sense of entitlement originate? In Saddam's case, Post believes it came from his childhood, which he implies held more deprivation than indulgence, while David Winter suggests that Saddam Hussein may have been more indulged than deprived. Clinically, however, an extreme experience in either direction can lead to the same result. If one is treated as extremely special, one can develop a lifelong sense of entitlement. If one is extremely deprived, the feeling can easily develop that the world must make up for it.

In either event, the assumption leads to the belief that one is entitled to take what one wants. Whatever the developmental origins of this sense of entitlement, it is clear that Iraqi politics provided a milieu in that Saddam Hussein acted out that assumption with increasingly successful effects. Moreover, an important aspect of this successful developmental experience is that particular means to this end were successfully developed and refined. These means entailed the exploitation of weakness, the masking where necessary of intentions (as for example, during Saddam's service as vice-president of Iraq), and ultimately the ruthless use of violence.

Post suggests that Saddam Hussein's propensity toward violence is defensive because of insecurity from childhood deprivation underlying the grandiosity. It is also possible, however, that the successful use of violence over time has its own nonchildhood-related effects on character development. The successful use of these tactics over decades of political struggle reinforces their utility and their appropriateness. Success proves one is right to have used such means in the first place. These dynamics help explain Saddam Hussein's calculated use of violence, but they do not by themselves explain why he was so atypically unsuccessful and unskillful during the Gulf War. True, Saddam Hussein's survival in power to this point can be taken as a partial vindication of one of the explanations for his behavior: that is, though he might have lost militarily, he triumphed politically. But there is no indication yet that he has triumphed politically, and in the meantime he has paid a high price (in his military and economic infrastructure) for this limited opportunity for eventual gain.

So, the question remains: Why did a skillful tyrant fail to heed the numerous signs that he was heading toward a disastrous outcome? An adequate, although not fully satisfactory, answer must consider two character elements: Saddam Hussein's grandiose ambition and his rage at having been challenged and stalled, first by Kuwait, which refused to accede to his threats and demands, and second by the United States and its coalition partners. Post's analysis provides very plausible evidence of the grandiosity but overlooks the rage. Certainly, Saddam Hussein's large regional ambitions, his view of himself as a great (and underappreciated) leader, and his encouragement of the personality cult all support the grandiosity thesis. What needs to be added to the Post analysis are the psychological mechanisms that are unleashed when such intense ambition and idealized view of the self are challenged or thwarted. In a word, one must deal with Saddam Hussein's narcissistic rage. *Narcissistic rage* is a term developed by Heinz Kohut (1972) to describe the extreme and emotionally violent reactions of patients to "narcissistic injuries," the most typical of which are empathetic failures—or more to the point here, challenges or experiences that tend to deny the person's intense narcissistic striving or call into question his highly idealized (grandiose) self-image.

Kohut notes that all narcissistic rage shares "the need for revenge, for righting a wrong, for undoing a hurt by whatever means, and a deeply anchored, unrelenting compulsion in the pursuit of these aims" (383). Among the triggering mechanisms are "conspicuous defeat." Once this rage is triggered, writes Kohut, "There is utter disregard for reasonable limitations and a boundless wish to redress an injury and obtain revenge" (385). Sometimes it is not enough to merely injure the offending party. "The narcissistically injured . . . cannot rest until he has *blotted out* an . . . offender who has dared to oppose him or disagree with him." Such a person seeks to *"wipe out the evidence* that has contradicted [the] conviction that [he] is unique and perfect" (389, emphasis added). These observations about narcissitic rage are very significant in view of Saddam Hussein's attempt to dismantle Kuwait's social, political, and economic institutions after he had gained control of the country.

Whatever the political and economic reasons for Saddam Hussein's wish to gain control of Kuwait's resources—and there were many—the fact that a small, militarily insignificant country not only spurned his demands, but also said they would review even the limited concessions they had made was too much of an affront to Saddam Hussein. Kuwait's "intransigence" was public, well known to all Arabs, and therefore humiliating to Iraq—a larger, militarily superior country ruled by a leader with a hunger for regional importance.

Both grandiosity and rage interfere with good judgment, but in different ways. Grandiosity interferes with judgment because it leads to an overestimation of one's skills and ability to affect circumstances. Rage interferes with judgment because the emphasis is on getting even and proving one's opponents wrong (and oneself right) rather than finding an effective strategy to peruse realistic goals.

Saddam Hussein failed to take advantage of the many opportunities afforded him to extract himself from the situation because, first, he would have had to recognize and then publicly acknowledge his limits (that is, he had miscalculated greatly), second, he was blinded by revenge and wanted to teach those who frustrated his ambitions a lesson. From this perspective, the peace proposal Saddam Hussein put forward on February 15 after the bombing began and before the ground war started, adding new demands on top of old ones, makes some sense. An acceptance of that initiative would have vindicated Saddam Hussein's original decision to invade Kuwait and his subsequent strategy and would have made up for the losses (through reparations) he had suffered (in effect, undoing the results of his miscalculations). The February 15 initiative was a bold attempt (in keeping with his character) to repair the damage he has caused, but not an especially realistic one.

No information emerging during or since the war has made the judgments regarding Saddam Hussein's ruthlessness and ambition less credible. If anything, his behavior toward the Kurds, his treatment of the UN nuclear inspection teams, and his political use of his own people's suffering have only confirmed those judgments.

Saddam Hussein remains in power, wounded but unbowed. The forceful check on his ambitions, the loss of his economic and military infrastructure, and the public humiliation of forced compliance to inspection and reparations regimes have very likely fueled his rage and desire for revenge. Large-scale means to accomplish this are not now at his disposal, although terrorist attacks are. Having understood the political psychology of his ambition, we would be unwise now to underestimate the political psychology of his loss.

The Aftermath of the War

Any examination of the Gulf War must acknowledge that outcomes are varied and complex and that judgments, therefore, must be composite rather than absolute. In addition, the negative consequences of policy decisions are not always immediately apparent. Even successful policy outcomes sometimes have unanticipated results long after the event. With these cautions in mind, let us turn to a brief discussion of the war's policy and political consequences.[13]

For a confrontation that appeared so stark and a conclusion that appeared so decisive, the results of the war seem curiously opaque. Internationally, mounting violence in Eastern Europe and other areas has diverted attention away from the Middle East. Domestically, Americans appear to have turned inward, worrying about economic problems, racial tensions, and a presidential election. It is of course possible that the very ability to turn toward other issues is one indication of a satisfactory outcome. Nonetheless, as of this writing Saddam Hussein is still in power, and this fact and others have led some to question the war's purposes and success. Were the objectives for which the war was said to have been fought realized? And if so, to what degree?

Did the War End Too Soon?

Saddam Hussein's continued defiance of UN resolutions connected with arms inspections, coupled with his attempts to suppress Iraqi Kurds and Shiite Muslims militarily, have raised doubts about the ending of the Gulf War. The fact that Saddam Hussein continues to hold power has led some analysts to conclude that the United States achieved a "triumph without victory" (U.S. News and World Report 1992). One newspaper commentator wondered, "How many Americans who supported the war would have done so if they had known in advance that Saddam Hussein would remain in power?" (Rosenthal 1992).

"Did the war end too soon?" actually asks more than one question. It challenges the decision to allow Saddam Hussein to retain power. But it also raises a question about the decision to implement a cease-fire before the last portions of Saddam's elite Republican Guard units were destroyed, thus leaving them available for his use against the Kurds, Shiites, and perhaps—down the road—others. These questions are related, but they are not the same questions.

Let us turn first to the question of Saddam Hussein's remaining in power at the war's end. The four original goals and rationales for the war were to expel Iraq from Kuwait, to restore the Kuwaiti government, to protect U.S. citizens, and to maintain the security and stability of Saudi Arabia and the Persian Gulf. Only the last raises the question of Saddam's continuation in power.

Answering the question "Did the war end too soon?" requires therefore some assessment of the relative stability of the region before and after the war that is directly related to Saddam's presence, ambitions, and abilities. *Stability*, of course, is a relative and somewhat subjective term. Was not a certain degree of regional stability achieved by severely damaging Saddam's military infrastructure and weapons capacity? Is not some stability assured by UN monitoring of Iraqi nuclear, biological, and missile ambitions? Is Saddam Hussein less of an immediate and direct military threat to other regional countries because of the war? The answer to all three questions is yes.

Even so, one could ask: would not the removal of Saddam Hussein have resulted in greater regional stability? Hypothetical questions are difficult, but some observations are possible. The assumption that eliminating Saddam would have been preferable to merely wounding him militarily must examine the risks as well as the benefits of the former. The major benefit of the "no Saddam" solution would be the removal from power of a smart, skilled, and experienced dictator with hegemonic ambitions.

Preferring this outcome, however, assumes that whoever followed him would either have smaller regional ambitions or less skill in carrying them out. This is by no means certain, although Saddam's combination of intelligence, ruthlessness, and experience might be hard to match. The first and second traits are not always present in the same person, and even a leader with both is not guaranteed to stay in power long enough to accumulate experience. Yet intelligence and ruthlessness are not in short supply among ambitious persons. Anyone with enough skill to seize power might in time accumulate the necessary experience to threaten regional stability. Nonetheless, after the Gulf War, a new leader might well think twice before threatening or taking military action outside Iraq's borders.

Against this gain one must consider that an Iraq without a strong central leader and thus no longer a regional military menace would perhaps find its own security threatened. Shiites and Kurds could well press for regional autonomy, splintering Iraq, making it vulnerable, and perhaps encouraging the intervention of other regional actors. At least it would tend to strengthen other powers like Syria and especially Iran, whose commitment to regional stability continues to be uncertain.

Another critical point is what was required to remove Saddam Hussein from power. The United States targeted the command bunkers where Saddam Hussein and his advisers were thought to be. As General Schwartzkopf put it, "If he had been killed in the process, I wouldn't have shed any tears" (1992). Having failed to make Saddam Hussein a war causality during the bombing, the United States could only hope that he would be removed by those dissatisfied with him; if this did not occur, the allied forces would have to face the task themselves.

Saddam Hussein's removal by disgruntled Iraqis—a conceivable, though doubtful possibility[14]—may have seemed a more attractive alternative than driving toward and occupying Baghdad to remove him. This action would have exposed the United States to further military casualties, perhaps even heavy losses, given a need for house-to-house fighting in the city itself.[15] As Schwarzkopf contends, "There was not a single head of state, diplomat, Middle East expert, or military leader, who, as far as I am aware advocated continuing the war and seizing Baghdad" (1992, 497). The reasons are not hard to find.

Not only would such a move be militarily dangerous, it would also have tremendous political implications in the region and elsewhere.[16] An invasion followed by an occupation would open up a need for a continued U.S. presence in Iraq, but the UN did not authorize the United States to become an occupying army in an Arab country. Nor, given the history of Western behavior in the region, would a military occupation—even if temporary and for good reason—have been politically neutral. On balance, the "no Saddam" outcome might seem preferable in the abstract, but not when compared to the costs of a military occupation.

Once Saddam Hussein had survived the war and the decision was made not to send allied troops to remove him, asking whether the war ended too soon raises questions of containment and the validity of the decision, taken late in the war, to allow a trapped segment of Saddam's elite Republican Guard to escape with their lives and some weapons. Critics (such as Rosenthal 1991) have charged that decision makers "underestimated the military strength with which the cease-fire would leave [Saddam]" and refer to this decision as a major mistake of the war. In Rosenthal's view, leaving Saddam Hussein alive and in power, coupled with the failure to destroy more of his military assets—particularly the trapped Republican Guard units—almost guarantees future trouble.

This is a plausible argument, judging from Saddam's behavior before and after the war, but it overlooks the moral leadership and political repercussions of pursuing and destroying these battered but still somewhat intact fighting units. Moral leadership in war may seem to be an oxymoron, but war may actually intensify the need for sound moral judgments.[17]

At the war's end it was clear that Iraqi troops were in retreat, that they had suffered a major defeat and substantial losses, and that the goals of expelling Iraq from Kuwait, protecting its oil fields, and reducing Saddam's military and political ability to disturb regional stability had been largely realized. The question then turns on whether further military destruction—especially additional causalities on both sides— was necessary to assure greater regional stability.

Schwarzkopf notes that when the decision to stop the war was being made, his own calculations led him to accept the White House decision to end the war without decimating the remaining Republican Guard units (1992, 469–70). Elsewhere he says that while he was prepared to wage a "battle of annihilation," the White House decision to stop was "very humane and very courageous" (American Enterprise Institute, 1992, program 3, 18). National Security Adviser Richard Hass adds, "Yes, we . . . would have destroyed another hundred, two hundred pieces of artillery and armor. . . . But it is not clear to me that it would have really meant that much, and against what cost in human life, against what cost politically?" (ibid.).

Certainly these considerations were influential. But there were also practical issues: what would be the effect of Western forces savagely attacking defenseless, beaten, and retreating Arab soldiers along the "highway of death" on the coalition? What would be the impact of this mixture of fact and perception on the coalition's postwar unity and the need to contain a beaten but not vanquished Saddam? Would regret and ambivalence prevent coalition partners from enforcing a strict inspection regime? Certainly the forced removal of Saddam Hussein from power would have entailed further problems—chief among them the spectacle of a martyred army, country, and leader subjected to an unnecessary, immoral use of force.

A Concluding Note on the War

Several (not necessarily inconsistent) rationales were advanced by the coalition for its involvement. From the first, George Bush had three direct, measurable goals—Iraq's complete and unconditional withdrawal from Kuwait, restoration of the Kuwaiti government, and the safety and protection of U.S. citizens in Iraq—and one somewhat more elastic goal—the security and stability of Saudi Arabia and the Persian Gulf (see Bush's Speech on Iraq Policy 1990). These goals were supplemented by an economic concern and a political concern that ultimately became a military one. These concerns emerged as rationales for the actions taken.

From the beginning of the crisis, Bush saw the invasion of Kuwait as a major economic threat to U.S. economic independence. The United States imported half its oil, and with Kuwait's oil under Iraqi control, Saddam would control 20 percent of world oil production. The political and military concern was the possibility of Iraq becoming the predominant Arab power in the region. Bush noted that, with its large standing army and successful invasion, Iraq would be in a strong position to intimidate, if not invade other Arab oil-producing countries. There was also the worry that Iraqi hegemony over Middle East oil production would have given Saddam Hussein a powerful international influence and enormous and continuing wealth with which to build his military force. Bush's view was that the United States could not "permit a resource so vital to be dominated by one so ruthless" (President's Address 1990).

In short, had the invasion not been repelled, Saddam Hussein would have had the means to become a major, even *the* major, regional

Arab power. The implications for the conservative Arab countries in the region (Egypt, Saudi Arabia, the Gulf Emirates) and for Israel of such formidable military-economic power built on the foundation of a successful, uncontested invasion can only be described as extremely sobering. Down the road, all these consequences and implications would have confronted American policy makers with some difficult and perhaps dangerous choices.

A rationale articulated early in the crisis concerned the role of the response to the invasion as a model for future international behavior. As the first post–cold war military crisis in which responses would not necessarily be dictated by East-West issues, the invasion of Kuwait was played out with few of the previous rules operating. The international structure imposed by cold war politics had disintegrated, and no comparable set of norms had taken its place.

It is now clear that the first three goals of the coalition were achieved. Saddam Hussein was forced to withdraw from Kuwait, the Kuwaiti government was restored, and American citizens held in Iraq were freed. The fate of the fourth goal—securing stability in the Persian Gulf region—is more problematic. It is difficult to assess regional stability because it is hard to argue in support of a policy by weighing the significance of what did *not* happen.[18] It is far easier to evaluate what did happen than what did not. Yet it is appropriate to note the problems we don't face because of the war.

For example, Iraq did not keep Kuwait and thus gain access to its oil reserves and to the economic, military, and political power that would have followed. The heavy damage to Iraq's military-industrial infrastructure has curtailed its use of military force outside its borders for the near future. This means that the possibility for aggression against either Arab countries or Israel, with its requirement of a U.S. response, has been significantly reduced. Iraq's nuclear arms program, more extensive and sophisticated than previously thought, was severely damaged and put under strict international inspection, backed by the threat of force for noncompliance (Rosenthal 1991, 6).[19] Overall, the prospects for regional stability would have been impaired had Saddam Hussein succeeded in keeping all or part of Kuwait, retaining his military-industrial forces intact, or continuing to develop nuclear weapons capacity.

These results alone do not ensure regional stability, since Saddam Hussein and Iraq are only part of a complex amalgam of political and economic issues in the region. The peace process in the Middle East has started up again, but to date the results are small, and the difficulties large. Still, the revival of the process is a positive development. Perhaps as Marvin Zonis argues, the shattering of the Arab myth by the war loosened the hard alignments and made some progress possible.

As for the international system, the possibilities of change, as Alexander George points out, are complex. The alliance that developed and held during the Gulf War was a truly unusual collective achievement. Does it provide a model for the future? Perhaps. The United Nations has voted to impose economic sanctions against Yugoslavia for its aggression against its former member states (P. Lewis 1992b), but to date has been reluctant to take further economic steps—much less to initiate a military one. The collective response and the imposition of sanctions in the Gulf may make such an exercise easier to think about and to carry out in other regions. It is too early, however, to say whether a collective international response is the new international norm. The Gulf War seems to have established a model, but whether this model will hold or fade remains to be determined. As for the Persian Gulf, one of the chief accomplishments of the war, besides those discussed above, was to buy time—time that can be used to settle the region's economic and political disputes, to improve economic and political circumstances, and to build new and better regional frameworks. Whether this time will be used productively is one of the major, and as yet unanswered, questions of the Gulf War.

NOTES

1. Timmerman (1991) provides a journalistic investigation of the activities of the United States, France, Brazil, Germany, and others. Sciolino (1992a, 166–68) presents data supporting this view of U.S. policy. See Draper (1992b, 38) for a critical view of this aspect of the Gulf War, and Draper (1992a) on the war itself.

2. There is major disagreement about the extent of the military damage to Iraq by the end of the war. Woodward (1991, 207) quotes Walter Lang, a defense intelligence agency officer, who claims that by the end of the war Iraq waged increasingly sophisticated warfare, killing 20,000–30,000 Iranians in a single battle. In the last major ground battle, 65,000 Iranians died. At that point, Lang felt, Iraq could have moved its army anywhere into Iran, but chose to consolidate its gains and make peace.

In its interim report to Congress, the Pentagon suggests that Iraq emerged from the Gulf War war battle tested and hardened, able to conduct sophisticated military operations with large numbers of troops against Iran (U.S. Department of Defense 1991, 3–4). But this assertion must be read in the context of the controversy regarding whether substantial numbers of Iraqi troops were in and near Kuwait, necessitating the large buildup of U.S. forces. The Pentagon's official estimate was "over 500,000" and listed Iraq's other technical and strategic assets in the area (ibid., 4). But Draper (1992b, 41–43), relying on calculations of "an experienced British correspondent" who wrote that Iraqi military strength was vastly overrated, is skeptical of these numbers.

A study conducted by the House Armed Services Committee suggests that only 183,000 troops might have been in or near Kuwait (Schmitt 1992). However the committee chairman admitted that the estimates used in the analysis were "little better than an educated guess." Dunnigan and Bay (1991, 374) note that intelligence estimates were made on the basis of satellite information regarding the presence of certain combat groups. Troop strength was estimated from these data, but only a head count could determine whether all units were at full strength. Both the Aspin report (1991) and Draper suggest that the massive forces brought to bear on Iraq were unnecessary. But from the standpoint of U.S. planning, a different calculus must be allowed. Draper reports that Egypt's President Mubarak remarked to General Powell that he thought that many of Saddam's soldiers would run away, but Powell replied that he did not want to take a chance that Mubarak might be wrong (Draper 1992b, 43).

The full Pentagon report to Congress on the conduct of the Gulf War shows that the possibility of high casualities was taken very seriously (Cushman 1992, 4). Estimates of over 10,000 causalities were widely discussed. The report also reveals that the president, the secretary of defense, and the chairman of the Joint Chiefs strongly mandated an upper limit on causalities.

Assembling such massive forces seemed to have been a response to two concerns: that forces be sufficient (1) to carry out the expulsion of Iraq from Kuwait, and (2) in a direct and timely manner. Behind these concerns were political and strategic calculations and apprehensions. Political support for U.S. involvement would have seriously frayed, and perhaps unraveled, had the war dragged on indecisively with a high number of allied casualties. In making a major commitment of forces, George Bush was addressing both political and military issues.

3. There is some evidence that this was done despite concerns that the Iraqi government was misusing those funds (Baquet 1992a, 1992b).

4. After the invasion and the onset of war, some suggested that responding to Iraq's wish to be a major regional player might result in a willingness to withdraw from Kuwait. But this does not explain why a policy that did not work well before the invasion would succeed afterward. Moreover, an attempt to give Iraq a substantial regional role after the invasion ran the risk of showing that Saddam's ends had justified his means. The Bush administration's insistence that there be "no reward for aggression" reflected an intention to set standards of international behavior for the new world order. At a more psychological level, the Bush administration was clearly concerned that such a response might embolden Saddam. For example, in a late November speech, Bush noted, "Brutality . . . must not be rewarded, because a bully unchecked today is a bully unleashed for tomorrow" (Bush's Speech on Iraq Policy 1990). Rewarding a leader who used violence in his past and not making him confront its consequences might well serve as reinforcement.

5. Deputy Secretary of State Lawrence Eagleberger said in testimony before the House, "I'm here to defend the policy. It didn't work. When you've got a policy that didn't work, it's not easy to defend" (Sciolino 1992, 6). Draper (1992b, 38) describes U.S. policy toward Iraq during this period as "appeasement." Paradoxically, one of Iraq's complaints about U.S. behavior before the war was that it had suspended food shipments and had "decided to deny Iraq

the purchase of a very large list of items" (Iraqi Foreign Minister's News Session 1990). For this and other reasons, it is doubtful in retrospect that the term *appeasement* describes U.S. behavior toward Iraq. Generally that term refers to a policy of accommodation, even compromising one's immediate or long-term interests based on fear of confrontation with a powerful, ruthless adversary. Such policies are generally associated with a direct or implicit challenge to one's interests. There is no evidence that George Bush feared Iraq or pursued policies that favored it because of threats to the United States. Nor has the Bush administration always eschewed military confrontation (e.g., Panama). The U.S. tilt toward Iraq during the Iran-Iraq War was surely motivated more by self-interest than by fear. If fear did drive U.S. policy during that period, it was more a fear of a revolutionary Iran than of a dictatorial Iraq. Similarly, during the second phase of U.S.-Iraqi relations, Iraq did not directly challenge the United States. U.S. policy at this point is better explained by diplomatic strategy than by the psychology of fear.

6. An Energy Department official warned that the pattern of Saddam Hussein's acquisition of components appeared to reflect a program for developing nuclear weapons (Broad 1992a), but this warning did not proceed up the policy deliberation chain (Broad 1992b). The prevailing view was that Iraqi nuclear research was at a primitive stage and that Saddam would be unable to build nuclear weapons until the late 1990s. Bush seems to have adapted a more urgent view of Iraqi nuclear technology just after the invasion. This raises the question of what new information, if any, was the basis of these revised estimates.

7. A full evaluation of the administration's culpability would have to examine the specific technologies involved. Were they low level? Did the Iraqis already have them, or access to them? What is the exact relation between the technical components exported and weapons production, on the one hand, and peaceful nuclear energy uses, on the other? What time periods are involved and for what specific shipments?

8. See for example the analysis of the United States' prewar behavior in Iraq's proposal to end the war made on February 15, 1991 ("Iraqi Statement" 1991). Saddam Hussein broadcast a detailed version of his concerns on February 15 (Hussein's Radio Speech 1991) and in an April 7, 1991, letter to the United Nations accepting the conditions for a cease-fire (Letter to U.N. 1991).

9. Dick Cheney testified that Iraq could survive long periods of economic hardship; that while the boycott was going on, Saddam Hussein would still control Kuwait and would continue to dismantle its political, economic, and social institutions; that Iraq would have additional time to fortify its position and to mobilize and deploy more forces; that the boycott would impose economic costs on those participating; and that the coalition might not hold for a protracted period (Testimony of Dick Cheney 1990). Colin Powell testified that relying on an embargo would leave the initiative in Saddam Hussein's hands. "He makes the decision as to whether or not he will or will not withdraw. He decides whether he has been published enough" (Testimony of General Colin Powell 1990). William Webster testified that while "sanctions are hurting the Iraqi civilian economy, they are affecting the Iraqi military only at the margins"; that in the military area Iraqi "ground and air forces can probably maintain near current levels of readiness for as long as nine months"; that "we expect the Iraqi air

force to feel the effects of sanctions more quickly and to a greater degree than the Iraqi ground force . . . which is more immune to sanctions." James Baker asked, "What is the workability of economic sanctions? . . . I am personally very pessimistic [and] this pessimism . . . is shared by our recent intelligence estimates. . . . The four months of experience we have had is not very encouraging" (Remarks by Webster and Baker 1990). Several former defense secretaries supported extending the sanctions for a time to bring about Iraq withdrawal. Their estimates of the long-term effectiveness of the sanctions are in Gorden (1990).

10. Two other postwar experiences with economic sanctions may shed some light on their usefulness against dictatorships. The effort to reverse a military coup in Haiti through economic sanction has not worked and may have been counterproductive, and an air embargo against Libya has not produced results.

11. The interview project from which this material was drawn was conceived and arranged by the American Enterprise Institute and produced by Brian Lapping Associates for the Discovery Channel and BBC Television. It consists of interviews with senior administration officials (Baker, Gates, Cheney, Powell, Schwarzkopf, Quayle) senior national security, State Department, and White House staff (Ross, Miller, Haass, Perle, Wolfowitz, Eagleberger) and foreign officials (Ambassador Al-Sabah, Sir Charles Powell, and others). Transcripts can be obtained from the AEI, Washington, D.C.

12. One can argue that the pressure of the possibility of war drove these efforts, and this is partly accurate. Removing the possibility of war would have taken away the urgency to find a negotiated solution, but in its place one would have had to confront the emotional and psychological fatigue that accompanies long defensive, but highly charged, sieges.

13. I do calculate here the human costs of the war, which caused great economic damage, personal suffering, and death for many Kuwaitis, Iraqis, Americans, Israelis, and others. All are by-products of Saddam's original decision to invade Kuwait and the political and strategic need of the United States and its allies to respond. Actual losses suffered by all parties and the apportionment of responsibility, while important to assessing some aspects of the war, require more extensive analysis than can conducted here (but see Walzer 1992 for a view on whether the Gulf War was just).

14. This doubtful scenario assumes that Iraqi citizens would take the very dangerous step of rising up against Saddam, holding him both guilty and responsible for their country's sufferings.

15. One could hardly invade Iraq, occupy Baghdad, and then turn over the city and country to either the Egyptians, Kuwaitis, or Syrians.

16. There was no guarantee that Saddam Hussein would have remained in the city. Still, having Saddam Hussein away from the levels of power might have allowed the installation of a more acceptable government. But the legitimacy of any Western-imposed government would be strenuously challenged.

17. Examples include the issue of collateral damage during the war, the level of harm to Iraq's infrastructure and its effects on the Iraqi public, and the question of whether to pursue and destroy the Republican Guard units. In these controversies, moral leadership requires a consideration of the price to be paid in death and destruction (once you assume that war is necessary) against the need

to accomplish the purposes for which the war is being fought. Moral leadership recognizes that ethical concerns may rival military and political ones and that how goals are carried out has a different impact from one's success in achieving them.

18. Paul Wolfowitz, a senior administration official, noted in a postwar interview, "If the world had done what it should have done in 1936 or 1938, someone might have felt cheated that Hitler was still in power, but they wouldn't have known of the tens of millions whose lives had been spared from World War II, and I think we have accomplished maybe something not on that scale, but something similar" (American Enterprise Institute 1992, program 3, 20).

19. Prewar estimates of Iraq's nuclear ability suggested it might be able to produce a weapon in five years. In a November 1990 speech, however, Bush stated, "Those who would measure the timetable of Saddam's nuclear program in years may be seriously underestimating the reality of the situation and the gravity of the threat." He also noted, "Every day brings Saddam one step closer to realizing his goal of a nuclear weapons arsenal" but "no one knows precisely when this dictator will obtain nuclear weapons" (Speech by Bush at Marine Post 1990).

That same week, some members of the Bush administration estimated that Saddam Hussein would obtain a nuclear weapon within six months. When questioned, Bush denied that such estimates were misleading, citing intelligence estimates that he has never disclosed (President's News Conference 1990). Early inspections of Iraqi nuclear facilities after the war led one expert to conclude that Iraq could have produced a bomb in twelve to eighteen months had the war not occurred (P. Lewis 1992a). Other experts believed, after examining Iraqi facilities, that it would have been twice as long. The question of exactly when Iraq would have produced a nuclear device is analogous to the debate over the number of Iraqi troops in or near the Kuwaiti theater of operations. Without the rigid inspection regime imposed after the war, it would have been difficult to appreciate by routine inspection the extent and sophistication of the Iraqi program. The important issue is not whether Saddam Hussein would have obtained the bomb in six, twelve, or twenty-four months, but the implications for Middle East stability of his acquiring such a device, and what, given sophisticated deception techniques, could have been done to forestall this acquisition short of military action.

REFERENCES

American Enterprise Institute. 1992. *The Gulf Crisis: The Road to War.* Washington, D.C.: AEI. Transcript of a three-part television series aired in January 1992.

Aspin, Les. 1991. *Winning the War and Losing the Peace in Saddam Hussein's Iraq.* Memorandum, House Committee on Armed Forces, December 12.

Baquet, Dean. 1992a. "Investigators Say U.S. Shielded Iraqis from Bank Inquiry." *New York Times*, March 20.

——— . 1992b. "Documents Charge Iraqis Made Swap: Food for Arms." *New York Times*, March 27.

Broad, William. 1992a. "Data on Iraq Nuclear Warnings Released by U.S." *New York Times*, April 23.

———— . 1992b. "Warning on Iraq and Bomb Bid Silenced in '89." *New York Times*, April 20.

Bush's Speech on Iraq Policy. 1990. Transcript. *New York Times*, August 29.

Cushman, John H. 1992. "Pentagon Report on the Persian Gulf War: A Few Surprises and Some Silences." *New York Times*, April 11.

Draper, Theodore. 1992a. "The Gulf War Reconsidered." *New York Review of Books*, January 16, 46–53.

———— . 1992b. "The True History of the Gulf War." *New York Review of Books*, January 30, 38–44.

Dunnigan, James F., and Austin Bay. 1991. *From Shield to Storm: High Tech Weapons, Military Strategy and Coalition Warfare in the Persian Gulf*. New York: Morrow.

George, Alexander L..1991. *Forceful Persuasion: An Alternative to War*. Washington, D.C.: United States Institute of Peace.

Gorden, Michael. 1990. "Ex-Defense Secretaries Advise Patience in Gulf." *New York Times*, December 1.

Graubard, Stephen R. 1991. *Mr. Bush's War: Adventures in the Politics of Illusion*. New York: Hill and Wang.

Gulf Testimony. 1990. Excerpt from transcript. *New York Times*, December 4.

Herrmann, Richard. Forthcoming. "Coercive Diplomacy and the Crisis over Kuwait: 1990-1991." In *The Limits of Coercive Diplomacy*, rev. ed., ed. Alexander L. George, David K. Hall, and William E. Simons. Boston: Little, Brown.

Hussein's Radio Speech Dealing with War and Peace. 1990. Transcript. *New York Times*, February 22.

Iraqi Foreign Minister's News Session After Geneva Talks. 1990. Excerpts from transcript. *New York Times*, January 10.

Iraqi Statement: Baghdad's Offer and Conditions. 1991. Transcript. *New York Times*, February 16.

Kohut, Heinz. 1972. "Thoughts on Narcissism and Narcissistic Rage." *Psychoanalytic Study of the Child* 27: 360–400.

Lewis, Anthony. 1992. "Who Fed This Caesar?" *New York Times*, March 15, p. 17.

Lewis, Paul. 1992a. "U.N. Experts Now Say Baghdad Was Far Away From Making A Bomb." *New York Times*, May 20.

———— . 1992b. "U.N. Votes Trade Sanctions Against Yugoslavia, 13-0: Air Travel and Oil Curbed." *New York Times*, May 31.

List of Strategic Exports to Iraq. 1992. Transcript. *New York Times*, April 24.

Letter to U.N.: Iraqis Accept This Resolution. 1991. Excerpt from Transcript. *New York Times*, April 8.

Lohr, Steve. 1990. "Experts Say Embargo May Work if Nations Maintain Commitment." *New York Times*, July 6.

President's Address to Joint Session of Congress. 1990. Transcript. *New York Times*, September 12.

President's News Conference on the Crisis in the Gulf. 1990. Transcript. *New York Times*, December 1.

Proposals by Iraqi President. 1990. Excerpts from transcript of his address. *New York Times*, August 13.

Remarks by Webster and Baker on Embargo's Drain on Iraq. 1990. Excerpt from transcript. *New York Times,* December 6.

Rosenthal, A. M. 1991. "Mistakes of the War." *New York Times,* July 12.

────── . 1992. "Elections and the Gulf War." *New York Times,* July 3.

Saddam Hussein's Speech on the Withdrawal of His Army from Kuwait. 1991. Transcript. *New York Times,* February 27.

Schmitt, Eric. 1992. Study Lists Lower Tally of Iraqi Troops in Gulf War. *New York Times.* April 24, p. 6.

Schwarzkopf, H. Norman, with Peter Petre (1992). *It Doesn't Take a Hero.* New York: Linda Grey/Bantam.

Sciolino, Elaine. 1991. "Hussein's Errors: Complex Impulses." *New York Times,* February 28.

────── . 1992a. *The Outlaw State: Saddam Hussein's Quest for Power and the Gulf Crisis.* New York: Wiley.

────── . 1992b. "Bush Aides Attack Democrats on Iraq." *New York Times.*

────── . 1992c. "Bush Ordered Iraqis Plied with Aid." *New York Times,* May 29.

Smith, Jean Edward. 1992. *George Bush's War.* New York: Holt, Rinehart and Winston.

Speech by Bush at Marine Post. 1990. Excerpts from Transcript. *New York Times,* November 23.

Speech to the Arab Cooperation Council Summit. 1990. *FBIS Daily Report.* FBIS-NES-90-039, February 24, 1–5.

Taylor, Patrick E. 1991. "U.S. Has Trouble Maintaining Unity of Allies on Iraq." *New York Times,* July 28.

────── . 1992. "Confronting Hussein: Risky for Bush." *New York Times,* March 20.

Testimony of Dick Cheney. 1990. Transcript. *New York Times,* December 4.

Testimony of General Colin Powell. Transcript. *New York Times,* December 4.

Timmerman, Kenneth R. 1991. *The Death Lobby: How the West Armed Iraq.* New York: Houghton Mifflin.

U.S. Department of Defense. 1991. *Conduct of the Persian Gulf Conflict: An Interim Report to Congress.* Washington, D.C.: Government Printing Office.

U.S. News and World Report (1992). *Triumph Without Victory: The Unreported History of the Gulf War.* New York: Times/Random House.

Viorst, Milton. 1991. "Report from Baghdad." *New Yorker,* June 24, 55–73.

Walzer, Michael. 1992. *Just and Unjust Wars.* New York: Basic Books.

Woodward, Robert. 1991. *The Commanders.* New York: Simon and Schuster.

POSTSCRIPT

The Ides of January, 1993

■

Stanley A. Renshon

Almost two years to the day from the beginning of Operation Desert Storm, the United States and its coalition partners again became engaged in military action against Iraq. The immediate cause of the confrontations was a series of steps taken by Iraq that were viewed as increasingly provocative by U.S., allied, and UN officials. These steps appeared designed to test the boundaries and the resolve of coalition members, who were becoming increasingly preoccupied with other matters.

Saddam Hussein's actions, and the U.S. and allied response, have underlined the unresolved dilemmas of the Gulf War, notably the long-term consequences of having Saddam Hussein in power. But they have also raised the issue of the long-term viability of the present coalition policy after the chief architect of that policy, George Bush, has left office and Bill Clinton has become president. As a result, the relationship among the United States, its allies, and Iraq has become more complex, even as it continues to be hazardous and incendiary. In this postscript I explore some of the issues that have arisen in this context.

Post – Gulf War Patterns

The general outlines of the postwar relationships with Iraq of the United States, its Gulf War allies, and the UN are clear.[1] They are reflected in the military, economic, and political goals pursued by all sides. At another level, they also reflect the psychological goals and methods used by each of the parties.

The U.S. and its allies have followed a policy best described as intrusive containment. They have (1) imposed a postwar inspection regime on Iraq's biological and nuclear weapons facilities, (2) maintained their economic embargo (allowing only for humanitarian supplies), (3) tried to keep Saddam Hussein from reconsolidating his authority and power, especially in northern and southern Iraq, and (4) pressed (but not strongly) the issue of war reparations. Those policies have slowed, but not stopped, Iraq in its drive to restore its military and economic infrastructure and have limited Saddam Hussein's ability to reestablish and solidify his control over the country.

At the psychological level, the policies put into place by the Bush administration reflect a view of Saddam Hussein as an aggressive leader very capable of violent acts. It follows from this view that if allied policies cannot change Saddam Hussein's character, they can at least frustrate his means. U.S. and allied policies toward Saddam Hussein reflect both psychological as well as political-military considerations.

The psychological elements of coalition policy also enter the calculations in another way. A war was fought, after all, over Saddam Hussein's invasion of Kuwait and after commitments to contain him had been made. Failure to follow through on these commitments would have dramatically recast the psychological understanding of the war. Questions of will and resolve would certainly have been raised, as would the benefits of adamant refusal and persistence.

The United States and its allies clearly wish to see Saddam Hussein replaced. Brent Scowcroft revealed that the Bush administration took direct steps toward that end (*New York Times,* January 20, 1993, 10). It is therefore not clear whether present U.S. and allied policy is meant to be temporary or whether it represents a long-term strategy. Events unfolding since December 1992 have exposed some of that policy's limitations and potential dangers, prompting calls for its reconsideration.

Saddam Hussein has been equally consistent in his postwar policy goals. They are (1) to rebuild his country's economic and military infrastructure—a goal that has achieved substantial success given the amount of damage Iraq sustained in the Gulf War, (2) to evade and frustrate where possible the UN inspection regimes, (3) to secure the lifting of the UN economic embargo, (4) to solidify and/or reestablish his power and authority within Iraq, and (5) to continue to project his and Iraq's presence in the Middle East.

Saddam Hussein's political and military policies reflect his understanding of the psychology of the conflict as well as his psychological goals and motivations. Saddam Hussein wishes to demonstrate that although he received devastating military blows during the Gulf War, he remains unbeaten, unbowed, and undeterred. His capacity to absorb military punishment and remain defiantly unrepentant adds to his stature in some eyes. Indeed, provoking and taking military punishment (especially if on a small scale, like the bombing of a manufacturing facility or the destruction of some ground-to-air missiles), serves important strategic purposes.

The Developing Crisis

Between December 1992 and January 1993, Saddam Hussein has made a concentrated effort to challenge the United States, its allies, and the UN on a variety of fronts. It is important to take a closer look at these events, which reveal much about Saddam Hussein's strategy and the resulting complications, opportunities, and dangers for the coalition.[2]

During this period (1) Saddam Hussein continued in his defiance of UN resolutions regarding the inspection of Iraq's nuclear and biological weapons facilities; (2) he massed troops along the northern borders, leading to concerns about Iraqi military action against the Kurds (Gordon 1992a); and (3) he interfered with UN relief trucks providing humanitarian aid to the Kurds, including placing bombs on trucks delivering aid (*New York Times*, December 20, 1992, 9).

After "no-fly zones" in both southern and northern Iraq were established, allied patrol flights gradually decreased, as military forces were given other assignments. (4) On December 27, Iraqi jets breached the no-fly zone in southern Iraq and were reported to have to have fired a missile at nearby U.S. planes (Gordon, 1992b). U.S. jets shot down the Iraqi plane. However, other Iraqi aircraft later crossed into the no-fly zone when U.S. planes were not in the area. On December 28, two squadrons of American planes and other military assets were rushed back to the Gulf to buttress U.S. forces there (Gordon 1992c).

(5) On January 5, Saddam Hussein deployed surface-to-air missiles in southern Iraq "just south of the 32nd parallel, which marks the northern boundary of the air exclusion zone," that would be able to reach allied planes flying though it (Gordon, 1993a). (6) Despite an ultimatum and deadline to remove these missiles, Iraq's leader publicly defied allied demands (Gordon 1993b). (7) Iraq on January 8 indicated that they were moving some, but not all, of the missiles from their original sites (Schmitt 1993a), which ultimately did not fully comply with conditions imposed by the United States and its allies (Gordon 1993c).

(8) Next, on January 11 Iraq refused to let UN weapons inspectors enter the country except on Iraqi aircraft, which had been grounded by UN economic sanctions, or except by driving overland from Jordan (Ibrahim 1993a). (9) This move was accompanied by an incursion on January 10 of about 250 armed Iraqis into Kuwait to seize missiles and other weapons claimed by Iraq (Schmitt, 1993b). (10) A smaller but similar armed incursion occurred the following day (Ibrahim, 1993b).

(11) Iraq then shifted surface-to-air missiles into the no-fly zone in the north on January 11, again posing a direct threat to allied planes in that area (Gordon 1993d). When the United States threatened military action, on January 12 Iraq sent a letter to the United Nations asking for

a "dialogue" on these disputes (Gordon 1993e). In response to these events, on January 13 the United States and allied forces launched an air attack on Iraqi surface-to-air missile facilities in the south (Apple 1993). In an interview, President-elect Bill Clinton supported the action but mused about the possibility of a new relationship with Iraq—a view he then insisted had been misunderstood and he publicly disowned (Interview with President-elect Clinton 1993; see also Friedman 1993a, 1993b).

(12) Thereafter, on January 16 Iraq refused to ensure the safety of UN inspectors flying in the northern and southern zones (Gordon 1993f). Saddam Hussein continued to defy the United States and its allies by (13) "targeting" allied planes on patrol missions with radar for its surface-to-air missiles, (14) entering the northern no-fly zone, and (15) continuing its armed incursions into Kuwait. On January 17, the United States and its allies launched a missile attack on an industrial plant in the Baghdad suburbs that produced components needed for the recovery of Iraq's economic, military, and nuclear capacity (Gordon 1993g).

The next day, the United States and some of its allies launched another air attack against Iraqi antiaircraft sites (Gordon 1993h). Iraq then announced that it had ordered a cease-fire against American planes and agreed to let UN inspection teams enter Baghdad (Gordon 1993i). The Iraqi press characterized this announcement as an "expression of good intention toward the Administration of U.S. President-elect Bill Clinton" (*New York Times*, January 20, 1993, 10).

This situation held for one day into the new administration. (16) U.S. jets attacked and destroyed a surface-to-air missile radar site that was actively tracking an allied flight in the no-fly zone (Gordon 1993k). Iraq denied that it had turned on any radar since its announced cease-fire. (17) On January 22, the same tracking-attack sequence took place (Sciolino 1993). Iraq again denied that it had tracked any planes, calling it "a fabricated incident." The next day a U.S. fighter again fired on an Iraqi antiaircraft battery in somewhat ambiguous circumstances amid reports that new air defense sites were being constructed in the excluded zones (Cushman 1993). Iraq again denied that it had fired on or tracked any allied aircraft.

The Emerging Patterns: Their Meaning and Implications

It is possible to examine each of these seventeen incidents and the U.S. and allied responses to them individually, but it is more productive to look for broader patterns. It is a mistake, however, to seek a single meaning in each event or even in the patterns that emerge. Each event or pattern has multiple purposes and meanings.

In examining these incidents in the context of the Gulf War, one discerns four general characteristics. First, they both assert and reflect an element of power. The ability to command attention at will is a form of power, as is the ability to cause disruption. Second, with some exceptions (like threatening to fire a missle at an allied plane), these are not major events. Sending the Iraqi army into the northern provinces against the Kurds would be a provocation of more dramatic military and psychological significance.[3] Third, these actions on Iraq's part are finely calibrated explorations of ambiguities and challenge, sometimes mixing two messages (compliance and defiance) at once. Did the announcement of a cease-fire against allied planes mean they would not be tracked by radar? Does not every country have the right to monitor its own air space for self-defense? Fourth, Iraq risked small losses (several surface-to-air missile radar installations, one factory, a plane) in exchange for disproportionate political, psychological, and perhaps other more strategic gains.

The Potential Bases of Psychological, Political, and Strategic Gain

What are these psychological, political, and strategic benefits? Eight major potential avenues of gain emerge with some clarity. First, each incident represents a testing of boundaries to determine how much latitude, if any, exists within the system of constraints imposed on Iraq. Is there room for maneuver and assertion that can be uncovered or developed?

Each test is, at the same time, an assertion of Iraq's and Mr. Hussein's continuing courage, determination, and shrewdness. Each of these is psychologically significant for Saddam Hussein and his policy ambitions. His courage of course is reflected in his defiant stance toward U.S. and allied forces. Defiance against a militarily superior opponent is seen as strength, even when the opponent is constrained in many ways.[4] Somewhat paradoxically, the very severity of the military blows that Iraq received during the war have tended to magnify this aspect of Saddam Hussein's postwar behavior.

Mr. Hussein's behavior since the war also reflects and is meant to convey his shrewdness. Appreciating and choosing the right ambiguities, ones that will get attention but not be dramatically mobilizing, is itself an act of strategic intelligence. In exploiting ambiguities, pushing to limits (and then a little past) without more than a warning or with at most small losses, he demonstrates that he can make very good use of limited resources.

Saddam Hussein's determination is evident in his rise to power, his maintaining power, and his conduct during the Gulf War. It is therefore not surprising that it is again on display. This element of his character not only reflects Saddam Hussein's psychological nature; it has important policy uses. The capacity to persist in the face of severe adversity such as the military battering his country received during the Gulf War heightens the admiration of his followers, earns grudging respect for his tenacity (as well as anxiety) among his opponents, and fosters the belief that future policy decisions must take him into account. Considerations of accommodation are one possible outcome of such beliefs.

Fifth, each test is an assertion of real power elements that Saddam Hussein commands in this situation. By mounting many ambiguous tests, he projects at least three aspects of his power without taking active military action:

  a. He commands attention and other scarce resources that reflect and indicate to others his continuing importance.
  b. His actions require the redeployment of allied military forces, which cannot be used elsewhere and thus become in some respects hostage to his decisions.
  c. There are also opportunity costs involved for the United States and its allies. Attempts to interpret Saddam Hussein's most recent moves divert time, energy, and resources from other purposes.

The sixth and seventh major gains realized by Saddam Hussein from these tests are related: response fatigue and growing ambivalence on the part of the United States and its allies. It is important to remember that Saddam Hussein's aspirations for himself and for the reemergence of Iraq are his full-time concern; he has organized all of his government's and his country's resources around it. The United States and its allies find it difficult to keep Saddam Hussein and Iraq at the center of their attention for any extended period; sometimes, given other responsibilities and events, it is impossible.

Closely coordinated responses to Saddam Hussein's actions require continuous consultation between the United States and its allies, which at the same time links the allies psychologically and politically to Iraq. Paradoxically, this gives power to Iraq and adds to the vulnerability of present U.S. (and allied) policy. Each new act by Iraq, and hundreds more can be imagined, cannot be met with indifference; to do so would convey a lack of purpose and determination. Fatigue and its counterpart, impatience, are by-products of having to be on constant alert over extended periods to respond to what could be a daunting array of small but important challenges. Slippage in response or an erosion of allied support are the likely result.

The erosion of support among allies is a serious threat. Many of the Gulf War coalition partners have expressed doubts about the wisdom of one or another military response to Saddam Hussein's testing of limits. Saudi air bases were used to launch the air attacks against Iraq, but the Saudis themselves would not take part in them (Gordon 1993j). France, Britain, and Turkey expressed reservations about the missile attack on the manufacturing facility outside of Baghdad, and some UN members complained about the lack of U.S. consultation with them before the attacks (Lewis 1993; Cowell 1993). Arab countries were critical (Ibrahim 1993; *New York Times,* January 19, 1993, 9) of what they saw as a double standard in the treatment of an Arab country (Iraq) compared to others (including Yugoslavia, where Muslims were being attacked by Serbs, and Israel).[5]

An eighth and final avenue of gain for Saddam Hussein pertains to his support among the Iraqi people. While public opinion in a police state is difficult to gauge, it is not clear that he is widely viewed within Iraq as *the* cause of the Gulf War or its aftermath. The history of Western colonialism, nationalist sentiments favoring expansion of Iraq into Kuwait, resentment over being attacked and subjected to economic hardship (even given some appreciation of Iraq's role in these events), and Mr. Hussein's relative success in raising the general standard of living since the Gulf War make it less likely that Iraqis would hold him responsible for these hardships. When one adds to this the full-scale propaganda offensive against every allied action, one realizes that current policy will not necessarily lead to growing resentment against Saddam Hussein. The result could be the opposite.

Interestingly, the one major drawback to Saddam Hussein's actions are to be found in their flawed timing and scope—two deficiencies apparent in his previous judgments (see chapter 4). One could have predicted that George Bush would eventually respond to Mr. Hussein's actions. On the other hand, Bill Clinton had been an ambivalent supporter of the Gulf War. What if Saddam Hussein's probing of the boundaries had begun immediately before the inauguration, but at a relatively low level, and had been coupled with a diplomatic offensive directed toward the new administration and its allies?

Recall that Mr. Hussein began the current round of events with a direct military challenge to the UN and to the United States by bombing UN relief trucks and firing on U.S. aircraft. These actions were certain to revive memories of his dangerousness and probably contributed to the support that emerged for strong retaliatory action. Moreover, these challenges had another, easily anticipated effect on the range of actions available to the new Clinton administration.

The seriousness of Mr. Hussein's refusal to comply with the war-related UN resolutions almost guaranteed a strong response by President Bush. But it also reestablished a standard of enforcement that can be broached only with adequate political and military explanation. Whereas President-elect Clinton expressed a belief that a new relationship with Mr. Hussein is possible, it is unclear how far from Mr. Bush's policy President Clinton will be able to travel.

Whatever Bill Clinton's beliefs about his ability to bring about a new relationship with Mr. Hussein may be, he will have to contend with his unequivocal statements that his policies toward Iraq will echo those of George Bush. Moreover, President Clinton will also be constrained by criticism that he has backed away from a number of campaign pledges and by concerns that his wish to be inclusive and to be liked makes it difficult for him to take tough stands on principle. Whatever their merits, not taking these concerns into account could be attributed to another misjudgment on Mr. Hussein's part.[6]

The United States: Toward a New Policy?

In response to Saddam Hussein's actions, the United States has adopted a version of the "tit for tat" strategy. In this strategy, each action that violates a boundary is met with a proportional and appropriate response designed to be aversive. This strategy has the benefit of appearing on its face to be *fair* (the proportional and appropriate heuristics), a necessary benefit when others' views about one's actions are part of the calculation.

A military response has the advantage of being a manifest, dramatic action. This in turn signals seriousness of purpose and determination. Not incidentally, a military response also inflicts damage on the adversary's military assets, further weakening the possibility of retaliation.

There are several difficulties with the "tit for tat" strategy, however, some of which have been noted. First, the *fairness* heuristic is not a given in the present case. One can argue that the response of the United States and its allies is "limited," but that alone may not be enough to ensure the perception of fairness. Is it fair to bomb radar sites because the radar is turned on but no other action is taken? Is it fair to shoot down planes whose only transgression is the relatively passive one of crossing into an excluded zone within a nation's own territorial boundaries? Is it fair for a militarily superior country to bomb a country that is unable to defend itself?

Such questions suggest that the United States and its allies cannot expect that their view of their responses as proportional, limited, and appropriate will be uniformly accepted by others. The perception of unfairness is part of the dynamic that has fueled the uneasiness of some of the United States' allies. It has also helped to revive public criticism by those who did not support U.S. and allied policy during the Gulf War.

The "tit for tat" strategy also assumes that the costs to an opponent are proportional to the perceived advantages. It is not clear that this is the actual calculus operating here. I have already discussed the potential advantages that could motivate Saddam Hussein's behavior, and it is not certain that he is suffering a proportional cost relative to them. Does the loss of one plane, a factory, and several surface-to-air missile systems reach the level of loss required to deter future transgressions? Perhaps, but the amount of loss suffered by Iraq during the Gulf War was dramatically greater and yet appears to have had little effect in deterring these latest actions.

Last, the "tit for tat" strategy ordinarily requires both a consistent response and a commitment to it. Continuing a "tit for tat" strategy leaves the initiative to whoever decides whether or not to transgress the boundary. Also, if sustained for any time, it tends to make the specific kinds of responses that have already been taken the norm. It may freeze a situation so that the benefits to the transgressor outweigh the costs. Attempts to change that set of actions—for example, with a stronger response—run the risk of aggravating perceptions of unfairness. This in turn increases the danger of substantially damaging the overall consensus (as opposed to consensus on a specific response to a specific action) supporting boundary containment.

Saddam Hussein's recent actions and George Bush's responses have underscored the dilemmas of the current policy. President Clinton's initial reaction to those events has further complicated them.[7] When interviewed after the first air strike, Clinton regretted that over "the last year and a half [that is, the postwar period] we have sent mixed signals," referring later in the interview to accommodations made by the Bush administration in enforcing the inspection regime and developing the cease-fire agreement. He then expressed the hope that in the future "we will send a firm and consistent set of signals."

However, in the next sentence he somewhat ambiguously stated that "he wouldn't rule out reviewing our options in the future." It is unclear whether he referred to military changes, other policy changes, or both. When questioned as to whether a "fresh start between [Clinton] and Saddam" was possible, the president replied, as though addressing the Iraqi leader, "If you want a different relationship with me, you could begin by upholding the UN requirements to change your behavior."

Clinton's apparent willingness to entertain the possibility of a new relationship with Mr. Hussein has drawn the most comment (Friedman 1993b). However, as the above statement stands it is unexceptionable. Without knowing what would constitute such a change in behavior, it is difficult to tell whether this remark means continuity or change in U.S. policy. Does upholding UN requirements mean complete compliance with all UN directives, both in fact and in spirit? Must Iraq renounce its claim to Kuwait, pay reparations, stop attempting to evade UN inspections, and truly cooperate with the injunction to dismantle its nuclear and biological weapons facilities, and so on?

To state these requirements directly brings two points into clear focus. First, obeying many of the UN resolutions would require Mr. Hussein to renounce personal and regional goals that have characterized his leadership for decades. Second, these questions evoke a wide range of ambiguous issues about which there are "reasonable disagreements" and even direct conflict.

Attempting to resolve all these issues in the context of trying to develop a "fresh relationship" exposes the present policy to major dangers: (1) erosion of the present policy—intrusive containment—and (2) its loss of support in a series of endless disputes that must be "resolved." Americans generally believe that resolving disputes requires bargaining, give and take, and ultimate accommodation to another's "legitimate interests." An artful practitioner can make great use of such a procedure.[8]

The dangers just described are generally recognized; the real question is whether they will be sufficiently appreciated in this context. One striking aspect of President Clinton's interview is the remarkable self-assurance with which he discusses the possibility of a fresh start. After talking about Mr. Hussein's need to change his behavior and denying that he is obsessed with the man, Clinton goes on to state:

> *I think that if he were sitting here on the couch I would further the change in his behavior.* You know if he spent half the time, just a half, or even a third of the time worrying about the welfare of his people that he spends worrying about where to place his SAM missiles and whether he can aggravate Bush by violating the cease-fire agreement, what he's going to do with the people who don't agree with him in the South and in Iraq, I think he'd be a stronger leader and be in a lot better shape over the long run. (Emphasis added)

President Clinton appears to believe that he personally can bring about this change. In keeping with his respect for his own political skills, Mr. Clinton believes that he can persuade Saddam Hussein that he would be a better leader, that he would be better off, if he followed his—Clinton's—advice. To expect that people can be won over by words is plausible, given Mr. Clinton's successful experience in the election campaign, but it could be dangerously misapplied in this context.

There is a disturbing element of naive grandiosity reflected in these beliefs. It is naive to presume that anyone could overcome—indeed, reverse—the character patterns that have been evident in Mr. Hussein's adult career and behavior, and to do so by appealing to what Clinton sees as Mr. Hussein's long-run interests. The serene confidence that Clinton expresses in his ability to bring about such a change is a potential source of difficulty. The error of judgment that may await President Clinton is not that he will discount Mr. Hussein's shrewdness, but that he will overestimate his own.

Some Concluding Observations on Policy Alternatives

President Bush attempted to change Saddam Hussein's behavior by offering inducements. This policy failed either to deter Mr. Hussein or to modify his ambitions. It seems unlikely that the power of a convincing argument alone will prove more productive. On the other hand, the present policy of intrusive containment entails a number of risks.

From this dilemma several other policy options have emerged. One is to allow Iraq to continue its recovery as a hedge against Iran (Gelb 1993). The danger in this policy is that it assumes that Iraq would play this role without being allowed to rebuild economically and militarily. This in turn would mean dropping the economic sanctions, weakening the adversarial stance inherent in the inspection regime, and allowing Iraq to reassert its political authority throughout the country.

Such a move would represent a complete reversal of U.S. policy. It would bring about so many adverse consequences that it is difficult to treat it as a serious alternative. One such consequence would be to raise profound questions from our allies and others regarding the United States' determination and persistence, credibility, values, and ultimately its judgment in rearming a man whose ambitions it took a major war to slow.

A second policy option is to increase the costs to Mr. Hussein for noncompliance. This has advantages that reversing policy does not. However, unless the increments in costs are carefully selected, this option also adds costs for the coalition that has to date had difficulty in supporting "proportional" responses, much less stronger action.

The option of arming the Kurds has received some attention as one method of increasing the costs to Mr. Hussein for noncompliance. However, this option has a number of drawbacks. First, it cannot easily be started and stopped in response to Mr. Hussein's compliance or lack thereof. Second, a real commitment to this option exposes the United States and its allies to a major, long-term commitment, as well as to the charge that it has cynically used and/or abandoned a distressed and oppressed group. For a president who has frequently mentioned that values should inform U.S. military interventions in other countries, such behavior would represent a startling and politically costly departure. Third, the Kurds are not a viable counterweight to Mr. Hussein's power—they are merely a means of distracting his attention.

If this policy—increasing Saddam Hussein's costs for noncompliance—is to be effective, then other less costly increments on the part of the Western allies must be found. Extending the no-fly zone over most or all of Iraq is a possible means. It represents a substantial, direct, and highly visible but nonlethal increment in the level of costs imposed for noncompliance.

Third, there is the option of saving up provocations, issuing warnings, and then responding with disproportionate strength against a wide range of military and economic targets (Gordon 1993j). The advantage of such a policy lies in its direct impact on Mr. Hussein's plan to regain military power in order to be in a position to again pursue his regional ambitions. This third option would also demonstrate determination and seriousness, two qualities useful to the world's remaining superpower, one with worldwide responsibilities but more limited aspirations.

There are however several drawbacks to such a policy. First, it might not be particularly effective or defensible against the many "almost, but not quite" provocations that could occur. It is difficult to launch wide-ranging military attacks because UN weapons inspectors have to travel by bus rather than by plane. To be justified, provocations would have to be significant, blatant, and militarily threatening. While Mr. Hussein has, somewhat surprisingly, engaged in exactly the kinds of incidents that would provide justifications for such a response, there is no assurance that he will do so in the future.

Even if provocations were adequate, such a policy would run a substantial risk of undermining the coalition that has so far supported the policy of intrusive containment toward Iraq. Such a policy would also raise new questions and criticisms regarding its fairness. Last, the United States might well be left to carry out this policy virtually alone.

A fourth and last policy option is the one alluded to in the Clinton interview: not trying to convince Mr. Hussein that he would be better off if he renounced his ambitions and complied with UN resolutions, but carefully exploring the possibilities of a new relationship between Iraq and the United States and its allies.

How might such a policy evolve? It might begin with Mr. Hussein signaling his willingness to abide by some of the UN resolutions. He might, for example, call a cease-fire that would invite the Clinton administration to make an appropriate gesture in response.

This is an attractive and seductive policy option, but in many ways the most risky. It is attractive because resolving conflicts without war is preferable to settling them by direct military means. It is seductive because it promises change and could even deliver some, but with a subtle catch. The cease-fire presented to the Clinton administration as an "inaugural gift" is a case in point. In effect, Mr. Hussein is attempting to gain credit by promising not to do what he has already been prohibited from doing, while leaving his views of other matters unclear or unstated.

The policy is risky because it can be manipulated by a shrewd and calculating adversary. How? The policy could be exploited by Mr. Hussein to gain military, economic, and ultimately political advantage while biding his time and directing his resources toward the realization of his original ambitions. A president who believes in the sincerity of death-bed conversions and with a strong confidence in his own ability to change Mr. Hussein's character, beliefs, and behavior is particularly vulnerable to this strategic approach.

The policy has other hazards. It requires as much attention to details and the determination to deal with them, as does the present policy of intrusive containment. Indeed, in some respects it can be viewed as the same policy applied to a different process, one that is evolving rather than static.

The linchpin of such a policy would be verified compliance to significant elements of the UN resolutions for an extended period. This would lead to a *measured* easing of the economic costs imposed on Iraq—for example, allowing more imports of products particularly necessary to the Iraqi public.

This process appears to have some similarities to the GRIT proposal put forward by Charles Osgood (1962) some years ago: Osgood proposed that United States take unilateral initiatives to reduce tensions with the Soviet Union and await a favorable response. However, this option takes the opposite approach. It requires an initial and substantial compliance initiative from Iraq and does not necessarily promise an equal response in return. In these respects, it is actually the obverse of the policy that Osgood proposed; it approaches the possibility of an evolving U.S. relationship with Iraq on the basis of concrete changes in behavior over time, rather than reciprocal gestures. It does not promise an end to conflict, but rather (in the short term at least) a change of means. Even if such a policy were to succeed, it would entail an arduous process of negotiations with an smart, shrewd, and calculating adversary.

If such a policy were to be productive, what is entailed in compliance must be absolutely clear and unequivocal. Intense bargaining over these understandings must be expected. Linkages to larger issues, symbolic agreements, and other such mechanisms for evading real compliance must be anticipated and rejected.

To back up such a process, the United States and its allies must be willing to use military and other punitive options if necessary. These options represent a line of defense if other attempts and inducements to compliance should fail. Because punitive measures would of course be difficult to initiate after a "dialogue" has been publicly announced and initiated, the concrete steps that would indicate Iraq's acceptance of the terms of the agreement must be spelled out in specific detail, perhaps publicly.

Which policy option has the most potential? A prudent choice might be the last, holding the third in reserve. Whether the Clinton administration has the clarity of purpose, conviction, and energy to carry through such a policy, and whether Saddam Hussein would not ultimately become too frustrated by the rate of progress toward his goals remain major questions.

NOTES

1. Not not only are these three separate entities, but they also sometimes differ in important respects.

2. This section depends on news accounts, despite their limitations, as documentation of the major facts around a particular event: for example, planes were sent on a bombing mission, a letter was sent to the UN, and so on. News accounts provide at least three kinds of information: (1) to confirm that an an event took place; (2) to establish some of the circumstances surrounding an event; and (3) to convey the actors' understandings of an event as reflected in public statements or actions. (To be sure, in addition to their stated views, leaders have private understandings or motivations that they don't reveal and possibly are unaware of.)

In time, fuller knowledge and more informed interpretations of recent events will emerge that may modify tentative analyses based on news accounts. But the events described in this postscript are part of an ongoing series of events with which this book is concerned, thus giving somewhat firmer foundation to these analyses.

Admittedly, political psychology theory cannot reveal the deepest motivations of the actors involved or the means by which their calculations were translated into action. But such a framework for analysis can provide, especially for events that are part of an ongoing series, a systematic, integrated, and theoretically based explanation of the events and their possible significance.

3. Such an incursion against the Kurds would probably require a strong U.S. and allied response. It would also reveal a continuing capacity of Iraq's military in spite of the war and bring back memories of past Iraqi military moves, revitalizing the coalition against Iraq.

4. The U.S. public, its allies (especially Arab states), and UN officials would have great difficulty tolerating grossly disproportionate military action against Iraq for these "minor" transgressions.

5. These publicly voiced reservations must also be considered in the context of privately held sentiments with which they are sometimes at variance. Moreover, it is unclear that these reservations, when part of an overall agreement with goals and strategy, require a change in policy.

6. Possibly Mr. Hussein simply does not know enough about U.S. politics to have thought of these implications. But the question, "How are these actions likely to be viewed by the next administration?" was surely an obvious one to ask.

7. The following analysis and quotations are drawn from the published transcript of the *New York Times* interview with then President-elect Clinton.

8. President Clinton gave Mr. Hussein's the opportunity for the cease-fire gesture by publicly musing about the possibility of a changed relationship. This allowed Mr. Hussein to offer President Clinton a respite from the rigors of dealing with Iraq during his inaugural, an initiative that invited a similar relaxation in return.

REFERENCES

Apple, R. W. 1993. "U.S. and Allied Planes Hit Iraq, Bombing Missile Sites in South in Reply to Hussein's Defiance." *New York Times,* January 14.

Cowell, Alan. 1993. "Turks' Concern Grows on Tie to Anti-Iraq Block." *New York Times,* January 19.

Cushman, John N., Jr. 1993. "U.S. Watching Iraq for Air Defenses." *New York Times,* January 25.

Friedman, Thomas L. 1993a. "Clinton Backs Raids but Muses about a New Start." *New York Times,* January 14.

———. 1993b. "Clinton Affirms U.S. Policy on Iraq." *New York Times,* January 15.

Gelb, Leslie H. 1993. "Iraq Balancing Iran?" *New York Times,* January 17.

Gordon, Michael R. 1992a. "Iraq Reported to Mass Troops Near Kurds' Enclave." *New York Times,* December 18 [dateline December 17].

———. 1992b. "U.S. Shoots Down an Iraqi Warplane in No-Flight Zone." *New York Times,* December 28.

———. 1992c. "U.S. Sends Jets to Iraq Zone from a Carrier Off Africa." *New York Times,* December 29.

———. 1993a. "U.S. Urging Allies to Threaten Iraq on Action in South." *New York Times,* January 6.

———. 1993b. "Iraq Apparently Rebuffs Allies on Missiles Reported in South." *New York Times,* January 8.

———. 1993c. "U.S. Says That Baghdad Removed Missiles." *New York Times,* January 10.

———. 1993d. "Iraq Is Said to Shift Missiles into Excluded Zone in North." *New York Times,* January 12.

———. 1993e. "Bush Said to Plan Air Strike on Iraq over Its Defiance." *New York Times,* January 13.

———. 1993f. "Iraq Refuses to Assure the Safety of Inspectors' Flights in South." *New York Times,* January 17.

———. 1993g. "Bush Launches Missile Attack on a Baghdad Industrial Park as Washington Greets Clinton." *New York Times,* January 18.

———. 1993h. "U.S. Leads Further Attacks on Iraqi Aircraft Sites; Admits Its Missile Hit Hotel." *New York Times,* January 19.

————. 1993i. "Iraq Says It Won't Attack Planes and Agrees to U.N. Flight Terms." *New York Times,* January 20.

————. 1993j. "Raids on Iraq: Few Choices for Clinton." *New York Times,* January 21.

————. 1993k. "U.S. Jets Attack Iraqi Radar Site Seen as Threat." *New York Times,* January 22.

Ibrahim, Youssef M. 1993a. "Iraq, as Threatened, Prevents U.N. Inspectors from Flying in on Own Plane." *New York Times,* January 11.

————. 1993b. "Iraqi Aide Defends Removal of Equipment in Border Zone." *New York Times,* January 12.

————. 1993c. "Arabs Protesting Attacks on Iraq." *New York Times,* January 20.

Interview with President-Elect Clinton. 1993. Transcript. *New York Times,* January 14.

Lewis, Paul 1993. " Hussein Rebuilds Iraq's Economy Undeterred by the U.N. Sanctions." *New York Times,* January 24.

Osgood, Charles E. 1962. *An Alternative to War or Surrender.* Urbana: University of Illinois Press.

Schmitt, Eric. 1993a. "U.S. Tries to Verify Compliance As Iraqi Missile Deadline Passes." *New York Times,* January 9.

————. 1993b. "Iraqis Cross into Kuwait." *New York Times,* January 11.

Sciolino, Elaine. 1993. "New Iraqi Site Raided as White House Vows Firmness." *New York Times,* January 23.

NOTES ON CONTRIBUTORS

ASHER ARIAN is Distinguished Professor of Political Science at the Graduate Center, City University of New York, and is also affiliated with the University of Haifa. The second edition of his book *Politics in Israel* has recently been published.

L. CARL BROWN is Garrett Professor in Foreign Affairs and Director of the Program in Near Eastern Studies at Princeton University. He is the coeditor of *Psychological Dimensions of Near Eastern Studies* and author of *International Politics and the Middle East: Old Rules, Dangerous Game.*

ALEXANDER L. GEORGE is Graham H. Stuart Professor Emeritus of International Relations at Stanford University. His most recent books are *Avoiding War: Problems of Crisis Management* and *Bridging the Gap: Theory and Practice of Foreign Policy.*

CAROL GORDON is a member of the Center for Social Research at the Graduate Center, City University of New York, and the Winston Institute for the Study of Prejudice at Bar-Ilan University. Her work has appeared most recently in the *Journal of Conflict Resolution.*

FRED I. GREENSTEIN is Professor of Politics and Director of the Program in Leadership Studies at Princeton University. He has recently published *How Presidents Test Reality.*

ROBERT JERVIS is Adlai E. Stevenson Professor of International Relations at Columbia University. His most recent book is *The Meaning of Nuclear Revolution.*

HERBERT C. KELMAN is Richard Clarke Cabot Professor of Social Ethics at Harvard University and Chair of the Middle East Seminar at the Harvard Center for International Affairs. Among his most recent works is *Crimes of Obedience: Toward a Social Psychology of Authority and Responsibility.*

JAROL B. MANHEIM is Professor of Communication and Political Science at George Washington University, where he is also Director of the National Center for Communication Studies. Among his published books is *All of the People, All the Time: Strategic Communication and American Politics.*

John Mueller is Professor of Political Science at the University of Rochester. He is the author of *Retreat from Doomsday: The Obsolescence of Major War,* and he is currently completing a book, *Policy and Opinion in the Gulf War,* to be published by the University of Chicago Press.

Jerrold M. Post is Professor of Psychiatry, Political Psychology, and International Affairs at George Washington University, where he directs the Political Psychology Program. He has recently published, with Robert Robins, *When Illness Strikes the Leader: The Dilemma of the Captive King.*

Stanley A. Renshon is Professor of Political Science at Lehman College and at the Graduate Center, City University of New York. He is editor of the journal *Political Psychology* and is finishing a manuscript entitled "Selecting the President: The Psychological Assessment of Political Leaders."

Dankwart A. Rustow is Distinguished Professor of Political Science and Sociology at the Graduate Center, City University of New York. He is the author of *Oil and Turmoil: America Faces OPEC and the Middle East,* among other works, and editor of *Philosophers and Kings: Studies in Leadership.*

Janice Gross Stein is Professor of Political Science at the University of Toronto, where she specializes in deterrence theory, international conflict, and Middle Eastern studies. Her most recent work is *Getting to the Table: The Process of International Pre-Negotiations* and *Choosing to Cooperate: How States Avoid Loss.*

Shibley Telhami is an Associate Professor of Government at Cornell University specializing in international relations of the Middle East. He has recently published *Power and Leadership: The Path to the Camp David Accords.*

Stephen J. Wayne is Professor of Government and coordinator of the American Government Program at Georgetown University. His work, *The Road to the White House,* is now in its fourth edition.

David G. Winter is Professor of Psychology at the University of Michigan, Ann Arbor. He is the author of numerous research studies of personality and political psychology, among them *The Power Motive.*

Marvin Zonis is Professor in the Graduate School of Business at the University of Chicago, where he teaches international political economy and political psychology. His most recent work is *Majestic Failure: The Fall of the Shah of Iran.*

Pitt Series in Policy and Institutional Studies

Bert A. Rockman, Editor